From an oil painting, about 1845

HARRISON D. TAYLOR

Ohio County, Kentucky, in the Olden Days

*A series of old newspaper sketches
of fragmentary history*

By

HARRISON D. TAYLOR

Prepared for publication in book form
by his granddaughter

MARY TAYLOR LOGAN

With an Introduction by
OTTO A. ROTHERT

Southern Historical Press, Inc.
Greenville, South Carolina

This volume was reproduced from
An 1926 edition located in the
Publisher's private Library

All rights reserved. No part of this publication may be reproduced,
stored in a retrieval system, transmitted in any form, posted
on to the web in any form or by any means without
the prior written permission of the publisher.

Please direct all correspondence and orders to:

www.southernhistoricalpress.com
or
SOUTHERN HISTORICAL PRESS, Inc.
PO BOX 1267
375 West Broad Street
Greenville, SC   29601
southernhistoricalpress@gmail.com

Originally published: Louisville, KY. 1926
ISBN #0-89308-903-6
All rights Reserved.
Printed in the United States of America

CONTENTS

Introduction..........................Otto A. Rothert

		Page
I	Evidences of Prehistoric People and Early Pioneers...	1
II	Old Vienna and Calhoun, Barnett's Station, and Hartford..	6
III	Indian Depredations................................	10
IV	How Stephen Statler Came to Hartford..............	15
V	First Courts and Courthouse........................	19
VI	The War of 1812...................................	28
VII	"Ralph Ringwood"	33
VIII	Life in the Olden Days.............................	35
IX	Joseph Barnett and Ignatius Pigman, and Their Land Troubles..	42
X	Early Land Titles..................................	47
XI	Forests and Farms.................................	50
XII	The First Hanging.................................	53
XIII	Some Early Merchants..............................	57
XIV	Some Pioneer Families.............................	64
XV	Religion of the Pioneers...........................	69
XVI	Old-Time Schools..................................	73
XVII	Three Early Physicians.............................	76
XVIII	Ten Well-Known Lawyers..........................	80
XIX	Slaves and Slavery.................................	93
XX	Harrison D. Taylor's Autobiographical Notes.........	97
XXI	History of the Taylor Family.......................	101

APPENDIX

A.	Act Forming Ohio County in 1798.................	115
B.	Ohio County as Recorded by Collins in 1847 and in 1877	117
C.	Captain John Howell, Revolutionary Soldier.........	125
D.	Harrison D. Taylor—A Biographical Sketch..........	127
E.	Ohio County Biographies Published in 1885..........	131
F.	Ohio County Marriage Records, 1799 to 1840........	135

Index... 191

ILLUSTRATIONS

Harrison D. Taylor, 1845.........................*Frontispiece*
Mrs. Harrison D. Taylor, 1845........................*Page* 1
Map of Ohio County, 1800............................*Page* 20
Ignatius Pigman, 1800...............................*Page* 44
Map of Ohio County, 1886............................*Page* 68
Ohio County Courthouse, 1926........................*Page* 100

Introduction

More than a century and a quarter has passed since Ohio County was formed. Its pioneers have come and gone, and so have the sons of its pioneers. In many counties most of the local traditions—the so-called old traditions—now heard have undergone changes from generation to generation until the originals have become almost hopelessly lost in fabrications. Such, however, is less frequently the case in Ohio County, for Harrison D. Taylor, a pioneer and the son of a pioneer, wrote and published his own recollections and those of other early settlers from whom he gathered first-hand information.

Mr. Taylor was born in 1802. He came with his parents to Ohio County in his infancy and lived there until his death in 1889. From early childhood he mingled with the pioneers and heard their fireside stories. As the years rolled on, his interest in pioneers and olden times continued. He sought contact with men and women who, like himself, had participated in the making of early history. At the age of about fifty-five he wrote his recollections. He was a lawyer and was qualified to prepare them for print.

In 1857 he published a series of Ohio County sketches in the *Shield*, a newspaper of Owensboro, and twenty years later—from April 18, 1877, to March 27, 1878—he republished them, with a few additional chapters, in the *Hartford Herald*. Selections from these sketches constitute the first part of this volume.

His granddaughter Mrs. Mary Taylor Logan has gone over his various chapters for the purpose of presenting them in book form. Mr. Taylor refers to his loosely connected articles as "fragmentary history." They, however, are fragmentary only in that he wrote on subjects as they occurred to him, with little effort to present them in chronological sequence. Mrs. Logan has omitted his digressions into moral and political discussion. What has been selected for publication in this volume has been edited chiefly for the purpose of linking together the subjects and presenting them under selected headings. By such rearrangement an interesting history of Ohio County in the olden days has been produced. It is Mr. Taylor's story of his times and contemporaries from the days of the firstcomers down to about 1857, with a few fragments extending down to 1877.

Incidentally it includes his autobiographical notes, likewise a brief history of the Taylor family, one of the oldest and largest families in Ohio County.

The appendices and the footnotes that have been added contain many items with which Mr. Taylor, in all probability, was familiar, but which he did not embody in his newspaper sketches. It is likely, however, that he would have included some of them had he rearranged his chapters for publication in book form. During the course of the footnotes I cite every book, pamphlet, and manuscript bearing on Ohio County history known to me, and in the appendices quote some of the material heretofore published by other writers and call attention to the whereabouts of additional data in print.

This volume is Mrs. Logan's monument to her grandfather. It is a labor of love. No one could have been better qualified to prepare these sketches for publication in book form than she. Her parents died when she was a small child, and thereafter she made her home with her grandfather. From early girlhood on through the years that followed she heard her grandfather tell and retell these stories. It is to her fatherly grandfather that she dedicates this monument—a monument for the interest and instruction of the present and the many generations yet to come.

OTTO A. ROTHERT

Louisville, Kentucky
July 20, 1926

From an oil painting, about 1845

MRS. MARY DAVIS (HARRISON D.) TAYLOR

I

EVIDENCES OF PREHISTORIC PEOPLE AND EARLY PIONEERS

The author of the following fragments of Ohio County's early history gave a partial promise to the editor of the *Shield*,* of Owensboro, who announced the fact through his paper, thus committing both of us to the public; else this task might never have been undertaken.

After the inspection of the material left for the writing of a local history, we find that not a single pioneer or early settler is now living. Owing to the fact that Ohio County was first a part of Jefferson County which was formed in 1780, then a part of Nelson formed in 1784, and then a part of Hardin formed in 1792, it has no county records of its own until in July, 1799, when its official records as a county begin, the county having been formed by an act of legislature approved on December 17, 1798, and to take effect on July 1, 1799.

Like most of Kentucky and the other western countries, Ohio County has traces of having been settled by a different race of people at a day long prior to the advent of Europeans. Flints, arrowheads, hatchets, pestles, and other implements made of stone, also fragments of curious pottery, were numerous many years ago. In fact these flint arrowheads served our early settlers a valuable purpose, being the principal means of supplying the old-fashioned firelocks with flints. Mounds containing human bones were quite common. On many of these mounds the timber was as large as any in the adjoining forest.

Some years ago, while leveeing up a road near the banks of Muddy Creek, at the bottom of the ditches, which were some two feet or more deep, charcoal and ashes were found for the space of one or two hundred yards. These evidently showed that this place had been a favorite camping ground where some savage tribe had once probably hunted and fished, but how long ago none can tell.

The late Robert Render, Sr., a gentleman well-known and highly esteemed for his many virtues, used to relate finding a mound or grave near Green River, in which were bones of an enormous size: a

---

*The *Shield* was published in Owensboro. "During the Know-Nothing excitement in 1856 the *National American* was started in Owensboro by Joshua G. Ford, proprietor, and George H. Yeaman, editor. The first number was dated August 6, 1856. A. G. Botts succeeded Mr. Yeaman as editor and Colonel John H. McHenry was next, in 1857-58. About this time Mr. Ford changed the name to

human leg bone which, when stood on the floor beside his leg, when sitting down, would reach to the top of his knee, and a jaw bone which would fit loosely over his under jaw. Mr. Render was a man considerably over medium height, measuring over six feet and having large bones and face. It is estimated that the old bones belonged to a human one-third larger than Mr. Render, who ranked among the largest men in this country. It is now a subject of regret that this grave had not been thoroughly examined by scientific men, and a full skeleton procured of this semi-giant race. Nothing like fortifications have ever been found in this section. The mounds, so far examined, all contained bones.

The early pioneer, and Indian fighter, perhaps strode over these humble depositories of the dead without care or reflection, or perhaps with a feeling of triumph. But it was not so with the sensitive settler when rambling through the forest in after years. It would be difficult to imagine the strange feelings that would spring up in his mind when one of these mounds obstructed his way. With a thrill of superstitious awe and reverence for the dead he would turn his steps aside, and, no longer "whistling for want of thought," strange vagaries and inquiries would arise in his mind.

How long have they lain here? What manner of people were they? Whence did they come and whither have they gone? What

the *Shield*, and soon after the outbreak of the War to *Ford's Southern Shield*, which name it sustained until its discontinuance in 1875. For a year or so, however, during the War, it was located at Hartford."—From *A History of Daviess County*.

As stated elsewhere, these sketches were republished in the *Hartford Herald*. "The first issue of the *Hartford Herald* appeared January 6, 1875. The paper was founded by John P. Barrett, whose proprietorship continued nearly twelve years, with the exception of about five months when it was owned by James S. Glenn and Cicero T. Sutton, and about a year when it was owned by Mr. Sutton alone. On November 24, 1886, Frank L. Felix and McHenry Rhoads purchased the paper from its founder. In 1891 Mr. Rhoads sold his interest to Ben D. Ringo. On March 8, 1893, Mr. Felix became the sole owner and so continued until January 1, 1917, when it was sold to The Hartford Herald Publishing Company, by which corporation it was published until February 15, 1926, when it was consolidated with the *Hartford Republican*, which was established in July, 1889. The merger of the *Herald* and the *Republican* is now published under the name of the *Ohio County News*. The following have served as editors of the *Hartford Herald*: Wallace Gruelle, John P. Barrett, Nancy Jane Jones (said to have been the pseudonym of the wife of the founder), Lycurgus Barrett (brother of the founder), John O'Flaherty, Cicero T. Sutton, James S. Glenn, B. P. Robertson, Frank L. Felix, McHenry Rhoads, Ben D. Ringo, Heber Matthews, W. Harold Coombs, J. Walter Greep, Lyman G. Barrett (son of Lycurgus Barrett), McDowell A. Fogle (one of the present editors of the *Ohio County News*), and Miss Lillie B. Burton. Frank L. Felix was either sole editor or co-editor for about thirty years, while Heber Matthews served as co-editor with Mr. Felix for about twenty-one years. John P. Barrett and Mr. Felix were at the helm of the *Hartford Herald* for about forty-two years."—Letter from McDowell A. Fogle, May 21, 1926.

Prehistoric People and Early Pioneers

were their manners and customs? Do their spirits now mingle with the spirits of the palefaces, or do they chase the phantom buffalo, elk, and deer in their own spirit land?

No one can tell now what paleface first traversed the Green River wilds. Was he a marauding culprit banished by crimes he had committed? Or was he perhaps a land speculator seeking choice bodies of land on which to locate his entries and surveys? Or was he a second Nimrod, led only by his keen relish of slaughter in pursuit of the massive buffalo, stately elk, or sleek, symmetrical deer? Or was he the more humble but sly and cautious trapper seeking to divest the beaver, otter, mink, and coon of its fur?

None of these, nor even an amateur traveler, has left a record of his impression as he stood upon some lofty hill tops in the wilds that became Ohio County, and looked out over a virgin forest of magnificent trees, arbored over with a labyrinth of grape vines, through which marched tremendous herds of buffalo along their well beaten trace to their watering places. Nor has anyone left any record of the startled deer, that meek denizen of the woods, who, showing his white flag of danger as he bounded high over some obstruction, glided sylph-like below the tangled vines from which darted the nimble squirrel to a retreat upon the limb of the nearest tree, where in safety he chattered and barked braggart-like. What were his thoughts as, wending his way to the beautiful Green River unmarred by civilization, he beheld its limpid waters kissing the still greener canebrakes? Or when he looked at a shady bend where bevies of ducks, geese, and other wild fowls were diving, circling, and coquetting? Or, again, when standing on the sunny bank of the river where floated, on or near the surface, fish of all kinds in countless numbers?

Although we have no written description of those early sylvan scenes, a memory of them is still fresh in the minds of some of our oldest present citizens. From early boyhood I have talked to many an "oldest citizen," most of whom, each in his or her turn, have since passed away. Possibly some day I, too, will be an oldest citizen.

Notwithstanding that we have no written records or living witnesses, we still have some faint memorials of our earliest rovers. In 1836 a surveying and engineering party found a beech tree standing near the bank of Green River, marked "Leonard Helm 1776." The name was carved in neat Roman capitals. The up and down strokes had spread to near the width of a man's hand. Although the tree was from three to four feet in diameter, the name extended nearly around the tree, the date being below the name. Leonard Helm is spoken of in some of the early histories of the Carolinas and Tennessee. No doubt he extended his explorations across the country to Green River and followed it down to the Ohio and actually carved his name on the tree standing in what later became Ohio County.

Had we regarded the petition of the poet, "Woodman, spare that tree"—that beechen tree—we would still have memorials, though frail, of the trails used by our ancestors and other early pioneers of our country. An elderly gentleman gives the following narrative:

"About the year 1830 I was running out some old surveys of land on Caney Creek in Ohio County. I frequently saw marks of the old trail leading from Elizabethtown to Barnett's and Hartford stations. In running a line which crossed and recrossed it, we came to a stream of beautiful, clear running water. We stopped on the bank to quench our thirst and eat our dinners which we carried with us. While sitting there I discovered a large beech tree near by, literally almost covered with names carved in the smooth bark. Among them were Barnett, Cleaver, Rhoads, Pigman, Jackson, Taylor, Handley, Love, Isaacs, Baird, May, and many others of whom I had never before heard.

"The inquiry arose, why were all these names here? But upon surveying the locality this was easily explained. The stream, now called Richland, curved in, from a wide bottom lying on the south, to within a few yards of a bluff-point of a long sloping ridge running down from the north, leaving between the bluff and stream only room for a good camping ground. Right here had run the old trace or road along which had passed many early settlers of this and other sections of the Green River country."

The first formation of a state, or settlement of a colony, is always attended with such events as leave records or tradition accessible to the historian. Our territory was from 1780 to 1798 the lower or western outer border of the first three counties which embraced this section of the country: first of Jefferson, then of Nelson, then of Hardin. Such settlements as were made during those years were the result of individual enterprise without any concert or combination with others.

The veteran pioneer, Daniel Boone, was familiar, no doubt, with the Green River canebrakes at a very early period. There is on file in a suit in our court a patent, printed on vellum or parchment, signed P. Henry, Governor of Virginia, dated June 1, 1786, and issued on a survey dated December 19, 1784. It has endorsed on the back thereof the following certificate: "The one-fifth part of the within land is rich bottom, and I think the high land will produce sixty bushels of corn to the acre. I know the within land. Daniel Boone. January 7th, 1788. Test.—Baily Washington."

The name of Boone is written in a plain, unostentatious manner, reminding one of the man. There may be some doubt as to the name of Washington, as that part of the writing is somewhat defaced and worn, but the best of experts so read it. Furthermore, the high moral character of the patentee, the venerable William Duvall of Richmond, Virginia, father of the late William P. Duvall of Florida, is a guarantee of the genuineness of the certificate. There are also other, but somewhat slight, evidences of Boone's migrations through the Green River country, such as his name carved on trees.

II

OLD VIENNA AND CALHOUN, BARNETT'S STATION, AND HARTFORD

The first log cabin of which we have any proof was built in 1780 on what was called Muddy Creek, afterwards Blackford's Creek because the cabin was built by a man named Blackford. It also became well-known in consequence of a man named Cleaver, who, while with a hunting party, died there. It seems that hunters and land speculators usually passed down the Ohio and up Green River in their hunting and exploring expeditions.

It is not certainly known whether Vienna, now Calhoun, or Barnett's Station near the old town of Hartford was first settled. Nor is it known whether Hartford Station was started before or after either of these two. Owing to the convenience of water navigation down the Ohio and up Green River, it is probable that Vienna was the first point where anything like a permanent colony was planted.

From an old suit of John Handley against Myers, Chase, and John Dorsey's heirs, the following facts are gleaned: Jacob Myers issued his instructions to Henry Rhoads, Isaac Cox, and Isaac Morrison, dated February 23, 1785, authorizing them to lay off a town at the Long Falls on Green River, and to grant lots to settlers, upon their building cabins and actually settling on the same. From an old plan or plot of the town, it appears that they laid off a town containing 172 half-acre in-lots, with a public square of more than four acres, and numerous out-lots of eight acres each. This plan also shows that the following persons became settlers of the same: Henry Rhoads, Daniel Rhoads—senior and junior—Abel Undel, Adam Hay, Michael Hay, William Casebier, Nicholas King, Jacob Knight, Thomas Gardner, Henry Hatfield, Thomas Adam Young, James Clark, Daniel McCoy, William Kelly, John Keith, John Hogarth, Henry Grass, Isaac Vantrace, John Berry, Elias Moore, Aaron Rollins, Benjamin Huff, John Handley, Adam Shepherd, and others.

This town, it appears, had previously labored under the unpretentious name of Rhoadsville, and now assumed the name of Vienna. How it acquired so foreign a name is unknown. Perhaps some Austrian count (filled with admiration for her royal highness, Maria Theresa, who recently tarnished her good name by joining with

Old Vienna and Hartford

Frederic, whose extraordinary strategic duplicity had acquired for him the name of Great, and that cruel and soulless monster Catherine in partitioning proud but prostrate Poland) was for a time a denizen of this settlement of forty cabins, and as Americans always had an extraordinary admiration for foreign nobility, the settlers may have yielded to him the honor of naming this embryo town of the west, Vienna, in honor of his Austrian capital. He no doubt would have given the river, running by the new town, the classic name of Blue Danube, had not its green, deep waters proved its just title to that given by the earlier pioneers.

It appears that one of the original proprietors of the land at Vienna visited the country in March, 1786. In a letter of instructions directed to John Handley, whom he appointed his agent, among other matters is inserted the following clause: "As it appears that there is much danger from the Indians in that quarter, and the inhabitants think it dangerous to cultivate their respective out-lots, you will give them leave to cultivate the commons in common, observing only to kill the heavy timber."

From the tenor of Larkin Dorsey's letter of instructions the following facts may be inferred: First, that the country was much infested with the redskins; second, that the settlers were but slightly indebted to cultivation for support; and lastly, that Mr. Dorsey was no farmer: "observing only to kill the heavy timber." The idea of raising corn and potatoes among bramble bushes and briars! [1]

---

[1] Judge John A. Stevens, former judge of McLean County, says: "Calhoun was never called Long Falls, but was frequently spoken of as The Settlement at the Long Falls. At one time there was a long falls in Green River, at Calhoun, near the mouth of a little stream. This falls made it possible, at times, to walk across Green River at that point, but with the erection of the locks and dams in 1834 the falls were obliterated. The old fort was built about 1775 and the first settlement made the same year, and later called Vienna."

Collins in his *History of Kentucky*, under the head of McLean County, says, "The first fort or station in McLean County was built, where Calhoun now stands, in 1788, by Solomon Rhoads and called Vienna"; and in his list of pioneer stations he notes that "Barnett's Station, two miles from Hartford, Ohio County, was settled by Colonel Joseph Barnett before 1790," and that "Hartford Station, where Hartford, Ohio County, is, was settled before 1790." Lucius P. Little in his *Ben Hardin* remarks that William Hardin was at Fort Vienna about 1782. Rothert's *History of Muhlenberg County* says that in 1854, when McLean County was formed out of parts of Ohio, Daviess, and Muhlenberg counties, old Vienna became the county seat, its name having been changed to Calhoun in honor of Judge John Calhoun.

The origin, people, and events of old Vienna offer a good subject for original historical research for anyone interested in the beginnings of the lower Green River country. The same is true of Barnett's Station and Hartford Station. More of the history of these stations is given in our Chapter IV and Appendix B.

Ohio County in the Olden Days

We have no precise date as to the settlement of Hartford, but by reference to an old land suit we learn from the deposition of James Harrod, that he came up Green River in 1782, traveled up Rough Creek on the south side, and after traveling in company with John Isaacs and crossing a large stream which he then called Muddy Run, he came to a high bluff which he estimated to be fourteen miles from Green River, and, a short distance below that bluff, on a small white oak tree, cut the initials of his name as the beginning corner of an entry in the name of Gabriel Madison for four thousand acres.

A remarkable incident afterwards occurred in relation to this white oak. In 1821 or 1822 in an action of ejection, the plaintiffs, claiming under Madison's and defendants under Barnett's title, it became necessary to identify Madison's beginning corner. The same John Isaacs, who then resided in some of the upper counties of the State, was summoned and attended as a witness. When called to the stand, he gave positive testimony as to the oak still standing, a tree which he had not seen since the country was settled until his present visit.

As countervailing evidence, the defendants produced experts who carefully examined the tree and gave it as their opinion that it never had been marked. So confident was Mr. Isaacs of the truth of his statement that he requested the court to send the jury, under the care of the sheriff, to the tree, standing but a few hundred yards from the courthouse. The procession marched to the spot where stood the tree devoid of any mark or scar, but Isaacs, nothing daunted, seized an axe, soon split out a large block of it, and lo! there were the very marks he had stated, and upon a careful count of annulations, they agreed precisely with the date he had given. The reader can readily imagine with what a proud step the old veteran hunter, his character vindicated, went back to the courthouse and exhibited his blocks to the admiring crowd.

It also appears from the depositions of Isaacs and Matthias Shultz that Rough Creek was well-known as early as the year 1782, and that a company of men raised a field of corn at Barnett's Station in 1785. This old station was about two miles northeast of Hartford and was on the farm which included the late residence of Dr. Burr F. Nall [known as Fort Hill Farm].

How Hartford and the stream upon which it is located acquired their names is unknown. The stream near its head is called Yellow

Creek in various entries and surveys, but lower down it invariably bore the name of Rough Creek. The following seems the most rational solution of the question: Near the creek's source the country is broken and hilly; the rains washed the soil from the hillsides immediately into the stream and kept it turbid and yellow, while lower down in the wide, level bottom land the current lost its force, for the stream was greatly obstructed with logs and driftwood, giving it a rough aspect. Hence arose the name of Rough on the lower portion of the stream and Yellow on the upper. The name Hartford was probably derived from the ford on the stream where deer and other wild animals were in the habit of crossing in great numbers.

III

INDIAN DEPREDATIONS

Whether the Indians, from strategic motives, thought best to attack the larger and more populous settlements of the upper counties (and thus destroy the nucleus of white emigration, thereby restoring the country to its original owners and relieving their own territory on the north side of the Ohio River from repeated invasion, by which their own towns and corn fields were destroyed), or found their raids into upper Kentucky more productive of spoils and plunder, it is certain they made but feeble efforts to rid that portion of which Ohio County is composed of its white settlers. They seemed to have abandoned the idea of holding the territory as their own, and only visited it occasionally for the purpose of hunting or horse-stealing, always killing or taking prisoner such white stragglers as came in their way. Local tradition relates but a single instance of an attack upon any fort or station.

The town of Vienna was at one time regularly besieged by a large party of warriors who resorted to all their wily arts for several days to subdue the place. Things began to grow serious, and two daring men made their way through the Indian lines at night and reached Hartford in safety. A very short time elapsed until every man capable of bearing arms, who could be spared, was on the march to relieve Vienna, but before the rescuing party reached the place, the Indians had raised the siege and fled.

The names of the two gallant young men who thus risked the horrors of Indian torture to carry the news to Hartford should be handed down to posterity, but unfortunately tradition gives but one name, that of Stephen Rowan, the father of Dr. A. Rowan and William Rowan of Ohio County and John Rowan of McLean County.

Stephen Rowan will also appear in another incident which will be given later. Mr. Collins in his *History of Kentucky*, under the head of Ohio County, gives some very thrilling incidents in relation to depredations and therefore they will be omitted here, for his book is in reach of most readers. [Collins' chapter on Ohio County is reprinted in Appendix B.]

There are others, however, worthy of note. There are some facts in relation to the killing of the Anderson children that were omitted in the narrative published by Collins. The omissions are embraced

Indian Depredations

in the following version: Several women and children had left Barnett's Station to attend preaching in Hartford. The Indians had no doubt seen their tracks and waylaid them on their return. The road crossed a deep ravine less than a fourth of a mile from the fort. The Indians had concealed themselves in this ravine, covered with cane, and rushed upon the party as they passed, killing Mrs. Anderson's two children by dashing their heads against the root of a tree, and tomahawking and scalping Mrs. Anderson, who, however, survived and lived some years afterwards. They carried off Miss Barnett, quite a small but handsome girl. The appearance of John Miller—usually called Tick-eyed John—who happened to be near the place, and armed as usual, no doubt saved the lives of the others of the party. Harrison Taylor, Jr., had just arrived at the fort and was sitting with his gun across his lap when the screams of the women and children were heard. Springing to his feet he ran to the gate and saw an Indian running at his utmost speed through a small field that adjoined the fort. He gave chase and was gaining on the Indian, but as they were approaching the fence on the outside of which was thick undergrowth, he saw at a glance that his only chance was to fire before the Indian crossed the fence. He fired, but with a loud "Ugh!" the Indian disappeared. A few drops of blood was all that was found afterwards.

The citizens of Hartford had a field cleared on the farm now owned by Mr. Isaac Morton, near town, where they had a crop of flax. A party of women and children, guarded by armed men, went out one day to pull the flax. Among them was a foolish woman—but a few degrees above an idiot—who would go into the woods to gather flowers, and, regardless of warnings, ventured out of range of the guns of the men on guard. The report of a gun and the screams of the women alarmed the whole party. Samuel Neal ran to the fence and saw the poor woman running and an Indian after her. She soon fell and as the savage was preparing to take her scalp, Neal dispatched a bullet which caused him to stagger off. Other Indians ran to his aid and helped him away. The white men were too much encumbered with women and children to give chase.

Tradition gives two stories as to the fate of the wounded savage. One is that he was found in a gully covered with logs and brush, about a mile from where he was wounded. The other is that the party buried him under a pile of loose stones, near the present site of Concord Church. Such a pile heaped up some four or five feet high, nearly the shape in which earth is usually heaped over a grave, was to be seen at that place for many years afterwards.

While the people were confined to their fort, the cows were turned into the woods for the pasture. At Vienna one night they failed to come home, although the next morning their bells could be heard some distance away. Young Stephen Rowan, the same who had distinguished himself by passing the Indian lines, mounted his horse and, with his bright new rifle on his shoulder, was passing through the gate when his father called out: "Stephen, be on your guard. I fear the Indians are keeping back the cows to draw someone into ambush." Young Rowan hurried away and soon reached the vicinity of the cows. They were at the head of a very narrow ravine, where the bluff-hills were so steep that they could not climb up them. When he nearly reached them, his horse took fright and refused to advance. A blow caused him to rear and plunge into the air. This threw Rowan so high that he was enabled to see over a log, behind which an Indian, with a gun, was concealed. He instantly wheeled his horse, and, as he did so, saw another Indian on the opposite side of the ravine as he passed. He was met at the gate by a Mr. Downs, who asked in an imperious manner, "Where are the cows?"

"Indians! Indians! Indians!" shouted Rowan.

Mr. Downs made some contemptuous remark and said that the children should cry no longer for milk and that he would go himself for the cows. Rowan dared him to go and Downs immediately prepared to start. Several tried to dissuade him, and one man even caught him, but Downs jerked away. Many called out: "Mr. Downs, do not go out there; you will never come back alive." But he paid no heed and hurried away. Young Rowan now relented of his banter and called out, "I know there are Indians there. I saw them. Come back." But Downs was heedless of this appeal and hurried away. Then the men, women, and children gathered around young Rowan and after hearing his report of what he saw, they resolved on a reconnoissance, but before they were fully armed, they heard several gunshots in quick succession. As Downs did not return, a party cautiously approached the place of the shooting. They found poor Downs dead, scalped, and most savagely mutilated. The trail of a few Indians was discovered and followed to the Ohio River, but they had made their escape. Young Rowan was largely indebted for

Indian Depredations

his life to his fine horse and his bright, beautiful, silver-mounted rifle, which restrained the Indians from firing until he had passed so far up the ravine that he could not escape.[2]

A pet squaw was for some time living with the white families in Hartford, and was guilty of a most singular freak. The late William Sharpe, of Owensboro, was said to have been the first male child born in Hartford, and this squaw showed the greatest attachment for him, fondling and caressing him at every opportunity. About the time that he was beginning to walk he was missed, and the whole town was alarmed. His parents were in hopeless agony. For some cause the squaw was suspected and closely watched. She was finally found with young Sharpe concealed in the woods, where she seemed to have provided everything in her power for his comfort and safety.

In after years when the Indians would meet with our citizens on the other side of the river, they would frequently tell of their visits to the vicinity, and boast of passing through the village at night. An old chief used to inquire about that bright little boy, Joe Barnett, and tell how often he tried to entrap him and adopt him as his son. He used to watch and admire him in the woods, and had frequent opportunities to shoot him, but wanted to take him unhurt. He was always too fleet to be caught. At one time he had him penned in a narrow bend of Rough Creek and threatened to shoot him if he did not surrender, but he whipped his horse into the stream, swam across, and, with a loud laugh, hid behind a tree, and "cussed me for a dam old steal-hoss."

Indian depredations practically ceased after 1797. Save for an occasional band of friendly Cherokees, who continued to visit the country as late as 1802 or 1803, the citizens were uninterrupted, except by the needless alarm those friendly bands of redskins gave the women and children. It was perhaps to be relieved from these false

---

[2] Collins, under the head of Rowan County, says that William Rowan settled in Louisville in March, 1783, and in the following spring—when his son John was only eleven years of age—the Rowans with five other families made a settlement at the "Long Falls of Green River," and that the region was visited by a band of Shawnee Indians with whom the whites had many encounters. Under Jefferson County he gives a one-page story of how the Indians attacked these homeseekers while on the Ohio traveling in two flatboats from the Falls of the Ohio to the "Long Falls of Green River." The details of the trip and the arrival at what became The Settlement at the Long Falls are given in the Autobiography of Judge John Rowan (a sketch confined to the youth of Judge Rowan) written in 1841. It has not yet been published, but a copy of the manuscript was read before The Filson Club in October, 1923, by Willard R. Jillson of Frankfort.

alarms that some unprincipled white man shot one of their party. After that the Indians never returned to this locality, and most of the children thereafter grew up unfamiliar with the appearance of a savage, until a straggling band passed through the country a few years after the close of the War of 1812. All the men had certificates showing that they had fought bravely under General Jackson. Their progress was a great ovation. Their camp was crowded with admiring and curious visitors who loaded them with presents. This trip proved such a success that we soon had marauding bands of braves, squaws, and papooses in quick succession, of whom the settlers soon became weary. They treated them with less friendly attention, and the Indians gradually disappeared.

IV

HOW STEPHEN STATLER CAME TO HARTFORD

Among other remarkable men who were connected with the early settlement of Ohio County was Stephen Statler. He was of Dutch descent and was born and reared in the western portion of Pennsylvania. While quite a young man he was engaged to help run a trading boat to New Orleans. Their plan was to descend the river, stop at favorable locations, hunt and slaughter game, and load their boat with wild meats, skins, furs, and the like. The party consisted of a jolly band of flatboat men who glided along without mishap to a point a short distance below the mouth of Green River, where they landed on the north side of the Ohio, and commenced hunting for game.

Statler and another man rambled far into the woods and shot several deer. They came in at night loaded down with hams. To their great dismay they found that the boat had gone and had left them to their fate in the wilderness. Probably the dastardly conduct of the captain and his crew was occasioned by having seen fresh moccasin tracks in the canebrakes.

Statler and his friend concealed themselves for the night and next morning set about constructing a raft to cross the river. They embarked and had nearly reached the Kentucky shore when their raft, by the force of the current, was forced upon a snag, or sawyer, from which it was impossible to extricate it except by lightening the load. To keep his gun secure Statler adjusted the priming, shut down the pan, smeared it around and filled the muzzle with beeswax. After throwing to shore the venison hams, he plunged into the water and swam to the bank. He then suspended his gun from the limb of a tree. As soon as Statler got off the raft, it became disentangled from the sawyer, swung around into the strong current, and glided away with its only passenger on board.

Statler followed on and on, walking down along the shore, hoping to see his companion land, but finally gave him up in despair as the current bore him still farther into the middle of the stream and faster down the river and out of sight. After a long and anxious chase, Statler concluded to return and secure his venison and gun. But, alas! He had tarried too long, for when he reached the place, a gang of buzzards had devoured his meat and his gun had disappeared. He had to set out weary and alone to seek some habitation of his fellow-man.

He was entirely ignorant of the geography of the country, but had heard of such a place as Nashville and thought there might be some trace leading from this part of the Ohio River country to that point; so he concluded to follow up its bank. The water being at a high stage, his course was frequently obstructed. He waded, swam, and rafted himself over all these obstructions. When he reached the present site of Owensboro, he saw old signs of civilization and a trace leading off from the river. He concluded this was the Nashville trace and joyously followed it. He had nothing left but his tomahawk and butcher knife and flint and steel. He had lived on roots and bark since crossing the river, and now suffering an attack of rheumatism he was unable to get even them. His fate seemed sealed. While lying on the ground and thinking over his condition, he heard a noise in the leaves, and looking in that direction saw an opossum passing near him. What a joyful sight to him! With a well aimed throw of his tomahawk he killed it. With eager haste he crawled to it and kindled a fire, cooked his prize, and ate it. This, he said, although it had a very strong taste, was most delicious food to a starving man, and even though he could have devoured the whole, he wisely saved a portion for another meal.

The next day he was well enough to resume his journey. While in the flats of Panther Creek, he was overtaken by a tremendous rain and sheltered for the night in the hollow of a large sycamore tree. On the ninth day of his wanderings he reached No Creek, where he saw cattle with bells on. As he knew cows were in the habit of going home in the evening, he followed them, and they led him to the banks of Rough Creek near Hartford. The reader can well imagine the delight he felt at seeing the columns of smoke ascending from the chimney tops and hearing the sound of the woodman's axe and the voices of merry children at play.

But alas! How soon were these flattering hopes of again mingling with his fellow-men overshadowed and almost blasted. The first sound of his voice, as he called for help, produced almost a dead silence in the little town on the other side of the creek. Presently a few individuals, well armed and keeping behind the shelter of the trees and logs, cautiously approached to within speaking distance.

They questioned him over and over again, and finally left, apparently convinced that he was a spy or a decoy to lead them into danger. And to all appearances he was left to perish in sight of his own race who were living in plenty. After a considerable delay a large party of men again came to the top of the bluff. After they cautiously stationed themselves behind the most available shelter from an enemy's ball on the opposite side, Statler, hungry and weary as he was, had again to undergo another catechising.

Humanity finally prevailed over caution, and two men, well armed, pushed out from shore and came to his relief. When brought into the town, his worn, haggard condition fully corroborated, in the minds of all sensible and reasonable men, his story, but of that class who can always see several inches farther into a millstone than any of their neighbors, there was one who "knew" there was something wrong about him; she was the good old wife of the man who kindly invited the stranger to his house and administered to his wants. This old lady having been raised by Dutch parents could speak that language quite fluently and warned the family and the neighbors frequently, in that language, of the viper that they were warming to life in their bosoms, but the father and sons were kind to him, and as soon as he had recovered his strength, they took him about with them on their hunting parties.

After some days a number of men had to go across the big bend of Green River to see after horses which were running in the cane. The old gentleman offered a horse and gun to Statler and invited him to accompany the boys. At this the old lady became furious, predicting that she would never again see her sons alive, and heaped upon the "vagabond" all the epithets of abuse in her vocabulary—all in Statler's hearing. While she was talking, the party started off. They returned loaded with game, and it was hard to tell whether the old termagant was pleased or displeased. Her sons had come home alive; but she had proved a false prophet, which was very mortifying to her.

The next day was Sunday, and her "vagabond," shaved and smartly improved, took his seat at the breakfast table. After breakfast he took down the old Dutch Bible and read a chapter aloud. It would be impossible to describe the astonishment, mortification, and contrition of the old lady. She stood with tears in her eyes, and exclaimed: "Oh, mine Gott! mine Gott! Und you knows all I says about you. Vell, I did not know you vas Dutch, but now I knows you is a good, honest man. You does read de Bible so good. You must forgive me. I see I did not know vat I vas saying." Then a mutual forgiving and reconciliation took place, and they were ever afterwards the best of friends.

Through the summer young Statler joined in a few chases after Indians. One of these chases occurred when his party crossed the Ohio and followed the trail into the Indian country, where they overtook some of the redskins and exchanged shots with them. As one of the whites [John Miller] raised his gun to his face, a ball from the enemy struck him in the elbow and passed up his arm to his shoulder, shivering the bone as it went. The only remedy applied was a slippery elm bark poultice, and the entire bone came out of the wound in broken pieces. The man recovered, regained the use of his arm, and lived many years.

By fall Statler had become a favorite among the hunters. Several men volunteered to go with him in search of his rifle, which was a valuable possession in those days. Upon arriving at the Ohio River he pointed out the sycamore tree that stood near the place where he had lost his gun, and sure enough, they found it embedded in the sand on the spot under the limb where he had suspended it. And what astonished them more was that after a fresh priming it went off at the first trial. This was owing to the careful manner in which it had been closed up with wax.

He was so much charmed with backwoods life that after a three years' stay, he abandoned all ideas of making his native state his home. He visited his old home and after his return married in June, 1797, Miss Rhoda Pigman, daughter of Ignatius Pigman. They settled on a farm where they both lived to a good old age, pious and orderly members of the church.

Stephen Statler was a large, robust man, but never corpulent. He was commissioned by the governor the first sheriff of Ohio County. He never aspired to any other office. He had his rules of conduct for himself and family, with which he required strict compliance. He was a close observer of men and things, and was seldom at fault in judging the character of others. He was considered the weather prognosticator of the neighborhood, and many of his predictions were remarkably verified. To those he esteemed he was a kind friend and a most agreeable and social companion.[3]

---

[3] Stephen Statler was born in Pennsylvania in August, 1770. He married Miss Rhoda Pigman on June 18, 1797. She was born on April 25, 1778, and died in December, 1852. He died on June 9, 1856. They were the parents of four daughters and two sons: Mrs. Eliza (Nicholas C.) Taylor, Mrs. Mattie (Captain William) Duke, Mrs. Sallie (Richard) Duke, and Mrs. Susan Lamar (Henry) Stevens, and Ignatius Pigman Statler and Reverend Learner Blackman Statler.

V

FIRST COURTS AND COURTHOUSE

By an Act of the General Assembly approved on the seventeenth day of December, 1798, and amended by a supplementary act [a Resolution] passed on the nineteenth day of December, 1799, it was enacted that all that part of Hardin County, "Beginning on the Ohio River at the mouth of Blackford's Creek, running thence up the same to the head of the southeast fork that heads opposite the head of Harris's Fork of Rock Lick Creek, thence across the dividing ridge to said Harris's Fork, thence down the same to Rock Lick Creek, thence down the same to Rough Creek, thence a straight line to the Flat Clay Lick on Bear Creek and down the same to Green River, and down Green River to the Ohio, and up the Ohio to the beginning shall be one distinct county" and be called Ohio County. [The Act is quoted in full in Appendix A.]

The reader will be surprised to learn that this immense territory—embracing land enough for several German principalities, and including what is now the whole of Daviess, and parts of McLean, Butler, Grayson, Breckinridge, Hancock, and Henderson—had in 1801 only 347 titheables, which number fell off to 335 in 1802, and reached only 375 in 1803. A large portion of the revenue from these must have been exhausted in paying for wolf scalps. This seems to have been a charge upon the county, and was allowed for at the rate of eight shillings each at the yearly court of claims. The records show the number for each of the following years: The year 1800, 23; 1801, 63; 1802, 12; 1803, 33; 1804, 30; and 1805, 86.

The first county court was organized on the second of July, 1799, by the following gentlemen who were commissioned by the then governor, James Garrard. They were sworn and took their seats as justices of the peace, namely: Jesse Cravens, Stephen Cleaver, Harrison Taylor, David Glenn, Robert Barnett, and Christopher Jackson; and the court was fully organized by the appointment of William Rowan, clerk, and Stephen Statler, sheriff. A copy of a synopsis of the orders made at the first term may amuse the reader:

1, A deed from Jesse Cravens to James Keal; acknowledged. 2, Releasing John Howell from paying taxes. 3, Samuel York, sworn as an attorney at law. 4, Henry Davidge, sworn as an attorney at law. 5, 6, and 7, Ignatius Pigman's, John Howell's, and Joshua

Crowe's stock marks recorded. 8, Stephen Cleaver appointed county surveyor. 9, Viewers of roads from Smith's Ferry to Hartford appointed. 10, Like order for roads from Panther Creek. 11, Like order for roads from Milligan's Ferry. 12 and 13, Alexander Barnett's and William Smith's stock marks recorded. 14, Stephen Statler moves for leave to build a mill on north fork of Muddy Creek. 15, James Baird appointed coroner. 16, Road to county line in the direction of Hardintown [Hardinsburg]. 17, Leave for Christopher Jackson to keep ordinary [tavern or inn] at his house. 18, 19, and 20, Recording stock marks of Cleaver, Statler, and Glenn. 21, Establishing seat of justice at Hartford. 22, Cleaver and Cravens appointed commissioners to contract for building jail.

From these old records it will be seen that we had a brace of lawyers ready to begin business. It may be observed also that the long continued custom of recording stock marks, for which no legal enactment has ever been found, must have dated far back into antiquity. We find a large portion of the business of the subsequent courts composed of such orders as these:

At a court of claims held in the next October, we find the following allowances—pounds, shillings, and pence then being the currency: Charles Wallace for building jail, 53 pounds and 2 shillings; John Howell for building stray pen, 4 pounds and 16 shillings; Jesse Cravens for building pillory, 7 pounds and 4 shillings; clerk of court, extra services, 4 pounds and 16 shillings; sheriff for same, 3 pounds and 12 shillings; Cornelius Westerfield, for keeping James Briant, an idiot, 10 pounds; making a total of about 84 pounds sterling.

It will be seen that there is some difference between the county claims of that day and the present. The tavern rates established in 1801 read as follows: Diet per day, 1 shilling; whiskey or brandy per half pint, 9 pence; corn and oats per gallon, 6 pence; stabling and hay per night, 6 pence.

In July, 1800, the county was laid off into three constable districts. They were the same as the three militia captain districts. Joshua Barnard was appointed constable in Captain Crowe's company; Henry Field in Captain Travis's company, and Samuel Jackson in Captain McGrady's company. In August of the same year Samuel Work was appointed clerk to fill the vacancy occasioned by the death of William Rowan, father of the distinguished jurist and statesman Honorable John Rowan.

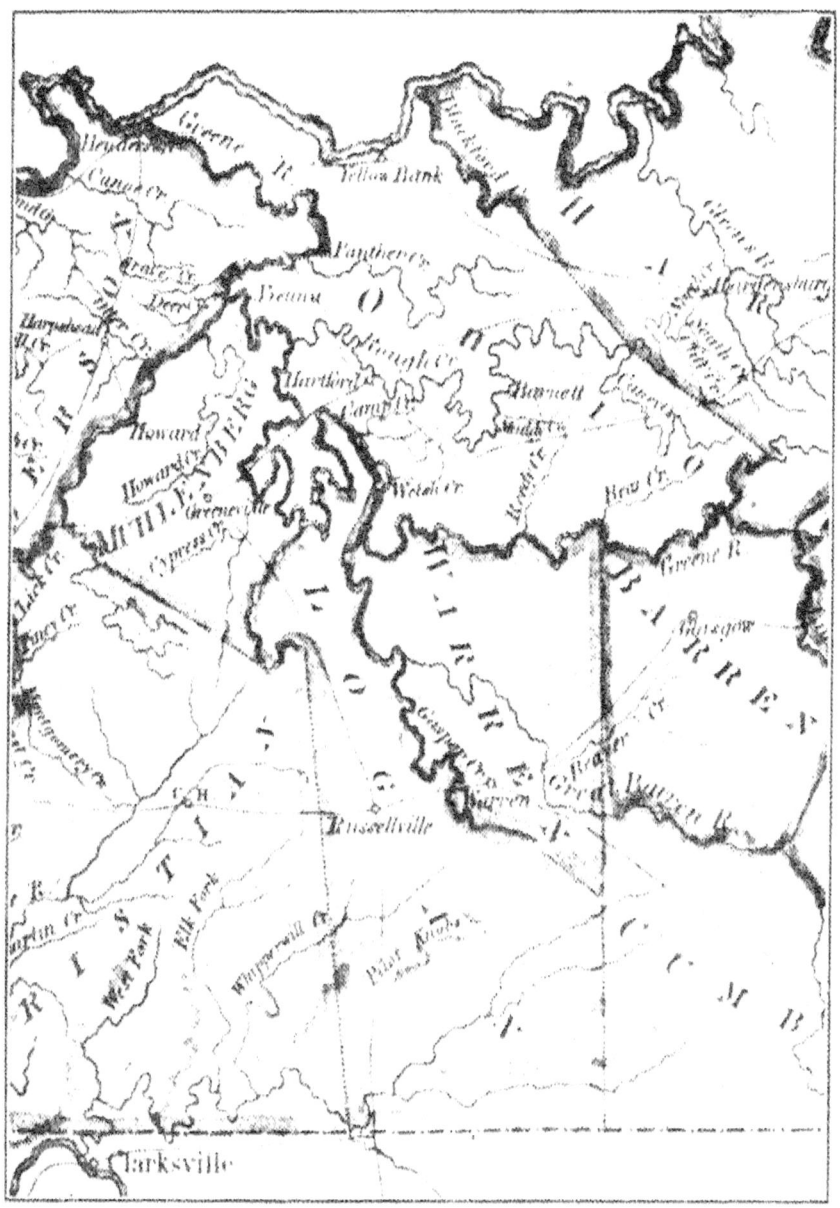

OHIO COUNTY, ABOUT 1800

This is an enlarged reproduction of a section of a map of Kentucky published in *Carey's Atlas of the World and Quarters* (1814). It is the only old map found showing the bounds of the original Ohio County. Like most early maps of a new and sparsely settled country it is inaccurate in some details, and, drawn on a small scale, does not show all important places. It represents the general outline of the county up to 1810, when Butler and Grayson were formed.

First Courts and Courthouse

The first term of court was held at the residence of Robert Moseley. In 1800 the courthouse was built. This house was a novelty in architecture. It was a log structure built on top of the jail, which was also of logs. The walls of the court room projected all around to enlarge its dimensions, and much resembled a huge balebox set on a smaller one. The jail was entered through a trap door in the floor of the court room.

An incident is related of the conduct of the prisoners there in the early days. During the session of the circuit court Judge Henry P. Broadnax—alike remarkable for his love of law and order, and his petulant, imperious temper—was presiding. He had just closed his charge to the grand jury and commenced the call of his docket when a most furious uproar was heard in the jail below. The sounds seemed to reverberate with increased force in the court room. "Silence!" called the judge. "Sheriff, keep silence!" The sheriff, in a loud, commanding tone, called to the prisoner below to be still, and the judge renewed the call of the docket, when again disturbing sounds arose. Loud shouts, songs, and hallelujahs came up from the prisoner's cell.

Then the judge sprang from his seat, took several strides across the floor, and commanded the sheriff to bring the noisy prisoner into court. The sheriff obeyed, and the prisoner greeted the judge with a most profound bow, saying in a submissive manner: "May it please your Honor, I did not think you would call my case so soon. I thought the grand jury had to find a true bill before a prisoner could be brought to trial."

"Scoundrel!" shouted the judge, "I did not have you brought up for trial, but to make you stop that infernal noise."

"Noise! Oh, I ask your Honor's pardon. Excuse me, and I will explain. You know there is a great religious excitement now prevailing in the country, and, like yourself, Judge, I am a very excitable man and I was at the time laboring under religious excitement."

"Scoundrel! Do not mock religion in my presence; I'll fine you!"

"Fine me, your Honor, but how will you collect it?"

"I will send you to prison," responded the furious judge.

"Prison, your Honor? Ain't I already in prison?"

The judge, now almost demented with rage, hesitated a moment, then, as if not knowing anything else to do, asked the sheriff to remove the "scoundrel" from the court back to prison. Before leaving the prisoner remarked:

"Judge, that jail is a very dry place. You know we all have our weak points, and mine is to become excited and noisy when dry."

The judge looked daggers, and would no doubt have adjourned court until the next term rather than comply with the hint. A friend in court—*amicus curia*, as the lawyers term it—left hastily, and returned soon, and with the sheriff descended into the prisoner's cell. Tradition says that the peace of the court was purchased at the rate of a tickler of whiskey per day.

This story, however, is a digression ahead of our history. We return to the old records of the county court. Our readers will be surprised at the immense territory sometimes assigned to surveyors of roads. One surveyor was given all the lands between Green River and Rough and Muddy creeks, with the hands living in Indian Camp to keep his road in repair. Another surveyor was given all the lands between the Ohio River and Panther Creek for a like purpose.

The first letters of administration ever granted were in February, 1804, to David Glenn, on Charles Travis's estate. It seems remarkable that nearly five years should elapse before such a thing became necessary. Was it the extraordinary health of the settlers or did the descendants have nothing to be administered on?

In 1806 an upper and a lower precinct, or place of voting, seems to have been formed. The upper place of voting was at the house of Stephen Cleaver; Thomas Gill and John Oldham were appointed judges, and Stephen Cleaver, clerk. The lower was at the house of George Ashley, with Benjamin Field and Anthony Thompson, judges, and Rev. William Downs, clerk.

The first common law court ever held in Ohio County was styled Court of Quarter Sessions, and was held on the fourth of February, 1800, by Benjamin Field, Stephen Cleaver, and Joshua Crowe, styled Justices of Quarter Sessions Court, of which Aquilla Field was appointed clerk.

The first suit in this court was Jacob Lewellin, complainant against Rachel Barnett and Joseph Barnett, son and heir of Robert Barnett, deceased. The bill is verbose and formal, but the summons in chancery is a curiosity. We give it as a sample of the legal verbiage of that day:

"The Commonwealth of Kentucky: To Rachel Barnett and Joseph Barnett [not to the Sheriff], of Ohio County, greeting:

"For certain causes offered before us in chancery, we command you and strictly enjoin you, that laying all other matters aside, and notwithstanding any other excuse, you be and appear before our

First Courts and Courthouse

said court of chancery on the first Tuesday of June next, to answer concerning those things that shall be then and there objected to you, and to do further and receive what our said court shall have considered in this behalf, and this you shall in no wise omit, under the penalty of one hundred pounds, &, &."

Now this summons seems ominous enough and broad enough for a summons to attend the final judgment day, and the poor widow and her son no doubt thought they were to be tried before this honorable court for all the sins of omission and commission of their whole lives. It seems, however, that these justices in their decisions were governed by good, strong, common sense and a love of justice. Only three of their decisions were reversed in the Court of Appeals, and those upon technicalities alone.

The Court of Quarter Sessions was superseded by a Circuit Court, for the counties of Ohio and Breckinridge. The first term was held in Hartford on the twenty-eighth day of March, 1803, by Benjamin Field and Joshua Crowe, associate judges, and Daniel Barry as clerk.

There were twenty-one grand jurors who were sworn in at this term. Their names were as follows: Massey Thomas, foreman; Jacob Lewellin, William Smothers, John Risbey, William Cooper, John Maddox, John Moseley, William Barnard, Joseph White, Josiah Hedges, Michael Myers, John Handley, David Miller, Richard Morton, William Stephens, Nathaniel Sipple, Anthony Thompson, John Powers, George Jackson, and Septimus Taylor. Out of this list of the early settlers twelve have left numerous descendants still remaining in the county, while no traces are left of the other nine or their descendants. This grand jury found only a single indictment, and that was one against Robert Price, for felony, who fled the county and was never tried.

Christopher Greenup took his seat at the June term, 1803, as circuit judge. William Fetherton and Horace Beardley were admitted attorneys of the court, but neither the records nor tradition give any further account of them, and their names are unknown to fame, at least here if not elsewhere. Judge Greenup, who presided in this court until the following April term, seems to have been an able and popular judge.

At the July term in 1804, Henry P. Broadnax took his seat as circuit judge. He was a man of many virtues, and perhaps some taults. He was high-toned, honorable, and sensible, but petulant, irascible, and imperious, and almost ungovernable in his prejudices when once excited. He was not well calculated to hold the scales and administer justice with a steady hand among a people in such a transition state as the people of this county then were.[4]

Our population was then divided into two almost distinct classes: one composed of peaceable, orderly, good citizens who were willing and anxious to sustain law and order, another of rogues and villains and rowdies who threw themselves on their reserved rights and claimed the privilege of living regardless of law. Judge Broadnax became very unpopular with this class of evil doers, and they in turn took very great pleasure in arousing his anger, and joined in every petty annoyance to provoke him and ridicule his high office. On one occasion they had his name presented to the grand jury for shooting caterpillars on the Sabbath day; yet, with an iron will, the old judge bore all this persecution, and before his removal to another circuit he had won the esteem of all of the better class of society. It was sometimes remarked that rogues could scarcely get justice at his hands, but that no man of character had a right to complain.

In the old records there were but few criminal prosecutions, but presentments for drunkenness were very numerous, and it may be inferred that our people swore like the army in Flanders, as it is recorded that on the same day several constables and one of the associate judges were fined for cursing—some their oxen and others their fellow townsmen.

---

[4] Charles Henderson was county and circuit court clerk for about forty years. He was a native of Albemarle County, Virginia. In 1808 when he was appointed clerk of the county and circuit courts he moved from Henderson to Hartford. He was the fifth county clerk and served from 1809 to 1847. The first was William Rowan, who was succeeded, in turn, by Samuel Work, Aquilla Field, and Daniel Barry. Mr. Henderson continued to live in Hartford until his death in 1871. He was blind during his last years. No man in Ohio County came in closer and more frequent contact with the citizens of his time. It is quite probable that if Mr. Taylor had added another sketch to his fragmentary history, it would have been one on Charles Henderson. In Mr. Taylor's scrap book is a clipping, about one column in length, dated and credited "Hartford, February 18, 1875: Correspondence of the Courier-Journal," and signed "Quits," the name used by Mrs. James (Kittie McElroy) Chapman. Further investigation revealed that it was published in the *Weekly Courier-Journal*, on March 3, 1875. Most of the sketch is devoted to Charles Henderson and Mrs. Elizabeth Foreman, who was a daughter of William Peyton and a sister of Dr. Samuel O. Peyton. Charles Henderson's children were: Beverly, John, James, and Thomas Henderson, and Mrs. John Gatewood (Emily A.) Nall, Mrs. Powhatan (Jeannette) Robertson, Mrs. Calvin (Elizabeth) Couch, and Miss Gabrielle Henderson.

First Courts and Courthouse

Only one or two assault and battery cases are found. Very few actions of debt occur, the declarations being generally in covenant, and the notes of the day were mostly payable in horses, cattle, salt, whiskey, skins, and the like.

Another old record is of a suit brought by Martin H. Wickliffe, then a merchant in Hartford, against William Wallace for damage resulting from his negligence to a load of cotton, and buffalo, deer, and coon skins which he had contracted to haul to the town of Lexington, Kentucky. This record shows that Lexington and Bardstown were the points to which merchants then had to ship their country produce, and from which they got their supplies of merchandise.

The majority of our early settlers were no doubt peaceable, orderly, and moral citizens, as our criminal records show. Few cases appear on docket except against overseers of roads, and against others for drunkenness, profane swearing, and occasionally a case of hog-stealing. Profane swearing seems to have been a luxury indulged in by the officers and attorneys of court and a few other individuals.

It was a common practice of persons who were in the habit of using profane language to watch the returns of the grand jury and pay up their fines in court, to save further cost. A rather pompous gentleman came into court one morning and paid his fine with quite a supercilious air, of which fact a wag, who was acting as deputy clerk, made the following record: "W. M., who was presented by the grand jury at the present term for swearing one profane oath, came into court and said he scorned to contend with the Commonwealth for the pitiful sum of five shillings, and thereupon paid his fine in court."

John Barnes in early life was a prosperous and well-to-do farmer. He was a worthy man in every respect except that he would come to town and take a long spree, for which he expected to be fined when the grand jury met. Charles Henderson, the clerk of the court, was in the habit of buying marketing from Barnes. Frequently when Henderson was in arrears in their settlement and would offer to pay up, Barnes would say: "Never mind, Uncle Charley, I'll take it out in fines next court."

The first trial for murder that appears to have occurred in the county was that of the celebrated Bill Smothers [also spelled Smithers and various other ways]. He was a man of extraordinary courage and boundless hospitality. He had a high sense of honor, but an uncontrollable passion for all kinds of fun and deviltry. A crowd hardly ever collected in those days without someone having a new story to tell about Bill Smothers's pranks.

He lived on the Ohio River near what is now Owensboro. A boat landed near his house, and some of the crew came up to it. The particulars of the difficulty are not recollected. It resulted in Smothers killing a big, overgrown ruffian. Then, making his escape from the killed man's companions, he came to Hartford and surrendered himself. The celebrated Joseph Hamilton Daveiss, alike remarkable for his legal abilities and eccentricity of character, volunteered for his friend Smothers. Perhaps no trial in the country had ever before collected so great a crowd, and no crowd was ever more completely absorbed with the incidents of any trial in our court of justice. Such a chain of logical argument, such bursts of eloquence, had never been heard before [April, 1809].

The incidents of this trial afforded gossip for the community for years afterwards. Joe Daveiss was said to have made his appearance in the county armed and equipped in complete hunter's garb, walking most of the time, with a negro boy riding his horse. He stayed all night with old Stephen Statler. Going to town to court he requested the old gentleman to accompany him through the woods and sent the boy and horse by the road to Hartford, some four miles. While in court arguing the case, instead of resorting to alcoholic stimulants he had a plate of boiled ham brought in and set by his side. In the midst of his speech he would pause, pick up a slice, and eat it with the gusto of a hunter at his camp fire.

Even at this trial Bill Smothers could not restrain his passion for fun and deviltry. Tradition has it that a young lawyer seeking a location "wrung" himself into the defense. Courtesy among lawyers required that he should be permitted to make a speech. It proved such a rigmarole of ranting and nonsensical flights that it was hard to tell whether it most amused or disgusted his hearers. Smothers saw at once how to perpetrate a joke and eradicate any unfavorable impression the speech might have made on the minds of the jury. Deliberately taking out a bright silver half-dollar and holding it up to view between his thumb and forefinger, he walked up to the young lawyer and said: "You volunteered in this case, sir, but I want to pay you for the full worth of your services. Take this." The burst

First Courts and Courthouse

of laughter—regardless of the cry for order and silence in the court—may well be imagined. The result of the trial showed that neither the young lawyer's speech nor Smothers' prank had seriously prejudiced the cause. It seems, however, that this young disciple of Blackstone came to the sage conclusion that the people of Ohio County were incapable of appreciating his transcendent abilities, and so left for parts unknown.

The acquittal of Bill Smothers was generally approved throughout the community. Even Judge Broadnax, who had been the victim of many of his pranks, was not accused of any rigorous rulings against the prisoner at the bar. Besides, it was looked upon as no more criminal to slay a drunken, lawless flatboatman of those days than to shoot a wolf or panther. In those days such characters would infest flatboats and become a nuisance to the river border.[1]

---

[1] Judge John B. Wilson, of Hartford, in a memorandum sent to the compiler of this fragmentary history, cites Order Book No. 3, page 16, for the time of the trial of William Smeathers (or Smothers): The April, 1809, term of court. No date of this trial is given in Mr. Taylor's nor in any of the other printed stories of Bill Smothers.

A fifteen-page sketch of Bill Smothers appears in *A History of Daviess County, Kentucky*, published in 1883 by the Inter-State Publishing Company of Chicago. It includes an account of this trial at Hartford and gives some details on the action of the prosecuting attorney, John Daveiss, brother of Joseph Hamilton Daveiss. Another appears in *An Illustrated Historical Atlas Map of Daviess County*, published in 1876 by Leo McDonough & Company. This Atlas contains many maps, a few biographical sketches, and a history of the county and its precincts, some of which pertains to Ohio County in the olden days.

VI

THE WAR OF 1812

Tradition has not retained any trace of the feelings or inclinations of the people of Ohio County in relation to what was called the Spanish Conspiracy, in which Judge Benjamin Sebastian and other prominent Kentuckians were accused of having been engaged during the latter part of the eighteenth century. The writer, however, has some recollections of the excitement produced in 1806 by the rumors relating to Aaron Burr's supposed rebellion or treason. If any secret organizations or cabals existed in Ohio County or any other part of Kentucky, they never made themselves known. All classes seemed open and outspoken in their denunciations of the so-called Spanish Conspiracy or the treasonable project of Aaron Burr.

The next great political excitement was the War of 1812. Ohio County then had a small portion of Federalists—a group violently opposed to all the measures of the administration. They were also bitter in their denunciation of the embargo and a declaration of war against England. This they called truckling to Napoleon and France; but when war really commenced, instead of following their brethren in the North and holding Hartford conventions and thwarting every measure of the government, they joined in the almost universal enthusiasm, and, like the immortal Blake, were for their country right or wrong. The people of Ohio County held mass meetings at which speeches were made and resolutions were adopted teeming with devotion to Kentucky and their country, no matter what the cost in self-sacrifice.

It was resolved that the people should wear nothing but homespun, and even recommended that the ladies should use thorns as a substitute for pins, and otherwise abstain from every article of English manufacture. The ladies of every neighborhood were ready to join together and knit socks and gloves and make hunting shirts and other garments for every new recruit. Certain individuals would go around and collect such articles to send off to supply their friends and other soldiers in the army. Thus, by the patriotism of the people, especially the women, Kentucky soldiers were equipped and sent to the field without a dollar's expense to the government. Few, if any, of these soldiers received a dollar of pay until after the close of the war, and then it was at the pitiful rate of eight dollars a month.

The War of 1812

The prices which the people had to pay for the actual necessities of life seemed almost fabulous. The writer, who was then the errand boy of the family, remembers paying six dollars in silver for fifty pounds of salt. It was so wet that the whole would not fill a half bushel measure, and dripped so on the horse's side that what was called "the bitter water" had to be washed off to keep it from taking off the hair of the horse. In purchasing indigo he had to put his silver in one end of the scales and get its equivalent in indigo in the other end. The few persons who could afford to pay a dollar a pound for coffee could afford to drink it only on Sunday mornings, yet, amid all these deprivations, there were no grumblings or complaints at the war; no longing for peace except on just and honorable terms.

Besides several small parties and companies who joined the cavalry expeditions into the Indian territory, Ohio County raised three companies during the war. One accompanied General Samuel Hopkins up the Wabash River, the other Governor Isaac Shelby to the Battle of the Thames, and another was under General Andrew Jackson at the Battle of New Orleans.

The company under General Hopkins, commanded by Captain Robert Barnett, was thought to be one of the most reliable and well-disciplined in the army. It was selected and prepared for critical and dangerous occasions, but never met the enemy.

So it was with the company with Governor Shelby, commanded by Captain James Tyler. His superiors in command had such confidence in his vigilance and courage that he was detailed for the important purpose of guarding a narrow neck of land forming a peninsula on which all the horses belonging to that part of the army were turned loose because transportation into Canada could not be procured. Anxious as Captain Tyler and his company were to follow the army after Proctor, they yielded to the hazardous and responsible duty assigned to them, and were not only deprived of the laurels won in the Battle of the Thames, but were entirely estopped from claiming the honor of killing Tecumseh.

The scene that occurred when Tyler's company was organized for Ohio County is still fresh in the recollection of the author of these sketches. It seemed as if the entire population of men and boys had assembled in Hartford on that occasion. After the company was made up, it was formed in line for the purpose of electing officers. It was arranged that, as each office was to be filled, the candidates

Ohio County in the Olden Days

were to step out in front of the line and march down it, each soldier following the man of his choice. The captain was the first to be elected. James Tyler, a fine looking specimen of the Kentucky hunter, dressed in hunting garb, was elected without much opposition. Then the choice of the lieutenant was announced, and Philip Thompson stepped to the front and made a speech full of wit, humor, and patriotism; but he did not get to walk to the head of the line, for several stout, brawny volunteers broke rank, reared him on their shoulders, and marched along the rank, the whole of them following with shouts of acclamation.

When Isaac Shelby's army reached The Lakes, it was necessary to leave most of the horses behind. As already stated a large peninsula afforded them range and pasture by the placing of sentinels across a narrow neck of land. It was necessary to detail men for this duty, and from the confidence that the superior officers had in Captain James Tyler's vigilance and prudence, his company was detailed for this purpose. But Lieutenant Philip Thompson was indignant at the order, and resolved to join the main army as a "high private." Jumping into a baggage transport he crossed to the Canada shore, followed the main army on foot, and was the only soldier from Ohio County who participated in the glory of the Battle of the Thames on October 5, 1813.

The company that went to New Orleans was the most unfortunate of all, unless consoled by the philosophy that

"He who fights and runs away
May live to fight another day."

The regiment to which this company belonged was landed at New Orleans on the eve of the great battle, and without arms. There were about one hundred and eighty men, of which Ohio Countians were a part. They were hastily armed with old muskets, shotguns, and other such make-believes, as would have scared only women and children, and sent across the river. There a line of battle was formed in something like the following manner: A battery of a few guns was erected near the river, and under the command of General Morgan and some Louisiana militia. A very slight breastwork had been extended at right angles from the river to a swamp. The Kentuckians were placed around this temporary breastwork. A mass of Creoles and undisciplined Louisiana troops formed the right wing of the American line in this swamp.

The War of 1812

The first object of the British command was to turn the Americans right in the swamp. This they did with ease, and then charged and took Morgan's battery and put his whole force to flight. In the meantime the Kentuckians maintained their position in the center, until it was evident they were liable to be enclosed by the enemy on each wing. Then they gave way, and Reuben Bennett—as stated in our chapter on Pioneer Families—was the last man to leave the field.

Notwithstanding the fact that General Adair with a large force of Kentuckians fought under General Jackson's own eye on this side of the river, the little band of Kentuckians on the west bank were all that the famed hero of New Orleans deigned to notice in his Report of the Battle of the Eighth of January, 1815. He therein branded them with "inglorious flight."

It is impossible to describe the emotions with which this Report was heard by the people of Ohio County when it reached Hartford. Its soldiery had never had a fair chance to display any gallantry and courage on the battlefield, although they had undergone the greatest privations and hardships; and now for them and their fellow-fighters to go down in history branded with "inglorious flight" was too bad to be borne with indifference. Old men held the paper with trembling hands, and with choked voices read the sad news—the great injustice done to the Kentucky troops in Jackson's Report.

During the War of 1812 the citizens were so patriotic they had to burn an old vacant house—and there were quite a few in Hartford then—whenever they heard of a victory.

The writer recollects the old Nathaniel Wickliffe building which stood where the Lyon House [later the Commercial Hotel] now stands. This old Wickliffe house had all disappeared except the frame of the roof, which rested on the ground, leaving the A-shaped garret intact. A celebrated victory had been reported, and this old roof was selected for a bonfire. Being very dry and combustible it was soon covered with flames. Patriotism and courage grew with the fire. Who would run through the roof? Several performed the feat successfully. The effect of the liquor on the crowd had increased in at least an equal ratio to the heat of the fire. Then old Major James Johnston, a stout, athletic man, was not to be outdone in feats of daring. He started through, stumbled and fell, rose again, and by a desperate effort got through, but terribly exhausted and singed. It is due to the old Major's memory to say that he was by no means an intemperate man. In early times—when they used the pure essence of corn, which did not make men mad and vicious, but inspired them with unbounded patriotism and benevolence—it was not uncommon for the best of men to become a little fuddled on an extraordinary occasion.

The writer does not now remember all of the victories thus celebrated. The old courthouse and jail were burned to celebrate the news of Perry's victory which had taken place on September 10, 1813. Another building was burned on the lot now occupied by Mr. Sandefer's residence, and another near what is now the home of John Thomas, but the last and most important bonfire was the old Crowe Tavern. This was quite a large building. It had been vacant for some time and was much out of repair. The Samuel, Isaac, and David Morton house then occupied the ground near by, and to all appearances would be greatly imperiled; but it was the last waste building in Hartford, and the battle at New Orleans, on the eighth of January, 1815, was too great a victory not to be celebrated by a bonfire, so the torch was applied to the vast pile, and the country was illumined for miles around.[6]

---

[6] Filson Club Publications No. 18 and No. 19 give many details pertaining to two of the battles fought during the War of 1812: No. 18, *The Battle of the Thames*, by Bennett H. Young, published in 1903, and No. 19, *The Battle of New Orleans*, by Zachary F. Smith, published in 1904. Each contains a list of Kentuckians—officers and privates—who took part in the battle described.

VII

"RALPH RINGWOOD"

Before writing of the manners and customs of our early settlers and contrasting some of them with those of the present day, we will give the story of "The Early Experiences of Ralph Ringwood"—a sketch by Washington Irving. Mr. Irving appends to this story of the Green River country the following explanation in the form of a footnote:

"Ralph Ringwood, though a fictitious name, is a real personage—the late Governor William P. Duvall of Florida. I have given some anecdotes of his early and eccentric career in, as near as I can recollect, the very words in which he related them. They certainly afford strong temptations to the embellishment of fiction; but I thought them so strikingly characteristic of the individual, and of the scenes and society into which his peculiar humors carried him, that I preferred giving them in their original simplicity."

In addition to quoting these remarks by Mr. Irving we would premise that in his sketch there are some inaccuracies in dates, names, and places, and in attributing some wrong qualities to certain individuals. For instance, he describes Bob Moseley as a great fiddler, but it is asserted by those who knew him well that he never played a fiddle in his life. Yet there were other persons answering to the character given Bob Moseley. His Bill Smithers is intended for Bill Smothers. John Miller, whom Irving also calls "Bluebeard Miller," was John Miller and is the same John Miller mentioned in our narrative of Stephen Statler as having his arm shivered by a bullet. It might be well to add that since publishing that narrative in the first issue of this fragmentary history, the writer has had an interview with his son Jacob Miller, now an old man, who says that his father was shot while on the Fork of White River, in what is now the state of Indiana, and he fully corroborated the statement as to the entire bone coming away and his still having his usual strength and use of his arm.

William P. Duvall, the "Ralph Ringwood" of Mr. Irving's narrative, was the owner of lands lying in Ohio County and frequently visited Hartford. He was a member of Congress from 1813 to 1815, residing at that time somewhere in Nelson County; and was appointed governor of Florida Territory in 1822, which office he held ten or twelve years. His visits to Hartford were perfect ovations. Crowds would gather around him, for his conversation abounded in wit, humor, and anecdotes. Some of the older citizens still recollect hearing him relate most of the incidents which are given in "The Early Experiences of Ralph Ringwood."

Upon the whole the individuals named by Mr. Irving were well-known among our early settlers, there being errors in the giving of the names of only two or three. Notwithstanding some small inaccuracies it is a very good description of early backwoods life. One of the principal scenes takes place at "Bob Mosely's own house, which was on the Pigeon Roost Fork of the Muddy, which is a branch of Rough Creek, which is a branch of Green River."[7]

[7] Mr. Taylor quotes the greater part of "The Early Experiences of Ralph Ringwood." The story is not reprinted in this volume for lack of space; furthermore, it can be found in full—about forty pages—in Washington Irving's *Wolfert's Roost and Other Papers*, or the *Sketchbook of Geoffrey Crayon*, or in some of his other books of *Sketches*. Mr. Taylor's introductory remarks are republished in full, for they will always be of interest to readers of the early history of Ohio County and of the Green River country. Besides Bob Moseley, Bill Smithers, or Bill Smothers, and John Miller mentioned by Mr. Taylor, the Green River characters, as named by Irving, in "Ralph Ringwood," are Simon Schultz, Patty and Polly Schultz, Jemmy Kiel, Bob Tarleton, Joe Taylor, Wesley Pigman, Sally Pigman, Peggy Pugh, Sukey Thomas, and Judge Broadnax. There is also an unnamed peddler.

Judge John B. Wilson, of Hartford, speaking of the location of Pigeon Roost Fork of Muddy Creek, recently said: "The stream referred to has its source just south of Rosine Tunnel and runs parallel with the railroad until it gets to Sandifur's Crossing, just below Horton, where it unites with Muddy Creek proper. From the best I can learn Old Bob Moseley's house was at or near what is now Excelsior School House which is on Muddy Creek proper and about one mile south of Pigeon Roost Fork. I have some records, also the testimony of some old citizens, that bear me out on this, but the fact that makes me feel most confident is that my grandfather Reverend George W. Jones, who lived on Muddy Creek and owned a tanyard there, often, in his talks, referred to this Pigeon Roost and Pigeon Roost Fork of Muddy Creek."

VIII

LIFE IN THE OLDEN DAYS

No "oldest inhabitant" now remembers when girls dressed in doeskins as described in "Ralph Ringwood's" tale. Our recollections reach back to the time when they mostly dressed in homespun. It was no uncommon thing to see men and boys clad in buckskin pants and hunting shirts, with moccasins to suit. This was a most convenient and excellent dress for dry weather, but a little worse than nothing when wet. It was their everyday apparel. The most respectable and well-to-do part of the community, however, was then provided with "store clothes" brought with them from old Virginia, Maryland, or other states. They were kept sacred for Sundays, weddings, and state occasions. Be it known to our present intelligent, refined, and progressive ladies, that a fine dress was a dress for life, and frequently passed for an heirloom from generation to generation, and had not to be recut or remodeled, rebuttoned, or reflowered and corded and spangled with lace, ribbons, and all the and-so-forths that now come in flaunting colors in the ladies' monthlies, which they gloat over and read with more intense devotion than they do their Bibles.

Notwithstanding the fact that the women of those days were free from the galling chains of fashionable foolery, they perhaps exclaimed: "Woman's work is never done." Many of them were the mothers of small children. They arose at break of day, milked the cows, cooked breakfast, cleaned up the house and table, spun, sewed, and knit until time to cook dinner. After dinner, without taking a fashionable sleep, they washed or worked in the garden or resumed their wheel or needle until milking or supper time. After the supperwork had been done, a mother generally sang her little ones to sleep to the cheerful, busy hum of the spinning wheel.

The reader must not infer that all our grandmothers were model housekeepers. It is the peculiar trait of some intellects to continually take hold of the wrong end of everything. By the time they get things turned right—if they ever do—they have lost much time and labor and let important matters suffer for want of attention. It requires a philosophic mind and strong will to adopt the great secret of life, which is: To have a place for everything and everything in its place. Without the application of this rule a household or farm is always a confused jumble; things are done in a hurry and are never well done.

Ohio County in the Olden Days

The men of those days were composed of the industrious, hard-working farmers and the lazy, lounging hunters, with an intermediate grade between the two.

The pioneers first waged perpetual war on the forests, adding acre after acre to their cleared lands, which, unfortunately, they wore out in a few years by injurious cultivation. The industrious farmer was not oblivious to the charms of a hunter's life. Frequently have we seen the rifle taken from its rack at early dawn, and ere breakfast the man would return with a deer or turkey, or both, to regale his family or neighbors. And when autumn came, it was no unusual thing to lay up a store of venison for the ensuing year. A fresh bear track produced as much excitement in a whole neighborhood as did the cry or alarm of Indians. The implements of husbandry fell to the ground, the gun was shouldered, and every one joined in the chase until bruin was slain, his carcass distributed, and his skin cast lots for.

Thrifty farmers soon acquired large herds of cattle, horses, and swine. They required little care save marking, handling, and gentling with salt and corn. All these did well through summer on the wild pea-vine—a good substitute for clover—and in winter they fattened on the canebrakes and mast.

The genuine hunter, owing to the abundance of game, lingered in Ohio County longer than in any other portion of the state. He was a peculiar type of *genus homo:* a squatter on people's land, paying no taxes, living in a log cabin, and with a few acres of cornland enclosed by a pole or brush fence he procured his bread. With his good rifle he threw himself on his "reserved rights," and, sitting in the shade, was "sovereign of all he surveyed"—except at times his better half. With his skins, venison hams, and wild honey he could always replenish his purse and keg. He seldom visited town except on election day, and as elections were then held for three days at a time, he was generally so dull of comprehension that it took all that time, with plenty of good feeding and treating, to make up his mind whom he should vote for. Nay, he was sometimes so overwhelmed with kindness that he could not vote, and so went his way.

The intermediate grade between the thrifty farmer and the lounging hunter was the lazy, indecisive mongrel. He was sometimes coaxed into fits of industry by an energetic wife, and then again driven into the forest by her scolding at his indolence and mismanagement. Like most persons destitute of will and energy he succeeded in nothing.

Life in the Olden Days

The officers, office-seekers, and politicians of those days may scarcely be named as forming a class as they do at the present day. As all the county officers, save the members of the legislature, were appointed by the governor or the county court and held office during good behavior, we were not annoyed with annual hordes of candidates. In those days people thought the members of the legislature were really of some utility, and consequently selected men whose characters and qualifications were considered the best in the community. Sheriffs and justices of the peace were recommended by the county court, and the commissioners by the governor. Constables and jailers were appointed by the county court alone. The different courts appointed their own clerks.

Our early settlers were by no means selfish or misanthropic. They were fond of social meetings and amusements. Visiting between families, quiltings, log-rollings, chopping-matches, cotton-pickings, corn-shuckings, and other such gatherings, including muster days, were great sources of pleasure.

The old militia muster! Every muster day was quite an affair. Company musters were held monthly from April until September. The climax of these great military affairs came off in a regimental muster in October, when all the militia of the county assembled.

It is true our tactics were not equal to those taught at West Point, but men and officers did the best they could. In the company musters especially, some ludicrous incidents would occur. One particularly is recollected. An awkward young fellow who had not studied the "discipline" was suddenly promoted to the office of captain. Muster day came. With a military strut he formed and dressed his men in line, gave the command, "Right face," setting the example of facing himself, by which he and his men got their backs to each other. Then with a loud commanding tone he gave the "Forward march." Off he stepped with the stride of a Wellington, and behold! his men marched directly from him instead of following him! This was more than his temper could withstand, and he shouted forth in a most unmilitary phrase: "Where the plague air you gwine there? Turn about and follow me."

These muster days were also recognized as a tournament in which quarrels, insults, and other wrongs were to be settled—not by the *code duello*, but by a game of fisticuffs, which game was governed by as equally fair and inflexible rules as the code of honor. If a difficulty occurred between two men, which could not be settled by friends, it was adjourned until the next muster day, when each of the parties met with their friends. Then, after the muster, the ground was selected and a ring formed, and a regular fist-fight settled it. This fight, where the parties were equally matched, would sometimes be long and bloody, but never dangerous to life or limb. No attempt at foul play or parting the combatants was allowed until one of them cried "Enough." Unfair or foul play was highly dishonorable, and the use of any weapons was branded as cowardly. Death or maiming was scarcely ever known.[8]

But the most hilarious, joyful occasions were weddings and infares. Good mothers looked upon their growing-up daughters as so many pledges of their future triumphs in their culinary and housekeeping arts. Few ladies ever passed their teens without marrying. Most young men, undeterred by the present expense of a fine lady's paraphernalia, sought a helpmate in some healthy, blooming, young girl, and generally found one.

At these weddings all the neighbors and most of the neighborhood were invited guests. Every family in reach tendered its delicacies—nicknacks—and even their personal services in contributing to the general feast. The table groaned with meats, fowls, custards, the whole family of pies, cakes, and other things to eat. The marriage ceremony was performed at early candlelight. Then the feasting commenced and continued until perfect satiety ensued. The table was then cleared and moved for plays or dancing—depending on the religious sentiments of the old folks—which continued until late bedtime, or until the small hours of the morning.

But the great excitement always came off the next day in running for the bottle. No matter how profound a secret the betrothal was considered, every youngster in the neighborhood who had a nag which had any pretentions to fleetness, would learn enough of

---

[8] A longer account of the old militia muster is given in Chapter XXII of *Lonz Powers or the Regulators*, a Romance of Kentucky, by James Weir of Owensboro, published in 1850, and now a rare volume. This account is republished in Rothert's *History of Muhlenberg County* (1913) with the following as a part of an introduction: "Up to the year 1850 every man in Kentucky considered himself a soldier, and was so considered in the eyes of the law. Until the Third Constitution was adopted, every male citizen from the age of twenty to forty-five, with a few exceptions, was on the enrolled militia and reported at a mustering place on specified dates and there took part in military drills. Such was the law old Virginia inherited from England, and it was also the law when Kentucky became a state, and remained a law until 1850."

Life in the Olden Days

the secret to put his nag in training. The program was as follows: The company met at the residence of the bride to accompany the happy pair to the infare. The cavalcade proceeded to within one or two miles of their destination where they came to a halt. All who wished to join in the race repaired to the front, and when they answered themselves ready, the signal was given, and away they dashed, helter skelter. But the race was not always to the swift. When there was a large bend or crook in the road, perhaps the very hindermost would take advantage of his woodcraft, and, by a nigh cut, be the first to reach the door of the bridegroom. At this door the jolly old folks were always ready with the capacious bottle to hand it to the first arrival. He received it with shouts and yells of triumph and rode back with the utmost speed to meet the company, who received him with a general shout of applause. The bottle was handed to the bridegroom, who gallantly held it to the lips of the bride, and next imbibed himself. Then, wiping the mouth of the bottle with his coat sleeve, he passed it round the company, all of whom went through the same process. Then a brisk canter brought them to their place of destination, where the same process of feast and frolic was acted over again.

If the bridegroom was a young man of prudence and forecast, he had nothing to do after the infare was over but shoulder his axe, pick up a chunk of fire, and march with his life-partner to their new-built cabin and there try the realities of "love in a cottage," but where this preparation had not been made by the bridegroom, an eligible site was selected, there friends and neighbors collected, and the domicile was reared almost as if by enchantment. There was not much of enchantment, however, in the mud and stick chimney, clay-back and jambs, puncheon floor and table, the clapboard door, and the wooden latch with the string always hanging out.[9]

But how in the world did people manage to live in those days? The answer to this question is simple: by limiting their wants to their

---

[9] Parental consent to a marriage was usually sought. The following letter of a father's approval was sent from "Yellow Banks," now Owensboro, on October 11, 1803: "To Daniel Morrison, Esq., Bairds Town. Dear Sir: In your request of the 25th of September, I answer in the affirmative. I was always partial to your deceased father from my first acquaintance with him. That first made me partial to yourself, which friendship has become stronger and more confirmed by time and circumstances, and as a proof of it, I am willing to give you my Sallie who is far dearer to me than language can express. I hope and trust that your goodness will render her as happy as I think she deserves. * * * Yours truly, Ignatius Pigman."

means. The real wants of life are few and simple. Anyone in good health is able to supply these wants by his own labors. When the law of our nature is violated, our wants soon overwhelm us. When a man begins to extend his wants to gin, mint-slings, broadcloths, fast horses, and fine turnouts, he has entered the whirlpool of wants that will sooner or later engulf him in ruin.

As a postscript to this chapter on life in the olden days the writer will append the old story about Peter Shown, a most remarkable and amusing character.

Among the early settlers were several German or "Dutch" families who were exemplary citizens, industrious, frugal, and neat. Their houses and farms were always a source of admiration. One of these settlers was Peter Shown. He was born and reared in Maryland, but spoke very broken English until the day of his death. He was of a slender, wiry form. He had an agreeable face, with pleasant, sparkling eyes. He was one of the best workers in his line of business in the country. He could build a post and rail or a paling fence, or a gate, that would last longer and stand more erect than any built by any other known man. Even his axe handles and ramrods were celebrated all over the county. No man could beat him making a grain cradle, or snead for a scythe, or in using it after made. He had his seasons of the year and the stages of the moon for doing everything, and would travel for miles to make his selections of timbers.

He settled on Rough Creek about three miles, in an air line, above Hartford, where he lived to a good old age. "Uncle Peter," as he was called, was a strictly honest and conscientious man, showing good sense and social judgment, but had the strangest combination of whimsical oddities of any man living. As a juror he was never known to agree with others. He could not agree about the weather or anything.

One evening when his work was done, he decided that he would go to town and have a spree to celebrate the completion of his log cabin. He had located in the county only a short while and up to that time had not been to Hartford. So that evening—with just a few inches of snow on the ground—he started for town. He knew that Hartford was on the creek and thought that all he had to do was to follow down its banks, but this was an unlucky conclusion, for besides several smaller creeks and ravines which intercepted his way the route by the meanders of Rough Creek was about nine miles.

Life in the Olden Days

The consequence was that before he reached town, night had set in, and he was serenaded by the hooting of owls and the howling of wolves. Peter went on, but becoming alarmed for his safety thought he would pray. In relating the incident afterwards he said in effect, "So I began to pray and I thought God said to me: 'Ah, Peter Shown, when you are snug and warm in your own cabin you never pray. Go your way, Shown, I will not hear you.' That made me so mad I would not pray another bit."

The owls and wolves, however, let him pass, and some time afterwards he saw a light, toward which he started in eager haste. He soon came to a tan-vat full of water, with a covering of only thin ice and snow. Into this he slipped and as he expressed it, "By sure, I thought I was going down to hell." Getting out of the difficulty the best way he could, he followed toward the light, and it led him to the tavern. After warming and drying himself he called for his supper, which, at that late hour, proved a very poor one. He next asked for a bed, which no doubt his fatigue and ducking rendered him more fit to enjoy. In the morning he called for his bill and was told that he owed two shillings and three pence. Reckoning was then still done in shillings and pence. "What is that for?" asked Shown, with an air of astonishment. "Eighteen pence for your supper and nine pence for your bed," replied the landlord. "I will not pay it," said Shown, with an indignant and determined air. Then, assuming a tone as if willing to compromise, he said: "I will tell you what I will do. I will pay you nine pence for my supper and eighteen pence for my bed."

The landlord, whose intelligence was not as accurate as some of the theologians of the present day, finally adopted Peter's views of the matter, as it became evident that a further discussion of the difference between them would not produce any practical results.

IX

JOSEPH BARNETT AND IGNATIUS PIGMAN, AND THEIR LAND TROUBLES

Among the early settlers of Ohio County were two celebrated land speculators and holders, Joseph Barnett and Ignatius Pigman. Joseph Barnett was the first of these two settlers, and being a deputy surveyor made early entries and surveys of the best portions of the lands lying in the neighborhood of Hartford. He sold a great many of these lands, only executing bonds for their conveyance. He died without making a will, leaving minors; consequently no one had power to convey. To escape from the difficulties of this situation the legislature passed an act vesting his estate in Stephen Cleaver, Harrison Taylor, and Henry Rhoads as trustees and commissioners. They were authorized to sell and convey and to settle up his estate. They went on to dispose of it pursuant to this act, but in after years, when Barnett's heirs became of age, they brought suit for and recovered most of these lands under the decision of Alney McLean, then circuit judge, who declared that the above act was unconstitutional and void. It may be here remarked that Judge McLean was an honest man, an incorruptible judge, who thought it his duty to guard well our sacred charter of rights against legislative encroachments.

The legal proceedings in these cases are a fit illustration of what a farce we make in our mode of dispensing justice of that provision of our constitution copied from the great Magna Charta of England which declares that justice shall be administered without sale, delay, or denial. Those poor men had bought and paid for these lands, and had spent the best periods of their lives in hard labor in improving them. After being kept in court term after term, spending every dollar that they could raise in paying fee bills, expenses, and law-fees, they were literally overwhelmed when the sheriff visited them to turn them out of doors, seizing most of their property to pay plaintiff's execution for cost, and yet were denied justice because they had not the means to buy it by taking their cases to the Court of Appeals. The same question arose some years afterward in an adjoining county, and the defendant, being a man of means, took the case to the Appellate Court, where the act appointing said officers was decided to be constitutional, but our sufferers were dead or had left the country, and it was too late to take an appeal in their cases.

Joseph Barnett and Ignatius Pigman

Ignatius Pigman was a Methodist preacher of widespread fame, both in Virginia and Maryland. He was an orator, a Christian gentleman, and an energetic business man. He came to this county and acquired titles to various lands, returned to Maryland and sold Kentucky lands to his neighbors and friends, and took in exchange their homes or the proceeds of their homes in Maryland. This perhaps was done in good faith, but it resulted disastrously for some who bought Kentucky lands. A good many persons had come to the county during the fall season when the low flats, or bottom lands, were most lovely to the eye of the beholder, and they bought such lands; but during the following winter and spring their lands were almost entirely submerged in water, and they abandoned them in despair. It was then thought that the value of the lands of the county was in proportion to their elevation. The whole face of the country was at that time covered with a rich, black loam-mould and a luxuriant growth of cane and peavines. Many of Pigman's emigrants, therefore, selected the most broken, hilly locations. It needed only a few years' cultivation for the rains to wash away their soil and their hopes. That fact accounted for so many abandoned farms in the county. The men owning the bottom or oldest title finally recovered most of their lands that had been sold. In the meantime Pigman became insolvent, and, with his only son, removed to New Orleans, where he died in 1815.

On a review of the whole case we may perhaps justly record Ignatius Pigman as a public benefactor. Nearly all of the early settlers he brought from Maryland were peaceable, industrious, and moral citizens. Many of them were strictly pious. The strict economy and unwearied industry which it required to live on their poor lands, or to purchase the better titles to them when lost, grew into a second nature or habit. This has been handed down from generation to generation, and we now number among our most peaceable, orderly, and prosperous citizens many of the descendants of those early Marylanders.

To attempt a true delineation of Mr. Pigman's character would be difficult. Tradition represents him censured by some and highly esteemed by others. That he stood high in the estimation of many is evident from the numerous children that were named after him, Ignatius, Ignatius P., and Pigman still being the given names of many of the men and boys of the county. On the other hand it is evident

Ohio County in the Olden Days

that many men suffered from buying lands from him to which their titles were defective, and others from buying land that proved poor and worthless. It may, however, be urged that few men in that early day were judges of the better titles, and that his own favorite son-in-law, who no doubt had choice of his lands, selected among the poorest. That Pigman was a public-spirited man is evident from the fact that at such an early day he built a cotton gin in Hartford. Upon a survey of the whole case it seems that bad luck or bad management, or both, were his only crimes. He had five daughters, all of whom married worthy men, whose descendants rank among our most respectable citizens.[10]

We will close this chapter with some anecdotes of another branch of the Pigman family. On the return of Ignatius Pigman to Maryland his nephew, a youth just verging into manhood, was so delighted with his uncle's description of the Green River country that by the time his uncle had completed his arrangements to return, young Levi Pigman had also completed his equipment to go to Kentucky. He mounted his horse and turned "Westward ho!" He was a young man of such a fine personal physique that a professed novel writer would have delighted to portray him. He was of medium height, plump, compact, erect, and yet agile, with a face beaming with intelligence and good nature. He was communicative and confiding in his manner, with, however, one slight foible: A love of high diction, preferring to talk on stilts even on ordinary occasions.

He had somehow imbibed the idea that the country to which he was bound was almost a dead level plain. One day while riding

---

[10] No printed biography of Ignatius Pigman has been found. He was born in Virginia or Maryland, and in 1777, while living in Montgomery County, Maryland, married Susannah Lamar, daughter of John Lamar. "The Minutes of the First Methodist Conference at Baltimore," a manuscript in possession of the Baltimore Historical Society, indicate that in 1782 he was "admitted as preacher," and served various churches in Virginia and Maryland until 1788. During that year, or shortly thereafter, he came to Kentucky in the interest of his church. His many land transactions, in all probability, were made primarily for the purpose of helping settle Ohio County and establish a stronghold of followers in his denomination. He failed in the land business chiefly for the same reason as many others of his time who suffered in consequence of unreliable titles. He evidently did not fail in his religious work, for tradition has it that he built one of the first churches in the county; but to what extent he succeeded is now not definitely known.

That he was highly esteemed by most of his contemporaries is inferred from the following tradition: Discouraged with his efforts in Ohio County and wishing to get into a milder climate, he moved to New Orleans about 1810. He aided

From a miniature, about 1800

IGNATIUS PIGMAN

Joseph Barnett and Ignatius Pigman

along indulging in all the hopes and fancies of his future life, as all young men will and should do, he turned to his uncle and said: "Uncle Ignatius, it would gratify me extremely if you could assign me an altitudinous eminence to erect my domicile upon." To which his uncle replied, turning his face from him: "I have no doubt that I can accommodate you, Levi." The promised land was finally reached, and Levi had his lot assigned to him—not on the other side of Jordan, but on the other side of the North Fork of Muddy Creek, it being an eminence better adapted to a windmill than to a domicile.

It does not appear that he demurred at his lot; at least he was content to seek a partner and soon found Miss Jane Taylor, fresh from old Virginia. Tradition does not say how the nuptials were celebrated, whether by an old Virginia or a backwoods wedding, or whether they ran for the bottle on their way to the infare. At any rate he and his wife were soon settled in their log-cabin domicile and had a large field ready for corn planting. After much hard labor, in which his good wife assisted him by dropping corn, the field was planted, but the labor was lost, for when the first rain came, every hill was entirely washed away, except an occasional one which was protected by stumps.

His brother-in-law John Taylor lived just over the high ridge separating the North Fork from the Pigeon Roost Fork of Muddy Creek. Levi and a neighbor, Wattie, concluded to visit Taylor one beautiful moonlight night. They had scarcely reached the summit of the ridge when they were alarmed by a bear in pursuit of them. They immediately took to trees. Levi, whether from accident or design, selected a small one, clear of limbs except near the top, while Wattie climbed one with numerous limbs and branches. Levi commenced hallowing to arouse his brother-in-law, and Wattie

---

the American soldiers—including the Ohio County boys—in their preparation for the city's defense against the English. Exposure resulted in pneumonia, of which he died. The Battle of New Orleans was fought on January 8, 1815, and two days thereafter the news that peace had been declared on December 24 preceding reached New Orleans. This same news had reached Hartford before the report of the battle. A peace celebration was in progress in Ohio County, with the Reverend Thomas Taylor as the chief orator, when the victory at New Orleans was announced to the assembled crowd. With the same messenger came the report that Ignatius Pigman had died, and the peace celebration was prolonged into a memorial meeting in his honor.

Ignatius Pigman was the father of five daughters and one son: Rhoda (Mrs. Stephen Statler), Anne (Mrs. Samuel Work), Sidney (Mrs. John Rice), Philena (Mrs. Harrison Taylor—Harrison, son of Richard), Polly (died at an advanced age unmarried), and Sallie (Mrs. Daniel Morrison), and Wesley Pigman, who, after the death of his father, made Ohio state his home.

commenced praying. Levi, being more exposed to the sight of the bear, was selected for the first victim; but the tree was too small for the bear to make good progress in climbing. He, however, got near Levi, who had taken hold of an upper limb, drawn up his feet, and before bruin was aware, kicked him with utmost force, which broke his hold, causing the bear to fall back to the ground. Being attracted by Wattie's prayers, he climbed after him. Wattie alternately appealed to Levi and heaven for aid, to which Levi each time answered, "Pray, Wattie, pray," or "Kick, Wattie, kick." The bear still made progress among the thick limbs. Wattie still appealed to heaven and Levi for help and climbed higher and higher, until the top swung from side to side. Then John Taylor and his dogs were heard near by, and the bear beat a hasty retreat.

X

EARLY LAND TITLES

The territory embracing what became Ohio County in 1798 was, no doubt, overrun and partially settled by land speculators and migratory hunters long before it became a separate county. Old records show that various entries were made in 1780, that surveys were made as early as 1782 and 1783, and that patents were issued between 1784 and 1788 for large bodies of land lying between Green and Ohio rivers. Most of these lands were obtained under settlement preemptions and Virginia land warrants, and are described as lying in Jefferson, Nelson, and Hardin counties.

Large portions of land obtained under the Virginia land warrants were located and patented in the names of wealthy Virginians at a very early period, and not being settled, or assigned, were lost sight of by subsequent locators, and, as a consequence, the whole territory was shingled over some two or three deep. The actual settlers sometimes bought their land three or four times as different claimants made their appearance. Others in despair and disgust abandoned their farms and moved to other states and territories where they could get Congress lands, the title to which was deemed indisputable.

No people, perhaps, upon the face of the earth were ever so cursed with land litigation as the people of Kentucky, all growing out of a defect in the laws of Virginia regulating the location of lands.

At the close of the Revolution the market was glutted with Virginia military grants and treasury land warrants. The rich lands of Kentucky lay open for immense land speculations, but marauding Indians were too numerous to have those lands regularly sectionized, and speculators could not wait. The Virginia legislature provided a mode of locating lands by entry. Any man or company of men could go to the surveyor's office and have entered in the surveyor's book of entry any quantity of land; the law requiring that the calls of the entry should be so specified as to give subsequent locators notice of the boundaries so entered. Had judges, lawyers, or even intelligent surveyors made these entries, perhaps a moiety might have proved good; but at that time no man was so great a fool as not to be able to make an entry of land.

The consequence was that every man who had the courage to brave the dangers or who could be hired or taken in as a partner was dispatched to the wilds of Kentucky to make land entries. These speculators, or agents, proceeded in something like the following manner. For their own protection and comfort two or more would band together and roam deep into the forest, and finding what they considered desirable land, would make a memorandum somewhat as follows, to be entered in the surveyor's book:

"John Doe enters ten thousand acres of land as follows: Beginning at a sycamore marked with the letters J. D., standing on a branch and near a deer lick, supposed to be a branch of Muddy Creek, which is a branch of Rough Creek, and to be run from said tree east and north for quantity. 7th May, 1782." "Richard Roe enters ten thousand acres of land, to lie on the east side of John Doe's entry of this date, etc., etc." In this way they would make some half dozen entries all calling to adjoin each other.

These speculators, with certificates of their entries in their pockets, returned to the settlements, awaiting more peaceful times to survey their lands and obtain patents. In the meantime subsequent locators commenced at the mouth of Muddy Creek, a well-known natural object, and made large entries covering all the lands of "Roe," "Doe," and the others.

The patents were obtained first on the latter entries, but "Doe" and others flourished their older entries to innocent, ignorant settlers. They fought, but how they fared when the younger entries—but older patents—were tested in court may be learned from various cases reported in *Hardin's Reports* and *Bibb's Reports* of the Kentucky Court of Appeals.

It seems as well a natural as a moral law that one extreme always produces another, nearly, if not quite, equal in another direction. Virginia had committed a great error, and to relieve her suffering citizens, Kentucky committed one nearly as great, and by her legislation not only violated her compact of separation with Virginia but approached the very border of injustice to non-resident land holders by the extreme measures resorted to in her limitation and occupying claimant laws, which produced conflicts between the state and Federal courts. The excitement soon wore off, and Kentucky and her suffering citizens submitted to the superior claims of law and justice. Time has almost removed the evil and given men assurances of their homes.

Early Land Titles

No portion of the State suffered more than Ohio County. Many of the best citizens left their lands and left the county. Many young men preferred seeking homes elsewhere to risking land titles here.

From all these causes, and from the continual migration of the old hunters and trappers to regions where game was more plentiful, a quarter of a century after our county was formed, we had but slightly increased our population. Everywhere over the county might be seen old, worn-out fields and dilapidated cabins, entirely abandoned. One dollar per acre was considered a good price for woodland, and most of the cleared land was so worn that it was not considered worth having. This was illustrated by the following story.

A very benevolent, kind-hearted judge, coming to our court, was passing by a solitary cabin—without any other buildings or fixtures—located in the center of a large old field, with not a rail in sight. At the door of the cabin sat a long, bony, sunburned fellow, in tow-linen shirt and trousers, barefooted and bareheaded, save the rim of an old straw hat, and about a dozen half-naked and half-starved children playing around him. The scene was too woebegone for our good judge to pass unheedingly. He had to pause and look around, evidently intending to offer commiseration at least, if not pecuniary aid. But the good fellow, feeling a little sympathy for the judge, and willing to relieve his embarrassment, cried out with the utmost sangfroid: "Judge, I reckon I ain't as dog-goned poor as you think I am, for I don't own a darn foot of this here land."

As evidence of the value of land and of the uncertainty of land titles about those times, it was a well-known fact that a note given for land could hardly ever be sold or shaved at any discount. To sue the obligor was more than likely to involve the plaintiff in a protracted contest, and the costs would probably amount to more than the note sued on, even if the plaintiff ultimately succeeded, and, if defeated, he only had to foot the bill, and like many another imprudent speculator, charge the account to his schooling expenses.[11]

---

[11] Persons interested in early land titles and names of early landowners will find valuable guides in The Filson Club Publications No. 33, published in 1925, and No. 34, published in 1926. Both were compiled by Dr. Willard Rouse Jillson: No. 33: *The Kentucky Land Grants*—a systematic Index to land grants recorded in the State Land Office at Frankfort, Kentucky, 1782 to 1924—a book of 1,844 pages; No. 34: *Old Kentucky Entries and Deeds*—a complete Index to the earliest land entries, military warrants, deeds, and wills of the Commonwealth of Kentucky.

XI

FORESTS AND FARMS

Green River is the most gentle, the deepest, and the most beautiful stream in the interior of Kentucky. In Ohio County it passes through a low, wide bottom, most of which is subject to overflow and is extremely fertile. Rough Creek is among the largest tributaries of Green River. Hartford is situated on this stream twenty-eight miles, by its meanders, from its mouth. It also has a deep, gentle current and a wide belt of bottom lands, many of which are equal in fertility to the Ohio River bottoms. Besides these two there are many small streams emptying into them. One is Panther Creek. Adjacent to all the streams of any magnitude the lands are flat or gently rolling. Ascending higher to the various grades of hilly, broken lands, we find some of them too poor and rocky for cultivation. The soil is a mixture of clay, sand, and loam with but little lime or limestone.

Coal is cropping out in almost every locality, not only in the beds of the streams but at various altitudes on the hillsides. Iron ore also is abundant, and small specimens of lead have been found, but not in any great amount. Other valuable minerals no doubt exist, but the coal, iron ore, and timber everywhere abundant are ample guarantee of the future prosperity of the county.

Perhaps no portion of Kentucky was ever covered with a more dense forest of large and valuable timber consisting of the different varieties of oak, poplar, hickory, gum, walnut, cherry, sugar maple, ash, sycamore, and beech. Some were of extraordinary size. A sycamore tree near Green River in the summer of 1836 measured forty-three feet around the base a few feet from the ground, and the body and top were proportionately large and well shaped. It looked sound and vigorous. On the same stream near the mouth of Rough Creek a wild grape vine measured three and seven-tenths feet in circumference. Another big sycamore is still standing on the farm of Mr. Warren Griffin, above Hartford, measuring sixty-three feet in circumference.

These dense forests are now beginning to be looked upon as a source of unbounded wealth. It was not so in the early settlement of the country. They were then the greatest obstruction to the farmer's progress. To cut down and clear up all the trees that stood on the ground was a herculean task. The usual mode was to "belt" or deaden all the timber save the smaller saplings, and commence cultivating before the roots were out of the way. The consequence was that but a small portion of the loose mould was plowed or brought into cultivation, and it required but a few rains to wash all the soil away if the ground was hilly, and by the time the roots and stumps were sufficiently decayed to render the land really fit for cultivation, it was worn out and worthless, or at least was then considered so. In addition to this, the dead timber left on the ground was continually falling and injuring the crops, and each spring the field required another clearing before it was ready for the plow.

It was this system of half-clearing of the lands, and wearing them out before the clearing was completed, that caused so much emigration to the prairie lands of the far west for many years. Corn was the principal crop of the county. This, when the ear had nearly matured, was stripped of the blades from the ear down, and the tops cut off immediately above the ears. These blades were cured, tied in bundles, and stacked around a pole in the field. The tops were put in shocks, and, when cured, spread as a roof over a frame of rails and poles, forming what was called the fodder-house. Convenient to this house the corn, when gathered, was hauled and thrown, and, when shucked, was hauled to the crib, and the shucks carefully packed away in the fodder-house. The blades were reserved for the horses; the shucks were carried out and scattered on the ground to the cattle, whether it was wet or dry.

A shucking was an event of next importance to a wedding, and was always well attended, especially if pretty girls were about. There generally were, notwithstanding the rules and regulations of corn shuckings, which imposed the severe penalty of a kiss upon any lady who happened to be so unlucky as to find a red ear of corn.

We cast no reflection upon the early settlers for their mode of agriculture. They had labors and difficulties under which most of us would now succumb. They had none of the present improvements in agricultural implements and practically no labor-saving machines. They had nothing but the old-fashioned bar-shear and shovel-plow, and the old-fashioned scythe and sickle. They labored and toiled as few men do in the present day. For a long time they did not have sufficient pastures and clover fields. They supposed the uplands would provide neither grass nor clover, and, therefore, they were almost entirely neglected. Most of the bottom lands were considered absolutely worthless. Hence it was that by the time a family of children was raised, the father had worn out his life and farm together, and, the children having sought homes elsewhere, the old homestead was left desolate and deserted, or it passed into the hands of strangers.

All changes in the manners and customs of society were then more the result of time, experience, and accidental discoveries than of any direct, scientific enlightenment, or teaching of philosophy. It was through the result of accident and repeated experiments that farmers found their worn and deteriorated land could be improved by clover and grass crops, and our wet and overflooded bottoms made the best of meadow lands. Large crops of tobacco yielded the most ready money, but after a series of years it was learned that if he who had devoted the time usually employed on a tobacco crop, had gone to improving his farm, increasing his meadows and pastures, and to using good stock of all kinds, he would be greatly ahead in real wealth of his neighbors—that is, the neighbors who wore out their lands and neglected their farms and stock while cultivating large crops of tobacco.

XII

THE FIRST HANGING

Francis Irvin, who was raised in the Adams Fork settlement, had become involved in a lawsuit with an old gentleman named William Maxwell in which Irvin's character and purse were involved. Maxwell gave a deposition and, after he had testified, mounted his horse to go home. That was the last seen of Maxwell alive. At a late hour in the evening his riderless horse reached the farm and whinnied for his master. The animal was found by a member of the family who at once saw that the empty saddle was covered with blood, indicating that the rider had been seriously hurt or killed.

Several days were spent in hunting the body, in which hunt Irvin joined. Being suspected of the crime he was constantly watched. It was afterwards observed that he always proposed searching in different localities from that in which the body was eventually found. It had been thrown into a slight pool or basin worn by the water of a small branch where it poured over the roots that partially obstructed the channel. It was there found covered with loose stones, logs, dirt, and leaves. A heavy fall of rain had washed away all the lighter covering, and after the high water subsided, the body was left exposed to sight.

Cowardly sneaks, although the most disposed, should never commit crime. Had Irvin been a man of iron nerve and will and boldly protested his innocence, he could never have been lawfully convicted, but his craven heart gave evidence as soon as the body was discovered. He trembled and turned pale, and although his confession might have been made under sufficient threats and persuasions to have excluded it as evidence on the trial, yet he gave facts which fastened the guilt upon him, such as telling where he had hidden Maxwell's hat and shoes and where they could find another bullet hole in the body, one which, up to then, had not been noticed.

Irvin was arrested and committed to the old log jail in Hartford. The old house was so weak that it had to be guarded at a great expense until he was removed to the Hardinsburg jail for safe-keeping.

His case lingered in court for nearly two years and at one time resulted in a hung jury. A final trial was had and the jury brought in a verdict of murder.

Joseph Allen, of Hardinsburg, had been a practitioner at the Hartford bar from perhaps the first circuit court held in the county. He was Irvin's lawyer, and was able, untiring, and devoted to his client. Great reliance was placed on the selection of juries in desperate cases. Next to the hardened villain who feared punishment himself, the mild, tender-hearted man who abhorred a murder and shrank from taking life, even by due process of law, was sought as a juryman. The panel was at last completed save one, and the defendant still had one or more peremptory challenges in reserve. Timothy Condit was called. There perhaps never lived a purer Christian or more tender-hearted man. He seldom listened to a tale of suffering or misery without tears.

Mr. Allen viewed him sternly and critically and took him without challenge, and during the trial and in his argument always aimed to excite the old man's sympathy. This he no doubt succeeded in doing, for tears were seen coursing down his cheeks during the trial, also when a verdict of guilt was announced. The able counsel for the defendant looked surprised, but no doubt still clung to the hope that Timothy Condit would "give down," so he called for a poll of the jury.

This was done by each juryman being called by name and asked whether he agreed to the verdict. Condit's name was the last on the list. When his name was called, Mr. Allen assumed a grave and solemn tone of voice, and, pausing on each word, said: "Mister Condit, do you agree to that verdict?"—with an emphasis on "you," "agree," and "verdict."

During all this time the courthouse was thronged with spectators. The interest felt seemed painfully intense. Every eye was turned on the meek, simple-hearted old man. Every ear was strained to hear his words. The good old man raised his eyes to heaven; tears trickled down his cheeks. His words were feeble, yet thrilling. Slowly he said: "In the name of the Lord, I do." A murmur of applause burst from the crowd. This was followed by a titter of laughter at an

The First Hanging

ill-natured remark by Allen about the old man and his Lord. Allen then threw down his papers and books and left the courthouse.

Judge Alney McLean, whose heart was always overflowing with human kindness, could not pass sentence with anything like due composure. He solemnly set the day of execution—May 13, 1826—but when he spoke the words "that you be hanged by the neck until you are dead, dead, dead!"—his voice became husky and almost inaudible as he wiped tears from his eyes.[12]

A hanging had never before occurred in Ohio County. Men, women, and children of every age and condition came not only from this county but also from Daviess, Breckinridge, Grayson, Butler, and Muhlenberg. Taverns, private houses in town, and even homes for miles in the country were crowded with visitors. Even the courthouse was filled over night with campers. The whole of the four acres of the public square was then unoccupied, except as a common, and was almost as green as a meadow, but the morning after the hanging it resembled a battlefield.

The erection of a gallows in the center of the town was unusual, but the reason was this: Shortly after the sentence was passed, remonstrances came in from every neighborhood to the sheriff, John Rogers, against erecting a gallows on the road they traveled to town. No man would give leave for its erection on his property. The sheriff did not wish to incur the ill will of the whole community, so, upon the advice of the county attorney, he built the scaffold in Washington Street, a short distance below the crossing of Market Street.

The night previous to the execution the poor wife of the condemned man brought him a new suit of snowwhite home-made linen and a very large twist of home-grown tobacco. Dressed in his suit

---

[12] In a subsequent article Mr. Taylor makes a correction to the effect that upon further reflection he found "the scene with Timothy Condit and Joseph Allen" took place at the first trial of Irvin and not the last. He attended all the trials and admits that "after a lapse of these many years these trials became blended together in the writer's memory."

Judge John B. Wilson, in a memorandum (1926) citing Order Book No. 7, pages 10 and 44, says that the last trial ended on Tuesday, April 4, 1826, and that the jury consisted of: George Oldham, Job Malin, Joseph D. McFarland, Ezekiel Kennedy, Cornelius Roach, Joseph Paxton, Stephen Rowan, Churchill Jones, Michael Myers, Nicholas Taylor, Allan May, and Ansel Watkins, foreman.

of white, with his big twist of tobacco protruding largely from his pantaloon pocket, he was driven to the gallows in a one-horse cart by the sheriff. He seemed determined to take the tobacco with him to another world, for, just before the rope was adjusted around his neck, he pulled out his twist, took an enormous chew, and then put the twist back in his pocket and buttoned the flap over it, apparently with anxious care.

Irvin's conduct upon the scaffold seemed to excite only pity and contempt. He showed nothing but a weak, cowardly fear of death— no courage, no stoicism to excite admiration, certainly nothing to stimulate the most depraved spectator to emulate his example. Whilst the sheriff was adjusting the cap over his face and the rope around his neck, he clung to him like a drowning man, and the sheriff had to pull from him. The cart moved suddenly away. A few convulsive struggles, a quiver of muscles, and the melon-stealing, orchard-robbing boy who had culminated into a vile murderer in middle age was no more.

XIII

SOME EARLY MERCHANTS

The first mercantile transaction of which tradition gives any account is the story of a Yankee peddler who came to Hartford with a barrel of whiskey—a story which we will retell presently. The next to come to this section was the peddler whose story is told in "Early Experiences of Ralph Ringwood." Whether "Ralph Ringwood's" peddler was a myth or not, he was at least a representative character of his trade of the day. It was to such itinerant "merchants" or peddlers as "Ringwood's" that the early pioneers looked for their few supplies. Besides, the early pioneer's means of purchasing were too scant to justify the permanent location of a store in any one special place.

Previous to Anthony Wayne's complete and decisive victory over the Indians in 1794, very few settlements were made below Elizabethtown, Kentucky, with a view of opening and cultivating farms. Forts and stations were erected in various localities; small parcels of land were cleared and cultivated by placing wary, expert riflemen as sentinels while others worked.

A few bushels of corn, with the aid of hand mills and hominy mortars, furnished their daily bread. The buffalo, elk, bear, and deer not only furnished them with an abundant supply of meat but also with bed clothes and wearing apparel. Geese, turkeys, and other wild fowls supplied them with meat more delicious than the chicken of the present day. Feathers, furs, skins, tallow, and wild honey formed the basis of trade and commerce.

Tradition does not give the palm of shrewdness and cunning always to the peddler of those days, as will be illustrated by the following story of transactions involving whiskey and coonskins.

Some enterprising Yankee peddler had managed to get a barrel of whiskey into Hartford. With it he proposed to accommodate the citizens, selling a gill for a coonskin, or nine pence in silver—the principal coins in circulation under a whole dollar, being dollars cut in halves, quarters, eighths, and sixteenths. To save paying rent, he, with the aid of some poles and boards, erected a shanty around his whiskey barrel, and, with a partition in the middle, he had the front for a salesroom and the back part for a storeroom. Business was not brisk the first day; only a few old loafers, who were too infirm or too lazy to hunt, or an occasional old lady who wanted a little spirits in her camphor bottle, came to the shanty to trade.

But after dark the scene changed: Scouts, hunters, loafers, and boys gathered around the whiskey; skins were pouring in as fast as the liquor could be poured out. The scene became absolutely uproarious with fifes and drums, songs and shouts of laughter, making a medley of sounds that might have prostrated the walls of Jericho. The peddler would hand out the liquor, seize the skin, and throw it back into his storeroom with an air of triumph. He became weary of success, and felt relieved when the crowd, or as many of them as could walk, retired. Mr. Peddler slept but little and reckoned much on the gains of the night, and, as soon as it was light enough, proceeded to count his enormous pile. To his bitter disappointment and utter astonishment, the pile seemed very little larger than it had been early the evening before. On further inspection he saw that a board had been removed from the back part of his shanty. A long pole with a hook at the end told the story—all night he had been buying his own skins over and over again.

The second day his sales were as dull as the day before, and when night came on, he gathered his skins into his salesroom, watching them closely, and refused to sell for anything but cash, which came in very slowly. Towards bedtime business revived and the Yankee thought that there might be a trick—counterfeit money about—and so rubbed each piece between his fingers. He found it too hard for pewter, and smelling it found it was not copper. Not until after he had deposited it in his leather purse did he hand out the liquor. Finally he retired to rest with the consolation that if he had not done a smashing business, he had at least done a safe one. He was aroused next morning by hearing a furious voice complaining behind the shanty, and upon walking out, saw a man's cross-cut saw despoiled of every tooth! With trembling and fear he stole back into his shanty, untied his purse, and poured out his receipts; then he discovered that he had scarcely anything but saw-teeth!

To return to the subject of our early merchants, or rather to begin it: The first store in Hartford of which we have any authentic account was that of Nathaniel Wickliffe. As already related, he seems to have drawn his supplies from Bardstown, as is shown by the old records of a suit he brought against William Wallace for damage

Some Early Merchants

done to a load of furs and hides Wallace had contracted to haul from Hartford to Bardstown. It appears that the firm of Rose and Fitzhugh also had a store of some note in the early days.

I remember Samuel Rose, who was a very popular man. He was also clerk of the court for a while. Some time previous to the War of 1812 he removed to Bardstown and was a soldier under General Samuel Hopkins in his march, in 1812, up the Wabash River, where Rose and his friends Murry and Dunn and others were caught in an ambush while on a reconnoitering party. They were slain and terribly mangled by the savages. Some Ohio County friends found Rose's body, recognized it, and had it decently buried. The *Bardstown Repository* of that period was full of eulogy of the three—Rose, Murry, and Dunn—all of whom were represented as men of sterling virtues and worth.

Perhaps the next store in Hartford was that of Lewis and Rogers, a branch probably of some Bardstown house; it was not of long duration. The writer recollects on his first visit to town of spending his first three fourpence, half pennies, for a small mustard cup, being, as he thought, the prettiest thing on the almost empty shelves.

Robert Moseley, Richard Taylor, and Harrison Taylor, as partners, at an early day bought a large stock of goods—large for that period—from Colonel Criss, of Bullitt's Lick. They traded largely in country produce. This speculation resulted in great loss, especially for the Taylor partners.

During the War of 1812, Samuel, Isaac, and David Morton built a storehouse and opened a very considerable stock of goods. Near their house stood the buildings that were burned to celebrate the Battle of New Orleans, of which we have written. William and Daniel McKenzie built a house which is still a part of the Lyon House [in earlier days Crowe House, later Commercial Hotel]. In it they opened a respectable stock. They, however, sold out in a few years and moved to parts unknown. Both were well esteemed while citizens of Hartford.

Up to the close of the War of 1812 the country needed but little, and had but little to buy with. Families made their own clothing and shoes. Such hats as they could not plait of straw or make of other home-made material, they bartered for with some country hatter. Nearly every family had a shoemaker at home, or, if not, exchanged work with some country cobbler. Most of the ladies had

Ohio County in the Olden Days

a Sunday dress of fine cotton for summer and a nice barred, or checkered, linsey-woolsey for winter. The most aristocratic seldom aspired to anything above calico.

At the close of the War of 1812 a period of credit and its concomitant extravagance and fashion set in. Pork which had sold from $1.50 to $2.00 rose to $5.00; tobacco to $10.00 and $12.00. It was supposed that any man able to work would be able at the end of the year to pay for everything that had been sold to him, hence, a system of almost universal credit sprang up, and Hartford became crowded with stores. Murry and Walker, Thompson and Moseley, Richard A. Jones, and the three Mortons, all had large and respectable stores for that period. Besides these there were smaller ones not now recollected. For several years all seemed to be on the high road to fortune. The merest country bumpkin was wrapped from head to foot in broadcloth. A clodhopper would mount his burr-tailed pony, rigged out with a forty-dollar saddle and a twelve-dollar bridle.

This *ignis fatuus* with which the whole state was carried away led on to the Eldorado of a universal banking system. The legislature passed a law chartering a bank in nearly every county, and in some of them two, as in Ohio County. For this our then representative Major James Johnston was most terribly vilified and abused for a time. He was, however, later highly commended for his sound sense and good judgment, which created for him a fund of popularity which lasted for years. How this great air-bubble burst, bankrupting the community and leading to other blunders in legislation, to litigation and party excitement, would require an entire chapter to relate.

The great South Sea bubble of England was scarcely a more laughable farce than this Kentucky banking scheme proved to be. Everybody wanted bank stock. It was greedily taken. The banks organized, and their notes were put in circulation. The Battle of Waterloo had settled the peace of Europe, and the close of our war with England rendered the United States a tempting field for the

Some Early Merchants

long pent-up workshops of the world, and we were flooded and overstocked with foreign merchandise.

To vend these overstocks of goods, peddlers swarmed over the whole country. They took notes of these independent banks and made regular raids upon them until their small specie deposits were exhausted. Only two of these banks in the whole State proved solvent. The notes of the balance proved an entire loss to the country; the poor merchants were among the principal sufferers.

In the meantime our Hartford merchants had shipped the tobacco of the county at highly remunerative prices for several years. That, of course, increased its production. Skilled as well as unskilled labor everywhere was engaged in its culture, which resulted in a tremendous over-crop, much of which was of the lowest grade. This crop was eagerly bought by the merchants and shipped to New Orleans. Because of over-supply on the market prices fell to a most ruinous rate. In some cases the whole crop did not sell for enough to pay the expense of shipment, inspection, commission, and other expenses.

These heavy losses from broken banks and the low price of tobacco fell so heavily on the merchants in Hartford that every store in the town was closed, or suspended business, save that of Samuel, Isaac, and David Morton, who were the sole survivors of the panic. This firm was a striking example of the strange freaks of the fickle goddess of fortune.

The routine of merchandising in those days was to ship produce to New Orleans, sell it, buy bills of exchange on New York or Philadelphia, and then proceed on vessels to the eastern markets and there purchase goods. The year previous to the great decline in tobacco, the Mortons had been quite successful in their shipments to New Orleans. There they sold their goods and received a draft on some eastern house. They left immediately for the East to lay in a stock of merchandise, but on arriving there the house on which their draft was drawn had failed. The consequence was that the Mortons bought no goods that year. They returned to New Orleans, and got their money out of the drawer of the draft, but only after a long and tedious course of law had been followed. Thus while their means were locked up in the courts, they were no doubt fretting and fuming at their ill luck. In the meantime their fellow merchants in Hartford were chuckling at their own good fortune at having monopolized the trade, not seeing that they were greedily running into ruin and disaster.

The Mortons, chagrinned at their apparent ill luck, and fearing the ultimate loss of their suspended New Orleans debts, set about a vigorous and vigilant collection of their home accounts in Ohio County. Thus by the time the panic and pressure set in, they had collected or secured the most of their home debts, and were ready with this capital to take possession of the vanquished field. They monopolized the trade of the whole country for years afterwards; then they divided their means. Samuel Morton removed to Palmyra, Missouri, William Morton to Hardinsburg, and David Morton to Owensboro. Isaac Morton continued business in Hartford, where he had little or no opposition for a considerable period of time.

After the palmy days of the Mortons there were no large stores until one was opened by Richard Elliott, who had been the cashier of the old Commonwealth Bank of Hartford, from its commencement. [This building is now the residence of James H. Williams.] Elliott was an excellent financier of indefatigable industry, shrewd but pleasant in his manners. He proved to be the most successful merchant of his time. His health failed, however, and he died in a few years. It was a matter of doubt as to what his ultimate outcome might have been, whether he would have become a millionaire or a bankrupt, as the times were so uncertain that no one could predict. When he commenced his career, the period was a very prosperous one; property of all kinds continued to rise in value. The improvements in machinery, in manufacturing, and the great reduction in the tariff on foreign merchandise had so reduced the price of goods bought at wholesale that merchants could sell them at retail at a heavy profit, and yet have the credit of selling them "dirt cheap," as their customers thought and said. This prosperous period continued during the whole of Mr. Elliott's time of merchandising. His estate wound up with a very large surplus for his heirs, as well as a formidable list of insolvent debts which were an entire loss to his estate, although the strictest vigilance was used in making collections.

Mr. Elliott's death was much lamented by the community. He was highly esteemed as a citizen. He devoted much of his time to reading and had considerable literary taste and attainments. He was liberal and generous in his dealings. It is useless now to speculate what would have been his financial success had he lived to pass the panics and pressure of the years 1837, 1842, and 1860, which not only tried men's souls but also merchants' solvency.

During the time of and shortly after the close of Mr. Elliott's career, various other stores were started in Hartford. Among other merchants were Logan Walker, Larkin and John G. Nall, John Phipps, W. W. Phipps, and Crowe and Taylor. They carried on a long career of merchandising with varied success. None of them became millionaires, but all escaped insolvency. All have given place to others whose operations are well-known to the present generation.

XIV

SOME PIONEER FAMILIES

In examining the old county records we find many names of early citizens who are now lost sight of and have passed from the memory of the present generations. In fact, much of the early population was of a very migratory, transient character. It is amusing to look over the delinquent list returned by the sheriff in early days. "Gone to Logan County," "Gone to Nelson County," "Gone to Post Vincent," "Gone to New Orleans," "Gone to Spanish Dominion," and various other places, known and unknown, followed the names of numerous delinquents. There are many other names whose descendants still constitute the bone and sinew of our present citizens and who are perpetuating the good qualities of their ancestors. The names of many of those early pioneers are now given, also, as far as can be ascertained, the country from which they came. This is done with the hope that their descendants who may know of any interesting facts in relation to their family record will make them known so that they may appear in this fragmentary history.

The Bairds, Barnetts, Statlers, and Browns were from Pennsylvania; the Condits from New Jersey; the Crowes, Addingtons, Leaches, Ambroses, Bennetts, Griffiths, Stevenses, Millers, Phippses, and Barneses from Maryland; the Bells, Fields, Hayneses, Rowes, Renders, Mays, Thomases, Walkers, Hendersons, and Taylors from Virginia. Besides these there are many other names quite familiar, but, owing to the imperfect knowledge of the writer, the country from which they came cannot now be designated. Among them are the Mortons, McFarlands, Smiths, Handleys, Faiths, Glenns, Hustons, Maddoxes, Ashleys, Rileys, Tichenors, Showns, Rhoadses, Rowans, Shultzes, Barnards, Shanks, Moselys, Wallaces, and others.

Perhaps the Bennett family has the most numerous descendants of any of the early settlers of Ohio County. Old John Bennett, called "Governor" perhaps from his numerous family, with his sons Jeffries, John, Samuel, Reuben, Asa, Titus, Obed, and George Bennett, were among the first settlers on No Creek. The old man and most of his sons were very industrious, frugal, sober, honest farmers. The descendants of the Bennett family are now intermarried and mixed with most of our population, and, with very few exceptions, perpetuate the virtues of their ancestors.

Some Pioneer Families

During the War of 1812 Reuben Bennett was, by seniority, entitled to the office of lieutenant in the company which went to New Orleans, but when the regiment rendezvoused at Henderson, by some legerdemain of superior officers, a more pert and showy youth was placed above him. Reuben was not to be bulldozed in that way, and instead of resigning and coming home, he went south as a high private. At New Orleans his regiment happened to be among that Kentucky force that General Jackson branded with "inglorious flight," and in which the young lieutenant who had supplanted him was said to have made two-forty speed in retreat, but Reuben Bennett was the last man to leave the field, and gallantly bore off a wounded officer under the fire of the enemy.

The Presbyterian and the Methodist camp meetings were located for many years in the No Creek neighborhood, and the hospitality of the Bennett family is still fresh in the memory of many survivors of those days.

The next most numerous family is Stevens. John, William, Thomas, Richard, and Henry Stevens all settled in this county in about 1800. They had two sisters; one married John Duke and the other Higginson Belt. Richard Stevens removed West at an early period. All the others lived and died citizens of the county, sober, honest, liberal, industrious farmers. Thomas Stevens was remarkable for his portly form and beaming, benevolent countenance. He was a class leader in his church from time unknown. "Uncle Henry" Stevens and his sister Mrs. Belt are still fresh in the memory of the writer. His strong sense and his stronger will made him as firm as a rock and as obstinate as a mule. He always sought the right and when he thought he had found it, he went ahead, like Davy Crockett. Honesty, frugality, benevolence, and industry were the rules of his life, which was prolonged in unusual mental and physical vigor to an extremely old age.

The writer has but an indistinct recollection of the head of the Render family in Ohio County. As far back as his recollection extends, he sees a large, portly old gentleman [Joshua Render, Sr.] whose head was silvered over with grey, and who rode a fat horse. Joshua, George, and Robert Render were his sons and the early settlers of those once thrifty farms in the vicinity of the Render and McHenry coal mines. All were strict members of the Baptist church and industrious, honest, and peaceable members of society.

Colonel Joshua Render died at about middle age, leaving a family of children, and grandchildren, all of whom, as far as known, are doing well.

George Render, the oldest son, was a preacher, well accepted where he was known, but spent most of his time on his farm. He preached only at such suitable times as occurred, receiving no pay or salary from the churches. He was a man remarkable for his strength and melody of voice, which was pleasing and enchanting to the hearer. The following story is told of an old sister's description of one of his sermons:

"Well, Sister H., did you hear Brother Render preach last Sunday?"

"Yes indeed I did."

"Well, what for a sermon did you have?"

"Oh, a most excellent one."

"Well, what was the text?"

"Now, I don't remember the text, but it was one of the best sermons I ever heard."

"Well, what was the subject?"

"Now, I can't tell you that, but I do believe it was the best sermon I ever heard; it had such a heavenly tone to it."

George Render's children, so far as recollected, died early in life. Green and George Render, and Reverend James Austin, his only grandchildren, rank among our best citizens.

Robert Render would have been a model citizen in any community; thoroughly modest and unassuming almost to a fault, he was a man of unusual good sense and sound judgment. He was seldom passed by when a juror, road viewer, commissioner, or arbitrator was needed, for his good, practical sense and scrupulous honesty always pointed him out as the best person. He left a long line of descendants, none of whom has ever tarnished the name of so good a man.

Largely intermingled with the population of our county is the Rowe family. George, Edmund, and Robert Rowe were among the first settlers and best farmers on Walton's Creek. Industrious in their habits, honest in their dealings, social and jovial in their intercourse with others, and fond of all kinds of jokes, they never failed to have some good-humored story to tell on each other.

George Rowe was a remarkable man in various respects, possessing a splendid physique, fine, intellectual head and face, and

Some Pioneer Families

sound practical sense. He, like many of the other earliest pioneers, could neither read nor write, yet his powers of mental arithmetic or calculation were remarkable. For many years he sold the greater amount of the meats and vegetables that were bought by the citizens of Hartford. He was never known to fail in filling his engagements. Regardless of the state of the weather or of how dark the previous night, he would be in town with his marketing and ready to sell before his customers were fairly out of their beds. No matter how many different articles the purchaser might buy, Rowe, without slate or pencil, could tell to a cent the amount of the bill, and with equal facility he could perform almost any ordinary calculation involving addition, subtraction, multiplication, or division. His marketing was always equal to what he represented it. With a proper education he might have become a leader among men.

George and Edmund Rowe left large families, and a large portion of their descendants are frugal, industrious, and punctual in their dealings—and remarkable for the good quality of their marketing.

The memory of no old settler occurs more vividly to the writer than that of old Elijah Williams, living near Hartford on the south side of Muddy Creek. Mild, modest, and unassuming; never involved in any family, church, or neighborhood feuds, he and his good old lady died at a ripe old age, leaving untarnished memories. Other parents pointed out as an example to their children the quiet good order and affectionate harmony of this family of children. It was, no doubt, a misfortune to our community that all the sons, save one, died in early life; for all those sons, unless they had been unfortunate in selecting wives, might have reared equally respectable families. The only surviving son, Mr. Jerry Williams, seems to have walked in the footsteps of his father.

There is perhaps no period in social life more agreeable than the midway point between the deprivations and hardships of pioneer days and the advanced stages of wealth and fashion. Hartford and Ohio County enjoyed this midway point between the years of 1820 and 1840. The most conservative families had acquired all the comforts and conveniences of life, not knowing or caring for its luxuries and fashionable fooleries. They had means to acquire an abundance of wholesome, substantial food and neat and decent apparel. All lived and dressed and entertained as their fancy dictated. In some of the homes there was substantial mahogany furniture which was purchased by the merchants either in New Orleans or in Philadelphia. It came by river to Owensboro and in wagons to Hartford for the more well-to-do citizens. Some of their cherished possessions had been brought with them from old Virginia. The writer well remembers an "old blue schooner" wagon, brought by the Taylor family from their home near Winchester, Virginia, in which they had hauled their household goods.

During the most of the period from 1820 to 1840 there were among the principal householders: Dr. Charles McCreery, Richard Elliott, Dr. Benjamin Smith, Charles Henderson, John McHenry, William B. Charles, Reuben Bennett, Harrison Taylor, and Reverend Thomas Taylor. All were fond of social enjoyment, and always kept their doors open, or at least the latchstring out, to young and old. All these families, as well as many others in the county, were of quiet, refined habits and literary taste. All of them were of our pioneer families.

Among the resident belles were the Misses Ferguson, Henderson, McCreery, Crutcher, Shanks, and Davis, besides a great accession of frequent visitors from Daviess, Muhlenberg, and other counties.

Among the single men and youths and widowers in Hartford at that time, 1820 to 1840, were William M. Davis, Dillis Dyer, Samuel O. Peyton, John M. Austin, Ben Duncan, James Smith, Joshua Ferguson, Martin D. McHenry, and Harold McCreery. All of these I have mentioned were endowed with a high degree of social, intellectual, and moral virtues, and were of pioneer parentage.

One or more social parties occurred every week at different private homes. The heads of the families justly believed that their company preferred "brains to bacon" and put themselves to no further trouble than that of furnishing houseroom, fuel, and light. They joined with a zest in the social intercourse and amusement, which consisted in discussing the news and literature of the day, telling jokes and anecdotes, singing songs, and—*sub rosa*—occasional love making. The writer cannot recall to mind a single incident that marred the social intercourse of those days of "auld lang syne." This happiness grew mainly out of the fact that the miss in her calico felt as well dressed as the madam in her silks; and the boy in homespun never thought of casting a glance of envy at the broadcloth of the gentleman.

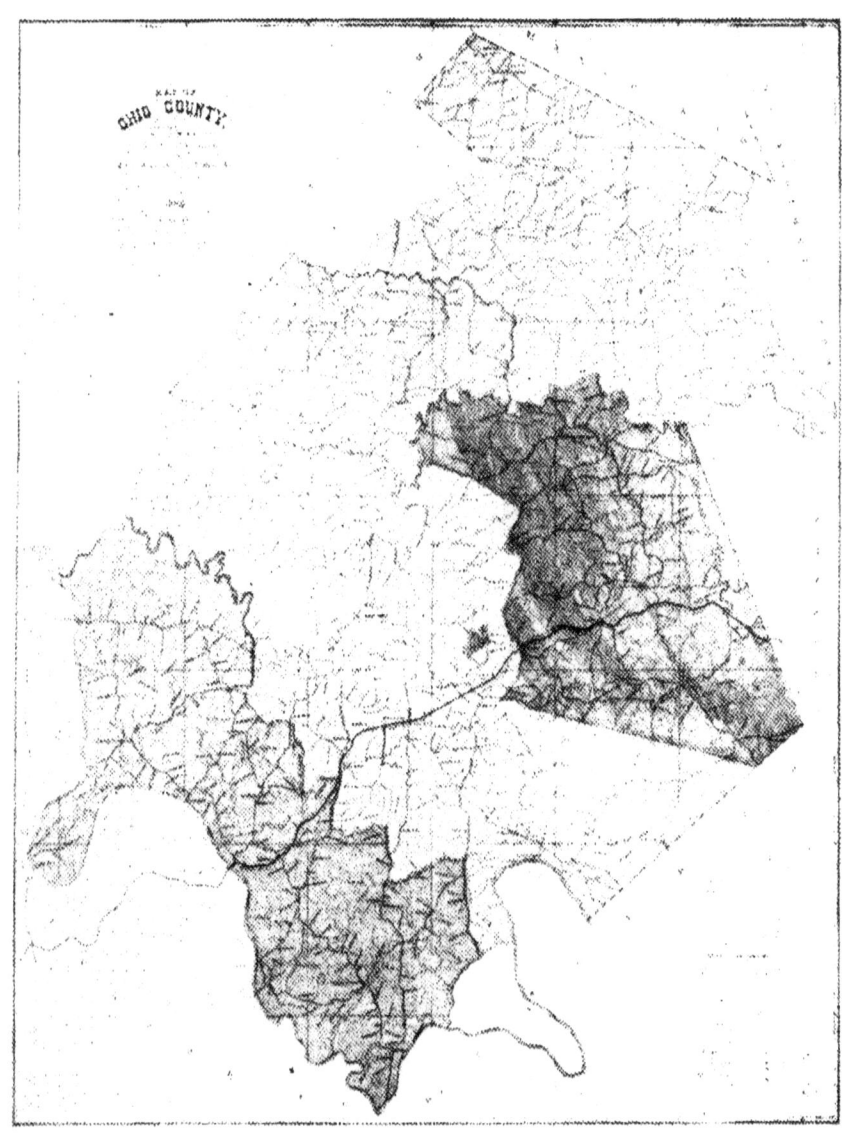

OHIO COUNTY, 1886

Reduced from a copy, thirty by thirty-six inches, entitled "Map of Ohio County, Kentucky, Surveyed and Drawn by J. F. McAdoo, C. E., and J. J. McHenry, Assistant. Scale: One mile to one inch. 1886. Jno. J. McHenry, Publisher, Hartford, Kentucky." In the lower righthand corner is a table giving "Statistics of Ohio County, 1885," and "Distances from Hartford." The six precincts are shown in colors. The original presents many details. The chief purpose of this miniature is to serve as a memorandum of the existence of the original. See footnote, page 120.

XV

RELIGION OF THE PIONEERS

It is probable that religion was at a tolerably low ebb in our early history—at least those aggressive, doctrinal discussions of the present day. There was, no doubt, a strong undercurrent of true piety and religious sentiment in the minds and feelings of the early settlers. The murders which occurred near Barnett's Station, of which an account is given under Indian Depredations, were committed on a party returning from meeting. Old ladies have been heard to boast of their feat of walking from Hartford to a log house near the site of the present Beaver Dam Baptist Church, a distance of five miles, to attend night meetings.

At a very early day a quondam Episcopalian or Church of England minister found his way to Hartford. Aquilla Field, an old invalid bachelor who was subject to most severe attacks of phthisic, but nevertheless, was a firm believer in good luck, had acquired the name of "Luck's All" from his frequent application of the phrase. He was reported to be at death's door. Our good minister, who had been indulging rather freely, as he was disposed to do, thought it his duty to visit Mr. Field and administer the consolation of religion. Straightway he repaired to the house and found him apparently on the very verge of the grave. No time was to be lost. Our minister with but a few preliminary remarks proceeded to inform the old gentleman that his end was near. Uncle Aquilla gasped forth: "Lu-lu-luck's all." This callous reply was like a wet blanket on the minister's religious zeal, and he immediately rose from his knees and affirmed with an oath, rugged for a preacher, that the man would die.

Benjamin Talbott was among the first Baptist preachers to organize regular Baptist churches in Ohio County. At that time he was first a resident of Logan then of Butler County. Beaver Dam and Walton Creek were the two most prominent and flourishing churches. The Ashleys, Mortons, Popes, Tichenors, and Rowes were the most zealous and active members and worshipers at Walton Creek, and the Athertons, Colemans, and Renders at the Beaver Dam Church.

George Render was a good, pious old preacher, confining his sphere of action mostly to his own neighborhood, and relying upon his own labors on his farm for his support—and was very successful.

Thomas Downs was another early Baptist preacher. The field of his labors was mostly in the section now included in McLean and Daviess counties, and consequently comparatively little is known here of his work. His brother William Downs was likewise a preacher of considerable ability, especially in controversial debate. He lived for many years in Hardin and Nelson counties, where he was said to have waged war to the knife with the Catholics.

Although there were several Methodist preachers, it seems that no itinerant formed a circuit of regular preaching until about the year 1804. The first camp meeting was held near the present Paradise Road, between the old Phipps and Johnston farms. The second was in what is known as the Milton Taylor Meadow, the land being covered then with spreading maple trees. The place was also used as a maple sugar camp by the Taylor family.

Camp meetings for a number of years afterward were held alternately at Bethel, No Creek, and Anthony Thompson's, and at points on the Ohio River. It will still astonish the preachers of the present day to learn that Hartford Circuit included a part of Muhlenberg, McLean, Butler, Grayson, Breckinridge, and Hancock, and all of Ohio and Daviess counties. It took four weeks to go around it, yet the people attended the regular appointments with utmost confidence that the preacher would be there, regardless of the weather. They were seldom disappointed.

That old veteran pioneer of Methodism, Jesse Walker, was the first circuit rider. Cold, hunger, fatigue, and danger were only incentives to further zeal and industry. The humble log cabin and the forest wilds were his favorite temples of worship and the glad tidings of salvation his constant theme.

That great ornament to the Christian religion, to his church, and to human nature, was the first presiding elder, William McKendrick. Among the first classes, or societies as they were called, which were formed in this circuit were those at Goshen, Bethel, No Creek, Thompson's, Duncan's, and Lewis's. Besides the laborious traveling preachers there was quite an array of zealous local preachers, among whom were Otho Williams, Daniel and John Pinkston, Lodewick Davis, John James, and Thomas Taylor. Several of these names are worthy of more than a mere mention.

For many years the Methodists and Baptists were the only churches of any note. Some time afterwards the Cumberland

Religion of the Pioneers

Presbyterians made their appearance, and were backed by preachers of most decided talents and energy. Among those who accepted this faith were the Barnetts, Chapmans, Harrises, and Hunters. Old Mr. Chapman was a model for a Christian and for that noblest work of God, an honest man.

One act of Mr. Chapman's worthy to pass down the "tide of time" was this: His negro man killed the negro man of his neighbor. The slave was tried, condemned, and executed for the crime. As our laws then stood, Chapman was entitled to, and drew from the state treasury, the full value of the executed slave. No sooner had he received this money than he mounted his horse, rode to his neighbor's house, and counted out to him one-half of the money. It is needless to comment on this noble act; it speaks for itself.

A great peculiarity, or rather mystery, called the "jerks" attended a great revival of religion in those early days. Many persons would be seized with an involuntary jerking and nervous or muscular excitement, throwing their hands and limbs in every direction with the utmost rapidity and force. Tradition says that women would spring to their feet and in an instant every fastening of their hair would be thrown from their heads; the jerking of the long tresses because of the rapid motion of their heads would result in a sound that much resembled the cracking of whips. Men would spring to their feet and plunge over benches and any other obstructions around the campground. They would seize upon trees or saplings, apparently endeavoring to hold themselves steady, but all the time were convulsed in every limb. Their countenances, so far from indicating that pleasing, hopeful enthusiasm which is indicated in extreme religious excitement, rather betrayed pain and suffering, if not horror. This excitement usually continued until the person sank in apparent exhaustion. The subjects of this peculiar agitation always professed that the whole thing was involuntary and beyond their power of resistance.

The whole subject of the "jerks" was the source of much annoyance. It caused much speculation among the more sedate and pious members and the clergy. Some members whose piety seemed beyond question were affected in this way; their actions seemed almost supernatural. If it were mere pretense, it far exceeded any acting that had ever been performed on the stage. The whole thing was permitted to take its course, with approval and condemnation, and finally died away an unexplained mystery.

The preachers and church members of the early times would suffer nothing by a comparison with those of the present day. It is true that they, too, were human beings and that it is humanity's fate to err. Some who were affected by the "jerks" fell by the way, but backwoods life, untrammeled by the follies of fashion and the allurements of wealth, had a natural tendency to give strength, vigor, and originality of thought to the intellect, and force and simplicity to language.

In the present day we hear from the pulpit much learning, much metaphysical display, and great historical research, but seldom see a congregation moved to tears. Our old-fashioned preachers preached the gospel in all its native purity and simplicity. They had no theatrical swagger and no reaching after high sounding, euphonious words. They poured forth ideas truly original and sublime in good old-fashioned Saxon phrases. We even now remember the very looks and the features of the old "brothers" and "sisters" at the church, who in their clean, neat homespun filled their seats at church as regularly as their preacher filled his appointment. We also recall their faces shining with pious devotion, which was not left at the church, but accompanied them to their homes, where they lived peaceable and orderly lives and died as only Christians can die. From such recollections even an infidel might exclaim: "Let me die the death of the righteous, and let my end be like his."[13]

---

[13] More or less detail of the early history of Methodism in Ohio County is given in *The History of Methodism in Kentucky*, by the Reverend Albion H. Redford, published in 1868, in three volumes. Chapter XIV in Volume I is entitled "From the Conference of 1803 to the Conference of 1808." In it Reverend H. C. McQuown and Harrison D. Taylor, of Hartford, are quoted—also cited as authorities for some of the local church history.

In a thirty-two-page pamphlet entitled "Local Preachers in Old Times in Kentucky," by Lucius P. Little—an address delivered in 1904 before the Louisville Annual Conference of the M. E. Church, South—sketches are given of eight pioneer preachers whose field lay in Ohio County and in what later became Daviess and McLean counties. Harrison D. Taylor is quoted in the biography of Anthony Thompson. The subjects are: Anthony Thompson, John Pinkston, Joseph Miller, Joseph L. Gregory, R. Thomas Stevens, Diocles Whitescarver, and Hiram Killam, also Nathan Bordley (colored).

XVI

OLD-TIME SCHOOLS

The educational record of the early days is very obscure. The first school teacher of which tradition speaks was James Shanks grandfather of Colonel Quintus C. Shanks. He was a well-educated man for that day and much esteemed as a teacher and disciplinarian.

The noted Robert Moseley, who was among the first urchins that bathed in Rough Creek and played "hide and seek" behind the stumps and logs in the then new town of Hartford, used to tell a story that illustrated his teacher's discipline. He—James Shanks—enjoined it upon his pupils to say their prayers night and morning, and punished them if they did not. This school teacher boarded at Moseley's father's. One night Bob Moseley fell asleep, before bedtime and before saying his prayers, as boys sometimes do, especially when they have to sit still and listen to their elders talk about affairs which they are too young to understand. At prayer time it was difficult to arouse him. Someone got him on his feet, and in this half-sleeping and half-waking state told him he must say his prayers. But Bob, still half asleep, swore with an oath that he would do no such thing. He looked around and there stood the school master. At the sight of him Bob fell on his knees and prayed like he was at a camp meeting. Colonel Shanks explained this feature of his grandfather's discipline by saying that it was only in compliance with the wishes of his employers that his grandfather thus taught his pupils, for he, like his own son and grandson, was a staunch unbeliever in religion.

At an early period the legislature passed an act incorporating the Hartford Academy and granted it several thousand acres of land. These lands were trusted to a surveyor to locate on shares, and, it was said, he had no difficulty in finding good salable lands on which to locate his own share. Tradition also says that he could find no place vacant except in the swamps of Cypress Creek on which to locate the Academy's share. That the grounds were so located is true. It is likewise true that the early trustees of the Hartford Academy paid no attention to their portion of the property. A new act of the legislature, passed between the years 1835 and 1840, vested the property of the Hartford Academy in the Hartford Seminary. The trustees of the latter institution procured copies of the original patents and sold those lands for a fraction of their real value, the proceeds of which aided in erecting the old brick building now called the Seminary.

Daniel Barry, a small-framed, mercurial Irishman, who, it was said, was never known to stand or sit still, was, as old records show, appointed clerk of the Ohio Circuit Court as early as 1803. He taught perhaps the largest and most popular school ever held in Hartford. Many of the most distinguished men of the state attended this school in their youth, among them Ben Hardin. Many are the stories told of pranks and frolics of the school days at Barry's, notwithstanding his most rigorous and strict discipline. He had the reputation not only of being thoroughly learned in all the branches which he professed to teach but also of having the knack of rapidly and thoroughly teaching each pupil to the full extent of his mental capacity. Nearly always on his feet, he was continually punishing or instructing or encouraging each scholar. He was the terror and the admiration of all. In after years it was thought an honor to have gone to school to Daniel Barry. It was not the good fortune, however, of the early settlers to have many such teachers as Daniel Barry. Some were cruel and inhuman in their punishment; others were lazy and careless; and others drunken and dissipated.[14]

The writer of these sketches was so unfortunate as to have for his first preceptor a fanatical, idiotic old hypochondriac. The older boys could manage him as they pleased, and procure a holiday whenever they wished by persuading him that he was very sick and looked

---

[14] A sketch of Daniel Barry appears in *Ben Hardin: His Times and Contemporaries, 1784-1852*, by Lucius P. Little, of Owensboro, published in 1887. Mr. Taylor is cited as the authority for many of the facts pertaining to Barry and to various other subjects presented by Judge Little. It may be well to call attention to the fact that shortly before Judge Little died (in December, 1918), he had almost completed his manuscript of a history he intended to call *Old Stories of Green River and Its People*. This book has not yet (1926) been published. If published, it will make available much new material bearing on the early history of Ohio County and of other sections of the Green River country.

Among the pupils of the Hartford Academy was Richard Parks Bland, who was born at Hartford in 1835, but reared in the country. He graduated from the Academy in 1854 and shortly thereafter moved to Missouri, where he practiced law. He became the father of the free silver movement and was the forerunner of William Jennings Bryan. Frank Griffin began teaching in Hartford in 1840 and was identified with its schools for many years. Ulysses T. Curran taught in Hartford for a short time until the spring of 1861. His son Charles Courtney Curran, of New York, was born in Hartford on February 13, 1861, and for many years has ranked among America's foremost artists. Among other well-known teachers at the Hartford schools were William B. Hayward, Malcolm McIntyre, and Wayland Alexander.

as pale as a corpse, upon which the good old creature would take an affectionate leave of us all and request us to meet him in heaven, as he felt sure that his end had come. Being too feeble and too cowardly to chastise the large scholars, he would, without cause, flog the little ones by way of caution to the older ones.

A severe but unjust reprimand of this kind administered to one of the youngest pupils set him so against the teacher that persuasion, bribes, and severe whippings were in vain. Nothing but actual force could ever make him enter the school again. When the parents gave way to this pupil's will, lest he would starve in the woods, he demonstrated how far the preceptor had succeeded in "teaching the young ideas how to shoot" by hanging around the schoolhouse and shooting at the old man through the crevices of the log walls with a popgun. The employment of such a teacher as this was a forcible illustration of the folly—nay, the almost criminality—of having utterly incompetent instructors. Perhaps there was not a single scholar who went any length of time to this school who ever entirely recovered from the defects of his early education.

XVII

THREE EARLY PHYSICIANS

DOCTORS CHARLES MCCREERY, BENJAMIN SMITH,
AND SAMUEL O. PEYTON[15]

There is no tradition of our having a regular doctor of medicine among the earliest settlers of the county. The people seemed to have had very little use for a professional doctor of medicine. Every neighborhood, however, had its own old lady or gentleman who was always ready, without fee or reward, to prescribe the proper compound of roots and barks for any disease. Wild ipecac tea was the principal emetic, and white walnut and may-apple pills were the usual cathartics of pioneer times. The first man, according to tradition, who was dubbed "Doctor" was a "Dutch Root Doctor" named Houseman. The first real physician was Dr. Charles McCreery.

Dr. Charles McCreery settled in Hartford as early, perhaps, as 1807 or 1808. He was a young man of fine personal appearance, of social and convivial habits, volatile in his manners, also energetic, and frequently original in his ideas and notions of matters and things. He enjoyed a very high reputation, not only as a physician, but also as a fine surgeon as well, having performed several bold—and then considered hazardous—operations many years ahead of the surgical science of the times. His practice extended into the territory that now embraces Muhlenberg, McLean, Daviess, and parts of Breckinridge, Grayson, and Butler counties.

It is a credit to his memory that he never neglected his poor patients, but visited them as readily as the rich or more influential ones. He was always revered for his kind heart and wise counsel. He was a remarkably interesting fireside companion, conversing

---

[15] The well-known Dr. John E. Pendleton belonged to a later generation of Ohio County physicians. He was born in Washington County in 1831. He came to Ohio County in 1852 and commenced the study of medicine under his uncle Dr. William J. Berry. In 1854 after receiving his degree in Louisville, he began the practice of medicine. In the fall of 1861 he organized a company at Hartford, and at its head entered the Confederate Army. He was rapidly promoted and became chief surgeon of his brigade. At the close of the Civil War he returned to Hartford and resumed his practice of medicine and surgery. He died in Hartford in 1897. A biography and sketch of Dr. Pendleton appears in *Kentucky, A History of the State*, by J. H. Battle, published in 1885. Another

logically on all matters, as well as those pertaining to his own domain of science. He was keenly alive to all wit and nonsense, but did not enjoy a practical joke upon himself.

His friend Judge John Calhoun esteemed the good doctor highly, but at the same time was ever ready to play a prank on him, as the following story will illustrate: It happened that the doctor and the judge were out together one day, and Dr. McCreery was descanting on the lack of general knowledge in the community of the principles of surgery and medicine. He stated, by way of illustration, that a man might be riding along and be thrown from his horse and have his neck dislocated, but not broken, and that the presence of an expert might save his life. Almost at this time the doctor's horse became frightened and jumped so violently that the rider was thrown full-length in the road. Calhoun, who was then young, dismounted, seized the doctor by the hair of his head before he had time to rise, placed his foot on his shoulder, and kept pulling with all his strength until the doctor fairly roared with pain. Then the expert "neck setter" helped him up and congratulated himself on having saved his friend's life. The doctor remounted and slowly rode along for several minutes, whilst Calhoun was convulsed with laughter to which he dare not give vent. Suddenly checking his horse, the doctor rose in his stirrups and with uplifted hand exclaimed: "John Calhoun, if you ever tell anyone of this affair, may I be ——" using a tremendous oath—"if I do not make it a personal matter with you." Of course Calhoun never could have kept so good a joke to himself. He told it often, but no one dared repeat it in the presence of the doctor.

Dr. McCreery died in middle age, in 1826, on August 26th. He had been to Shelbyville to bring home his eldest daughter from Mrs. Julia A. Tevis's school—Science Hill. He was taken sick and died at a house on the road between Shepherdsville and Key's Ferry on Salt River. His remains were afterwards brought to his old home for

---

sketch, with portrait, is given in the *History of the Orphan Brigade*, by Ed Porter Thompson, published in 1898.

Dr. William J. Berry, kinsman and preceptor of Dr. Pendleton, was born on January 9, 1816, in Washington County. He came to Hartford in 1838 and in the same year married Sarah M. Walker, daughter of R. L. Walker, merchant of Hartford. Dr. Berry continued a successful practice in Ohio County until his death on December 17, 1893. Mrs. Berry was born on November 8, 1822, and died on August 5, 1894. Dr. Berry served several terms in the legislature. "It is worth noting that he was the fourth physician, in the history of medicine, who successfully removed the clavicle bone from a patient," says the writer of a sketch of Dr. Berry published in 1878 in *Biographical Encyclopedia of Kentucky*.

burial. His wife, who was a daughter of Joshua Crowe, lived many years a citizen of Hartford, where she was universally beloved and esteemed. She reared a large family of children and with them removed to St. Louis. [She died in St. Louis, and her remains were brought to Hartford and placed by the side of her husband.][16]

Dr. Benjamin Smith moved to Hartford about the year 1822, from Shelbyville, Kentucky. He was a high-toned, hospitable gentleman of retiring modesty, a skillful and reliable physician, always retaining his practice in a family when once employed. He enjoyed the confidence and esteem of his many friends and acquaintances. He died during the summer of 1840.

Dr. Samuel O. Peyton was the next distinguished physician. He was a son of William Peyton and a grandson of Craven Peyton, early surveyors in Louisville and central Kentucky. He came to Hartford when a boy. He was a student of Dr. Charles McCreery, graduated at a medical school in Lexington, returned to Hartford and commenced the practice of medicine when quite a young man, and soon grew into eminence as a practicing physician. His practice

---

[16] Two pages are devoted to Dr. McCreery in *A Report on Kentucky Surgery*, by Dr. S. A. Gross, published in Louisville in 1853, and one page in *A Cyclopedia of American Medical Biography*, compiled by Dr. Howard A. Kelly, published in Philadelphia in 1912. The latter—in a sketch contributed by Dr. August Schachner of Louisville—gives a brief biography of Dr. McCreery, stating among other things that he was born in 1785 near Winchester, Kentucky, studied medicine under Dr. Goodlet of Bardstown, then moved to Hartford, where, in 1811, he married Ann Wayman Crowe. Dr. Schachner adds that Dr. McCreery's brother Robert was the father of United States Senator Thomas Clay McCreery of Daviess County, and that the Doctor's brother James was the grandfather of the Kentucky Governor and United States Senator James B. McCreary.

Both books referred to give a brief history of an operation Dr. McCreery performed in Hartford in 1813 on a boy of fourteen, named Irvin, by the excision of the clavicle, or the removal of the entire collarbone—the first known successful operation of its kind. Irvin lived in Muhlenberg County, where he died in 1849. In 1828, two years after Dr. McCreery's death, Dr. Valentine Mott of New York performed the same operation, and believing he was the first to do so, proclaimed his success to the world. When Charles Fox Wing of Greenville, Kentucky, heard of this claim, he came to the defense of his friend the late Dr. McCreery and called attention to the fact that Dr. McCreery had performed the operation successfully fifteen years before Dr. Mott, citing the case of Irvin. "Notwithstanding Dr. McCreery's large practice in Ohio and adjoining counties," continues Dr. Schachner, "he found time to deliver lectures regularly in his home to his own as well as to other students. His surgical instruments were made under his own supervision by an expert silversmith in Hartford."

for many years was laborious and lucrative. He turned his attention to farming too, and was not only a successful but also a model farmer.

Possessing all the hospitality and social qualities of the true Kentuckian—pleasant manners and fluency of speech—Dr. Peyton was soon drawn into the arena of politics and became the Democratic leader of this section of the country. With a large Whig majority in the county he was elected to the state legislature in 1835, and afterwards was elected to Congress [1847-1849, 1857-1861]. He was an acute and able debater on the stump, and, perhaps, no man in this district could mingle more successfully with the crowd or enlist more warm friends in his cause. [He died in January, 1870.]

XVIII

TEN WELL-KNOWN LAWYERS

HENRY DAVIDGE, SAMUEL WORK, JOHN DAVEISS, SAMUEL TEVIS
MOSES CUMMINS, PHILIP THOMPSON, JOHN CALHOUN,
DILLIS DYER, HENRY PIRTLE, AND JOHN H. MCHENRY

The first two resident lawyers in Hartford and Ohio County were Judge Henry Davidge and Samuel Work, both of whom, after a successful career here, moved elsewhere.

Henry Davidge, although he had the reputation, so far as manual labor was concerned, of being the laziest of men, was perhaps the most formal, painstaking draftsman of his time. He kept up all the formula of "Lincoln's Inn," leaving nothing to implication or inference, having his case always ready and well prepared for trial. He, however, left no reputation behind him as an orator or declaimer. His manner was calm, dignified, and dispassionate, quiet, retiring, and unobtrusive. His conversation in a social circle, or with a fireside friend, was deeply imbued with philosophy, morality, and religion. A junior member of the bar was heard to say that Judge Davidge came nearer being a Socrates than any other man he ever knew. He represented Ohio County in the legislature for several terms beginning about 1802. He was finally appointed to a judgeship in the upper section of the State and removed to Henry County, where he lived to an advanced age.

Samuel Work, except in moral worth and integrity, was unlike Judge Davidge in every respect. As a draftsman he was very short, condensed, and pointed. As a speaker he was fluent, impassioned, and frequently quite eloquent. As a boon companion he was jovial and hilarious, but irritable and passionate. It is related that several times he became so irritated with Davidge that he made assaults upon his person; but Davidge, being far his superior in physical strength, would catch and hold him until Work's passion subsided or friends interfered. One amusing instance particularly is related. The two were returning home from court in a neighboring county; they stopped to rest in the cool shade; a discussion sprang up in which they differed. Work became excited and finally attacked Davidge, who calmly caught him and had to hold him on the ground until Work promised to behave; this he did, for he was a man of his word, and they rode into town as if nothing had occurred. Samuel Work finally moved to Bowling Green, where, for a long time, he stood at the head of the bar.

John Daveiss was one of the next lawyers to practice at the Hartford bar. He was a resident of Hartford for some years, and was both commonwealth and county attorney. The pleadings and other papers drawn up by him indicate good, plain, practical sense, and there is no want of the essential legal formula, although stripped of its surplus verbiage. Tradition speaks of him as a promising young man, little, if any, inferior to his celebrated brother, Joseph Hamilton Daveiss, possessing, however, some of the latter's eccentricities. The hopes entertained by his friends of a brilliant career at the bar were cut short by his marrying and retiring to a farm on the Ohio River. There he devoted his time to what in these days would be considered a most incompatible and antagonistic trio, namely: Farming, politics, and religion. It is due, however, to his memory to say that he succeeded better at all three than most men.

As a politician he was frequently elected to the state senate and legislature, before and after Daviess County was formed in 1815. He made several races for Congress, but was defeated. This was partly because of the late period at which his friends forced him "on the track" against his will, but mainly because of his manly independence in refusing to submit to the party shackles and drill so necessary to secure success in political life. Few men surpassed him as an orator or offhand debater. Modest and unassuming in his private intercourse, none would suspect, until he was aroused in public discussion, the fiery eloquence that lurked within his brain. Old Remus Griffith, an observant but eccentric character, was heard to swear, after listening to him, that "John Daveiss can get up and say things in a public speech that he had never thought of before and would never think of again." As a farmer he was hospitable, industrious, and frugal. He lived to a good old age and died in the Christian faith.

His brother, Joseph Hamilton Daveiss, was, for a period of years, a citizen of the county, residing on the Ohio River near the present city of Owensboro. Though never a resident of, he was frequently at Hartford. He seems to have been the agent and owner of most of the lands now constituting Daviess County. A suit which he prosecuted for those lands constitutes the most voluminous record now on file in our court. He also defended Bill Smothers in his celebrated trial for murder, a description of which is given in our chapter on the First Courts. To give all the traditionary stories of the eccentricities of Jo Daveiss would swell a volume. One fact, however, may be stated to show that his physical power was a full match for his mental: He spent the whole of the celebrated Cold Friday of 1805 [February 6, 1807?] in the woods surveying the big pond above Owensboro, which pond, many years afterwards, was drained, cleaned, and put in cultivation. Its first crop of corn produced a lawsuit, and at the trial the insult originated which resulted in the celebrated duel between Robert Triplett and Philip Thompson.

Samuel Tevis was one of the next lawyers to appear. He came from Shelby County, practicing here only a few years, then returning to Shelby, where he was clerk of that court for many years. While in Hartford he was looked upon as a young lawyer of promise and got a fair portion of practice.

Moses Cummins came to Hartford at an early period. Few men of his time were his superior in high intellectual endowments or moral worth, but he had one vice, and one virtue in excess, both of which stood in his path and barred his way to honor and distinction. His vice was intemperance; his virtue in excess was his most consummate modesty and want of self-reliance. Charles Henderson, who was clerk of the court for fifty years, was often heard to remark that he never knew Cummins to say or do an unwise thing in court. Phil Thompson, a competitor at the bar, said that he would as soon have Cummins draw up the pleadings in a suit as John Marshall, then the Chief Justice of the United States, yet, with all these legal and intellectual qualifications, he would resort to almost any subterfuge rather than speak in public. There are many records still in our court showing the chastity, force, and perspicuity of his intellect. Whether acting as surveyor, or commissioner of court, or attorney, every instrument of writing drawn by him is remarkable for its clearness and brevity. In society he was mild, gentle, and retiring, never assuming the lead in conversation, and always expressing his views in the fewest possible words.

A story is told of his attending a party at the home of my grandparents Harrison Taylor and his wife, old Aunt Jane, as she was familiarly called, who was remarkably social. Observing his extreme modesty and retiring manner she several times endeavored to engage him in conversation, but, meeting with such little success, exclaimed: "Well, well! They say your name is Moses, and you are a young lawyer. Have you a brother Aaron to do your talking? I think you will have to have one before you make a great lawyer of yourself." She was a shrewd observer of human character, and her prediction proved too true, for, with all his intellectual and moral worth, he never reached fame or distinction, but remained poor, gaining only a meager support by practicing law, surveying, and sometimes teaching school. It is to be regretted that he did not devote his whole time and attention to teaching, for few men excelled him in the art of conveying ideas to the pupil of meagerest capacity. Although he seldom resorted to the use of the rod, yet the continual smile playing upon his countenance and in his jet-black, sparkling eyes seemed to be foreboding disaster and punishment to the indolent and naughty boy, and approbation and love to the timid and diligent.

We have endeavored to portray Moses Cummins in his sober hours. When partially intoxicated, however, he was quite different: talkative, witty, and sarcastic, bold and daring, but never aggressive or quarrelsome unless ill-treated. He was always polite and good-natured in his most withering sarcasm, never uttering a word that would be out of place in the most polite society. In a word, his brilliant fancy, wit, and sarcasm while drinking were far more enjoyed by his best friends than his retiring, unassuming modesty while sober. His drinking was no doubt too often winked at, if not encouraged, by many who should have been better friends. He removed to Daviess County, where he resided for many years, but finally went to Texas, where he died.

Philip Thompson, the next resident lawyer at the Hartford bar, was a striking contrast to the foregoing. Thompson was by no means the superior of Cummins—not even his equal in intellect. He was of small stature and had a stammering impediment in his speech; yet by force of an indomitable will and untiring industry he rose to wealth and distinction.

He came to Hartford, when quite a youth, with his license signed. He was ever a close student and was seldom seen on the street. He soon acquired the reputation of being a safe and capable legal adviser. His devotion to his client's interest was untiring, as he was ever ready to fight to the bitter end, either intellectually or physically. Even the stammering or halting speech that sometimes occurred in his delivery he seemed to have turned to his advantage. Like the pause between the vivid lightning flash and the thunder clap, his manner of hesitating seemed but the gathering of his forces for the impassioned burst of eloquence which followed. He was remarkably acute in his judgment of human character, and during the days of early practice, when jurors were summoned indiscriminately from the crowd, he was noted for his knack in selecting men. His selection of jurors and his eloquence gave him fame as a criminal lawyer. It was not many years until he had acquired a lucrative practice.

He took an active part in the War of 1812; besides volunteering in several cavalry excursions into the Indian territory, he went with Governor Isaac Shelby's forces to Canada. He was elected to the legislature and served the session of 1815, when Daviess County was formed, and shortly afterwards moved to Owensboro. The county was named after Joseph Hamilton Daveiss and the town after Abraham Owen, both of whom fell in the Battle of Tippecanoe in November, 1811, fighting for their country. Philip Thompson was by no means an office seeker. He was elected only once to Congress, and was present when John Quincy Adams was elected president of that body.

It is the duty of the biographer to record the failings as well as the virtues of our distinguished men, in order that their failings may be shunned and their virtues followed. Although the subject of this sketch had most of the qualities that should exalt men in society, he was extremely high tempered, hasty, and excitable. When he conceived the idea that he had been insulted or injured, his temper was ungovernable. This failing led to several personal difficulties: first, the almost fatal duel between himself and Robert Triplett, and finally the encounter which resulted in his lamentable death in 1836.[17]

After the removal of Moses Cummins and Philip Thompson there was an interregnum, or vacancy, of several years in the Hartford bar. John Calhoun was the first to fill the vacancy. A few years afterwards Dillis Dyer, Henry Pirtle, and John H. McHenry became resident lawyers, and perhaps no bar in Kentucky, at that time, excelled that of Hartford in legal, moral, and social worth.

---

[17] The details of the duel between Philip Thompson and Robert Triplett are given in the *History of Daviess County*, also in Robert Triplett's autobiography entitled *Roland Trevor or The Pilot of Human Life*, published in 1853. It is now a very rare volume.

Ten Well-Known Lawyers

John Calhoun was the son of old Judge Calhoun of Daviess County. He was reared in the wilds and swamps of Green River, with most limited education, and had looked into *Blackstone* only far enough to answer such stereotyped questions as judges were in the habit of asking. He came to town, as his brother George afterwards said, "in a perfect state of nature." He was rather too prone to fall into the wild, rollicking customs of the day indulged in by too many citizens of the town, but his fine personal appearance, his pleasant address, strong common sense, clear, discriminating intellect, and personal combat during the sitting of court with old Philip Thompson, who was then looked upon as the lion at the bar, soon rendered him a popular lawyer.

It was frequently remarked that without any apparent embarrassment, or any reference to law books or legal authority, he would argue profound and intricate questions of law, relying alone upon the broad principles of natural justice and equity. His social qualities were most fascinating, and his love of fun unbounded. Of this an amusing incident is given in our sketch relating to his "setting" Dr. Charles McCreery's neck after a fall from his horse. Another story illustrative of the manners and customs of the times may amuse the reader.

There was a whole neighborhood on Caney Creek remarkable for its love of fun and frolic. Young and old delighted to "trip the light fantastic toe" on every occasion. It was Christmas time, and John Calhoun had been invited to the Caney Creek festivities. Frollicking kept up as they went from house to house for several days and nights. John Calhoun had participated until worn out. "Tired nature's sweet restorer, balmy sleep" invited him to repose in the first bed he could procure. The grand field marshal of all this fun and frolic was Old Jake, of African descent, who, with his wooden leg and fiddle was seated in a corner like

"A towzie tike, black, grim, and large;
To give them music was his charge."

Now the same human nature that abolitionists claim should bring about an amalgamation of the races induced Old Jake to seek repose also, and where he sought it we will proceed to relate. Some time in the night Calhoun's lower extremities came in contact with something too hard and cold for human flesh and blood. Half frightened, half asleep and half awake, he gave a tremendous kick which landed Old Jake on the floor. Calhoun, indignant at the insult, was about to pounce upon him, but Old Jake in an entreating voice exclaimed: "'Fore Heaven, Massa, I didn't know it was a gentleman in that bed. I thought it was Massa Frank." Master Frank had been a ringleader in all the hilarities. This made Calhoun reflect on his associations, and the result was he mounted his horse the next morning for home.

Had John Calhoun confined himself to law alone, few men in the State, although it was then shining with a galaxy of stars in the legal profession, would have surpassed him. He had every qualification except close application to study, yet what he failed to acquire by reading he seemed to absorb and gather up by his intercourse and practice at the bar.

His personal magnetism, love of excitement, and young ambition soon drew him into the great vortex of politics, in which he had a tolerable success. He was elected without much trouble to the A-B-C school of young politicians—our state legislature. Next [in 1824] he became a candidate for Congress against Dr. William S. Young of Elizabethtown. Dr. Young's location in the most populous portion of the district, and his extensive family connections gave him a decided advantage; yet he beat Calhoun by only twenty or thirty votes. This only inspired Calhoun with increased ambition. Hardinsburg being a more central point in the district than Hartford, he removed to that place. In the meantime the "Gog and Magog," the Jackson and Clay contest that convulsed not only Kentucky but the whole Union, had loomed up.

Mr. Calhoun, true to the instincts of a Kentuckian, was for the Great Commoner; the hero of New Orleans was represented by the celebrated Thomas Chilton. No man was more thoroughly ridiculed, vilified, and abused than Mr. Chilton on his first appearance on the political stage, but justice compels the admission that he was highly endowed with all the qualifications of a public speaker. He was enthusiastic and honest in his belief, as was afterwards proved by his denouncing his party and again taking the stump against the political prescriptions and vindictive partisan measures of the Administration.

Mr. Calhoun made his second race against this man, and was again defeated by only about twenty votes. In some obscure precinct the election had not been conducted in due accordance with the requirements of law. The sheriffs of the district, who then met and compared the polls, refused to count the votes of that precinct, which being excluded gave Calhoun a majority and certificate of election. In the then feverish state of public opinion Mr. Calhoun, although entitled to his seat by the strict rules of law governing elections, threw up his commission, and the governor issued a new writ of election, which took place in the month of November. Almost the whole of the political world seemed to sympathize with the election in this district. Barrels of whiskey were shipped from Louisville to most of the prominent voting places; Jackson's deeds were immortalized; "Adam's brass carpets" were wrung in every ear; Calhoun's magnanimity was lost sight of; even nature's elements, by pouring upon the earth the greatest flood that had occurred for years, could not keep the voters from the polls. They swam, they waded, seized on skiffs and canoes, built rafts, and rushed to their places of voting. The result of this excitement was another defeat for Mr. Calhoun by a very few votes.

However, Mr. Calhoun was finally successful in being elected to one or more sessions of Congress [1835-1839], which seemed to satisfy his political aspirations.

After the death of Judge Alney McLean [in December, 1841] Mr. Calhoun was appointed to succeed him as circuit judge. His sound common sense, clear and discriminating intellect, and wonderful memory of the decisions of superior courts upon similar questions, soon distinguished him as an able judge. After several years he wearied of this office and removed to Calhoun, where he engaged in milling and where he died. [He was born on April 13, 1793, and died on October 15, 1852.]

Like most men who take a prominent part in active life, Judge Calhoun had his friends and his enemies. It would have been almost impossible during the excitement of the times to have evaded having enemies. He was accused of being fickle in his friendships, and it was said that:

"He threw off his friends like a huntsman his pack,
For he knew when he wished, he could whistle them back."

Ardent and impetuous in his manner and feelings, he frequently, on the stump and at the bar, gave offense to persons professing to be his friends, but no man surpassed him in the pleasing, winning way in which he could conciliate and win them back again. Taking him altogether he was an impulsive, talented, generous, manly Kentuckian.

Ohio County in the Olden Days

Dillis Dyer came to Hartford from the North when quite young. He was small, neat, and symmetrical; correct in his dress and pleasing in his manners. He commenced the study of law and the teaching of school at the same time. He also had a practical knowledge of surveying, which rendered him a good assistant counsel in land suits, a great many of which were being presented at that time. He was public spirited and entered into various enterprises. He and John Hale owned and operated the wool-carding machine and cotton gin in Hartford, the first in this part of the country. He was also partner in a merchandising firm. Strictly honest in all his transactions, cool and deliberate, and self-poised and pleasing in his address, he was selected by the old Whig party as their standard bearer. His first race was with Henry Pirtle, during the Old and New Court questions. He was elected over Mr. Pirtle by one vote only. He afterwards ran repeatedly for the legislature as the Whig candidate, alternately beating and being beaten by William M. Davis and Elijah Crowe, the principal leaders on the other side. He was also elected to the State senate while living in Hartford and after his removal to Rumsey.

Having been appointed as one of the commissioners to superintend the building of the locks and dams on Green River, he became in possession of a part of the land on which the town of Rumsey was laid out. He moved to that place, where he continued to reside [until his death on June 27, 1858]. Few men, entire strangers, ever came to Hartford who had more warm friends than he. This is evidenced by the number of young men with the name of Dillis and Dyer attached to their names.

Henry Pirtle came to Hartford from Washington County, the home of his father, Reverend John Pirtle, where he was born in 1798. He was a student of the celebrated John Rowan. Perhaps few young men had ever more thoroughly studied and investigated the standard works which were then prescribed as constituting a student's course of studies before becoming a lawyer. His studies were not confined to law alone, for he had acquired a wonderful knowledge of general literature for one of his age. His moral habits, high sense of honor, modest deportment, and general intelligence made him a great favorite with all the better classes of this community.

He soon acquired a fair practice throughout his whole circuit. Lawyers in those days had their regular circuits, as well as the judge. Generally their circuits were the same as that of the judge of the district. The circuit of the Hartford lawyers was then composed of Muhlenberg, Hopkins, Union, Henderson, Daviess, and Breckinridge counties, in addition to their home court. No one court offered business enough to support a resident lawyer, for they stood on the dignity of their profession and never thought of practicing in a magistrate's court. The fact is that, in those times, a man would have been fooling away his money to have feed a lawyer to plead his case before an old country squire, for the squire would have come at once to the conclusion that the lawyer had been brought there to hoodwink him, and to show him his independence—for a squire was not then elected to office, and, of course, he felt independent—he would almost strain his conscience to decide against the lawyer.

Mr. Pirtle was defeated in the incipient stage of his political aspirations. This was, no doubt, fortunate for his future welfare. His first race for the legislature was against Robert Moseley, an old citizen who had lived in Hartford from his infancy and who was a man of vast popularity and influence and very respectable mental qualifications. In this race Mr. Pirtle was beaten by only about twenty votes. His next race was with Dillis Dyer, and he was again defeated, but by only one vote.

Being a man of the most delicate sensibility and of inflexible honor, and having a love of justice and right, Henry Pirtle could never have condescended to the means which are now too often resorted to to gain in an electioneering canvass. His early defeats in Ohio County were, no doubt, the cause of his removal to Louisville, where he won esteem and honor, discharged the duties of a good citizen, and filled high and honorable offices without stain.

John Hardin McHenry [Senior] was the son of Barnabas McHenry, one of the best known Methodist preachers that crossed the mountains to preach the gospel in the western wilds. John H. was raised in Washington County and studied law under his uncle Martin D. Hardin, a very distinguished lawyer of Frankfort. He first commenced the practice of law in Leitchfield, in 1819, but having been appointed commonwealth attorney for this district, he removed to Hartford shortly after Mr. Dyer and Mr. Pirtle settled here, and in a short time married Miss Hannah Davis, of Muhlenberg County. He became a prominent citizen of Hartford, living here for more than thirty years and moved to Owensboro in 1853.

As a lawyer he soon acquired the reputation of an able, safe, and reliable one. Although possessed of few of the natural gifts of an eloquent declaimer, he was a close, cogent reasoner. He was candid in his manner, seized on the strong points in a case, and urged them with logical force. He seldom failed to win the confidence of a jury, and from his thorough knowledge of law always had the respect and attention of the court. His retentive memory was also remarkable. He never took notes of the evidence in a trial, yet never garbled or misstated it or forgot or neglected to use an important fact in an argument before a jury.

As commonwealth attorney he seemed to thoroughly understand his duty; that is, to see that justice was done to the criminal as well as to the state. No laurels of victory or triumph of success could ever tempt him to urge the conviction of anyone he really believed to be innocent. In this way he acquired the confidence of jurors, and being one of the best special pleaders at the bar, his indictments were always drawn with such legal precision that they were seldom, if ever, demurred to successfully. The consequence was that the prisoners never escaped on a technical quibble; and if the evidence failed to make out reasonable grounds for guilt, a *nolle prose qui* was entered or a verdict of not guilty was found by the jury. If there were any reasonable grounds for guilt—having an honest jury—a verdict of guilty was the usual result.

An incident is recollected of a trial in which Philip Thompson was counsel for the prisoner, in the argument of which trial he had made one of his most powerful efforts, with a telling effect, to all appearances, upon the minds of the jury. It was his practice to promenade back and forth behind the railing that enclosed the bar while the opposing attorney was speaking. McHenry was making the closing speech. Step by step he took the facts in favor of the prisoner, admitted their full force and weight, but countervailed them with other facts. All this time Thompson was casting anxious glances at the jury. He saw how McHenry was winning them over, and, turning to a young friend, he almost peevishly whispered: "Damn McHenry's candor! It is playing hell with the jury."

Having been reared in the best moral and social circles, he was always aware of all the amenities due society, and was a welcome guest everywhere. He was a boon companion of his fellow members at the bar, and a very especial favorite of the younger members, to whom he was ever ready to lend a helping hand. No one could surpass him in telling anecdotes, as he never failed to remember a good one. No one could tell a story with better zest or happier effect, and he never missed telling a story when it was applicable in his speeches.

The writer remembers an amusing case in court that occurred in Owensboro. Two tailors who worked in the same shop fell out and came to blows. The goose, shears, pressing-board, tongs, and shovel had been used as weapons of warfare. Philip Triplett, a first-rate lawyer, had been employed by one of the parties to bring an action of assault and battery, and John McHenry and John Calhoun appeared for the defendant. The trial came on at a term to which a number of Ohio County citizens had been summoned—all old, grave, and sedate men by whom it was expected to prove facts that had occurred in the early settlement of the county. These old gentlemen were among the crowd that filled the court room when the trial of the tailors came off. Even the pleas were tendered with a view to fun and ridicule. Triplett foresaw this and did his best to have them ruled out; but in vain.

The evidence was heard and the argument opened—if a succession of wit, sarcasm, story, and anecdote could be called argument. It was hard to tell which surpassed, Calhoun or McHenry. The courthouse roared with laughter. The grave old gentlemen from Ohio County laughed until the tears ran down their cheeks. The judge tried, but all in vain, to preserve the dignity of the court. Triplett strained every nerve to look as if he were at a funeral; but couldn't. Like a boy in school, he had to laugh, although he knew he would be whipped for it. He rose to reply and poured out a terrible philippic against the manner of conducting trials; but all in vain. His cause, although it had some justice in it, was completely laughed out of court.

At no period of time, perhaps, did the lawyers of the Green River country ever enjoy more true, friendly intercourse than during the time John H. McHenry traveled his circuit as commonwealth's attorney. A very large proportion of the bar were men of refined manners and strict moral integrity, meeting and mingling together in friendship. A rivalry would sometimes spring up as to who could tell the best anecdotes—those north or those south of Green River. McHenry was always selected as the standard-bearer of the north side, and generally bore off the palm of victory.

One of his best traits as a lawyer was his candor in giving counsel. He told a man plainly what would be his chances of success, and would never encourage him to go to law if his cause was an unjust one. His fees were always reasonable, and he never refused to render service to anyone too poor to pay him a fee, if he thought the cause a just one. As a private citizen he was beloved and esteemed by all the better class of the community. Hospitable and obliging as a neighbor, kind and sympathetic with the sick and the afflicted, liberal almost to prodigality in public or charitable causes, he was looked up to and consulted as the leader in all measures of that character.

As a politician he, perhaps, met with better success than most men of his inflexible adherence to right. He was elected to the State legislature, to one term of Congress, and to the convention which in 1849 formed the new Constitution; all of which offices he filled with dignity and honor. His removal to Owensboro in 1853 was universally regretted by the citizens of Ohio County. At Owensboro [on November 1, 1871], after lingering for years in feeble health, life's sun set in a clear sky, leaving not a cloud or a vapor to dim the love and esteem of the many who knew him long and well.[18]

[18] This sketch of John Hardin McHenry (Senior) was rewritten and published about 1878 and appeared in the *Hartford Herald* among the chapters added to Mr. Taylor's sketches printed some twenty years before. Had his sketches included some of the men who were prominent after the olden days, he, no doubt, would have devoted a chapter to some of the children of John Hardin McHenry (Senior) and his wife Hannah Davis: Henry D., John H. (Junior), William H., W. Estill, and Lemuel S. McHenry, and Emma, wife of Dr. Josiah Hale, and Jenny, wife of Robert Craig. Sketches of Barnabas McHenry, John H. McHenry (Senior and Junior), and Henry D. McHenry appear in *Biographical Encyclopedia of Kentucky* (1878). One of John H. McHenry (Junior) in *Biographical Cyclopedia of the Commonwealth of Kentucky* (1896) contains much genealogical data on the McHenry family.

XIX

SLAVES AND SLAVERY [19]

The writer of these fragments has serious doubts as to whether he should make any allusions to the early political sentiments of Ohio County upon the slavery question. That question having been settled by the wager of battle, it seems no doubt the duty of all good citizens to use their best efforts to heal the bleeding wounds inflicted in that deadly strife. Those wounds are still kept bleeding by a few soulless, heartless fanatics of the North who seize every occasion in Congress and elsewhere, even polluting the sacred pulpit, to heap the vilest abuse on the slaveholders, a class of men whose chivalry, honor, benevolence, and humanity would have scorned to reduce their very slaves to the scant, meager subsistence to which capitalists of the North subject their wretched laborers.

The writer, therefore, thinks it not improper to place upon record the various phases of the slavery question, with its alternate ebbings and flowings in this county. From his earliest recollection he was always hearing it discussed as an evil which had been entailed upon us without our consent. But what to do with that evil was the vexed question.

Quite a number of the early settlers of this country were slaveholders and also members of the Methodist church. During a great revival it happened that both the elder and the circuit rider in charge were extremists on the slavery question. The slaveholding members were importuned and threatened with the anathemas of the church until finally most of them consented to the gradual emancipation of their slaves.

These slaves, with many others who had been emancipated by kind masters, soon became a nuisance to the community. They were despised by the owners of slaves, who accused them of making their slaves disobedient and worthless. The emancipated ones soon lost the industrious and moral habits taught them by their former owners, and sank into idle, dissipated lives, and disease and crime. Emigration to other states had so completely extirpated the whole

---

[19] This chapter and the next—Harrison D. Taylor's Autobiographical Notes—are the only historical sketches published in the *Hartford Herald* in which Mr. Taylor deals with a period later than the olden days. All the others that were printed about 1878 and added to those originally published about 1857 pertain to the days preceding the Civil War.

of them that in less than twenty years scarcely one could be found here. This experiment was quite a defeat to the emancipation doctrine, and relieved the consciences of the slaveholders by the assumption that although slavery might be wrong, yet it would be a greater wrong to turn loose on society the freed slaves.

The following is an illustration of the public sentiment between the years 1830 and 1835. About that period the writer was a member of a literary club which held regular meetings.[20] Among other things it was the rule for members to prepare essays to be read at meetings. "Is Slavery an Evil?" was a question announced for a topic at one of these meetings. Every member had an essay ready, and every member pronounced slavery a great evil to the country. It is well recollected how eloquent one young man was in pointing out the evil of raising a family of children in idleness, the fruits of which evil in after life helped to hasten him to a premature grave.

Every member of this club, except the writer, was in after years an aspirant to political honor and distinction. Most of them had their ambition gratified. It was later a source of amusement to the writer to hear those very men defending the pro-slavery cause and to reflect on how much like a thunderclap from a clear sky would sound their old essays on the evil of slavery, if read in reply to their later speeches. They were all, no doubt, as sincere in their last as they were in their first faith. As a proof that popular opinion was against slavery in the abstract, the legislature about 1832 or 1833 passed a law prohibiting the importation of slaves as merchandise. Had the people of Kentucky been let alone, there is little doubt that the State at some future day would have adopted a system of gradual emancipation.

This feeling in the public mind was having a happy effect on the condition of the slave himself, the master trying to make the yoke as

---

[20] Hartford in those days, like most other towns, had its literary societies, and, like most of them elsewhere, each, having helped its members in literary lines, has come and gone. Mr. Taylor was a member of a number of organizations of that kind. Some of the later clubs had members whose work appeared in print beyond the local press.

In 1867, Mrs. Jennie T. McHenry, wife of Henry D. McHenry, published, in Louisville, a book of sixty-two poems entitled *Forget Me Not*. Most of them had been printed previously in newspapers and magazines, principally in the *Louisville Journal*, over the name "Rosine." A second edition appeared in 1907. One of her poems is "To Jennie C. Morton." Mrs. Jennie Chinn Morton, of Frankfort, was the wife of John C. Morton (son of the pioneer merchant Isaac Morton) and the Regent of the Kentucky State Historical Society. About 1885

light as possible. A feeling of mutual confidence and affection existed in most slaveholding families. Unfortunately for the human race there are always such men as Homer described as: "Thou dog in forehead, but in heart a deer." Such men as these, resorting to the popular cry of "universal freedom of mankind," became so aggressive toward Kentucky by stealing and demoralizing the slave property and heaping upon slaveholders all the epithets of abuse in their vocabulary, that most of our citizens abandoned their long cherished ideas of gradual emancipation, and sought for reason and argument not only to maintain their legal and vested rights in their slave property but also to justify their own good characters. The whole country teemed with speeches, pamphlets, and Bible defense of slavery.

So unpopular had the question of gradual emancipation become that few, if any, of its friends dared to brook the torrent in the Convention which formed the present State constitution. The result was that the constitution [of 1850] was almost radical in its features. To rebut the "higher law" assumptions of the abolitionists the zealous and energetic Garrett Davis procured in the declaration of rights the assertion that "the right to property was above law." It was thus the contest grew, until the abolitionists, under the false pretense of saving the Union, abolished slavery, thus perpetrating the most cruel outrage on a crushed people and reducing thousands of families from wealth and affluence to the most abject poverty.

Thirteen long years have gone, and the doomed old slaveholder has lived on through wrong and oppression. His innate patriotism

---

Miss Lizzie Walker, daughter of E. Dudley Walker, issued a booklet of fifteen poems entitled *Not Altogether Fanciful*. There is nothing on its pages to indicate when or where it was published. When, in 1892, Mrs. Fannie Porter Dickey compiled her selection of Kentucky poetry in a volume entitled *Blades of Bluegrass*, she included one of Mrs. McHenry's and three of Miss Walker's poems, also a portrait of Miss Walker.

Mrs. Tula Pendleton Cummins, daughter of Dr. John E. Pendleton, wrote a number of prose sketches over the name of "T. D. Pendleton." Some of them appeared in the *Youth's Companion*; one entitled "A Month in a Tent" in the *Outing Magazine*, in July, 1909; and another, "The Life Belt," in the *Bellman*, in October, 1914. The latter story is favorably mentioned in *The Best Short Stories of 1915*, compiled by Edward J. O'Brien.

Another Ohio County author is Dr. William Foster, son of William and Sarah Jane Carter Foster. He was born in 1869 in Hartford, where he lived until he reached early manhood. He has been at the head of the Department of Chemistry, Princeton University, for many years, and has published a number of articles in scientific journals. His books are *A Laboratory Manual of General Chemistry* (1905) and *Introduction to General Chemistry* (1922).

and love of country smothers his sense of injustice and makes him willing to live in fraternal union with his fellow countrymen and restore the nation to its once happy condition. It is the nature of ignoble minds never to forgive those whom they have grossly wronged; hence, we hear such characters in Congress, and elsewhere, still boasting of the victories they snuffed at a safe distance, but never participated in; still heaping calumny on the old slaveholders, and trying to grind to the earth the people whom they so grossly injured.

It is true that there are some evils attending slavery. Some men will always be tyrants unless they are themselves slaves. There is no doubt that there exists as much petty tyranny in the North as in the South, but taking the old slaveholders as a class, their descendants need feel no blush of shame for their ancestors, for they stood as high in principles of honor, integrity, charity, and benevolence as any race of people on the earth.

XX

HARRISON D. TAYLOR'S AUTOBIOGRAPHICAL NOTES

Whether the reader concurs with him or not, the writer has arrived at the conclusion that this fragmentary history should come to a close. The seventy-sixth year of his life is about complete, and owing to his failure of sight, what was once a pleasure has now become a burden. He prepared these sketches hoping to preserve some of the history of the early times. It has been his aim to instruct and to amuse the reader. He has given a number of amusing stories and anecdotes, some of which may not be in accordance with other persons' recollections or with traditions familiar to them. However, in every statement relating to persons or events he has endeavored "Naught to extenuate or aught to set down in malice" and to give the true facts in each case.

He did not commence this fragmentary history nor intend it as a novel—made up of heroes and heroines, playing their parts in blood-and-thunder scenes on the stage—but wrote it as a plain narrative of the manners and customs and the virtues and vices of the olden days as they had been daguerreotyped on his brain from early boyhood.

He now regrets that he had not prepared something of the kind at an earlier period, while many of the pioneers of the county were still living. One by one they sank beneath the waves of time and left him with only his boyhood memories of them. In this, his last chapter, he will write a few lines about himself.

The writer was born in Frederick County, Virginia, on March 31, 1802. His parents started late that fall for Kentucky, but when they reached the Monongahela River at what was then called Red Stone, the point at which emigrants usually embarked on flatboats, an early winter set in, and, owing to the low water and later the ice in the river, navigation was entirely suspended. Here he stayed until the following fall. Then he again set out on horseback for Kentucky, and reached Ohio County in safety.

The country around his father's dwelling was for years thinly settled, and there the writer, young as he was, gained an inkling of Indians, canebrakes, bears, wolves, panthers, and most of the other excitements of pioneer life. His father's residence was only three miles from the county seat at Hartford. He had a very extensive acquaintance and his house often resembled a tavern, except that there was no innkeeper's bill, not even on court and muster days. At night the writer learned from these visitors many a legend of early times and the then passing events.

He was but little, if any at all, indebted to the schools of that early day. In fact the most that he then learned took him years to unlearn. In one or two instances he almost suffered martyrdom at home rather than suffer worse than martyrdom in a school house, under an ignorant, peevish, petty tyrant of a teacher. His troubles in this way were not of long duration, for he soon grew large enough for errand boy, plow boy, and any other kind of boy that is of use in a large family on a farm. In this occupation he remained until of age.

In the meantime, however, he had, during Sundays, and rainy days and at night, seated on the hearth, read and studied every useful book that he could lay his hands on. Thus, with the exception of two months' aid at grammar school, he had become pretty thoroughly acquainted with ancient and modern history, mental and moral philosophy, English grammar, also geometry, trigonometry, and practical surveying, all by his own exertions. He does not recite these facts in a boasting way, but to encourage youth to surmount any difficulty that stands in the way of acquiring a useful education.

The writer had as much patriotism and as much desire to contribute to the public good as most young men of his age. He devoted much study to the theory of government, but was always too modest—or perhaps too proud the reader may term it—to thrust on the public his claims for political preferment. He had always admired the Washington theory of neither seeking office nor declining it. He would have felt himself as much disgraced in thrusting himself on the people as a candidate and begging their vote as in being a tramp and asking their charity; hence it was that he never became a candidate before the people for any office of honor or profit. During his whole career he filled only such offices as were thrust upon him without solicitation, the duties of which almost always required industry, investigation, and determination of purpose. It is useless to say that in the faithful discharge of any office whatever, offense is given to someone; yet the writer can look back upon no dereliction of duty in any official act he ever performed.

In his boyhood he always admired Henry Clay. In fact much of his learning to read came from his poring over Clay's speeches in Congress in early days. He generally concurred in the views of the

Autobiographical Notes

Whig party and in the policy of the protective system, until the American manufacturer no longer needed protection, having become the aggressor, instead of the suppliant for help.

For a short time he was fooled into becoming one of the Know-Nothing Party, because of the belief that its real object was to break down party strife and party corruption, in fact to slip the halter from the old political heads and party leaders and call honest, sensible, and pure men to office. To his great surprise and mortification, however, the doors of the lodges were thrown open to everyone who wished to enter, and we beheld our same old masters, with whips and halters in hand, ready to mount and drive the car of state. The general scramble for office that ensued disgusted and drove from the party most of its original members, and the whole attempt at reform proved worse than a farce.

Unfitted by nature alike for a party leader or a party hack, he has for years abstained from party strife—which only leads to scrambles for office, and makes availability the only qualification regardless of the true questions, "Is he honest? Is he capable?" While the logic of events—which is the true test of the correctness of human judgments—has sometimes proved that he was mistaken in results, he is sorry to find that his predictions of other events have been fully filled, and that the present deplorable state of our country was fully foreshadowed and predicted by him years ago—and, worst of all, there is little hope of improvement under the present state of society.

It would not be proper for anyone to attempt to give his own moral or social standing in society. The fact is so many persons seemed to have formed such incorrect opinions of their own standing that it may be well questioned whether anyone sees his own character in the proper light; and then again, whether the public always forms a true estimate of our character.

The writer is aware that he has had warm-hearted, true personal friends. He is also aware that he has had enemies. He generally felt proud of both his friends and his enemies. There is no doubt that he has sometimes incurred the dislike of good and honest men, by means of prepossessions, prejudices, and mistakes on one or both sides. Such mistakes were always painful, and he always has been, and is now, ready to make the amende honorable, and ask forgiveness of all such persons. For a mean, dishonest man he has always felt a natural repulsion, and felt consoled at his hatred, and, while having no wish to do him wrong, could not but pass him by with contempt as a blot on the human race.

The age in which the writer has lived has, perhaps, surpassed any other period of time known to history for the rapid advance in the arts and sciences. Invention after invention, discovery after discovery, have been witnessed almost every day, until scarce a tool or an implement of the household, of the farm, or the workshop, is left to remind an old man of his early days.

How it would have cheered the patriot's heart to have witnessed a like improvement in the moral and social conditions of the human race! These great changes in the physical conditions of society have aroused the cupidity of mankind, have led to enormous fortunes and to enormous extravagance, luxury, and dissipation, which are corrupting and enervating all classes of society and plunging us into debt, disease, and crime.

If a portion of the great intellect of the country could—uninfluenced by the hope of gain and the scramble for high salaries—be honestly and earnestly directed to the improvement of the moral and social conditions of the human race, the next generation might witness the same rapid advance in that direction that the man of seventy-odd years has witnessed in its physical condition.

And now, kind reader, farewell. If the writer has presented any history that you will remember, or portrayed any virtues you will emulate, or any vices you will shun, he will feel that he has done some good in publishing this fragmentary history of Ohio County.

From a photograph by Emory G. Schroeter, 1926

OHIO COUNTY COURTHOUSE, ERECTED 1865-1870

The present Ohio County Courthouse was erected during 1865 to 1870 on the site of the one burnt in December, 1864, by General Hylan B. Lyon. General Lyon was then on his raid through western Kentucky, and, "as a military necessity," burned every courthouse used as a Federal garrison. When he approached Hartford, the Federal guards took shelter in the old Courthouse. They were captured and paroled, and the building burned. Dr. Samuel O. Peyton implored the invaders to spare the Clerk's Office, a one-story two-room brick which stood on the southeast side of the courthouse yard. His request was granted, and the records were saved.

The front and the rear of the Courthouse are very much alike, and so are the two sides. This picture shows the rear and the north corner, and the northwest side.

XXI

HISTORY OF THE TAYLOR FAMILY [21]

The object of this meeting may be explained thus: Old Harrison Taylor, with eight sons and four daughters, with their wives and husbands, emigrated to this county in the latter part of the last and the beginning of the Nineteenth Century. He, with his sons and daughters, and their wives and husbands, has been swept by time to the spirit land. The children of those sons and daughters now alive have grown to hoary age, mostly ranging from seventy-odd to ninety-odd years. Another cycle of years will scarce leave one of this third generation. In the meantime the connections by intermarriages have become so enlarged that they are not half known to each other. It was, therefore, thought proper that they should meet and mingle together in this grand reunion—not for any selfish, clannish, or political purpose, but to talk over and recount the virtues of their good old sires and grandsires, who, though unheralded by fame, filled all the duties of private citizens with more true usefulness, more virtue, and honest integrity than a whole host of political humbugs and office hunters.

The most that is known of old Harrison Taylor is that, though unknown to fame, he was of just such a community of men as would render any country famous. He was honest, industrious, benevolent, mild, and reticent. Untainted by avarice and ambition, he glided along in the quiet undercurrent of life from whence the purest virtues flow.

He was born in the central part of Virginia. His parents were of Welsh and English origin, and derived the name of Harrison from an intermarriage of their ancestors with the Harrison family of Virginia. His father died without a will, and, under the feudal laws of the age, the oldest son took the property, which was said to be large, and left Harrison shareless. Instead of lying around a lackey and pensioner on his brother, he boldly struck out for the frontier and located at Winchester, Virginia, then but a village, where he took up the trade of house carpenter.

---

[21] This chapter is a reprint in full of a fifteen-page pamphlet entitled "A Sketch of the History of the Taylor Family, written by Harrison D. Taylor and read by Dr. [John E.] Pendleton at the Taylor Reunion, at Beaver Dam, Kentucky, September 9, 1875." Most of its contents appears in a disconnected form in some of Mr. Taylor's fragmentary sketches. It was not included in the foregoing selections, but reserved for presentation as compiled in this pamphlet.

Here it was that he evinced the only known instance of an ill temper and an ungovernable rage. A British officer located at that place in the recruiting service took a fancy to him and often tried to induce him to enlist as a soldier, but in vain. It was this officer's practice to gather a crowd about the tavern of nights, and drink and carouse until someone became so drunk and insensible that he either took the bounty or had it slipped into his pocket, and was then forced into the ranks as a soldier. As young Taylor was strictly temperate, he never could be caught in this way. However, one night after a hard day's labor, he took a seat in a quiet, retired corner and fell asleep. The officer observing this slipped the bounty into his pocket. Then he awaited until his supposed victim awoke. Blandly addressing him, he remarked that it was time that they should go home to the barracks. Taylor looked at him with astonishment and asked what he meant. The officer, who had formed an incorrect idea of his man, with a haughty air informed him that having taken the bounty he was now a soldier of King George, and the barracks were now his proper home. Taylor denied ever taking the bounty, when the officer, in like haughty tone, asked him how he could deny it when he had King George's coin in his pocket. At the word pocket the youth suddenly ran his hand into his, grasped the coin, threw it with his utmost strength at the head of the officer, and flew at him with all the fury of an enraged tiger. He was caught and held by his friends whilst the King's representative beat a hasty retreat. He gave this recruit a wide berth ever afterwards.

It was not long until he married Miss Jane Curlet and settled far back in the woods, where, with a single horse, he commenced clearing the forest and cultivating the land. This horse had to be belled and turned to the range at night and hunted up in the morning. Taylor, like all frontiersmen, carried his gun when he went to the woods, and one morning shot a deer just as he came up with his horse. He had just commenced reloading when he heard a turkey gobble, and then another, and another, until the "calls" had nearly formed a ring around him. He at once comprehended his danger, turned his horse's head towards home, struck it a blow, and then crept off in another direction through the undergrowth, until he thought himself entirely outside of the gobbling ring, when he made for home with utmost speed. He had barely arrived there when a messenger announced an Indian raid upon an adjoining settlement.

History of the Taylor Family

The horse, in passing through the gobbling ring, had been greatly alarmed by the redskins and made his way home, where he stood ready to bear the young wife and husband to the nearest fort.

As the country improved, he built a mill on a stream in Frederick County, by which mill passed the main road leading from the east across the Alleghany Mountains to the then great west. There he raised a large family, bore the reputation of a peaceable, quiet citizen, and, what is more remarkable, had the reputation of being an honest miller, which the following story, as related by one of his sons, will show:

His son Harrison, even before he had arrived to full manhood, had Kentucky on the brain, and solitary and alone set out for that Eldorado. On a summit of the Alleghany Mountains he stopped for the night at a wayside inn crowded with travelers. A youth and a stranger, he sat almost unobserved in a corner, until the landlord saw him. Book registers not then being in use, this landlord usually kept his register in his head, and blandly inquired of his young guest his name, residence, and destination. On being told he exclaimed "What! a son of Honest old Taylor that kept the mill on the road? Why I was a wagoner for years on that road, and we wagoners would drive for miles to get feed from him rather than buy elsewhere. We were always sure of honest measure and fair prices. In fact he used to go by the name of 'Honest old Taylor at the mill.'" Right-minded persons may well imagine the feelings of the young wayfarer at this encomium on his meek and modest old sire.

This old sire's wife and partner through life was as unlike him as it was possible, except in honest integrity and unbounded benevolence, yet this dissimilarity seemed to strengthen the bonds of mutual affection and render their love and esteem everlasting and sincere. Demonstrative, possessed of powerful will and strong sense, abounding in wit and anecdote, and having an almost infallible memory, she was ever remarkable for her great social qualities. Her mother had lived to the extraordinary age of ninety-odd years. The tenacious memories of these two women are a remarkable illustration of how the unwritten history of a nation can be preserved from generation to generation. There are some still living who, in their childhood, used to hear old Mrs. Taylor relate incidents of English history, as far back as the days of Cromwell, which facts were afterwards corroborated in reading the written history of that country, yet this was all traditional lore. Her kind-hearted benevolence was the leading feature of her character. That it was not always bestowed in vain, the following story will illustrate:

At their mill daily assembled men and boys from far and near, awaiting their turns. It was her custom daily to march down to the mill, with loaf and knife in hand, and cut and distribute bread to each of the hungry turn-awaiting urchins. Among these was often a poor, ragged, orphan bound boy who never escaped her eye. He was frequently taken to the house and fed to his heart's content, and many a garment belonging to her boys went to clothe his almost naked body. Stackhouse was his name; but the community would not allow him the whole of the only thing inherited from his parents, and called him Stack for short. He grew up under a sense of oppression and wrong, and it was natural that he should wish to retaliate his wrongs upon society. Shrewd, daring, and active, he was soon selected by old, hardened villains to become an accomplice in horse stealing. From his knowledge of the country he could skulk and hide in the spurs of North Mountain, steal any horse he wished, and transfer him to a regular band of horse thieves—a band that was supposed to extend to South Carolina and Georgia. The people of Frederick and adjoining counties were thus annoyed for years until the Governor ordered the military authorities to call out a sufficient force to scour the country and take Stack and his accomplices, dead or alive.

Richard and Thomas Taylor were among those detailed for that purpose. They took their range for exploration, and separated to meet at a designated point. Thomas had not gone far before he discovered smoke, and, approaching it cautiously, saw Stack busily engaged drying or jerking the choice parts of a mutton he had stolen the night before. At this critical moment Thomas tread upon a stick; it broke and gave the alarm. A race ensued in which little was lost or gained; it was rather far to fire with certain aim, and to fire without effect was placing himself at the mercy of his adversary, for guns in those days would not fire a second time without reloading. Stack, however, was approaching a precipitous hillside, which, if once gained, would hide him from sight. Thomas raised his gun while running, determined to fire at the first open range, but was so unfortunate as to get his foot so entangled in a vine as to stumble and fall. On raising up, his intended victim had entirely disappeared and, notwithstanding the most diligent search, no traces of him could be found.

He was banished for a time from his old haunts, but frequently returned. Finally he was caught, tried, and convicted. While Stack was in prison, Thomas Taylor visited him, and, alluding to their race, inquired how he had made his escape. "I was," said Stack, "within a few feet of the entrance to my den when you fell, and I immediately dodged into it. Its entrance was so concealed that no mortal, but myself, perhaps, has ever discovered it. Several times while you were hunting around, you were in range of my rifle. It was once aimed at you, my finger on the trigger, but I thought of your mother, and it dropped from my grasp. Ah, had I been raised by such a mother, I would never have been the wretched outcast that I am"—and tears trickled down the bronzed cheeks of the poor, degraded outcast.

Old Mrs. Harrison Taylor, believing in that text which says that "Man shall not live by bread alone," did not confine her benevolence to the hungry mill boys, but was ever ready to relieve the sick and suffering, no matter what their condition in life. Poor, dying mothers would often bequeath their children to her care, and in this way her house became almost an orphan asylum during the ravages of the Revolutionary War. It is said that at times she would have as many as thirty-odd children dependent on her for food and raiment. She, too, was the principal surgeon and physician of the then backwoods settlement. With her lancet in her pocket she was always ready to replace dislocated limbs, set broken bones, and lance or bleed as required, with the steady nerve of a hospital surgeon, although the wail of a feeble infant, or any tale of suffering or sorrow, would at all times bring tears to her eyes.

By the most untiring care and industry these old people—Old Harrison Taylor and his wife—acquired property and raised a family of eight sons and four daughters. Several of those sons had visited Kentucky, and because of their representations of the country the old folks were induced to sell out and remove to Ohio County. There all of the sons and the three daughters then living finally settled. The old folks bought the farm now occupied by Mr. Hamilton Barnes, where they retired until too old and feeble to keep house, after which they removed to their son Thomas, where they lived the remainder of their days, and were buried side by side in the family graveyard.

Old Harrison Taylor was born on August 11, 1735, and died on November 22, 1811, in the seventy-seventh year of his age. Mrs.

Taylor was born on September 5, 1742, and died on August 5, 1812, in the seventieth year of her age.

In selling his mill and farm the old man took a bountiful supply of such store goods as he thought would be useful in the new-settled country. These goods excited almost as great a curiosity as the glass lockets worn by the two girls at the party on Pigeon Roost Fork of Muddy Creek as described in "Ralph Ringwood's" story. The following story illustrates how they were appreciated by the young hunters and belles of the day:

At a social party at the house of the old folks one night, a pert, flippant young gentleman was seated nearest the candle, by which lay a pair of bright, polished snuffers. On being requested to snuff the candle, he picked it up and licked his thumb and finger, making ready to pinch it off, when he was told to use the snuffers there. Upon hearing this he set down the burning candle, picked up the snuffers, opened them, licked his thumb and finger again, pinched off the snuff, and placed it in the snuffers. He closed them and laid them on the table with the remark, "Ain't they nice and handy?"

As long as health and strength permitted, their house was the resort of the sick and afflicted who needed aid, also of the gay and witty who wished to measure lances with the unpolished backwoods, offhand wit, humor, and sarcasm of the old lady. Even the most sober and sage-like were fond of her society. The late eccentric James Axley, who preached her funeral, delighted in her company, and was heard to say that she had more native good sense and natural eloquence than any woman he ever knew.

We have given some of the details of the life of Old Harrison Taylor—"Honest old Taylor at the mill"—and his good wife. None should wish to trace their origin to a higher source, for "An honest man is the noblest work of God." We will try to give a brief sketch of their eight sons and four daughters.

Their oldest daughter, Elizabeth, was married, and afterwards died in Virginia. Little is known of her children; one, Peggy Pue, accompanied her grandparents to Kentucky and was married to a Mr. Keel. She died without children.

Richard Taylor, the oldest son, was twice married. By his first wife he had Harrison, Thomas, and, as well as I now recollect, five daughters. Katy married a Coleman and afterwards Thomas Ashby; Peggy married the Reverend John James; Sally married

History of the Taylor Family

Philip Falheron; and the other two, whose names are not recollected, married the one a Leach and the other a Tarleton. By his second wife he had Richard, John, Blackstone, and Mason, and three daughters: Susan, who married Richard Stevens; Henrietta, who married Daniel Stevens; and Clarissa, who married Ignatius Barrett. Richard Taylor lived to his eighty-fourth year, and throughout his life was celebrated for industry, honest integrity, and hospitality.

Thomas Taylor, the second son, united himself to the Methodist church at the early age of twelve years. He became a local preacher while quite young, and remained one until the day of his death. Although throughout life a large contributor in the aid of the church, he never asked nor received a cent for his own services. While in the vigor of manhood, it was his constant practice to labor hard through the week and then at the end ride miles away to preach in some place where there was no regular preaching. A file of old almanacs, still in the family, in which he used to note his appointments, will show that he frequently went to Hopkins, Muhlenberg, Grayson, and Breckinridge counties, and even to Hardin, to preach. Yet, to do this, he seldom left home until Saturday, returning home on Monday; then by almost superhuman exertion he made up the lost time throughout the rest of the week. If it were possible for any man to have too much physical, moral, and intellectual industry, he was the man. His life was a continual effort to improve the soil, the morals, and the intelligence of the country. Of him it may be truly said that his heart was always right, his failings were but virtues in excess.[22] Thomas Taylor had five sons—Nicholas, Wesley, Harrison D., Milton, and Thomas—and a daughter Frances, all of whom are dead, save Harrison D. and Milton.

Harrison, the third son, was said to have been a man born without fear; and I may add that he died without reproach. Whilst quite a youth he visited Kentucky and was intrusted with the location of lands in this part of the country. He made several trips through the wilderness alone, and was known to remain at the surveyors' camps when older and more experienced men would fly to the settlements. He was a plain, simple-hearted, honest man. His house for years was the headquarters of land claimants who came to the

---

[22] Tradition has it that old Harrison Taylor took an active part in the Revolution and that his three oldest sons, Richard, Thomas, and Harrison Taylor, served during the latter part of the war. Their Revolutionary records have not yet (1926) been investigated and compiled.

country to look after their lands, and his thorough knowledge of the country rendered his services highly important. In this way he often spent days and weeks, not only in entertaining them but in showing them their lands, for which his old Virginia ideas of hospitality would not allow him to charge a cent. There was one extraordinary trait in his character. Although remarkable from childhood for his fearless courage and, although he served as justice of the peace and as sheriff in the then chaotic state of society, was an extensive trader, and served as wagon-master to the army in Hopkins' campaign, yet he was never known to have had a fight, a recontre, or personal difficulty with anyone. He left four sons and four daughters: John A., Thomas Alfred, Harrison, and Washington, and Jane, Cynthia, Ann, and Rachel.

William Taylor, the fourth son, was a man of powerful frame, will, and energy all combined. He was distinguished as one of the best farmers, as the builder of the first brick dwelling house in the county, and as the first to thoroughly utilize our swamp-lands for meadows. He had four sons—Septimus, Richard, William, and Harrison—and an only daughter, Christina.

John Taylor, the fifth son, died about middle age, yet lived long enough to establish himself as a man of unbounded liberality. He was his own worst enemy, believing everyone as honest as himself. He liked everybody, believed everybody, and could be cheated by anybody who tried, which qualities he imparted to most of his children. It is thought, however, that his son "Coffee" John has drunk coffee enough to brace his nerves so that he holds his own with the world pretty well. The names of his children were Ignatius, Benjamin, Lorenzo, Stephen, Fleming, "Coffee" John, Hannah, Margaret, Sally, and Elizabeth.

Septimus Taylor, the sixth son, died early in life, leaving a reputation, however, of untiring industry. The following named are his children: Richard M., William S., Septimus, Levi, Harvey, and Jane, and another daughter, who married years ago and moved to Indiana. All these are good livers and have inflicted no disgrace on their ancestors.

Suffice it to say that Simon and Joseph, the two younger sons of old Harrison Taylor, like most pets, were a little spoiled in the raising and were bad managers. They thought Kentucky soil too poor and removed West, but at last accounts had failed, either from not being

History of the Taylor Family

rich enough themselves or from not finding lands rich enough to buy for farms, and were still renters. Little or nothing is known of their families.

Of the daughters of Old Harrison Taylor, Hannah married Samuel Brown, both of whom lived and died in this county. Margaret married James Harsha, who removed to Illinois. Jane married Levi Pigman, who removed to the state of Ohio. All of these daughters reared numerous children.

We have now sketched a brief notice of the second generation of the Taylor family, all of whom have gone to their long homes, and a large portion of the third generation have followed them. We who are left are in the sere and yellow leaf; the blandishments of life are gone, and our only care should be to guard well the family escutcheon and maintain the reputation of "Honest old Taylor at the mill." We have none of us been wise as Solomon, brave as Caesar, or renowned as Clay or Webster. We have had our foibles and follies, but thus far none of us have been stained with crime and dishonor. We will soon transmit the care of our family name and record to the fourth, fifth, and sixth generations. If there be any here today who have blotted that record, who have sullied that name, let them this day resolve to spend the balance of their lives in wiping out that stain. Let them one and all, like their ancestors, regardless of the allurements of wealth and fame, resolve to live industrious, honest lives, adding daily and yearly to their faith, virtue, knowledge, and charity, discharging all the duties of social and civil life, and, whether they die with wealth and distinction or sink to rest in the humble log cabin, a good conscience will whisper peace to the departing spirit, and their virtues will be cherished and remembered by those who come after them.

To the young men and boys just verging into young manhood, let one whose sands of life have nearly run give a word of advice. In our physical formation the spine or backbone is the grand support of our bodies. Weaken or destroy that, and the whole body is paralyzed. It is just as necessary to have a moral or intellectual backbone, a will, a firmness, and a fixed determination to carry out and finish anything we undertake or to refrain from doing what we think wrong. The boy that can be influenced to do anything which he knows is wrong, or has not the energy to carry out and do what he knows to be right, will never make a man worth rearing; he will always be a poor drone or ninny among men.

Without wishing to be at all egotistical, I will tell how this backbone of principle was serviceable to me at one period of my life, and in all probability saved me from ruin. When nearly of age, I resolved on studying a profession. My father contracted with the landlord of our principal Hartford tavern for my board and incidentals. Well, I packed up and went to town, as "green" as a cucumber in the usages of town life, dressed from head to foot in homespun, home-made clothing, as unlike town-folks as a gosling is unlike peacocks. The landlord assigned me to a little eight-by-ten room immediately over the bar-room; I was to cut my own wood and make my own fires.

Because of old decks of cards lying around I suspected that this was a resort of gamblers, and that it was intended I should be fireman for their benefit. Well, sure enough, on the next morning three gentlemen whom I knew by their voices to be the leading doctor, a well-known lawyer, and the most accomplished young gentleman of leisure and fortune in the community came into the bar-room below and requested to have a room to play a game. "Oh, yes," said boniface, "walk up those stairs; you will find a good fire. A young Mr. Taylor is up there, but he will have no objection." All this was loud enough for me to hear distinctly. Heavens, what a fix! What a current of thought rushed through my mind! Before they had ascended the stairs, I had argued the question *pro* and *con*: "I am here a lone boy, noticed by no one. How pleasant it will be to accommodate and become intimate with such distinguished gentlemen! How will it look for such an uncouth chap as I"—casting a glance at my homespun—"to refuse them so small a favor?" This was the argument *pro*, but by the time they had entered the room and politely asked leave to play, I had made up the following opinion *con* and thus delivered it: "Gentlemen, I am here for the purpose of studying and learning, and although I would be glad to accommodate you, yet, if I were to do so, others would expect the same privilege; so I think it best to allow no gaming at all."

The old doctor, who was slightly "corned," wheeled around, audibly muttering curses as he retired, but the other two politely bowed themselves out, and to my surprise, I heard the young man defending me downstairs. Here let me remark that this young

History of the Taylor Family

man, distinguished for his wealth, family connections, and mental endowments, was ever after my warm friend. Ah! How it grieved me to see him gradually sinking into an inebriate's grave. But to my story. After the excitement abated, for I stammered with bashfulness as I spoke, I began to think, "Every person has a backbone to his principles if he would use it, but what have I done? My landlord will be mad. These gentlemen may persecute me, and the loafers and gamblers laugh me to scorn, but I know I did right; and, like Davy Crockett, I'll go ahead." Then I commenced my reading in good earnest.

After a while a young man, a boarder, came in and congratulated me for breaking up the gamblers' den. When I went downstairs, the landlord treated me with unusual respect, the landlady was delighted with my pluck, and I soon became a favorite among the ladies. In fact, the affair, small as it was, soon became noised over town and instead of being passed without notice, or with a snarl of contempt, I was generally met with a friendly greeting. I believe I was the only country lad that ever came to town whom the boys never tried "to run the green off of." People will admire pluck and backbone in even a puppy.

Now let us look at the other side of the picture. Suppose I had let these gentlemen play. I might have been fascinated with their wit, perhaps their wisdom. I might have taken a hand just to make up a game. I might have tasted their liquor just to be social. I might have become their boon companion, and I might—nay, I would certainly—have become a drunkard. All three of those men met that fate. I have never seen it fail.

Boys, one more remark and I am done. Stick to your father's farms and shops. Learn to earn your bread by the sweat of your face. It is the surest way of living a respectable, honorable, honest life. Do not be led astray by the fascinations of town and city life. I would not give one sober, honest boy, with face bronzed by the sun and hands hardened by industrious toil, for a whole team of city fops with patches of down on their lips, cigars half-way down their throats, and wearing dainty kid gloves and boots that make poodle dogs bark at themselves. Such youths are taking tickets in life's lottery, it is true, but most of their prizes will be disappointed hopes, a loafer's calling, a blackleg's hardened life of fraud and crime, a felon's cell, or a drunkard's grave.

Appendix

A

ACT FORMING OHIO COUNTY IN 1798 [23]

An act for erecting a new county out of the County of Hardin. Approved on December 17, 1798.

Be it enacted by the General Assembly that from and after the first day of July next, all that part of the county of Hardin that is included in the following bounds, viz: Beginning on the Ohio River at the mouth of Blackford's Creek, thence up the same to the head of the southeast fork that heads opposite the head of Harris's fork of Rock Lick Creek, thence across the dividing ridge to said Harris's Fork, thence down the same to Rock Lick Creek, thence down the same to *Rough Creek, thence a straight line to* Flat Clay *Lick* [the first printing reads Flat Clay Creek] on Bear Creek, and down the same to Green River, and down Green River to the Ohio to the beginning, shall be one distinct county, and called and known by the name of Ohio. But the said county of Ohio shall not be entitled to a separate representation until the number of free male inhabitants therein contained above the age of twenty-one years shall entitle them to one representative, agreeable to the ratio that shall hereafter be established by law.

A court for the said county shall be held by the justices thereof on the first Tuesday in every month, except in the months the court of quarter sessions are hereafter directed to be held, after said division shall take place, in the manner as is provided by law in respect to other counties and as shall be by their commissions directed.

The justices to be named in the commission of the peace for said county of Ohio shall meet at the house of Robert Moseley, in the said county, on the first court day after said division shall take place, and having taken the oaths prescribed by law, and the sheriff being duly qualified to act, the justices shall proceed to appoint and qualify a clerk, and fix upon a place to hold courts in the said county, at or as near the center thereof as the situation and convenience of

---

[23] Ohio County was formed by an act of the legislature approved on December 17, 1798. A year later—on December 19, 1799—a resolution was approved by the legislature because "an error hath been made in printing the first section of the Act" which created Ohio County out of a part of Hardin. The error was in the omission of the words *Rough Creek, thence a straight line to* and in the name Flat Clay Creek, which should have read Flat Clay *Lick*. The addition and the change are inserted in italics in the copy here presented.

the place will admit; and thenceforth the court shall proceed to erect necessary public buildings at such place, and until such buildings be completed, to appoint such place for holding court as they shall think proper: Provided always, that the appointment for a place for erecting the public buildings, and of a clerk, shall not be made unless a majority of the justices of the court of the said county concur therein; but such appointment shall be postponed until some court-day when a majority shall be present, but the court may appoint a clerk *pro tempore.*

And be it further enacted, that the court of quarter sessions for the said county shall be held, annually, in the months of November, February, April, and June.

It shall be lawful for the sheriff of Hardin to collect and make distress for any public dues or officers' fees which shall remain unpaid by the inhabitants thereof at the time such division shall take place, and he shall be accountable for the same in like manner as if this act had not been made.

And the court of the said county of Hardin shall have jurisdiction in all actions and suits in law and equity which shall be depending before them at the time of such division, and shall try and determine the same, issue process, and award execution thereon.[24]

---

[24] In 1780 the District of Kentucky was divided into three counties: Jefferson, Fayette, and Lincoln counties, Virginia. In 1784 Nelson was formed out of part of Jefferson. In 1792 on June 1, Kentucky was admitted into the Union as a state. In 1792 Hardin was formed out of part of Nelson. In 1798 Ohio was formed out of part of Hardin. In 1799 Breckinridge was formed out of part of Hardin. In 1810 Butler was formed out of part of Logan and Ohio. In 1810 Grayson was formed out of parts of Hardin and Ohio. In 1815 Daviess was formed out of part of Ohio. In 1829 Hancock was formed out of parts of Breckinridge, Daviess, and Ohio. In 1854 McLean was formed out of parts of Daviess, Muhlenberg, and Ohio.

By an act of the General Assembly the whole of the Richard Henderson & Company's grant of land not already in Henderson County was taken into that county. This was done by "An Act to add part of Ohio County to the county of Henderson," approved on January 16, 1809: "Be it enacted by the General Assembly that, from and after the first day of April next, all that part of Ohio County comprised within the following bounds shall be added to and considered a part of the county of Henderson, to-wit: Beginning on the Ohio at the mouth of Green River and running up the Ohio to where the line of Henderson & Company's grant strikes the same, thence with said line to Green River, thence down the same to the beginning." By this act what is known as the Point Precinct was added to Henderson County, says Edmund L. Starling in his excellent *History of Henderson County*, published in 1887.

B

OHIO COUNTY AS RECORDED BY COLLINS IN 1847 AND IN 1877 [25]

As Recorded in 1847

Ohio County was formed in 1798, and named from the Ohio River. It is situated in the west middle portion of the State, lying on the waters of Green River, which forms its southern and a part of its southwestern boundary—Rough Creek, quite a considerable stream, flowing, in a meandering course, through its northern territory; bounded on the north by Hancock; east by Grayson; southeast by Butler; southwest by Muhlenberg; and northwest by Daviess. The soil of this county is considered equal to that of the Green River lands generally, producing excellent crops of corn, tobacco, oats, potatoes, clover, and other grasses, but supposed not to contain sufficient lime for the profitable growing of wheat. The timber is heavy and of a superior quality. Iron ore abounds in the county, and the beds of excellent coal are inexhaustible. The *morus multicaulis* flourishes here, and the culture of silk might be carried on to any extent. Some specimens of the manufactured article have been pronounced equal to the best Italian.

---

[25] In 1847 Lewis Collins published a one-volume edition of his *History of Kentucky*, and reprinted it in 1850. In 1874 Richard H. Collins enlarged and extended his father's work and published a two-volume edition, which, in 1877, was followed by a second edition. Several reprints of the two-volume edition have appeared, but none include any history later than 1877. In the one-volume and in the two-volume edition is a chapter devoted to Ohio County. Both are here quoted in full, notwithstanding that much of it is repetition. The killing of the two Anderson children, the escape of Martin Vannada, and the flax field episodes are word for word alike in both editions and, therefore, are not duplicated in our reprint. The flax field and the Anderson incidents were revised by Mr. Taylor, and appear in their revised form in his chapter on Indian Depredations. In the one-volume edition Collins acknowledges his indebtedness to "Charles Henderson, H. D. Taylor, and Stephen Statler."

In 1877 Richard H. Collins published a one-volume edition of nine hundred pages known as the Common School District Edition, copies of which were presented by the State to the public schools. The first part is local history, a reprint in full of Volume II of the two-volume edition; the last part—one hundred pages—is a general history of the State, a much condensed outline of the contents of Volume I.

Ohio County in the Olden Days

Valuation of taxable property in Ohio County, in 1846, $1,280,237; number of acres of land in the county, 309,630 [?]; average value of land per acre, $2.08; number of white males over twenty-one years of age, 1,407; number of children between five and seventeen years old, 2,032. Population in 1840, 6,592, but supposed to be one-third greater in 1847.

Hartford, the seat of justice, is situated on the bank of Rough Creek, about twenty-eight miles by water from its junction with Green River, and one hundred and sixty miles from Frankfort. Its location is pleasant and agreeable, remarkable for its fine water and the general health of the population, which numbers about 400. It contains a brick courthouse and other county buildings, two churches (Methodist and Free), [and has] six lawyers, six physicians, two taverns, fifteen stores and groceries, and ten mechanics' shops. Established in 1808.

Ohio County was the first county formed below Hardin, and once included all of the present counties of Ohio, Daviess and Hancock, with portions of Breckinridge, Grayson, and Butler. [As recorded in 1847 is continued on page 122, under Early Settlement, as published in both editions.] [26]

---

[26] In 1840, when the United States census was taken, the names of the Revolutionary soldiers then living were compiled. According to Collins (Volume I, page 8) nine were reported from Ohio County, with the age of each at that time: Zebra Arnold, 83; William L. Barnard, 81; Chesley Calloway, 81; William Campbell, 87; William Carter, Sr., 80; John Maddox, Sr., 78; Peter Parks, 81; Francis Petty, 87; Diadama Shutts, 78.

The Year Book, 1896, *Kentucky Society Sons of the American Revolution*, gives a roll of citizens of Kentucky who were granted pensions for services in the Revolutionary War under the various pension acts up to 1832. Sixteen appear under the head of Ohio County. Pensioners under the act of March 18, 1818: Peter Brandon, William Cooper, William Campbell, John Howell, Moses Johnson, Robert Mosely, Thomas Pender, and Peter Parks. Under the act of May 15, 1828: Benjamin Burch. Under the act of June 7, 1832: William L. Barnard, Seley Burton, Chesley Calloway, William Carter, Sr., John Monroe, John Sorrels, and Matthias Shultz.

In Daviess County, according to Collins, four Revolutionary soldiers were alive in 1840: Benjamin Field, then aged 84; Charles Hansford, 80; James Jones, 79; Benjamin Tayloe, 84.

According to the Year Book, 1896, S. A. R., cited above, there were ten soldiers in Daviess County who were granted pensions for services in the Revolutionary War under the act of June 7, 1832: Zachariah Briant, George Calhoon, Benjamin Field, James Hall, Samuel Johnson, Sr., James Jones, James Kelley, Anthony Thompson, James Tannehill, and Benjamin Taylor. It is quite probable that most of these old soldiers settled in Daviess County before 1815, that is, when its territory was a part of the original Ohio County.

Recorded by Collins in 1847 and 1877

As Recorded in 1877

Ohio County was formed in 1798, out of part of Hardin County, the thirty-fifth in order of formation, and named after the beautiful river that forms the northern boundary of the State. From its territory has since been taken the entire county of Daviess in 1815, and parts of Butler and Grayson in 1810, Hancock in 1829, and McLean in 1854. It is situated in the west middle portion of the State, on the waters of Green River; is bounded north by Daviess and Hancock counties, east by Breckinridge and Grayson, southeast by Butler, southwest by Muhlenberg, west by McLean, and northwest by Daviess. Besides Green River, the streams are Rough, East Fork of Panther, Muddy, White's Fork, Walton's, Barnett's, and Caney creeks. The soil is considered equal to that of the Green River lands generally—producing excellent crops of corn, tobacco, oats, potatoes, clover, and other grasses, but supposed not to contain sufficient lime for the profitable growing of wheat. The timber is heavy and of a superior quality. Iron ore abounds, and coal is inexhaustible. In 1842–1848, the *morus multicaulis* was tried extensively and flourished, showing that the culture of silk might be carried on to any extent. Some specimens of manufactured silk were produced, equal to the best Italian.

Towns: *Hartford*, the county seat, is pleasantly situated on the bank of Rough Creek, twenty-eight miles by water from its junction with Green River, 110 miles from Louisville by the Elizabethtown and Paducah Railroad, and 160 miles from Frankfort. It was incorporated in 1808, and was quite stationary in population for over twenty years, but bids fair to grow steadily under railroad influences; population in 1870, 511. *Rockport*, on Green River and the E. & P. R. R.; population in 1870, 173. *Cromwell*, on Green River, twelve miles from Morgantown; population in 1870, 149, a decrease of 58 since 1850. *Ceralvo*, on Green River, five miles from South Carrollton; population in 1870, 60. *Beaver Dam*, *Buck Horn*, *Buford*, *Cool Spring*, *Fordsville*, *Hines' Mills*, and *Point Pleasant*, are railroad stations, small villages or post offices.

Ohio County in the Olden Days

STATISTICS OF OHIO COUNTY

Population from 1800 to 1870: In 1800 it was 1,223; 1810 was 3,792; 1820 was 3,879; 1830 was 4,715; 1840 was 6,592; 1850 was 9,749; 1860 was 12,209; 1870 was 15,561. Population, white and colored, 1840 to 1870: White in 1840 was 5,747; 1850 was 8,568; 1860 was 10,868; 1870 was 14,168. Free colored in 1860 was 29; 1870 was 1,393. Slave in 1840 was 823; 1850 was 1,132; 1860 was 1,292. Number of white males over twenty-one years old in 1846 was 1,407; 1870 was 2,880. Number of children between six and twenty years old in 1870: Whites was 4,724; negroes was 282; total was 5,006.

Population of towns: Hartford in 1810 was 110; 1830 was 242; 1840 was 309; 1850 was 496; 1870 was 511. Rockport in 1870 was 173. Cromwell in 1850 was 207; 1870 was 149. Ceralvo in 1870 was 60.[27]

Crops and live stock in 1870: 2,691,250 pounds of tobacco; 3,490 tons of hay; 506,617 bushels of corn; 37,012 bushels of wheat; 15 bushels of barley. Live stock in 1870: 5,230 horses; 823 mules; 9,343 cattle; 14,657 hogs over six months old.

Valuation of taxable property: In 1870 it was $3,343,006. In 1846 it was $1,280,237. Number of acres of land in 1870 was 335,192, valued at $6.48 per acre. In 1846 it was valued at $2.08 per acre. [The Fourteenth Census of the United States, 1920, gives 375,760 acres, or 584 square miles, and John H. McHenry's Map of Ohio County (1886) gives 591 square miles as the area.]

---

[27] Collins in his Volume II, beginning page 635, gives a list of post offices in Kentucky in March, 1874. Eighteen appear under the head of Ohio County: Beaver Dam, Buck Horn, Buford, Centretown, Ceralvo, Cool Springs, Cromwell, Elm Lick, Fordsville, Hartford, Haynesville, Hogg's Fall, Horse Branch, Point Pleasant, Render Coal Mines, Rockport, Rosine, and Sulphur Springs.

The following is printed on the margin of John J. McHenry's Map of Ohio County (1886): "Statistics of Ohio County for 1885: Total assessed value of property, $2,681,964. Number of legal voters, 4,613; children between six and twenty years, 6,658; pounds of tobacco, 4,633,132; tons of hay, 4,875; bushels of corn, 561,295; bushels of wheat, 36,506. Area of Ohio County, 378,560 acres or 591.5 square miles. Distances from Hartford: To Beda, 4.6 miles; Beaver Dam, 5.1; Borah's Ferry, 14.5; Bell's Run Church, 11.3; Buford, 9.2; Ceralvo, 10; Centertown, 7.1; Cromwell, 13; Fordsville, 20; Horton, 7.7; Hines' Mills, 12.7; McHenry, 6.2; Paradise, 14.6; Pleasant Ridge, 12; Point Pleasant, 12; Rockport, 11.2; Rochester, 19.2; Rosine, via Leitchfield Road, 11.4; South Carrollton, 18; Sulphur Springs, 11; Sutton, 11.4; and Select, via Cromwell, 17 miles."

It may be well to add that a map of the greater part of Ohio County is embraced in six of the Topographical Sheets recently issued by the Kentucky Geological Survey in co-operation with the United States Geological Survey. These sheets are designated Central City, Dunmor, Hartford, Spring Lick, Southerland, and Whitesville Quadrangles. With the Map of Northeastern Ohio County, published by the Kentucky Geological Survey, they form a complete recent map of the county.

Recorded by Collins in 1847 and 1877

MEMBERS OF THE LEGISLATURE FROM OHIO COUNTY

Senate: William Campbell (from Ohio, Muhlenberg, Henderson, and Livingston counties), 1800; John Handly (from Ohio, Hardin, and Breckinridge counties), 1814; James Hillyer, 1816-1818; James Johnston, 1819; Nathaniel D. Anderson (from Ohio, Daviess, and Breckinridge counties), 1820-1823; Dillis Dyer, 1840-1846; Robert S. Russell (from Ohio, Muhlenberg, and Butler counties), 1850; William J. Berry, 1851-1853, 1873-1877; E. Dudley Walker, 1857-1861; Henry D. McHenry, 1861-1865.

House of Representatives: Henry Rhoads, 1800; Henry Davidge, 1802, 1805, 1806, 1807; Charles McCreery, 1809; John Daviess, 1811; Remus Griffith, 1813; James Johnston, 1814, 1817, 1818, 1837, 1842; Philip Thompson, 1814 (from Ohio and Daviess counties), 1815; Moses Cummins, 1816; Richard Taylor, 1819; John Calhoun, 1820, 1821; David J. Kelley, 1822; Robert Mosely, 1824; Dillis Dyer, 1825, 1830, 1831, 1834; William M. Davis, 1826, 1827, 1828; Elijah Crowe, 1829, 1832, 1833; Samuel O. Peyton, 1835; William H. Rumsey, 1836, 1839, 1841; Alexander R. Rowan, 1838; John H. McHenry, 1840; Larkin G. Nall (from Ohio and Hancock counties), 1843; John W. Crowe, 1844; Elisha M. Ford, 1845, 1848; Robert T. Bell, 1846, 1847; Quintus C. Shanks, 1849; Henry D. McHenry, 1851-1853, 1865-1867; Henry Thompson, 1853-1855, 1857-1859; William J. Berry, 1855-1857; John Haynes, 1859-1861; Remus Gibson, 1861-1863; W. H. Miller, 1863-1865; W. Estill McHenry, 1867-1869; Alfred T. Coffman, 1869-1871; J. S. Taylor, 1871-1873; Richard P. Hocker, 1875-1877.

A Giant.—Early in 1872, in prospecting for coal in Ohio County, about a mile from Rockport, the complete skeleton of a human body of gigantic size was found, six feet below the surface. The lower jaw-bone, when fitted over the lower portion of a man's face in the party of explorers, completely covered it; the thigh-bone, from the hip-bone to the knee, was forty-two inches long, and the forearm bone from wrist to elbow measured twenty-two inches. This would indicate a giant over ten feet high.

The Compass and Chain used in laying out the city of Louisville, at some time before 1800 (it was first laid out on August 1, 1773), was, in 1871, in possession of Colonel Quintus C. Shanks, of Hartford, Ohio County. It was formerly owned by William Peyton, who in early days made many surveys in company with James Shanks, the father of Colonel Shanks. The story of all its wanderings in detail would be thrilling, and rescue much local history that is lost forever.

Ohio County in the Olden Days

EARLY SETTLEMENT, AS PUBLISHED IN BOTH EDITIONS

Early Settlement.—The immediate vicinity of Hartford was settled at a very early period, and was often the scene of bloody strife and acts of noble daring. Hartford and Barnett's stations were about two miles apart, and although never regularly besieged, were frequently harassed by straggling parties of Indians, and a number of persons who imprudently ventured out of sight of the stations [were] killed or captured. The following facts we derived in 1846 from Stephen Statler, a pioneer, and a venerable and esteemed citizen of Ohio County.

In April, 1790, the Indians waylaid Barnett's Station, and killed two of the children of John Anderson. One of the party assaulted Mrs. Anderson with a sword, inflicted several severe wounds upon her person, and while [the Indian was] in the act of taking off her scalp, John Miller ran up within about twenty steps, and snapped his rifle at him. The Indian fled, leaving his sword, but succeeded in carrying off the scalp of Mrs. Anderson. She, however, recovered and lived some ten or twelve years afterwards. The same party captured and carried off Hannah Barnett, a daughter of Colonel Joseph Barnett, then a girl of about ten years of age. They retained her as a captive until October of the same year, when, through the instrumentality of her brother-in-law, Robert Baird, she was recovered and restored to her friends.

In August of the same year, three men were attacked by a party of Indians, near the mouth of Green River. John McIlmurray, one of the whites, was killed, a man named Faith was wounded, and Martin Vannada was made a prisoner. The Indians immediately crossed the Ohio River, and, after traveling for some days in the direction of their towns, struck, as they supposed, the trail of some white men. In order to pursue them with the utmost celerity and without impediment, they tied Vannada to a tree. With the view of rendering his escape hopeless during their absence, they spread a blanket at the root of a tree, and caused him to sit upon it, with his back against the tree. His hands were then pinioned behind him, and fastened to the tree with one rope, while they tied another rope around his neck,

Recorded by Collins in 1847 and 1877

and fastened it to the tree above. In this painful position they left him, and commenced the pursuit of their supposed enemies. But no sooner had they departed than he commenced the work of extricating himself. With much difficulty he succeeded in releasing his hands, but his task appeared then only to have begun. He ascertained that he could not reach round the tree so as to get to the knot; and it was so twisted or tied between his neck and the tree that it was impossible for him to slip it one way or the other. Without a knife, he made powerful efforts to get the rope between his teeth, that he might gnaw it in two. Failing in this, he almost regretted having made any effort to effect his escape, as, upon the return of the Indians, the forfeit of his life would, in all probability, be the consequence. At this moment he recollected that there were some metal buttons on his waistcoat. Instantly tearing one off, he placed it between his teeth, and, by great efforts, broke it into two pieces. With the rough edge of one of these, he succeeded in fretting rather than cutting the cord in two which bound his neck to the tree, and was once more free. But in what a condition! In a wilderness and an enemy's country, with no clothing save a shirt, waistcoat, breeches, and moccasins!—no provisions, no gun, no ammunition, no knife, not even a flint to strike fire with! He did not, however, hesitate or falter, but instantly struck into the trackless forest, in the direction of home,—and, under the direction of a kind Providence, reached Hartford the ninth day after his escape, having subsisted upon such small animals and insects as he could catch and eat raw. He was nearly famished, and greatly emaciated; but having fallen into good hands, he was soon recruited, and returned to his family in fine health.

In the year 1786 or 1787, an incident occurred at a fort on Green River, which displays the dangers which beset the emigrants of that period, and illustrates the magnanimity of the female character.

About twenty young persons—male and female—of the fort had united in a flax pulling in one of the most distant fields. In the course of the forenoon two of their mothers made them a visit, and the youngest took along her child, about eighteen months old. When the whole party was near the woods, one of the young women, who had climbed over the fence, was fired upon by several Indians concealed in the bushes, who at the same time raised the usual war-whoop. She was wounded, but retreated, as did the whole party, some running with her down the lane, which happened to open near that point, and others across the field. They were hotly pursued by the enemy, who continued to yell and fire upon them. The older of the two mothers who had gone out, recollecting in her flight that the younger, a small and feeble woman, was burthened with her child, turned back in the face of the enemy, they firing and yelling hideously, took the child from its almost exhausted mother, and ran with it to the fort, a distance of three hundred yards. During the chase, she was twice shot at with rifles, when the enemy was so near that the powder burned her and one arrow passed through her sleeve; but she escaped uninjured. The young woman who was wounded almost reached the place of safety, when she sunk, and her pursuer, who had the hardihood to attempt to scalp her, was killed by a bullet from the fort.

C

CAPTAIN JOHN HOWELL, REVOLUTIONARY SOLDIER [28]

A joint resolution was adopted by the legislature at its last session, approved January 27, 1874, appropriating a sum of money and authorizing the Governor to use same for the purpose of removing the remains of Captain John Howell, a soldier of the Revolution, from Ohio County to the State Cemetery at Frankfort, and erecting over them a suitable monument. Pursuant to this resolution, Governor Leslie appointed Mr. Harrison D. Taylor, a venerable and highly esteemed citizen of Hartford, to superintend the removal of the remains to this city [Frankfort, Kentucky].

Mr. Taylor, with the remains, arrived here yesterday, and informed us that, although he had some difficulty in finding the grave—Captain Howell having died in 1830—yet in the end he was entirely successful in fully identifying the remains. The re-interment, in accordance with the resolution of the legislature, will take place this morning. Mr. Taylor kindly furnished us with the following interesting and valuable memorandum of the military life and services of this Revolutionary worthy, together with a striking reminiscence of the esteem in which he was held by the famous LaFayette:

"Captain John Howell was a native of New Jersey. From his declaration made on November 20, 1820, for the purpose of procuring a pension, it appears that he volunteered for one year in the First Jersey Regiment, commanded by Lord Sterling, in 1775. In 1776 he was detached to Canada. In 1777 he was an officer in the said regiment on the war establishment, and was with the main army at Germantown and Brandywine. In 1778 he was with the main army at Monmouth. In 1779 he was detached against the Indians on the waters of Lake Ontario. In 1780 he was generally with the main army. In 1781 he was with the Morgans in Virginia and with the main army at the capture of Cornwallis. In 1782 he was Captain of Light Company in the same regiment. In 1783 he was regularly discharged. He seems to have been among the earliest settlers of Ohio County, where he died about October, 1830, aged about seventy-five years. He ever bore the reputation of a liberal, honest gentleman.

---

[28] This is a reprint of a clipping found in Mr. Taylor's scrap book, evidently from a Frankfort, Kentucky, newspaper of 1874. *A History of the Frankfort Cemetery*, by L. Frank Johnson, published in 1921, devotes a paragraph, on page 28, to Captain John Howell.

"As an evidence of his high standing as a brave and reliable officer I will state that the now venerable ex-chancellor, Henry Pirtle, of Louisville, but then a citizen of Hartford, was in Lexington when General LaFayette passed through that place in 1825, and in conversation with him Captain Howell was named as a resident of Ohio County; upon hearing his name the old hero and companion of Washington immediately remembered him and spoke of his gallantry and good conduct as an officer and his fidelity as a man, and sent Captain Howell a most kindly greeting. I was present when La-Fayette's message was delivered to the then feeble old Captain, and he wept like a child, and I will not assert that others did not shed tears also.

"Having myself known Captain Howell from my infancy until his death, I feel assured that none stood higher in the community in which he lived as a kind, honorable, and honest man. As a soldier, or citizen, his remains are fully entitled to a resting place in the beautiful depository of the good and great of our state. H. D. T."

D

HARRISON D. TAYLOR—A BIOGRAPHICAL SKETCH [29]

Harrison D. Taylor was born March 31, 1802, in Frederick County, Virginia, and died April 8, 1889, after a successful and useful life, at the advanced age of eighty-seven years. His parents were of Welsh and English origin and derived the name of Harrison from an intermarriage into the Harrison family of Virginia. His grandfather, also named Harrison Taylor, emigrated to Ohio County, Kentucky, the latter part of the last century. His father having died without a will, the eldest son inherited the property, under the feudal laws of that time, and left Harrison shareless, who, declining to be a pensioner on his brother's bounty, boldly struck out for the frontier. It was not long until he married Miss Jane Curlet and settled far back in the woods. As the country improved, he built a mill on a stream in Frederick County, by which mill passed the main road leading from the east across the Alleghany Mountains to the then great unexplored West. He raised a large family and bore the reputation of an honest miller, which, in after years, gained him the title of "Honest Old Taylor at the mill." Who should wish to trace his origin to a higher source? "There is no legacy so rich as honesty."

The subject of this sketch was the son of the Reverend Thomas Taylor, a pioneer Methodist minister in Ohio County. Although through life a large contributor to the support of his church, he never asked nor received a cent for his services as preacher of the gospel. While in the vigor of his manhood it was his practice to work at hard labor through the week and ride many miles on Sunday to fill some appointment, frequently going to Muhlenberg, Grayson, and Breckinridge counties and even to Hardin, to preach. Of him it may be truly said that his heart was always right, his failings were but virtues in excess. He had five sons—Nicholas, Wesley, Harrison D., Milton and Thomas—and one daughter, Frances.

The third son, Harrison D., was a man who lived without fear and died without reproach. His boyhood days were spent on his

---

[29] This sketch of Harrison D. Taylor is from *Biographical Cyclopedia of the Commonwealth of Kentucky*, published in 1896 by the John M. Gresham Company, of Chicago and Philadelphia. It was written about seven years after Mr. Taylor's death. A shorter sketch of Mr. Taylor, written twenty years before his death, appears in the *Biographical Encyclopedia of Kentucky*, published in 1878, by J. M. Armstrong and Company, of Cincinnati.

father's farm, where he had but small chance of obtaining an education, but such was his burning ambition for knowledge that, whilst he followed the plow, he carried his grammar in his pocket and conjugated his verbs as he went along. At night, by means of a bright wood fire, he pursued his studies. At last, upon attaining his majority, he decided upon law as a profession, and moved to Hartford, the county seat, where he studied with Judge Henry Pirtle, one of the most distinguished lawyers of the state. His mother, one of the illustrious women of her day, a model of all the duties of social, religious, and domestic life, had instilled in him the principle to do right whatever else might happen. * * *

He was admitted to the bar in 1825. As a practicing lawyer he was a model of industry and fidelity to his clients, of which he had a large share. He had the confidence of the people as an honest, fair dealing, truthful, noble-spirited man. His practice at the bar was restricted by his own choice and taste to chancery causes and for many years after his retirement from active practice his opinion on the vexed questions which so frequently arise in equity was sought after and esteemed by the Hartford bar.

His habits of close study, formed in early life, clung to him in old age. His mind was broad and liberal, and he had a most extensive knowledge of all subjects. In the domain of history, the sciences, literature, politics, and religion he possessed a vast and varied store of accurate information. He made the first authentic survey of Rough and Green rivers by direction of the Government, which resulted in establishing permanent navigation of Green River. His excellent knowledge of land titles and of surveying enabled him to acquire a vast amount of real estate in Ohio County. It has been said of him that by his leniency and indulgence he afforded many struggling young farmers the opportunity of retaining their homes. His influence was on the side of every good enterprise and every broad charity. His house was the home of the friendless and especially was he interested in those struggling to acquire an education. He wrote a valuable history of Ohio County and many other interesting papers; he was a member of The Filson Club, the principal historical

Harrison D. Taylor

society of the State. He never aspired to political honors and never held office but once [county attorney], and was elected to that without being a candidate. He was in early times a Whig and great admirer and personal friend of Henry Clay, but after the retirement of the great Commoner he affiliated with the Democratic party.[30]

His first marriage was to Miss Mary Davis in 1828, by whom he had several children: Henry Pirtle, Fannie, Randall, Thomas, and

---

[30] The following data pertain to Harrison D. Taylor's parents, his brothers and sisters, and his children and grandchildren. Some of the facts appearing here are given elsewhere in this book, but are repeated in order to present more clearly the additional data.

Old Harrison Taylor was a son of John Taylor who, in 1726, married Hannah Harrison. John Taylor was a son of Simon and a grandson of Richard Taylor who came from Kent County, England, in 1608.

The Reverend Thomas Taylor, son of Old Harrison Taylor, was born in 1764. On November 24, 1793, at Winchester, Virginia, he married Margaret Curlet (daughter of Nicholas Curlet). They came to Ohio County in 1802, where he died in 1836. She was born in 1772 and died in 1855. Both are buried in what later became known as the Milton Taylor Cemetery, about three miles east of Hartford. The Reverend Thomas Taylor's father and mother were the first to be buried in this graveyard, where now lie many of the five generations that followed. The Reverend and Mrs. Thomas Taylor were the parents of six children: Nicholas C., Wesley, Harrison D., Milton, Thomas, and Miss Frances Taylor. Milton, Thomas, and Miss Frances Taylor never married. Wesley Taylor was born in 1799 and died in 1824. Wesley's age and the absence of any known tradition or further record leads to the inference that he, too, had not married.

Nicholas C. Taylor, oldest son of the Reverend Thomas Taylor, was born in 1794 and died in 1873. In 1817 he married Eliza Statler, daughter of Stephen Statler. They were the parents of Colonel Marion C. Taylor (a bachelor), Hester Ann (who first married Thomas Davis, then Mr. Grissom), Susan (Mrs. Joseph Miller), Margaret Curlet (Mrs. William Harbison), and Julia (Mrs. Thompson Mitchell). Colonel Marion C. Taylor was born in Ohio County in 1822. On his maternal side he was a grandson of Stephen Statler and Rhoda Pigman, and a great-grandson of the Reverend Ignatius Pigman and Susannah Lamar. In early manhood he moved to Shelbyville and was identified with the social and political development of Shelby County. His diary written while with the Cardenas of the Lopez Expedition to Cuba in 1850 is published in the September, 1921, issue of *The Register* of the Kentucky State Historical Society. His services in the Fifth Kentucky Infantry are commented upon in *The Union Regiments of Kentucky*, published in 1897.

Harrison D. Taylor, son of the Reverend Thomas Taylor, married Mary Davis in 1828. She was born on November 11, 1802, and died on January 3, 1862. They were the parents of five children (not including John McHenry Taylor and Harrison Taylor who died in infancy): Dr. Henry Pirtle Taylor, Randall, Frances, Thomas, and Margaret Taylor. Margaret Taylor was born in 1839. She married Junius May of Daviess County. After her death, which occurred in 1867, Mr. May married again and continued to live in Daviess County. Thomas Taylor was born in 1837. He married Margaret Young Davis. They had no children. He died in 1903 and she in 1907. Frances Taylor was born in 1835. She married Dr. Burr F. Nall, who became a leading physician of Hartford. She died in 1868. Dr. Nall died the following year. Randall Taylor was born in 1833. He married Miss Lucy Griffin, daughter of Warren Griffin of Culpeper,

Margaret, all of whom are dead but Thomas, who is a farmer near Hartford. His second marriage was to Mrs. Kittie Trible, of Owensboro, who survived him.

His eldest son, Dr. Henry Pirtle Taylor, married Miss Sallie May of Daviess County. Two of their children are living [in 1896]: Harrison P. Taylor and Mary Taylor. The former married Miss Mary Pendleton, daughter of Dr. John E. Pendleton of Hartford, Kentucky, to whom were born two children, Sallie and John Pendleton.

Virginia. After his death, which occurred in 1870, his widow married James Luther Collins. Her only child was by her second marriage and was named Randall Taylor Collins.

Dr. Henry Pirtle Taylor, the oldest of the children of Harrison D. Taylor to reach maturity, was born in 1831. In 1858 he married Sarah (or Sally) Mildred May (sister of Junius May and a daughter of John and Elizabeth Davis). He died in 1866. She was born in 1835 and died in 1871. They were the parents of Harrison Pirtle Taylor, John Junius Taylor (who died aged three years), and Mary (Elizabeth) Taylor.

Many years after the death of his first wife Harrison D. Taylor married Mrs. Kittie Trible, widow of Barnett Trible and mother of Mary Ellen Trible who married Clarence E. Walker of Louisville. Mr. and Mrs. Walker are the parents of E. Helm Walker. Mrs. Kittie Trible was a daughter of John Wallace and his wife Jane Taylor Wallace, who was a daughter of pioneer Harrison Taylor and his wife, Elizabeth Allen.

Harrison Pirtle Taylor, son of Dr. Henry Pirtle Taylor, was born in 1859. In 1884 he married Mary Pendleton, who was born in 1858 and was a daughter of Dr. John E. Pendleton. She died in December, 1919, and he in May, 1920. They were the parents of two children: Sallie M. Taylor, who was born in 1885, and married Dr. Woolfolk Barrow of Lexington, and John Pendleton Taylor, who was born in 1887 and married Marie Cook of Vicksburg. These, in turn, are the parents of Woolfolk Barrow, Jr., Mary Barrow, and Harrison Taylor Barrow; and Esther Stuart Cook Taylor. In its obituary comments on Harrison Pirtle Taylor the *Hartford Herald* said: "For many years Mr. Taylor has been considered one of the most prominent members of the bar in western Kentucky. He was attorney for the Illinois Central Railroad during the past thirty-five years, and for the Central Coal and Iron Company for twenty years or more. He was a lifelong Democrat and represented the Fourth Kentucky District in the Democratic National Convention at Denver in 1908. During the World War he was very active in his support of all patriotic movements. He died at his residence on Main Street, this city, Monday, 3 A. M., May 17, 1920, after an illness of only two days of double pneumonia. He was born July 9, 1859 * * * He was a son of Dr. Henry Pirtle Taylor and a grandson of Harrison D. Taylor, pioneer attorney and financier of Ohio County."

Mary Taylor, only daughter of Dr. Henry Pirtle Taylor, and only granddaughter of Harrison D. Taylor, was born in 1863. In 1913 she married Abram Winter Logan, a native of Canada, who died in Hartford in 1922.

E

OHIO COUNTY BIOGRAPHIES PUBLISHED IN 1885

Biographical sketches of two hundred and seventy-five Ohio County citizens appear in *Kentucky, a History of the State*, by J. H. Battle [and W. H. Perrin and G. C. Kniffin], published in Louisville and Chicago in 1885. This is a volume of about a thousand pages: the first half is devoted to a history of the State, and the last half to biographical sketches. The edition here referred to includes Ohio County and twelve other counties: Butler, Caldwell, Crittenden, Hancock, Hopkins, Livingston, Logan, Lyon, McLean, Muhlenberg, Union, and Webster. Most of the sketches contain more or less early local history and genealogical data pertaining to the subjects' ancestors, many of whom were pioneers. We present a complete list of the names of the citizens of Ohio County whose biographies are published, each followed by the year of his birth.

SUBJECT OF SKETCH	BORN	SUBJECT OF SKETCH	BORN
William Henry Acton	1834	B. M. Bennett	1832
William Porter Allen	1829	Charles N. Bennett	1811
James Ferdinand Ambrose	1845	Jacob T. Bennett	1837
Henry Frederick Armendt	1853	John B. Blankenship	1848
Hardin Ashley	1836	Wm. H. Blankenship	1838
Albert S. Aull	1840	Thomas Bowles	1823
Edward G. Austin	—	W. L. S. Brackin	1825
William McKendree Awtry	1842	George A. Brown	1819
Levi Marion Axton	1845	Isaac Brown	1807
Alexander B. Baird	1821	Isaac Sylvester Brown	1847
Samuel L. Baird	1824	James B. Brown	1838
Augustus Baker	1839	John Sep. Brown	1837
Isaac H. Baker	1823	Asberry Anderson Bryant	1833
J. W. Baker	1846	Charles W. Butler	1831
George W. Barnard	1832	William Spurrier Byers	1829
Ignatius P. Barnerd	1846	Marcy T. Cain	1847
Mrs. Amanda P. Barnett	1830	John Wesley Cannan	1829
James M. Barnett	1854	Archie Little Chick	1839
John L. Barnett	1850	Robert Enos Childs	1835
Joseph C. Barnett	1818	John Chinn	1842
The Bean Family	—	Josias Chinn	1831
Dr. Henry F. Bean	1853	Charles Valentine Christian	1836
Henry William Bean	1846	Samuel Meritt Christian	1834
John D. Bell	1825	William Stewart Cole	1837
Alexander B. Bennett	1819	William D. Coleman	1822

Ohio County in the Olden Days

J. Will Cooper	1852
Lorenzo Dow Cooper	1819
James R. Coppage	1833
Dr. Leonard Thomas Cox	1843
Samuel K. Cox	1838
Charles Wintersmith Cromes	1850
Joseph Daniel	1832
Robert J. Daniel	1829
James Clinton Davis	1834
John F. Davis	1818
Edward Davison	1830
John Doherty	1836
Robert J. Duff	1838
Isaac N. Duke	1828
John D. T. Duke	1835
Robert N. Duke	1848
William Henry Duke	1843
David Duncan	1842
William G. Duncan	1851
Alexander C. Ellis	1842
Henry M. Eskridge	1861
James Eudaley	1827
William J. Everly	1827
Charles B. B. Felix	1847
Frank L. Felix	1858
James Thomas Felix	1831
William Logan Felix	1828
Charles L. Field	1852
James W. Ford	1842
John A. Ford	1819
William Ford	1824
Isaac Foster	1825
William Foster	1823
Absalom P. Frazier	1827
Septimus P. Fulkerson	1845
William H. Fulkerson	1822
William W. Gaines	1843
Thomas Gillstrap	1837
George W. Gordon	1846
William A. Gordon	1844
Bluford C. Greer	1840
John C. Greer	1831
Samuel H. Greer	1829
William F. Gregory	1837
Louis G. Haden	1846
Clarence Hardwick	1851
Eli Milton Hart	1824
Francis M. Hatler	1848
John A. Hawkins	1838
Wm. Bramwell Hayward	1832
Samuel E. Hill	1844
Alfred Thomas Hines	1816
John Birks Hines	1832
John W. Hines	1848
Thomas Henry Hines	1827
George B. Hocker	1832
James B. Hocker	1867
Philip M. Hocker	1827
Richard P. Hocker	1845
Asa W. Hodges	1830
John D. Holbrook	1851
Edward Clarence Hubbard	1840
Joseph A. Hudnall	1826
Elias Gess Hunley	1826
William M. Hunter	1826
Charles W. Hussey	1826
Rev. Benj. T. Iglehart	1835
James B. Iglehart	1842
Eugene P. James	1844
Rev. Benj. F. Jenkins	—
Thaddeus S. Jett	1837
John H. Jewel	—
Elijah Johnson	1832
John M. Johnson	1850
Samuel Jones	1825
Ezekiel V. Kimbley	1817
Isaac F. Kimbley	1821
W. T. King	1841
Robert E. Kinnimonth	1855
Herbert B. Kinsolving	1860
Dr. Charles W. Layton	1839
John Jay Layton	1821
Alfred K. Leach	1839
Henry Clay Leach	1845
Leonard H. Leach	—
James Stone Lee	1831
John W. Lewis	1817
Henry J. C. Lindley	1822
Adam Liter	1822
William Lyons	1847
Henry D. McHenry	1826
Azariah Peck Maddox	1824
David J. K. Maddox	1836
George M. Martin	—

Biographies Published in 1885

Wade N. Martin............... 1827	John L. Ralph................. 1824
Robert J. Mason............... 1829	George W. Reid................ 1845
Charles W. Massie............. 1845	Mosby J. Reid................. 1846
Chamburs I. Maxey............. 1851	Elijah Franklin Render......... 1853
Rev. Milburn A. Maxey......... 1848	George W. Render.............. 1824
Dr. James W. Meador........... 1838	John Render................... 1816
Wm. Paton Medkiff............. 1845	Joshua L. Render.............. 1821
William Mercer................ 1819	William P. Render............. 1841
Henry S. Metcalf.............. 1821	Mark Renfrow.................. 1843
Elijah Miller................. 1834	Virgil Renfrow................ 1837
James Miller.................. 1821	William H. Reynolds........... 1834
James Barney Miller........... 1847	Daniel James Rhoads........... 1834
James P. Miller............... 1850	McHenry Rhoads................ 1858
Joseph T. Miller.............. 1840	John C. Riley................. 1849
Dr. G. F. Mitchell............ 1843	Sylvester W. Roberston........ 1844
Dr. J. J. Mitchell............ 1847	John Butler Rogers............ 1851
John H. Monroe................ 1861	Christopher C. Rone........... 1849
Mrs. Nancy I. Montague........ 1832	George Rowe................... 1816
John Wilson Moore............. 1839	William L. Rowe............... 1841
Robert Y. Morehead............ 1858	Dr. George R. Sanders......... 1836
David Morton.................. 1842	Samuel F. Sharp............... 1843
Dr. James S. Morton........... 1828	Wm. Henry Sherrod............. 1836
John P. Morton................ 1843	Wm. Henry Shively............. 1837
Louis C. Morton............... 1850	Wm. D. Shrewsbury............. 1847
Timoleon Morton............... 1834	George C. Shultz.............. 1834
Benjamin Newton............... 1831	David L. Smith................ 1844
George W. Newton.............. 1859	George N. Smith............... 1832
Mrs. Catherine O'Brien........ 1833	John K. Smith................. 1856
James A. Park................. 1838	Joseph H. Smith............... 1840
William H. H. Park............ 1841	Thomas J. Smith............... 1835
Dr. Beverley N. Patterson..... 1834	Richard Henry Stevens......... 1833
George W. Patterson........... 1840	Rev. James C. Stewart......... 1813
Jonathan H. Patterson......... 1816	Lafayette Sublett............. 1834
Langston M. Patterson......... 1831	Cicero Truman Sutton.......... 1859
James H. Patton............... 1839	John T. Sutton................ 1838
Dr. John Wm. Patton........... 1835	Pardon Tabor.................. 1823
Joel Payton................... 1835	A. Donnie Taylor.............. 1858
Wm. Dawson Pemberton.......... 1847	John Alexander Taylor......... 1812
Dr. John E. Pendleton......... 1831	Leonard L. Taylor............. 1838
John William Petty............ 1831	Richard Stevens Taylor........ 1834
Francis M. Pharis............. 1842	S. Calvin Taylor.............. 1847
Ferdinand W. Pirtle........... —	Mrs. Sarah A. Taylor.......... 1838
Timothy C. F. Pirtle.......... 1857	Squire L. Taylor.............. 1827
William H. Porter............. 1818	Virgil Taylor................. 1837
John Walker Ragland........... 1834	William A. Taylor............. 1836
Moses Smith Ragland........... 1845	The Thomas Family............. —
James Raley................... 1818	Christopher Thomas............ 1835

Ohio County in the Olden Days

James A. Thomas	1823	Dr. Sylvester J. Wedding	1849
James William Thomas	1857	Jacob Weller	1830
George Bell Thomson	1855	John C. Westerfield	1832
James A. Tichenor	1846	Wm. H. Westerfield	1842
John W. Tichenor	1847	Uriah J. Westerfield	1852
Lavega W. Tichenor	1851	Edward R. Williams	1848
Silus N. Tichenor	1836	Gross B. Williams	1855
Squire W. Tichenor	1849	Jesse S. Williams	1845
Henry Tinsley	1836	Samuel A. Williams	1854
Daniel F. Tracy	1842	Thomas Williams	1832
Daniel B. Trout	1840	W. H. Williams	1818
Green Berry Van Nort	1838	Felix G. Willis	1839
David Vaughan	1809	Ansel Wilson	1834
E. Dudley Walker	1827	John Calvin Wilson	1842
Samuel Wallace	1825	Samuel Martin Wilson	1836
John Walle	1833	Daniel Wise	1817
Barnett C. Warden	1828	Henry P. Wise	1823
Thomas E. Webb	1849	Marion Yates	1836
The Wedding Family			

By far the greatest number of biographical sketches of Ohio County citizens published in any book are the two hundred and seventy-five in *Kentucky, A History of the State* here tabulated.[31]

[31] As already stated, the history of Daviess County up to 1815 is a part of the early history of Ohio County. The biographies of some of the pioneers given in *A History of Daviess County* (1883) contain much pertaining to Ohio County in pioneer times. Sketches of Ohio County citizens appear in other books. Among such publications are *Biographical Encyclopedia of Kentucky* (1878), *Biographical Cyclopedia of the Commonwealth of Kentucky* (1896), *A History of Kentucky and Kentuckians* (1912) by J. Polk Johnson, and *History of Kentucky* (1922) edited by Charles Kerr. In 1898 W. P. Greene, of Bowling Green, compiled a hundred-and-forty-page book entitled *The Green River Country from Bowling Green to Evansville*. It is devoted to the traffic, resources, towns, and people of that section. Fourteen pages are given to the history of Ohio County, including biographies of a few men of comparatively recent times.

In the archives of The Filson Club, Louisville, is an unpublished paper prepared by Mrs. Francis E. Merriman and read before the Club in April, 1920, entitled "A History of Hartford and Ohio County." Among her cited sources is the Harrison D. Taylor scrap book. It may be well to add that a more careful examination of the Draper Manuscripts in the Wisconsin Historical Society, Madison, may reveal unpublished material pertaining to some of the pioneers of Ohio County; also that the *History of Kentucky*, the Blue-Grass State, by Temple Bodley and Samuel M. Wilson, now in preparation by the S. J. Clark Publishing Company of Chicago, may have some Ohio County citizens in its list of biographies.

F

OHIO COUNTY MARRIAGE RECORDS, 1799 TO 1840

The following list of early marriages was compiled from the original certificates returned by the ministers or county officials who were authorized to perform the ceremony. These more or less loosely filed documents [supplemented by a book of copies of records from 1808 to 1828, indexed and neatly written by Charles Henderson] constituted the only record of early marriages until 1923, when Miss Amelia May Barnett [now Mrs. Whittier W. Rogers], at the request of Mrs. Mary Hale Dean, arranged the mass of papers in chronological order and listed them in à ledger.

It is probable that in Ohio County, as in other counties in early times, ministers sometimes failed to return the certificates until months after they had performed the ceremony, and in some such cases, through error, gave the date of the marriage the same as the date of the belated report. A few marriages are twice recorded; all such entries show a variation in the date and in some of the names. How many of the records are missing will never be known, for in those days no memorandum was kept of the blanks that were called for nor of those that had been returned. Some returns may have been lost many years ago after they had been deposited in the county clerk's office, and, as was the case elsewhere in pioneer times, some may never have been turned in at all.

The frequency of bad penmanship and phonetic spelling makes it impossible to prepare a list in which every name and date can be given with exactitude. Erroneous spelling has not been corrected. The only changes made are in some of the Christian names which have been abbreviated to prevent the entry from exceeding one line. In some instances the name of the minister or the bondsman could not be deciphered.

The entries are here published in duplicate with the names of the brides and grooms in alphabetical order. The date of marriage

Ohio County in the Olden Days

is followed first by the name of the person who performed the ceremony, and second by the bondsman who declared that he knew of no legal objection to the proposed marriage.

This Appendix is not embraced in the Index at the end of this volume.

GROOM OR BRIDE	DATE	OFFICIATOR	BONDSMAN
Abner, Edward, and Watson, Elizabeth, Dec. 31, 1806.	John Davis	Robert Watson
Acker, William, and Harris, Sally, March 5, 1813.	John Davis	Jesse Harris
Acton, America, and Ardell, James, March 20, 1828.	Ancil Hall	Richard Wathen
Acton, Francis, and Casey, Didamah, Jan. 23, 1839.	J. G. Ward	Caleb Boswell
Acton, Francis, and Casey, Catherine, Nov. 26, 1840.	———	Caleb Boswell
Adams, John, and Wilson, Mary Jane, Dec. 9, 1839.	John Phipps	Thomas Wilson
Adams, Sally, and Lee, Abner, May 19, 1807.	John Davis	Lewis Adams
Addington, Dorcas A., and Duke, Thomas, March 28, 1837.	J. A. Holding.	H. Addington
Addington, Henry, and Barnard, Dorcas, Dec. 1, 1799.	Ignatius Pigman.	Josh. Barnard
Addington, Jemima, and Coleman, Henry, Dec. 11, 1835.	John Phipps.	Josh. Addington
Addington, Joshua, and Cooper, Sally, July 28, 1828.	Loderic Davis	Henry Cooper
Addington, Joshua, and Ingleheart, Sally, Oct. 7, 1834.	Wm. Sandefur	H. Addington
Addington, Sally, and Cane, John, March 5, 1830.	Loderic Davis	Henry Addington
Adle, Margaret, and Roberts, Willis, June 28, 1814.	John Weldon	Chas. Thrift
Adle, Nancy, and Meeks, Hardin, Oct. 5, 1829.	Ancil Hall	James Adle
Albin, Joshua, and Cox, Polly, March 11, 1835.	George Render	Nathaniel Howard
Albin, Malinda, and Beasley, Robert, Sept. 28, 1828.	Paul Abney	A. Albin
Albin, Polly, and Wilson, John, April 5, 1823.	William Harlt	Absalom Albin
Albin, Rebecca, and Marlowe, Thomas, Nov. 25, 1837.	Ancil Hall	Absalom Albin
Alin, Elizabeth, and Duvall, Benjamin, Feb. 19, 1820.	Thomas Taylor	Dillis Dyer
Allen, Alfred, and Harlong, Mitalda, Jan. 31, 1840.	Paul Brey	James Izel
Allen, Henry, and Leatherman, Jane, Feb. 28, 1821.	Benj. Burton	Theophelum Allen
Allen, Mahala, and Stevens, Joshua, Jan. 13, 1838.	Basil Ward	Isaac Keown
Allen, Mary, and Moseley, Robert, Sept. 16, 1823.	William Harlt	Jacob Wood
Allen, Milly, and Cooper, Wesley, Sept. 22, 1831.	Thomas Taylor	Benj. Duvall
Allen, Nathan, and Webb, Titha, May 3, 1829.	John Denham	John Webb
Allen, Usa, and Campbell, Abagaile, July 18, 1822.	Wm. Hart	Zachariah Roberts
Allen, William, and Huston, Ann, Feb. 8, 1813.	Job Hobbs	Nathaniel Hamilton
Allen, William, and Wilson, Rhoda, July 4, 1831.	Thomas Taylor	James McKenzie
Alm, James, and Hodden, Rosey, May 21, 1808.	John Grower	Jones Alm
Alphine, Sutton, and Taylor, Martha, Aug. 23, 1810.	John Davis	Henry Taylor
Ambrose, Henry, and Crowe, Eliza, Aug. 30, 1836.	Wm. Sandefur	Sam Hendricks
Ambrose, Jacob, and James, Mariah, June 18, 1823.	William Hart	John Calhoun
Ambrose, John, and Hoover, Sally, July 28, 1828.	William Hart	James Jones
Ambrose, Lewis, and Chapman, Frances, April 18, 1833.	Wm. Hart	Samuel Huston
Ambrose, Michael, and Ward, Delilah, March 18, 1840.	Basel Ward	Nathan Bennett
Ambrose, Samuel, and Duke, Polly, June 28, 1832.	Buford Henry	Thomas Duke
Anderson, Amos, and Hatcher, Elizabeth, Feb. 5, 1820.	Davis Loderic	Wm. Hatcher
Anderson, Anna, and Deweese, Benjamin, June 25, 1802.	Ignatius Pigman.	———
Anderson, Athel, and Byers, Margaret, Jan. 8, 1810.	L. Davis	George Hoover
Anderson, Elizabeth, and Brown, Jonathan.	———	———
Anderson, Hannah, and Brown, Henry, Jan. 19, 1803.	Benj. Talbert	Reuben Brown
Anderson, Henry, and Beasley, Malinda, Jan. 7, 1838.	Jos. Ward	Absalom Albin

Marriage Records, 1799 to 1840

Anderson, John, and Gardner, Fanny, Mar. 7, 1817. Thomas Taylor....Henry Evans
Anderson, Mary, and Crowe, Jesse, Oct. 1, 1814. Thos. Taylor......N. H. McFarland
Anderson, Nelson, and Glenn, Martha, Dec. 17, 1808. John Davis........Wm. Glenn
Anderson, Patsy, and Dexter, Joseph, Dec. 20, 1825. Wm. Kincheloe...Jesse Anderson
Anderson, Peggy, and Bracher, Thomas, April 22, 1810. Wm. Anderson....J. Anderson
Anderson, Sarah, and Smith, Joseph, April 19, 1813. Thos. Taylor....Leonard Hoover
Archibald, Nancy, and Moseley, Robert C., Jan. 10, 1827. Ancil Hall......B. B. Malin
Ardell, James, and Acton, America, March 20, 1828. Ancil Hall.....Richard Wathen
Armstrong, Polly, and Linn, James, May 15, 1810. John Davis......William Wright
Armstrong, Thomas, and Head, Polly, Aug. 8, 1832. Ancil Hall..........B. Barnett
Arnold, Amanda, and Arnold, Brockel, Dec. 3, 1832. William Hart.......John Daniel
Arnold, John, and Jackson, Catherine, Dec. 2, 1818. Thos. Taylor......Julius Jackson
Arnold, William, and Miller, Amanda, Jan. 12, 1835. William Hart....John D. Miller
Ashby, Charlotte, and Hedges, James, Oct. 23, 1806. John Davis......Warren Ashby
Ashby, David, and Rowe, Elizabeth, March 25, 1812. Joe Anderson...Edward Rowe
Ashby, Fronie, and Williams, Evan, March 14, 1807. Benj. Talbert....Jesse Ashby
Ashby, George, and Rowe, Elizabeth Crowe, Sept. 13, 1836. Geo. Render....J. Stewart
Ashby, Horiteo, and Field, Hannah, March 28, 1804. Thomas Taylor.....Sally Field
Ashby, Jesse, and Ingleheart, Elizabeth, March 22, 1830. Wm. Downs......J. Inglehart
Ashby, Katy, and Ross, Ervin, Sept. 5, 1804. John Davis...............Jesse Ashby
Ashby, Peter, and Rowe, Sally, Aug. 7, 1817. George Render..........Robert Rowe
Ashby, Polly, and Little, David, Jan. 15, 1808. John Grower.........Warren Ashby
Ashby, Polly, and McNeely, Ezekiel, Sept. 30, 1819. John Phipps.....William Ashby
Ashby, Rebecca, and Lindsey, William, April 22, 1819. John Phipps....William Ashby
Ashby, Rebecca, and Williams, Warden, Sept. 25, 1839. Thomas Downs....Wm. Ashby
Ashby, Sanford, and Bell, Mary R., April 2, 1839. William Downs......John Crowe
Ashby, Susannah, and Hocker, John B., Dec. 10, 1831. John Phipps....Thomas Ashby
Ashby, Tanna, and Haskins, Charles, Dec. 9, 1836. George Render.....Jesse Ashby
Ashby, Tanner, and Miller, Elizabeth Ann, June 30, 1836. John Phipps....W. Phipps
Ashby, Warren, and Hedges, Mary, Feb. 18, 1807. John Davis......Josiah Hedges
Ashby, William, and Rowe, Nancy, March 29, 1816. George Render....Thomas Rowe
Ashley, Elizabeth, and Coffee, Philip, Dec. 29, 1813. ―――――.....James Rogers
Ashley, Jesse, and Ingleheart, Eliza, June 27, 1800. Wm. Davis........Wm. Dauney
Ashley, Thomas, and Coleman, Catherine, June 18, 1806. Thomas Taylor....Sam Ross
Askins, Elizabeth, and Malin, John, Aug. 29, 1812. Loney Jackson....Harrison Askins
Atherton, Aaron, and Hoover, Millie, Mar. 21, 1819. Thos. Taylor....Jacob Hoover
Atherton, Amelia, and Hugh, Joel, Oct. 6, 1825. Loderic Davis.......Nicholas Hocker
Atherton, Ann, and Pender, Thomas, Oct. 14, 1817. Loderic Davis....Abednigo Baize
Atherton, Benjamin, and Far, Sarah, Jan. 15, 1806. Benj. Talbert.......Henry Brown
Atherton, Delilah, and Riggs, Isaac, Dec. 29, 1823. Jared Tichenor......Joseph Riggs
Atherton, Elizabeth, and Biggerstaff, Wm., Nov. 14, 1811. Lon. Jackson....A. Atherton
Atherton, Hannah, and Davis, Nelson, May 6, 1822. Loderic Davis.....Jeremiah Cox
Atherton, John, and Atherton, Unis, Feb. 9, 1811. Benj. Talbert........John McLean
Atherton, John, and Morgan, Elizabeth, March 4, 1837. Ancil Hall....James Tanner
Atherton, Joseph, and Davis, Mary Ann, March 30, 1830. Ancil Hall......A. Atherton
Atherton, Moses, and Tanner, Eliza, Dec. 21, 1830. William Downs....Zachariah Field
Atherton, Peggy, and Wafford, Wm., Aug. 16, 1810. Joe Anderson.....Moses Atherton
Atherton, Unis, and Atherton, John, Feb. 9, 1811. Benj. Talbert.......John McLean
Atterberry, David, and Moore, Sally, April 6, 1809. John Grower.......Geo. Matthews
Atterberry, Eliza, and Maheuren, Frederic, Sept. 18, 1828. A. Hall.....W. Atterberry

Ohio County in the Olden Days

Atterberry, Rebecca, and Lamb, John P., Jan. 3, 1831. Ancil Hall......Henry Edison
Atterberry, Reuben, and Weeks, Catherine, Jan. 1, 1814. Joseph Wilson..⎯⎯⎯⎯⎯⎯⎯⎯
Atterberry, Reuben, and Weeks, Catherine, Dec. 22, 1823. Joseph Wilson. R. Eskridge
Atterberry, Richard, and Moore, Patsy, April 19, 1807. John Davis....Walker Moore
Atterberry, Stout, and Crash, Fanny, Dec. 8, 1824. Joseph Wilson....Saul Whittier
Aubrey, Benjamin, and Likens, Sally, Feb. 1, 1836. John Phipps......Mark Likens
Aubrey, Emilie, and White, Lewis, Aug. 19, 1831. David Kelley.......John A. White
Aubrey, Jacob, and Crawford, Fanny, Sept. 28, 1840. Oscar Bishop......J. Crawford
Aubrey, John, and Cannon, Nancy, Sept. 20, 1821. Benjamin Burton....Pardon Taber
Aubrey, William, and Wilson, Betsy, May 13, 1828. William Hart......Robert Wilson
Austin, Andrew, and Chinn, Dorothy B., Aug. 31, 1840. John Phipps....Raley Chinn
Austin, Barnch, and Render, Polly, Aug. 10, 1818. John Phipps.......George Render
Austin, Elizabeth, and Taylor, Blackstone, Jan. 10, 1828. Wm. Harlt....Thomas Austin
Austin, Helen, and Miller, Joseph, Nov. 10, 1818. Loderic Davis.........John Austin
Austin, John, and Redman, Polly, Oct. 9, 1932. John Phipps............John Phipps
Austin, John, and Redmond, Ann, Oct. 25, 1837. John Phipps............John Phipps
Austin, Margaret, and Borah, Willis, Feb. 15, 1830. Wm. Harlt..........Thos. Austin
Austin, Margaret, and Leach, Talbert, March 25, 1839. ⎯⎯⎯⎯⎯⎯⎯......T. J. Benton
Austin, Nancy, and New, James, Jan. 19, 1818. Benjamin Kelley........Joseph Wallace
Austin, Philner, and Marletts, Mabel, April 27, 1837. Wm. Sandefur......J. Hoover
Austin, Robert, and Render, Mary, March 17, 1829. George Render....Robert Render
Austin, S. C., and Bailey, Theodicia, Jan. 10, 1840. ⎯⎯⎯⎯⎯⎯⎯.........James Lewis
Austin, Sarah Emily, and Stevens, James, Oct. 14, 1839. Mino Ford....Brooks Austin
Austin, Thomas, and Basford, Amelia, Sept. 6, 1830. Loderic Davis........W. Barnes
Austin, William, and Lanham, Henrietta, Mar. 29, 1826. Thomas Taylor. W. M. Davis
Austin, William, and Taylor, Sarah Ann, Oct. 31, 1836. Geo. Render.....John Phipps
Austin, Wisas, and Stevens, Minerva, Nov. 6, 1838. John Pinkston......David Stevens
Autory, Elizabeth, and Ezel, Thomas, Jan. 11, 1822. William Harlt......John Autory
Autory, Giles, and Miller, Siticia, March 28, 1822. William Hart........John Miller
Autory, Patsy, and Autory, Simon, Jan. 19, 1822. William Hart..........John Autory
Autory, Simon, and Autory, Patsy, Jan. 19, 1822. William Hart..........John Autory
Autry, Burrel, and Wiley, Lucinda, March 10, 1834. John Phipps........Simon Autry
Autry, Emeline, and Shields, James, Sept. 3, 1839. ⎯⎯⎯⎯⎯⎯⎯........Simon Ashby
Avery, Milly, and McDaniel, Collen, July 12, 1808. William Anderson.....John Pult
Axton, Margaret, and Robertson, Henry, Aug. 25, 1825. Benj. Talbert....Benj. Axton
Axton, Nancy, and Evens, Francis, Aug. 31, 1818. Benj. Kelley........Philip Axton
Bailey, Martin, and Spence, Sarah, Sept. 8, 1834. Allen Boyd............John Spence
Bailey, Theodicia, and Austin, S. C., Jan. 10, 1840. ⎯⎯⎯⎯⎯⎯⎯........James Lewis
Baird, James, and Barnett, Rebecca, Oct. 24, 1803. John Davis..........W. F. Smith
Baird, Jane, and Stevens, John, March 10, 1830. William Harlt ....James Baird
Baird, Martha Isabel, and McSherry, Henry, Sept. 22, 1840. Basil Ward...Thos. Baird
Baird, Martha Jane, and McSherry, Hiram, Jan. 14, 1840. Basil Ward.....Thos. Baird
Baird, Mary, and Stevens, William M., Feb. 25, 1833. R. Y. Reynolds....James Baird
Baird, Polly, and Hopkins, James, Dec. 17, 1803. John Davis............James Baird
Baird, Rachel, and Barnett, Thomas, Nov. 14, 1825. Thomas Taylor.......James Baird
Baird, Wm. L., and Wallace, Nancy, Oct. 22, 1837. John Pinkston......Richard Walker
Baize, Isaac, and Shepherd, Sarah, Dec. 5, 1840. Basil Ward.............J. Shepherd

Marriage Records, 1799 to 1840

Baize, John, and Shultz, Nancy, Oct. 6, 1807. John Davis...........Matthew Shultz
Baize, Margaret, and Wright, Aaron, Jan. 7, 1830. Thomas Taylor....Emanuel Bracher
Baize, Nathan, and Hall, Betsy, Feb. 10, 1825. Loderic Davis...........Samuel Lee
Baize, Polly, and Hall, James, Sept. 13, 1823. Loderic Davis..........Nathan Baize
Baker, Elizabeth, and Evans, Allen, Aug. 2, 1838. Ancil Hall..........Harris Evans
Baker, Wm., and Overlin, Lebiba, Nov. 4, 1826. William Harlt.......William Overlin
Ball, Tucky, and Field, Henry, June 23, 1805. John Davis...........Mark Florence
Balmain, Henry, and Peyton, Ellen, Sept. 28, 1833. William Hart.......Lucien Peyton
Banks, Nancy, and Hardin, David R., May 18, 1839. Ancil Hall..........David Banks
Bannon, Sally, and Hale, William, Oct. 25, 1825. _____........John Bannon
Barker, Elisha, and Rusher, Elizabeth, Aug. 19, 1839. Ancil Hall........John Banner
Barkin, Sanders, and Greer, Mary, Nov. 5, 1833. John Phipps........George Greer
Barnard, Ann, and Phipps, John, Nov. 18, 1819. Loderic Davis......Ignatius Barnard
Barnard, Dorcas, and Addington, Henry, Dec. 1, 1799. Ignatius Pigman. Josh. Barnard
Barnard, Dorcas, and Barnard, Ignatius, Feb. 18, 1812. Francis Travis....H. Cooper
Barnard, Helen, and Cox, Joseph, Dec. 6, 1811. Loderic Davis............John Cox
Barnard, Ignatius, and Barnard, Dorcas, Feb. 18, 1812. Francis Travis......H. Cooper
Barnard, Jared, and Morton, Ann, Nov. 27, 1833. William Downs......Thomas Morton
Barnard, Josiah, and Hocker, Dorcas, Dec. 24, 1805. Thomas Taylor....Philip Harker
Barnard, Lloyd, and Hocker, Nancy, Jan. 30, 1824. Loderic Davis......Martin Hocker
Barnard, Matilda, and Cox, Wm., Mar. 7, 1822. Loderic Davis.....Ignatius Barnard
Barnard, Mema, and Brown, James, Feb. 5, 1803. John Davis........William Barnard
Barnard, Milton E., and Field, Almenda, Sept. 20, 1836. John Phipps.....Jack Field
Barnard, Minerva, and Pedicord, Jonathan, Aug. 24, 1836. _____. Ignatius Barnard
Barnard, Miranda, and Simmons, Albeun S., Dec. 16, 1833. Wm. Downs. Thos. Hudson
Barnard, Nina, and Brown, James, Dec. 9, 1813. Thomas Taylor...... _____
Barnard, Sally, and Phipps, Thomas, Nov. 2, 1829. John Phipps........John Phipps
Barnard, Sarah, and Riley, Higginson, March 30, 1840. John Phipps....J. Reddison
Barnes, Elenor, and Worthington, Thomas, Nov. 18, 1806. John Davis. Weaver Barnes
Barnes, John, and Hocker, Sally, Jan. 5, 1836. John Phipps..........Charles Lawton
Barnes, Joseph, and Barrow, Elizabeth, July 28, 1821. Jared Tichenor....Rob Rowe
Barnes, Joseph H., and Miller, Dorcas Jane, April 20, 1840. J. Phipps......J. Miller
Barnes, Mary, and Moseley, Elijah, Jan. 24, 1811. Thomas Taylor....Higgerson Belt
Barnes, Weaver, and Miller, Betsy, April 6, 1809. Thos. Taylor.....Thos. Worthington
Barnett, Abigail, and Rowan, William C., Dec. 24, 1829. Wm. Harlt....Robert Barnett
Barnett, Alex., and Bennett, Sally Mary Ann, Jan. 29, 1838. J. Ward....Robert Barnett
Barnett, Hannah, and Meyers, Elijah, June 24, 1801. Ignatius Pigman. John Mosely
Barnett, Isaac, and Williams, Mary, July 30, 1814. Benj. Kelly.......William Whitt
Barnett, Jacob, and Lewellen, Martha, Aug. 27, 1812. Benj. Kelley..Jacob Lewellen
Barnett, James, and Ingleheart, Julian, Sept. 14, 1817. Benj. Kelley...Jared Tichenor
Barnett, Jean, and Barnett, Joseph, July 20, 1799. Ignatius Pigman. Robert Baird
Barnett, Joseph, and Barnett, Jean, July 20, 1799. Ignatius Pigman. Robert Baird
Barnett, Joseph, and Midkiff, Polly, Nov. 30, 1817. Thomas Taylor....Joseph Midkiff
Barnett, Joseph, and Stevens, Charlotte, Oct. 28, 1821. Wm. Foulks......M. McClean
Barnett, Joseph B., and Carson, Sally, Oct. 20, 1829. Wm. Harlt....Lindsey Carson
Barnett, Lucretia, and Bennett, Samuel, May 31, 1810. Loderic Davis....Rob Barnett
Barnett, Margaret, and Lee, Abner, Feb. 22, 1810. John Davis........Robert Wall

Ohio County in the Olden Days

Barnett, Martin, and Morris, Nancy, April 1, 1826. Ancil Hall..........James Miller
Barnett, Palcy, and Chapman, Moses, Feb. 13, 1817. Benjamin Malone....W. Calloway
Barnett, Rachel, and Sprigg, Thomas, Jan. 20, 1803. Ignatius Pigman. Robert Baird
Barnett, Rachel, and Prudden, James, Nov. 4, 1839. Basil Ward......Joseph Barnett
Barnett, Rebecca, and Baird, James, Oct. 24, 1803. John Davis..........W. F. Smith
Barnett, Rebecca, and Johnson, Philip, Aug. 18, 1820. Wm. Harlt....Jeffries Barnett
Barnett, Robert, and Condit, Betsy, March 23, 1816. Wm. Kincheloe......Uzal Condit
Barnett, Robert, and Bennett, Elizabeth, Oct. 28, 1834. Wm. Hart....Phipps Johnson
Barnett, Sarah, and Pemberton, William, April 2, 1839. Wm. Brown....Robert Brown
Barnett, Thomas, and Baird, Rachel, Nov. 14, 1825. Thomas Taylor....James Baird
Barnett, William, and Gibbons, Lydia, April 30, 1812. Thos. Taylor......Wm. Wallace
Barrett, Ignatius, and Taylor, Clarice, May 17, 1826. Thos. Taylor...Richard Taylor
Barrett, Joshua, and Tongon, Priscilla, April 1, 1819. Thos. Taylor. Richard Barret
Barrett, Matilda, and Fitzhugh, James, Oct. 3, 1825. Wm. Harlt........Samuel Pate
Barrett, Richard, and Wedding, Mary, May 1, 1820. John Rillney......John Ridgeway
Barrett, Thomas, and Keath, Elizabeth Ann, June 21, 1837. John Phipps.....B. Malin
Barrett, Thomas, and Lindley, Elizabeth, June 27, 1840. Basil Ward.....Wm. Lindley
Barrett, Wm. S., and Blacklock, Mary E., Mar. 26, 1829. Wm. Harlt. Harold McCreeny
Barrow, Elizabeth, and Barnes, Joseph, July 28, 1821. Jared Tichenor.....Rob Rowe
Barry, Abraham, and Underwood, Elizabeth, May 10, 1813. Thos.Taylor. Joshua Crowe
Basford, Amelia, and Austin, Thomas O., Sept. 6, 1830. Loderic Davis......W. Barnes
Bates, Winifred, and Howell, John, May 30, 1813. Loney Jackson....Chas. Nothington
Baynes, Mary, and Mobberly, John, March 21, 1832. David Kelley.......Dillis Dyer
Bean, Polly, and Crawford, Granite, Jan. 30, 1830. John Phipps......Leonard Leach
Bean, Wm. R., and Taylor, Sarah Ann, Aug. 29, 1833. Wm. Downs...Thomas Taylor
Bearden, Thomas, and Bell, Catherine, August 1, 1814. Thomas Taylor. Robert Bell
Beardon, Nancy, and Richard, William, July 16, 1826. Ancil Hall....Elijah Phipps
Beasley, Malinda, and Anderson, Henry, Jan. 7, 1838. Jos. Ward....Absalom Albin
Beasley, Robert, and Albin, Malinda, Sept. 28, 1828. Paul Abney...........A. Albin
Beck, Becky, and Culberson, Joseph, March 21, 1805. Thomas Taylor....Steven Beck
Beck, Polly, and Stocumband, Samuel, March 20, 1804. John Davis....Steven Beck
Bell, Abigail, and Tumbaugh, William, Oct. 14, 1817. Benjamin Kelley...Joe Allen
Bell, Catherine, and Bearden, Thomas, Aug. 1, 1814. Thomas Taylor. Robert Bell
Bell, David, and Inglehcart, Polly, Feb. 12, 1824. Jared Tichenor.....John Inglehart
Bell, Elenor M., and Sullenger, Birch, Sept. 27, 1836. John Phipps......Robt. T. Bell
Bell, Elizabeth, and Smeathers, James, April 4, 1805. John Davis.........___
Bell, Jane Eliza, and Berryman, Thomas, Dec. 10, 1829. Wm. Harlt.....Wm. Edison
Bell, Mary, and Walker, Wm., Sept. 14, 1804. Thos. Davis.....Higgerson Petticunard
Bell, Mary R., and Ashby, Sanford, April 2, 1839. William Downs......John Crowe
Bellance, Cynthia, and Jones, Gabriel, May 3, 1809. John Davis.....William Johnson
Belt, Henry, and Crowe, Mary Ann, April 15, 1838. F. Tanner......Higgerson Belt
Belt, Higginson, and Stevens, Charlotte, Jan. 10, 1805. Thos. Taylor......Wm. Stevens
Beng, Eliza, and Brown, David, Nov. 22, 1808. John Davis..........Evan Williams
Bennett, Alexander, and Benton, Frances, Oct. 1, 1838. J. G. Ward.......A. R. Rowan
Bennett, Amanda, and Douglas, John, Nov. 14, 1837. John Phipps....Quintus Shanks
Bennett, Amelia Ann, and Inglehcart, Henry D., Dec. 10, 1834. W. Sandefur. ___
Bennett, Ann, and Brian, Samuel, Jan. 25, 1827. William Harlt........Samuel Howard

Marriage Records, 1799 to 1840

Bennett, Asa, and Woodward, Delilah, Feb. 9, 1817. George Render.....Hezekiah Ford
Bennett, Chas., and Lindley, Margaret, Dec. 23, 1835. Wm. Sandefur....Dan Lindley
Bennett, Elenor, and Brian, Asa, Nov. 9, 1830. Wm. Sandefur......Samuel Bryant
Bennett, Elizabeth, and Shown, Peter, Aug. 30, 1820. Thos. Taylor... John Bennett
Bennett, Elizabeth, and Sandefur, Wm., Sept. 9, 1825. Sam Julian...Alford Bennett
Bennett, Elizabeth, and Barnett, Robert, Oct. 28, 1834. Wm. Hart...Phipps Johnson
Bennett, George Plummer, and Benton, Lydia, Dec. 14, 1826. Geo. McNelly. L. Bryant
Bennett, James, and Moore, Rebecca, Jan. 13, 1838. B. Burdon......Jacob Inglehart
Bennett, Jesse, and Henman, Maria, Nov. 2, 1804. Thomas Taylor........A. Henman
Bennett, John, and Underwood, Elizabeth, Aug. 14, 1823. Wm. Hart. Richard Elliot
Bennett, Lewis, and Fuqua, Eliza, Sept. 3, 1831. Ancil Hall......William Fuqua
Bennett, Lucretia, and Bryan, William, Dec. 18, 1832. Wm. Hart......Samuel Ford
Bennett, Margaret, and Tichenor, James, Mar. 28, 1814. Geo. Render....Jas. Tichenor
Bennett, Maria, and Stevens, Richard, Aug. 3, 1805. Thomas Taylor...Aquilla Field
Bennett, Mary, and Sandefur, Francis, Nov. 7, 1822. Wm. Hart......Jeff Bennett
Bennett, Mary Jane, and Stevens, Nathaniel, Mar. 25, 1833. R. Y. Reynolds. S. Bennett
Bennett, Matilda, and Wallace, Franklin, Jan. 25, 1836. Wm. Sandefur. Jas. Bennett
Bennett, Minerva, and Ward, John, June 17, 1835. William Hart....Joseph Bennett
Bennett, Nathan, and Ward, Martha, Jan. 5, 1831. Wm. Sandefur.....Ezra Ward
Bennett, Nelson, and Fuqua, Lucretia, Sept. 29, 1831. David Kelley......Wm. Fuqua
Bennett, Polly, and Woodward, Benjamin, May 23, 1820. Wm. Barnett. R. Bennett
Bennett, Rachel, and Clark, William, April 26, 1838. Basil Ward......Samuel Hedrick
Bennett, Sally Mary Ann, and Barnett, Alex., Jan. 29, 1838. J. Ward...Robt. Barnett
Bennett, Samuel, and Barnett, Lucretia, May 31, 1810. Loderic Davis...Robt. Barnett
Bennett, Sarah, and Sandefur, John, Sept. 21, 1832. W. Hart.......Jeffries Bennett
Bennett, Susan, and Taylor, Joseph, July 18, 1809. Thomas Taylor.....Thos. Bennett
Bennett, Theodocia, and Benton, Allen, Jan. 7, 1838. James Ward......Robt. Barnett
Bennett, Thomas, and Tichenor, Polly, July 24, 1819. John Phipps ....Tim Tichenor
Bennett, Thomas, and Tichenor, Polly, 1820. Benjamin Talbert.........———
Bennett, Thomas, and Cox, Minerva, July 14, 1838. Benj. Burdon......Joseph Cox
Bennett, Titus, and Davis, Mirinda, Aug. 22, 1820. Wm. Allison ....Henry Sallee
Bennett, William J., and Owen, Sarah J., Jan. 17, 1840. R. Holding...Richard Stevens
Benton, Allen, and Ward, Rebecca, March 16, 1820. Benj. Kelly........Wm. Carter
Benton, Allen, and Bennett, Theodocia, Jan. 7, 1838. Jas. Ward....Robt. Barnett
Benton, Bassett, and Carter, Polly, Mar. 5, 1808. Wm. Anderson.........C. Jackson
Benton, Edward, and Carter, Dorcas, Dec. 16, 1835. Ancil Hall.........Geo. Carter
Benton, Elizabeth, and Greer, George, Sept. 17, 1811. Thos. Taylor.....Silas Benton
Benton, Erasmus, and Howard, Elizabeth, March 27, 1830. Wm. Harlt......Wm. Leach
Benton, Frances, and Bennett, Alexander, Oct. 1, 1838. J. G. Ward......A. R. Rowan
Benton, James, and Ward, Susan, Jan. 9, 1827. John Pinkston..........John Ward
Benton, James, and Fulkerson, Nancy, July 25, 1829. Chas. Henderson ...A. Fulkerson
Benton, Joseph, and Woodward, Matilda, Feb. 24, 1835. Wm. Hart. Richard Walker
Benton, Lydia, and Bennett, George Plummer, Dec. 14, 1826. Geo. McNelly. L. Bryant
Benton, Miranda, and Whittaker, Lee, Dec. 8, 1817. Thomas Taylor....Benj. Benton
Benton, Nathan, and Johnson, Elizabeth Ann, Jan. 5, 1826. Wm. Harlt. R. Bennett
Benton, Nicholas, and Wallace, Elizabeth, Nov. 8, 1830. Wm. Harlt....Peter Shown
Berry, William, and Walker, Sarah Ann Martha, July 20, 1838. J. G. Ward. R. Walker

Ohio County in the Olden Days

Berryman, Elvina, and Taylor, John, July 4, 1833. R. Y. Reynolds.....John Calhoun
Berryman, Frances, and Nall, Gatewood, Sept. 2, 1828. Wm. Harlt. Richard Hall
Berryman, Isabelle, and Fraze, Robert, July 15, 1837. Jacob Miller.....J. B. Rogers
Berryman, Lucinda, and Berryman, Weeks, Oct. 29, 1828. Thos. Downs. Ashum King
Berryman, Thomas, and Bell, Jane Eliza, Dec. 10, 1829. Wm. Harlt. Wm. Edison
Berryman, Thomas, and Thompson, Margaret, Aug. 8, 1831. Wm. Hart. Francis Black
Berryman, Weeks, and Berryman, Lucinda, Oct. 29, 1828. Thomas Downs. Ashum King
Bigger, Widow Sarah, and Finley, Sam, July 6, 1805. T. Taylor........G. Willingway
Bishop, Ann, and Rowe, Broxton, June 2, 1831. Wm. Downs.........Eramus Bishop
Biggerstaff, Wm., and Atherton, Elizabeth, Nov. 14, 1811. Lon. Jackson. A. Atherton
Biggerstall, John, and Wilkins, Elizabeth, Oct. 10, 1807. Benj. Talbert....M. Atherton
Bishop, Annie M., and Wallace, John Benton, July 29, 1828. Wm. Harlt. Josh. Bishop
Bishop, Erasmus, and Kerfold, Ann, Feb. 12, 1812. Joe Anderson......John Taylor
Black, Henry, and Carter, Catherine, Oct. 29, 1833. David Kelley....John Phipps
Black, Lucinda, and Groves, William, Nov. 29, 1822. Benj. Kelley...Willis J. Black
Black, Willis, and Phillips, Polly, June 5, 1828. Ancil Hall..........Solomon Phillips
Blacklock, Adeline, and Stevens, John, Mch. 4, 1839. Basil Ward. Richard Blacklock
Blacklock, Clarissa, and Taylor, Mason, Oct. 18, 1830. D. Kelley...Thos. Blacklock
Blacklock, Edmond, and Landrum, Nancy, Aug. 30, 1814. Nathan Pulliam. Sam Burch
Blacklock, Mary E., and Barrett, Wm. S., Mch. 26, 1829. Wm. Harlt. H. McCreeny
Bland, Slaughter E., and Nall, Margaret P., Oct. 9, 1834. Wm. Hart.....Richard Nall
Blevins, Betsy, and Clannah, John, Oct. 8, 1816. George Render......Thomas Ray
Blevins, Betsy, and Clouch, John, Nov. 10, 1816. Geo. Render.....Walter Calloway
Blevins, Charlotte, and Grigsby, Nath., Jan. 17, 1825. Loderic Davis....J. Blevins
Blevins, Irene, and Wise, William, March 10, 1831. John Phipps....J. R. Williams
Blevins, John, and Gray, Nelly, Dec. 28, 1819. John Phipps.............
Blevins, John, and Grey, Nancy, Jan. 6, 182[?]. Lodowick Davis........
Blevins, Keturah, and Ross, Willis, June 24, 1821. Thos. Taylor....Barnett Clouch
Blevins, Linsey, and Warden, Even, Aug. 22, 1820. Benj. Talbert.......Wm. Ashby
Blevins, Patsy, and Robinson, Philip, Dec. 26, 1822. Loderic Davis. Phil Fulkerson
Blevins, Sally, and Tichenor, John, Oct. 15, 1823. Jared Tichenor....James Hatcher
Blevins, William, and Vickory, Rosa, Jan. 5, 1819. Loderic Davis.......John Shultz
Blevins, William, and Coleman, Mary, Oct. 1, 1838. Geo. Render.....P. Robertson
Boas, Sally, and Wilkins, James, Sept. 29, 1825. Thomas Taylor.....W. E. Probert
Borah, Jacob E., and Taylor, Susan, Sept. 30, 1833. John Phipps....Harrison Taylor
Borah, Lee, and Render, Catherine, June 18, 1831. Geo. Render........Nat. Howard
Borah, Noah, and Ross, Lucinda, Oct. 31, 1835. George Render......Thomas Ross
Borah, Willis, and Austin, Margaret, Feb. 15, 1830. Wm. Harlt........Thos. Austin
Borer, Valentine, and Grant, Elizabeth, Dec. 2, 1824. Benj. Talbert. Elijah Phipps
Borough, John, and Miller, Mary Catty, April 11, 1809. John Davis. John Armstrong
Boswell, Alex. H., and Stephens, Ann, Oct. 11, 1819. Thos. Taylor.....James Johnson
Boswell, Caleb, and Duke, Lydia, Nov. 22, 1825. William Hart..........John Duke
Boswell, Caleb, and Watson, Cynthia, April 29, 1840. John Phipps........B. Watson
Boswell, Polly, and Miller, David, Oct. 10, 1825. Wm. Harlt.......Caleb Boswell
Boswell, Trycy, and Crowe, John, April 27, 1812. Thomas Taylor....Leonard Bean
Boyle, Alexander, and Hopkins, Ruth, July 13, 1820. Joseph Tichenor....Wm. Hill
Boyle, Alford, and Condit, Elena, Nov. 15, 1823. Richard D. Neal.....Uzal Condit

Marriage Records, 1799 to 1840

Boys, John, and Shulch, Nancy, Oct. 7, 1801. James Keele............._____
Bozarth, Jeremiah, and Glever, Sally, Feb. 28, 1814. Joseph Faulks. Geo. Matthews
Bozarth, Mary, and Brown, Reuben, July 28, 1806. Thomas Taylor..Henry Brown
Bozarth, O. H. Perry, and Brooks, Elizabeth J., July 20, 1840. F. Farmer. J. Stewart
Bozarth, Rebecca, and Rowe, Randolph, Sept. 24, 1808. Wm. Anderson. J. Bozarth
Bozarth, Washington, and Peddicord, Eliza, Dec. 12, 1838. Ancil Hall. L. Peddicord
Bozarth, William, and Stewart, Elizabeth, Nov. 14, 1817. J. Pinkston. Alex Stewart
Bracher, Thomas, and Anderson, Peggy, April 22, 1810. Wm. Anderson. J. Anderson
Brandon, Polly, and Martin, Reuben, Feb. 7, 1828. Ancil Hall......John H. McHenry
Brandon, Robert, and Loyal, Leticia, Sept. 23, 1827. Ancil Hall.....Wm. B. Charley
Brant, Hannah, and Warren, Moses, Oct. 15, 1807. John Davis............Ed Brant
Brant, John, and Harris, Betsy, Feb. 10, 1811. John Davis............Jesse Harris
Brashers, Emanuel, and Humphrey, Margaret, Jan. 9, 1830. J. Phipps. Benj. Humphrey
Brashiers, Thomas, and Powers, Judith, Nov. 16, 1814. Benj. Kelly......John Powers
Breamer, Mary, and Reed, George, June 25, 1807. Samuel Hodge......Samuel Hodge
Breshoro, John, and Powers, Hannah, May 24, 1813. Benj. Kelly......Isaac Covens
Brevins, Polly, and McClain, Matthew, April 27, 1809. Wm. Anderson.......J. Crowe
Brian, Asa, and Bennett, Elenor, Nov. 9, 1830. Wm. Sandefur......Samuel Bryant
Brian, Samuel, and Bennett, Ann, Jan. 25, 1827. Wm. Harlt..........Samuel Howard
Brian, Sarah, and Newcome, Samuel, Feb. 4, 1825. Wm. Harlt.....Jeffries Bennett
Bright, William, and Phipps, Rebecca, Jan. 5, 1805. John Granmer......Wm. Phipps
Bristoe, Lovey, and Potts, Martha, April 22, 1809. Wm. Anderson........Jesse Potts
Brooks, Elizabeth, and Brown, Albert, Jan. 24, 1835. Ancil Hall........John Clement
Brooks, Elizabeth J., and Bozarth, O. H. Perry, July 20, 1840. F. Farmer. J. Stewart
Brooks, John, and Campbell, Polly, April 25, 1814. Thomas Taylor......Wm. Condit
Brooks, Leah, and Hall, Mingo, Jan. 18, 1806. Thomas Taylor........Joseph Dunlap
Brown, Albert, and Brooks, Elizabeth, Jan. 24, 1835. Ancil Hall........John Clement
Brown, Alexander, and Coolman, Elizabeth, Dec. 8, 1819. Thos. Taylor. Peter Foster
Brown, Ann, and Hedges, Josiah, March 11, 1818. George Render......Joshua Brown
Brown, Ann, and Loney, James, May 29, 1821. Jared Tichenor.......Armstead Brown
Brown, Ann, and Taylor, William, Jan. 20, 1824. Thomas Taylor......John Kenney
Brown, Ann L., and Williams, Taylor, _____, 1825. Thomas Taylor. John Kenney
Brown, Charlotte, and Render, Robert, Dec. 9, 1801. Ignatius Pigman. Jos. Barnes
Brown, David, and Beng, Eliza, Nov. 22, 1808. John Davis...........Evan Williams
Brown, Eliza, and Taylor, Silas, April 15, 1832. John Phipps.........George Brown
Brown, Eliza, and Southard, Thomas, March 26, 1838. George Render. James Brown
Brown, Elizabeth, and Eatheruton, Jonathan, Nov. 1, 1802. James Keele. _____
Brown, Henry, and Anderson, Hannah, Jan. 19, 1803. Benj. Talbert....Reuben Brown
Brown, Horace, and Brown, Nancy, Aug. 4, 1836. James Taylor..........._____
Brown, Isaac, and Tichenor, Sally, Dec. 23, 1833. Thomas Taylor......Jared Tichenor
Brown, Isaac C., and Reddecood, Mary, March 20, 1840. Basil Ward. L. Reddecood
Brown, James, and Barnard, Mema, Feb. 5, 1803. John Davis......William Barnard
Brown, James, and Barnard, Nina, Dec. 9, 1813. Thomas Taylor........_____
Brown, James, and Wakeland, Polly, Oct. 5, 1820. Loderic Davis......Wm. Wakeland
Brown, James, and Lucas, Polly, March 30, 1837. Jacob Miller............I. Lucas
Brown, Jane, and Pool, William, Dec. 25, 1826. Charles Tanks......William McLough
Brown, Jane, and Condit, William, Aug. 5, 1833. Thomas Taylor.....Isaac Brown

Brown, Jane, and Lee, Talbert, Sept. 29, 1835. William Sandefur.   Archibald Taylor
Brown, Janet, and Matthews, William, Aug. 22, 1827. Geo. McNeely.   Philman Moore
Brown, John, and Thornback, Phoebe, Feb. 21, 1814. Benj. Kelly......James Salice
Brown, John, and Morgan, Jane, Oct. 10, 1835. William Sandefur.....George Brown
Brown, Jonathan, and Anderson, Elizabeth, ————————————————————
Brown, Joshua, and Wilcher, Nancy, Sept. 14, 1812. John Davis......William Wilcher
Brown, Judy, and Loney, John, Aug. 18, 1821. Jared Tichenor........Robert Brown
Brown, Margaret, and Rowe, Thomas, Feb. 1, 1812. George Render. Armstrong Brown
Brown, Mary Ann, and Taylor, Archibald, Oct. 23, 1826. ——— ———, John Brown
Brown, Milly, and Wise, Daniel, July 26, 1840. G. Garrett............
Brown, Milly, and Brown, Robert, July 20, 1840. ——— ———..........Dan Wise
Brown, Nancy, and Brown, Horace, Aug. 4, 1836. James Taylor........
Brown, Presley, and Humphrey, Sarah, Sept. 24, 1829. Wm. Downs....Benj. Humphrey
Brown, Pretius, and Payner, Mitchell, Dec. 19, 1800. Ignatius Pigman. Jonathan Brown
Brown, Reuben, and Bozarth, Mary, July 28, 1806. Thomas Taylor.   Henry Brown
Brown, Rhoda, and Condit, James, Oct. 14, 1826.   Jared Tichenor.....James Brown
Brown, Robert, and Rowe, Judy, Nov. 8, 1816. George Render.........
Brown, Robert, and Pemberton, Beny, March 9, 1835.   Ancil Hall....William Brooks
Brown, Robert, and Brown, Milly, July 20, 1840. ——————............Dan Wise
Brown, Sally, and Travel, John, Sept. 13, 1809. Thomas Taylor......Henry Brown
Brown, Samuel, and Taylor, Jane, Nov. 22, 1831. Ancil Hall...........Levi Taylor
Brown, Susanna, and Johnson, Marcus, May 6, 1818. Geo. Render.......Ancil Brown
Brown, Theby, and Jones, William, Oct. 10, 1804. ——————..........Reuben Brown
Brown, Thomas, and Hedges, Mary, June 11, 1834. ——————......Jas. Hedges
Brown, William, and Corley, Judith, July 1, 1816. Geo. Render........Wm. Corley
Brown, William, and Johnson, Elizabeth, June 9, 1817. Geo. Render...Moses Johnson
Brown, Wm., and Montgomery, Margaret, Jan. 22, 1828. A. Chapman. J. Montgomery
Bruce, Polly, and Johnson, James, March 13, 1809. Wm. Anderson.....Moses Cummins
Bruner, Peter, and Davis, Hannah, Jan. 8, 1827. ——————...........Hardin Cale
Bryan, William, and Bennett, Lucretia, Dec. 18, 1832. Wm. Hart.......Samuel Ford
Bryant, Amelia, and Logston, Philip, April 29, 1840. John Phipps..........F. R. Hall
Bryant, Horatis, and Wallace, Nancy, Aug. 22, 1829. Wm. Harlt......John Wallace
Bryant, Margaret, and Givins, John, Dec. 2, 1810. John Davis........John Bryant
Bryant, Mary, and Hunter, Reuben, April 2, 1810. Wm. Anderson.......John Bryant
Bryant, Rebecca, and Davis, Garret, Oct. 22, 1827. John Phipps.........Wm. Bryant
Bryant, Rebecca, and Davis, Jared, Oct. 25, 1827. Thomas Taylor.......
Bryant, William, and Sutherland, Susanne, Sept. 12, 1804. Thos. Taylor. Benj. Benton
Burch, Elenor, and Mason, Joseph, Sept. 3, 1825. Thomas Taylor.......Benj. Burch
Burch, Henley, and Matthews, Nancy, Nov. 9, 1829. Ancil Hall......John Johnson
Burch, Margaret, and Tuttle, William, Dec. 23, 1831. Ancil Hall........Wm. McIntire
Burch, Mary, and McIntire, William, Jan. 3, 1830. Jacob Miller.......Wm. S. Barrett
Burden, Cynthia Ann, and Pearce, Wm., June 18, 1833. Benj. Burden. John W. Crowe
Burden, Delilah, and Coy, Allen, Nov. 13, 1829. Benj. Burden..........Wm. Evans
Burden, Eli D., and Norris, Meriah, July 8, 1830. Benj. Burden........V. W. Peyton
Burden, Jane, and Langley, Bartholemew, Jan. 7, 1837. Ancil Hall....Clement Langley
Burden, Jemima, and Green, John, Sept. 12, 1832. Benjamin Burden. Absalom Peace
Burden, Osaah, and Pearce, Susan, Oct. 2, 1837. Wm. Anderson.....Absalom Pearce

Marriage Records, 1799 to 1840

Bureman, Nancy, and Moorman, James V., Sept. 30, 1823. Ben H. Johnson. Jas. Edison
Burkes, John, and Roach, Eliza, Nov. 17, 1836. Ancil Hall............Edward Roach
Burks, Davis, and Ralph, Nancy Jane, May 18, 1839. Thomas Downs. Wm. Ralph
Burton, Horace, and Miller, Mary Ann, Nov. 25, 1837. John Pinkston. Robert Miller
Burton, James, and White, Mary Ann, Oct. 18, 1838. Ancil Hall........Dewey White
Burton, Polly, and Taylor, Absalom, Nov. 8, 1826. Thos. Downs....Redding Taylor
Burton, Rebecca, and Lashbrook, John, Oct. 6, 1826. David Kelley ...James Burton
Butler, John, and Rogers, Nancy Ray, June 16, 1839. Alfred Taylor....Fleming James
Butterworth, Eliza, and Clifford, William, Aug. 4, 1824. Thos. Taylor....Wm. Leach
Byers, Margaret, and Anderson, Athel, Jan. 8, 1810. L. Davis........George Hoover
Cain, Elizabeth, and Davis, Amos, Aug. 4, 1823. Loderic Davis.........Dillis Dyer
Cain, Jane, and Humphrey, Ranghley, Feb. 15, 1827. Wm. Kincheloe....Amos Davis
Cain, John, and Addington, Sally, March 5, 1830. Loderic Davis....Henry Addington
Cain, Rebecca, and Williams, Evan, Aug. 8, 1808. William Anderson. James Baird
Calhoon, John, and Kelly, Amy, _____, 1800. Benj. Talbert.........._____
Calhoun, John, and Lamb, Sarah, Dec. 25, 1806. John Davis........Henry Jones
Calhoun, John, and Morton, Polly, Dec. 25, 1819. _____......Charlie McCreney
Calloway, Chester, and Gilbert, Elizabeth, Oct. 24, 1809. John Davis....A. Hepsley
Calloway, Frances, and Crowe, Elijah, Jan. 21, 1811. Lon Jackson........Z. Calloway
Calloway, James, and Mills, Mehila, March 23, 1823. William Harlt....Abe R. Rowan
Calloway, Sarah, and Tarlton, Robert, Feb. 10, 1810. John Davis....Charles Calloway
Calloway, Tomzay, and Simmons, William, Feb. 18, 1820. Wm. Harris. Dillis Dyer
Calloway, William, and Williams, Rebecca, June 2, 1836. Wm. Downs. David Williams
Calloway, Zacariah, and Cleavir, Phebe, August 7, 1805. _____...Jas. Cleavir
Calvert, Payton, and Warden, Ella, Feb. 14, 1835. Geo. Render........Jas. Warden
Campbell, Abigaile, and Allen, Usa, July 18, 1822. Wm. Hart.....Zachariah Roberts
Campbell, Andrew, and Lanham, Polly, Sept. 8, 1804. Thos. Taylor. Richard Lanham
Campbell, Ann, and Duvall, Nicholas, Dec. 23, 1819. Thos. Taylor. John S. Brooks
Campbell, Elizabeth, and Stewart, John, March 18, 1839. J. G. Ward. Richard Stevens
Campbell, James, and Tuell, Matilda, May 1, 1838. Ancil Hall....Archibald Stewart
Campbell, John, and Cooper, Polly, June 18, 1810. John Craig......Cornelius Cooper
Campbell, Lucinda, and Underwood, John, Aug. 20, 1827. Jared Tichenor. John Loney
Campbell, Maria Jane, and Stewart, Jas., Jan. 22, 1827. Loderic Davis. Alex. Cooper
Campbell, Martha, and Lewellan, John, Sept. 17, 1810. John Davis....Jacob Lewellan
Campbell, Mary, and Stewart, Richard, Jan. 14, 1837. Ancil Hall....Wm. J. Stewart
Campbell, Polly, and Brooks, John, April 25, 1814. Thos. Taylor ....Wm. Condit
Campbell, Rebecca, and Railey, Benjamin, Dec. 19, 1825. Wm. Harlt. Jonathan Railey
Cannon, John, and Iler, Nancy, Jan. 5, 1826. William Harlt..........L. McReynolds
Cannon, Nancy, and Aubrey, John, Sept. 20, 1821. Benj. Burton......Pardon Taber
Carson, John, and Hynes, Sally, Oct. 21, 1812. Francis Travis.........Levi Hynes
Carson, Lindsey, and Stevens, Elizabeth, Oct. 24, 1826. Wm. Harlt....Thos. Stevens
Carson, Sally, and Barnett, Joseph B., Oct. 20, 1829. Wm. Harlt......Lindsey Carson
Carter, Abraham, and Felix, Elizabeth, Feb. 7, 1828. D. J. Kelley......Philip Felix
Carter, Alford, and Phillips, Betsy, July 15, 1835. Ancil Hall........Nathan Howard
Carter, Amy, and Crowe, Henry, Nov. 4, 1822. Benj. Kelley............Wm. Kelley
Carter, Carolina, and Phillipes, Philip, Oct. 22, 1827. Ancil Hall......Henry Crowe
Carter, Catherine, and Black, Henry, Oct. 29, 1833. David Kelley......John Phipps

Ohio County in the Olden Days

Carter, Delilah, and Kelly, Lendon C., Oct. 5, 1825. David Kelley......Wm. Carter
Carter, Dorcas, and Benton, Edward, Dec. 16, 1835. Ancil Hall......George Carter
Carter, Fanny, and Kelly, David, Feb. 16, 1810. Thos. Taylor........John Carter
Carter, George, and Neville, Emeline, May 3, 1839. John Pinkston......Ed Turner
Carter, James, and Coleman, Nancy, Oct. 9, 1825. Benj. Talbert......Geo. Coleman
Carter, John, and Kelly, Amy, March 11, 1809. William Anderson......Joe Haynes
Carter, Martha, and McDaniel, Gobel M., Nov. 15, 1832. Ancil Hall. Chas. McDaniel
Carter, Moses, and Thorp, Ann, Dec. 23, 1817. Benj. Kelley............Terry Thorp
Carter, Peggy, and Jackson, Roby, March 4, 1814. Loderic Davis......Wm. Carter
Carter, Polly, and Benton, Bassett, March 5, 1808. Wm. Anderson......C. Jackson
Carter, Polly, and Coleman, Martin, Jan. 27, 1821. Loderic Davis......John Shields
Carter, William, and Haynes, Hannah, May 2, 1824. Benj. Kelley.....Alex. Barnett
Carter, Wren, and Wakeland, Plemelia, Dec. 9, 1831. Geo. Render. Allen Wakeland
Casey, Catherine, and Acton, Francis, Nov. 26, 1840. _____.........Caleb Boswell
Casey, Didamah, and Acton, Francis, Jan. 23, 1839. J. G. Ward......Caleb Boswell
Chamberlin, Liles, and Taylor, Sarah, Feb. 10, 1824. Warner Crowe. Archibald Davis
Chambers, Abrin, and Miller, Sally, July 2, 1828. Ancil Hall........Jacob Miller
Chambers, Elizabeth, and Oldham, George, Feb. 14, 1818. J. Bristow. John L. Smith
Chapman, Eliza, and Heck, Randall, Aug. 22, 1839. Alfred Taylor. Ezekiel Chapman
Chapman, Ellis, and Southard, Nancy, Sept. 14, 1820. Loderic Davis....Amos Davis
Chapman, Ezekiel, and Mason, Catherine, Oct. 15, 1840. Alfred Taylor. John Mason
Chapman, Frances, and Ambrose, Lewis, April 18, 1833. Wm. Hart....Samuel Huston
Chapman, James, and Taylor, Margarie, Feb. 4, 1819. John Phipps. Richard Taylor
Chapman, Levina, and Grigsby, Aaron, Aug. 25, 1813. Thomas Taylor. F. Fulkerson
Chapman, Moses, and Barnett, Palcy, Feb. 13, 1817. Benj. Malone....W. Calloway
Chapman, Nancy, and Rogers, Edward, Jan. 22, 1818. John Phipps....James Chapman
Chapman, Rachel, and Hall, Ancil, Feb. 7, 1840. J. Bristow........Squire Whittaker
Chapman, Robert, and Porter, Sally, Jan. 12, 1836. John Phipps......Virgil Porter
Chapman, Sally, and Ford, William, Feb. 10, 1813. Thomas Taylor....Samuel Lewis
Chapman, Sally, and Smith, William, Dec. 19, 1832. John Phipps....Robert Chapman
Chapman, Solomon, and Render, Sarah, June 4, 1824. William Harlt. Robert Render
Chapman, Willis, and Render, Nancy, Dec. 13, 1805. Benj. Talbert....Robert Render
Chapman, Wilson, and Nicholas, Ellen, Jan. 31, 1838. Ancil Hall....Squire Whittaker
Chinn, Ann Eliza, and Cooper, John, March 8, 1837. Ancil Hall......Wesley Phipps
Chinn, Catherine, and Cooper, Wesley B., March 11, 1840. John Phipps. J. P. Cooper
Chinn, Dorothy B., and Austin, Andrew, Aug. 31, 1840. John Phipps. Raley Chinn
Christian, Charles, and Wylee, Dolly, Dec. 23, 1816. Benj. Malone......Wm. Wylee
Christian, James, and Wilcher, Nancy, Sept. 18, 1813. Benj. Kelly....Wm. Galloway
Christian, Walter, and Smith, Eliza, Sept. 26, 1833. Benj. Burden....Andrew Balmain
Christian, William, and Welcher, Malinda, Aug. 7, 1821. _____......F. Fulkerson
Clannah, John, and Blevins, Betsy, Oct. 8, 1816. George Render........Thomas Ray
Clark, Andrew, and Clifford, Catherine, Dec. 23, 1820. Benj. Talbert....M. Clifford
Clark, Anthony Ann, and Earp, James, Oct. 5, 1840. John Phipps........L. D. Earp
Clark, Elenor, and Wilson, George, Aug. 26, 1808. Wm. Anderson......Sarah Clark
Clark, Sarah Ann, and White, Alfred, July 11, 1839. Alfred Taylor.......James Clark
Clark, Wilford, and Langley, Susan, Jan. 9, 1839. John Wathen......James Langley
Clark, William, and Overtin, Delilah, July 8, 1806. Thomas Taylor....Wm. Overtin

Marriage Records, 1799 to 1840

Clark, William, and Bennett, Rachel, April 26, 1838. Basil Ward......Samuel Hedrick
Cleavir, Phebe, and Calloway, Zachariah, August 7, 1805. _____....Jas. Cleavir
Clement, William, and Thorp, Sally, April 3, 1812. L. Jackson......Stephen Thorp
Clever, Stephen, and Topsley, Elenor, April 22, 1810. John Davis..........J. Crowe
Clifford, Betsy, and Houtchins, Jesse, April 8, 1818. Geo. Render....Mitchell Clifford
Clifford, Catherine, and Clark, Andrew, Dec. 23, 1820. Benj. Talbert......M. Clifford
Clifford, Michael, and Rice, Nelly, Jan. 6, 1820. John Pinkston.........Peter Foster
Clifford, Nancy, and Taylor, John, June 22, 1813. John Davis.........James Marks
Clifford, William, and Butterworth, Eliza, Aug. 4, 1824. Thos. Taylor......Wm. Leach
Clouch, John, and Blivens, Betsy, Nov. 10, 1816. Geo. Render.......Walter Calloway
Clutter, Delilah, and Reed, James, July 18, 1804. Thomas Taylor....Stephen Taylor
Cobb, Elizabeth L., and Wilson, Warren, Nov. 6, 1832. Ancil Hall....Warren Cobb
Cobb, Henry H., and Huff, Nancy, Feb. 10, 1840. John Kelley.........._____
Cobb, Jesse, and Lamb, Sally Ann, Sept. 30, 1831. Ancil Hall............John Lamb
Cobbs, Forbetha, and Hall, John, Feb. 3, 1835. Ancil Hall...........Henry Cobbs
Cochran, John, and Davis, Peggy, Sept. 23, 1813. Loderic Davis........Nic Hocker
Cochran, Polly, and Warnell, Richard, Feb. 19, 1818. Loderic Davis.....John Shultz
Cochran, Rachel, and Hocker, Philip, June 1, 1816. Loderic Davis....Hezekiah Davis
Coffee, Cleo, and Hudson, William, Aug. 29, 1810. John Craig.........Philip Coffee
Coffee, Philip, and Ashley, Elizabeth, Dec. 29, 1813. _____........James Rogers
Cole, Mary, and Leach, Leonard, Feb. 4, 1824. Thomas Taylor......Septimus Taylor
Coleman, Ann, and Williams, Erezine, Nov. 7, 1831. John Phipps....Mallam Coleman
Coleman, Catherine, and Ashley, Thomas, June 18, 1806. Thomas Taylor. Sam Ross
Coleman, Christine, and Williams, Amos, Feb. 22, 1825. Loderic Davis....H. Coleman
Coleman, Elisha, and Mattox, Susan, _____, 1826. Wm. Harlt......Wm. N. Davis
Coleman, Elizabeth, and Durlap, Henry, Sept. 7, 1811. Benj. Talbert. Henry Coleman
Coleman, Elizabeth, and Brown, Alexander, Dec. 8, 1819. Thos. Taylor. Peter Foster
Coleman, Henry, and Addington, Jemima, Dec. 11, 1835. John Phipps. Josh Addington
Coleman, Martin, and Taylor, Catherine, Oct. 2, 1799. John Mosely....Henry Coleman
Coleman, Martin, and Carter, Polly, Jan. 27, 1821. Loderic Davis......John Shields
Coleman, Martin, and Williams, Harriet, Nov. 7, 1831. John Phipps.... Elijah Williams
Coleman, Martin, and Leach, Martha Ann, Feb. 25, 1840. Alfred Taylor. Joseph Leach
Coleman, Mary, and Blevine, Wm., Oct. 1, 1838. Geo. Render.....Philip Robertson
Coleman, Nancy, and Carter, James, Oct. 9, 1825. Benj. Talbert.....George Coleman
Coleman, Polly, and Fulkerson, Fulkerd, March 30, 1818. Loderic Davis. H. Coleman
Coleman, Richard, and Hocker, Rebecca, Jan. 23, 1823. William Harlt......N. Hocker
Coleman, Sally, and Williams, Isaac, Feb. 10, 1824. Loderic Davis......Henry Coleman
Coleman, Sarah, and Wise, James, Jan. 5, 1828. Jared Tichenor......Philip Williams
Collins, Sarah, and Davis, Churoe, Sept. 6, 1814. Thomas Taylor....John McLean
Combs, Eden, and Tilford, Mary, May 8, 1839. John Phipps..........Jesse Ward
Compton, Susanna, and Edmund, Isaac, Oct. 1, 1804. John Davis........Wm. Weeks
Compton, Winney, and Herrald, Richard, July 25, 1800. John Grammar. Jas. Skiman
Condit, Abigail, and Housley, Robert, Feb. 6, 1832. Wm. Sandefur......G. Condit
Condit, Allen, and Hostute, Catherine, April 14, 1810. John Davis.......James Lin
Condit, Angelina, and Tichenor, Bennett, Aug. 30, 1831. Wm. Hart....Jacob Condit
Condit, Ann, and Elliott, John, July 18, 1812. Loney Jackson.........Byron Condit
Condit, Betsy, and Barnett, Robert, March 23, 1816. Wm. Kincheloe.....Uzal Condit

Ohio County in the Olden Days

Condit, Elena, and Boyle, Alford, Nov. 15, 1823. Richard D. Neal......Uzal Condit
Condit, Emeline, and Ingleheart, John, Nov. 28, 1832. Wm. Downs....Jacob Condit
Condit, Jacob, and Brown, Rhoda, Oct. 14, 1826. Jared Tichenor......James Brown
Condit, Jemima, and Tumnondy, William, July 28, 1818. Nall Overale. Moses Condit
Condit, Jonathan, and Duke, Mary, June 14, 1834. William Hart......John Crowe
Condit, Moses, and Condit, Sally, Dec. 8, 1812. Thomas Taylor.......James Pleden
Condit, Peter, and Housley, Elizabeth, Dec. 7, 1826. Jared Tichenor. Robt. Housley
Condit, Rhoda, and Ingleheart, William B., Oct. 1827. Geo. McNelly.....Wm. Condit
Condit, Ruth Ann, and Davis, Miles H., Feb. 17, 1823. Wm. Kincheloe. Wm. Simmons
Condit, Sally, and Condit, Moses, Dec. 8, 1812. Thomas Taylor......James Pleden
Condit, William, and Brown, Jane, Aug. 5, 1833. Thomas Taylor.....Isaac Brown
Condit, Uzal, and Lindley, Mary, Nov. 1, 1832. William Kincheloe....David Lindley
Conner, William, and Potts, Rachel, March 7, 1807. John Davis......John Conner
Cooksey, Eliza, and Iler, Perry, Feb. 11, 1831. William Hart............Lewis Smith
Cooksey, Victoria Ann, and Earp, Nicholas P., July 27, 1840. J. G. Ward. J. H. Blane
Cooper, Alexander, and Miller, Sally, June 7, 1814. John Weldon........Wm. Cooper
Cooper, Betsy A. I., and Hocker, Quisenberry, April 13, 1840. J. Phipps. Wash. Phipps
Cooper, Clarissa, and Hocker, Nicholas, Sept. 25, 1827. Loderic Davis......H. Cooper
Cooper, Elenor, and Wallace, William, June 8, 1803. _____..........Henry Cooper
Cooper, Elizabeth, and Cox, Benjamin, April 12, 1807. John Davis......William Cox
Cooper, Elizabeth, and Embry, Isaac, Feb. 11, 1833. Benj. Burden.....Wesley Cooper
Cooper, Henry, and Phipps, Nancy, Oct. 31, 1803. Ignatius Pigman......Wm. Phipps
Cooper, Jacob, and Hoover, Milly, Nov. 18, 1839. Basil Ward......Leonard Hoover
Cooper, Jane, and Miller, David, Jan. 25, 1810. Wm. Anderson........Sam Cooper
Cooper, Jane, and Embry, William, April 12, 1834. Paul Abney.........Wm. Keown
Cooper, John, and Chinn, Ann Eliza, March 8, 1837. Ancil Hall......Wesley Phipps
Cooper, Martha, and Stewart, Henry, March 22, 1837. Wm. Anderson....Jas. Campbell
Cooper, Polly, and Campbell, John, June 18, 1810. John Craig......Cornelius Cooper
Cooper, Robert, and Neal, Delilah, March 28, 1809. Wm. Anderson......Sam Cooper
Cooper, Sally, and Addington, Joshua, July 28, 1828. Loderic Davis....Henry Cooper
Cooper, Sarah, and Shiveley, John L., Feb. 9, 1830. J. Bristow........David French
Cooper, Wesley, and Allen, Milly, Sept. 22, 1831. Thomas Taylor......Benj. Duvall
Cooper, Wesley B., and Chinn, Catherine, March 11, 1840. John Phipps. J. P. Cooper
Corley, Judith, and Brown, William, July 1, 1816. Geo. Render.........Wm. Corley
Corn, William, and Show, Edith, Dec. 31, 1831. William Downs......John Bozarth
Cortland, John, and Talmon, Sally Ann, Oct. 22, 1824. Wm. Harlt......Jas. Talmon
Covington, Edward, and Fulkerson, Rebecca, Oct. 25, 1836. Geo. Render. Geo. Smith
Cox, Althae, and Cox, Philip, Sept. 24, 1838. George Render........Thos. Jeff. Cox
Cox, Anderson, and Mitchell, Sally, April 27, 1820. Benj. Burden......Jesse Craddox
Cox, Ann, and Shultz, John, Sept. 18, 1831. John Phipps............William Cox
Cox, Benjamin, and Cooper, Elizabeth, April 12, 1807. John Davis......William Cox
Cox, Elizabeth, and Six, David, Dec. 23, 1819. Benj. Burden......Frederic Trunell
Cox, Elizabeth, and Robel, Logustain P., April 5, 1828. Jasper Bristow....Wm. Barrett
Cox, Elizabeth, and Pool, Allen P., Nov. 29, 1836. _____............Thomas Cox
Cox, Finis, and Napier, Mary, Feb. 17, 1807. Benjamin Talbert........Rene Napier
Cox, James, and Leach, Elizabeth, May 13, 1806. Thomas Taylor........John Cox
Cox, Jane, and Troxal, Frederic, April 13, 1818. _____........ Solomon Kissinger

Marriage Records, 1799 to 1840

Cox, Jeremiah, and Davis, Dorcas, Dec. 21, 1819. Loderic Davis......Gideon Davis
Cox, Joseph, and Barnard, Helen, Dec. 6, 1811. Loderic Davis..........John Cox
Cox, Joseph, and Tanson, Elizabeth, Jan. 17, 1825. Loderic Davis....Thomas Davis
Cox, Lucinda, and Wallace, Washington, Aug. 29, 1833. Wm. Hart....Robert Johnson
Cox, Minerva, and Bennett, Thomas, July 14, 1838. Benj. Burdon.......Joseph Cox
Cox, Philip, and Cox, Althae, Sept. 24, 1838. George Render.......Thos. Jeff. Cox
Cox, Polly, and Albin, Joshua, March 11, 1835. George Render......Nathaniel Howard
Cox, R. E., and Payne, Emily Ann, Sept. 28, 1840. John Phipps.......F. R. Robertson
Cox, Sally, and Green, William, Jan. 2, 1836. George Render...........James Cox
Cox, Susan, and Davis, Alford, June 4, 1830. Thomas Reese........Wesley Davis
Cox, Thomas, and Leach, Miranda, Dec. 24, 1829. Loderic Davis.......John Crowe
Cox, William, and Barnard, Matilda, March 7, 1822. L. Davis......Ignatius Barnard
Coy, Allen, and Burden, Delilah, Nov. 13, 1829. Benjamin Burden.....William Evans
Crabtree, Abraham, and Potts, Johanna, Dec. 13, 1810. Loderic Davis....Ralph Hunt
Crabtree, Isaac, and Lamb, Sally, March 5, 1814. John Davis..........Robert Lamb
Crabtree, Isabel Elizabeth, and Morris, Amos, Aug. 13, 1827. Paul Abney....Wm. Six
Crabtree, Jane, and Six, William, Dec. 26, 1821. Benjamin Burden......David Six
Craddock, Margaret, and Taylor, Nicholas, Oct. 8, 1833. Thos. Taylor. Richard Taylor
Crash, Fanny, and Atterberry, Stout, Dec. 8, 1824. Joseph Wilson.....Saul Whittier
Crash, Phebe, and Matthews, James, Aug. 22, 1818. Joseph Wilson......Wm. Matthews
Cravens, Dorcas, and Gibson, Daniel, April 22, 1832. John Phipps.....Jesse Cravens
Cravens, Jane, and James, William, July 28, 1825. L. Davis............Jesse Cravens
Cravens, Jesse, and Tarlton, Rebecca, Sept. 17, 1802. Ignatius Pigman. John Mosely
Cravens, Jesse, and Namny, Ann, Aug. 23, 1832. John Phipps.......Edward Namny
Cravens, Jessie, and Royal, James, Aug. 4, 1831. Ancil Hall..........Jesse Cravens
Crawford, Fanny, and Aubrey, Jacob, Sept. 28, 1840. Oscar Bishop......J. Crawford
Crawford, Granite, and Bean, Polly, Jan. 30, 1830. John Phipps.....Leonard Leach
Crawford, Jossie, and Wooley, Levi, Aug. 1, 1814. Benj. Kelley.......Thomas Baird
Crawford, Mary Elizabeth, and Thrasher, Eli, Nov. 3, 1822. John Hart. Ed Blacklock
Crawford, Mason, and McCary, Mary Polly, Feb. 10, 1805. Wm. Davis......N. Ross
Crockin, John, and Hall, Peggy, March 26, 1820. Benj. Kelley............
Crowder, Ann, and Stewart, Cornelius, Jan. 24, 1835. Wm. Sandefur. Thomas Crowder
Crowder, Lucinda, and Daugherty, Moses, May 3, 1838. Ancil Hall......Chest. Cole
Crowe, Ann, and McCreery, Charles, Oct. 28, 1811. Thomas Taylor. Samuel Lewis
Crowe, Caroline, and Lightfoot, Pendleton, Feb. 21, 1832. Wm. Hart. Robt. McCreery
Crowe, Elijah, and Calloway, Frances, Jan. 21, 1811. Lon Jackson........Z. Calloway
Crowe, Elijah, and Johnson, Judy, Jan. 2, 1814. Benj. Kelley........James Johnson
Crowe, Eliza, and Ambrose, Henry, Aug. 30, 1836. Wm. Sandefur.....Sam Hendricks
Crowe, Elizabeth, and Woodward, James H., April 8, 1833. Wm. Hart. Elijah Crowe
Crowe, Henry, and Richard, Elizabeth, Feb. 24, 1820. Benj. Kelley. Edward Marlow
Crowe, Henry, and Carter, Amy, Nov. 4, 1822. Benj. Kelley..........Wm. Kelley
Crowe, Hyram, and Whittier, Elizabeth, July 25, 1827. Ancil Hall.......Jacob Miller
Crowe, Jesse, and Anderson, Mary, Oct. 1, 1814. Thos. Taylor......N. H. McFarland
Crowe, John, and Boswell, Trycy, April 27, 1812. Thomas Taylor......Leonard Bean
Crowe, John, and Jackson, Polly, July 8, 1835. William Hart..........John Smith
Crowe, Louise, and Hamilton, Samuel, April 17, 1834. Wm. Hart......Geo. Hamilton
Crowe, Mary Ann, and Belt, Henry, April 15, 1838. F. Tanner......Higgerson Belt

Crowe, Nancy, and Smith, John J., Feb. 22, 1832. Wm. Sandefur........Dillis Dyer
Crowe, Sarah Ann, and Woodward, Stephen, Oct. 24, 1838. J. Phipps....Quintus Shanks
Culberson, Joseph, and Beck, Becky, March 21, 1805. Thomas Taylor....Steven Beck
Cummins, Jacob, and Williams, Polly, March 11, 1824. J. Tichenor......Jas. Williams
Cummins, Moses, and Griffith, Ruth, Oct. 23, 1810. John Davis.........J. Thompson
Cumpton, Molly, and Young, William, March 13, 1806. John Davis....John Barnett
Cumpton, Theodocia, and Shane, Thomas, Jan. 9, 1809. Wm. Anderson. Charles Scott
Curd, Daniel, and Upton, Edvina, Nov. 11, 1830. Wm. Downs........S. G. H. McGary
Curd, Mary, and Moseley, Jesse, Aug. 12, 1824. Richard Neal........Robert Lightfoot
Curlet, Margaret, and Moseley, Robert, Jan. 22, 1829. Thos. Taylor....Thos. Taylor
Daniel, Ann, and Smith, Thomas, Dec. 10, 1831. John Phipps........Thomas Ashby
Daniel, Brockel, and Arnold, Amanda, Dec. 3, 1832. Wm. Hart........John Daniel
Daniel, Doranda, and Ross, John, March 30, 1840. _____.....William Daniel
Daniel, George, and Tilford, Nancy, March 18, 1827. David Kelley. Walker Daniel
Daniel, Martha, and Thomas, Nathaniel, April 18, 1833. Wm. Downs....John Daniel
Daniel, Mary Ann, and Plumer, Caleb, June 3, 1819. Thos. Taylor. Jeremiah Tilford
Daniel, Vivian, and McCreery, Vitula, Sept. 25, 1836. James Taylor....Rob. Brown
Daniel, Walker, and Smith, Maryan, Aug. 22, 1825. Wm. Harlt.......James Smith
Daugherty, Andrew, and Evans, Sarah, June 3, 1837. Ancil Hall.......T. W. Rosdale
Daugherty, Moses, and Crowder, Lucinda, May 3, 1838. Ancil Hall....Chest. Cole
Davenport, Robert, and Wise, Katie, Nov. 13, 1817. George Render..Philip Fulkerson
Davenport, Sam A., and Funk, Nancy H., Sept. 18, 1840. Alfred Taylor...._____
Davenport, S. A., and Turner, Nancy, Sept. 18, 1840. Alfred Taylor.....W. Turner
Davenport, William, and Meyers, Ellen, Feb. 21, 1838. B. Ward......Richard Tarfa
Davis, Alford, and Cox, Susan, June 4, 1831. Thomas Reese.........Wesley Davis
Davis, Amelia, and Talbert, Benjamin, Dec. 7, 1838. Wm. Hart......James Albin
Davis, Amos, and Cain, Elizabeth, Aug. 4, 1823. Loderic Davis......Dillis Dyer
Davis, Baxter, and Owen, Frances, July 12, 1830. James Miller........Henry Owen
Davis, Betsy, and Lanson, John, June 29, 1820. Loderic Davis......Ignatius Barnard
Davis, Beverly, and Landrum, Priscilla, Dec. 8, 1825. Ancil Hall.......W. Winter
Davis, Churoe, and Collins, Sarah, Sept. 6, 1814. Thomas Taylor......John McLean
Davis, Cynthia Ann, and Shultz, Nicholas, Oct. 6, 1832. John Phipps. Gideon Davis
Davis, Dorcas, and Welcher, William, Sept. 5, 1810. John Davis......Henry Davis
Davis, Dorcas, and Cox, Jeremiah, Dec. 21, 1819. Loderic Davis......Gideon Davis
Davis, Elizabeth, and Hillman, Benj., Sept. 19, 1809. Thos. Taylor.....Forrest Davis
Davis, Garret, and Bryant, Rebecca, Oct. 22, 1827. John Phipps.....William Bryant
Davis, Garrett, and Elin, Mary Ann, Sept. 14, 1829. John Phipps......Walter Earp
Davis, Hannah, and Bruner, Peter, Jan. 8, 1827. _____..........Hardin Cale
Davis, Harriet, and Redmond, Robert, March 2, 1811. Thomas Taylor. Forrest Davis
Davis, Hezekiah, and Hatcher, Elenor, July 21, 1813. Loderic Davis....Philip Hocker
Davis, Isabella, and Royal, John, Jan. 14, 1830. Thomas Taylor....William Royal
Davis, James, and Field, Lucy, Feb. 20, 1810. John Davis...........William Field
Davis, Jared, and Bryant, Rebecca, Oct. 25, 1827. Thomas Taylor........_____
Davis, Jerimiah, and Ross, Aaron, Dec. 23, 1819. Loderic Davis........Amos Davis
Davis, Joseph, and Shepherd, Nancy, Jan. 25, 1840. John Phipps........_____
Davis, Lucy, and Hanshaw, William, Oct. 12, 1814. Thos. Taylor.....Matthew Adams
Davis, Malinda, and McKay, Allen, April 17, 1822. Jared Tichenor......Caleb Hedge

Marriage Records, 1799 to 1840

Davis, Margaret, and Shepherd, William, Feb. 26, 1840. John Phipps....Theo. Davis
Davis, Mary, and Taylor, Harrison D., Nov. 11, 1828. W. Kincheloe. Christ. Jackson
Davis, Mary Ann, and Atherton, Joseph, March 30, 1830. Ancil Hall. A. Atherton
Davis, Mary Ann, and Hocker, Richard Weaver, July 30, 1836. ——— S. Huston
Davis, Miles H., and Condit, Ruth Ann, Feb. 17, 1832. Wm. Kincheloe. W. Simmons
Davis, Mirinda, and Bennett, Titus, Aug. 22, 1820. W. Allison........Henry Sallee
Davis, Nathan, and Grigsby, Eliza, ———, 1840. Alfred Taylor.........John Grigsby
Davis, Nelly, and Hocker, Martin, April 12, 1829. Loderic Davis.........Dillis Dyer
Davis, Nelson, and Atherton, Hannah, May 6, 1822. Loderic Davis.....Jeremiah Cox
Davis, Owen, and Gentry, Polly, Nov. 8, 1834. William Sandefur......James Atherton
Davis, Peggy, and Cochran, John, Sept. 23, 1813. Loderic Davis........Nic Hocker
Davis, Richard, and Neal, Elizabeth, Nov. 4, 1824. Loderic Davis........W. Handy
Davis, Solomon, and Ross, Jemima, Nov. 29, 1829. Loderic Davis........John Cox
Davis, Thomas, and Ingleheart, Rhoda, April 18, 1836. W. Green......Wm. Condit
Davis, Thomas Y., and Taylor, Hester Ann, Dec. 23, 1840. C. J. Ward.....J. Mason
Davis, William, and Haynes, Elizabeth, Jan. 11, 1832. David Kelley......D. Baker
Davis, Willis, and Lawton, Ann, Aug. 9, 1839. T. J. Ward...........Thomas Lawton
Dean, Summers, and Robertson, Amanda, April 30, 1826. Ancil Hall......W. Austin
Deering, S. S., and Nall, Martha Jane, Sept. 22, 1840. A. H. Shown......John Nall
Dehaven, Edward, and Hall, Dosha, May 15, 1828. Ancil Hall......Armstrong Hale
Dent, Peter, and Phipps, Martha, Aug. 23, 1838. C. J. Ward..........Henry Board
Deweese, Benjamin, and Anderson, Anna, June 25, 1802. Ignatius Pigman. ———
Deweese, Dan, and Kuykendoll, Louise, Oct. 12, 1840. A. H. Shown ....A. Kuykendoll
Deweese, Farmer, and Haynes, Nancy, Feb. 25, 1837. John Pinkston....John Haynes
Deweese, Martin, and White, Sarah, Jan. 25, 1830. Paul Abney........Thomas White
Dexter, Benj., and Warden, Betsy, Jan. 29, 1827. Jared Tichenor....Joseph Warden
Dexter, Joseph, and Anderson, Patsy, Dec. 20, 1825. Wm. Kincheloe....Jesse Anderson
Dexter, Rebecca, and Hedges, James, Nov. 8, 1809. John Davis........James Dexter
Dexter, Silas, and Woodward, Ann, July 4, 1825. William Harlt......John Barnett
Dickey, Elijah, and Ervin, Polly, Jan. 1, 1810. Thomas Taylor.........John Dickey
Dickey, Sarah, and Durbin, William, July 16, 1814. George Render....Robert Crump
Dodson, Dolly, and Martin, Monroe, Jan. 4, 1827. John Pinkston.....George Dodson
Dodson, George, and King, Deborah, Nov. 13, 1828. Thomas Downs....Ashum King
Donaldson, Patrick, and Goff, Betsy, Aug. 6, 1805———..........Robert Mosely
Dougherty, Chesterfield, and Ezell, Levice, Jan. 7, 1835———......Wiley Peasley
Dougherty, William, and White, Abagile, March 17, 1836———......Lewis White
Douglas, John, and Bennett, Amanda, Nov. 14, 1837. John Phipps....Quintus Shanks
Douglas, Jonathan, and Wilson, Martha, Nov. 11, 1809. John Davis....George Wilson
Dover, Abraham, and Stone, Celia, Aug. 20, 1805———..........William Watson
Downey, Alex., and Taylor, Ann, April 14, 1826. H. B. Hunter........John A. Taylor
Downs, William, and King, Penelope, Jan. 5, 1836. Thomas Downs......———
Dozier, James, and McFabes, Betsy, Dec. 29, 1813. Thomas Taylor....Joshua Crowe
Dragoo, John, and Lanham, Easter, Jan. 9, 1809. Wm. Anderson.....Andrew Campbell
Drake, Rice, and Tichenor, Elizabeth, Oct. 27, 1840———......Dan Tichenor
Dubois, Stephen, and Williams, Rebecca, May 23, 1819. Benj. Talbert....Nat Thomas
Duke, Dolly, and Stevens, John, Sept. 17, 1819. Loderic Davis........Richard Duke
Duke, John, and Mason, Elvira, June 4, 1831. William Hart..........John H. Mason

Ohio County in the Olden Days

Duke, Lydia, and Boswell, Caleb, Nov. 22, 1825. William Hart..........John Duke
Duke, Mary, and Condit, Jonathan, June 14, 1834. William Hart........John Crowe
Duke, Polly, and Ambrose, Samuel, June 28, 1832. Buford Henry......Thomas Duke
Duke, Richard, and Statler, Sally, Feb. 24, 1823. William Harlt.........Caleb Boswell
Duke, Susannah, and Sullenger, Francis, Feb. 19, 1840. John Crouch....John Huston
Duke, Thomas, and Taylor, Elizabeth, Sept. 6, 1832. Bluford Henry... Thomas Barnett
Duke, Thomas, and Addington, Dorcas A., Mch. 28, 1837. J. A. Holding. H. Addington
Duke, Washington, and Tinsley, Martha, March 21, 1840. Basil Ward....J. Tinsley
Duke, William, and Statler, Matty, _____, 1818. Thomas Taylor...Nicholas Taylor
Duke, William, and Neely, Julian, Feb. 28, 1836. William Davis........J. L. Condit
Duncan, Samuel, and Thompson, Catherine, Dec. 15, 1810. J. Rogers. Joe Thompson
Dunn, Mrs. Lebina, and Floyd, Jasper, May 28, 1800. Carter Tarrent.....Wm. Jones
Duposter, William, and Land, Polly, July 17, 1827. Loderic Davis.....Joseph Land
Dupoy, James, and Taylor, Rebecca, Dec. 19, 1801. James Keele......Philip Taylor
Durbin, William, and Dickey, Sarah, July 16, 1814. George Render....Robert Crump
Durlap, Henry, and Coleman, Elizabeth, Sept. 7, 1811. Benj. Talbert. Henry Coleman
Duvall, Benjamin, and Alin, Elizabeth, Feb. 19, 1820. Thomas Taylor. Dillis Dyer
Duvall, Nicholas, and Campbell, Ann, Dec. 20, 1819. Thomas Taylor. John S. Brooks
Duvall, Nicholas, and Mitchell, Sally, April 3, 1824. Thomas Taylor......Isaac Six
Earp, James, and Clark, Anthony Ann, Oct. 5, 1840. John Phipps........ L. D. Earp
Earp, Josiah, and Storm, Elizabeth, April 7, 1837. Jas. Holding....Nicholas Earp
Earp, Nicholas, and Storm, Abigail, Dec. 19, 1836. Jas. Holding..........L. D. Earp
Earp, Nicholas P., and Cooksey, Victoria Ann, July 27, 1840. J. G. Ward. J. H. Blane
Eastland, Robert, and McGee, Polly, April 10, 1810. John Davis......James Mosely
Eatherington, Aaron, and Hoover, Millie, March 24, 1819. Thomas Taylor_____
Eatherington, Polly, and McClain, John, Oct. 14, 1805. John Davis.....A. Eatherington
Eathernton, Jonathan, and Brown, Elizabeth, Nov. 1, 1802. James Keele_____
Edmunds, Isaac, and Compton, Susanna, Oct. 1, 1804. John Davis.....Wm. Weeks
Edmunds, Jane, and Harris, James, Nov. 17, 1825. Loderic Davis. James Hamilton
Edwards, William, and Nash, Peggy, March 25, 1800. Benj. Talbert......_____
Eidson, Lucy, and Webb, William, Jan. 23, 1839. J. G. Ward........Wm. Mooreman
Eidson, Molly, and Morgan, John, Feb. 10, 1834. William Hart........John Eidson
Eidson, Morning, and Rosedale, Tucker, July 20, 1823. Wm. Harlt......John Eidson
Elin, Mary Ann, and Davis, Garrett, Sept. 14, 1829. John Phipps.....Walter Earp
Elliott, John, and Condit, Ann, July 18, 1812. Loney Jackson.........Byron Condit
Ellis, Joseph, and Taylor, Jane, Sept. 15, 1835. Wm. Hart........Washington Phipps
Ellis, William, and Nichols, Polly, June 18, 1838. Ancil Hall..........Jesse Chapman
Elm, Rebecca H., and Embry, John, Sept. 27, 1833. Stephen Harber....Isaac Embry
Elms, Jane, and Shultz, John, June 10, 1829. Loderic Davis......... Charles Shultz
Elms, Thomas, and Keown, Elizabeth, Sept. 12, 1833. Benj. Burden......Ab. Pearce
Embry, Isaac, and Cooper, Elizabeth, Feb. 11, 1833. Benj. Burden....Wesley Cooper
Embry, John, and Elm, Rebecca H., Sept. 27, 1833. Stephen Harber....Isaac Embry
Embry, William, and Cooper, Jane, April 12, 1834. Paul Abney........Wm. Keown
English, Betsy, and Watson, John, May 1, 1806. John Grammar........John Powers
Ervin, Jane, and Heet, Nicholas, June 2, 1813. Thomas Taylor.....Richard Barnett
Ervin, Polly, and Dickey, Elijah, Jan. 1, 1810. Thomas Taylor........John Dickey
Ervin, William, and Whittehill, Elizabeth, Dec. 1, 1815. Benj. Kelley......_____

Marriage Records, 1799 to 1840

Erwin, Elizabeth, and Myers, Benjamin, Dec. 26, 1816. Benj. Kelley. Francis Erwin
Erwin, Mrs. Mary, and Wade, Ballanger, Oct. 20, 1833. Wm. Hart......Edmund Roach
Eskridge, Robinson, and Weeks, Elizabeth, Oct. 7, 1818. Jos. Wilson....Jas. Mathews
Evans, Allen, and Baker, Elizabeth, Aug. 2, 1838. Ancil Hall........Harris Evans
Evans, Hatfield, and Leathermon, Polly, Mch. 26, 1821. Benj. Burden. E. Kennedy
Evans, Jefferson, and Wiley, Mahala, Jan. 4, 1830. Philip Abney........Wm. Campbell
Evans, Sarah, and Daugherty, Andrew, June 3, 1837. Ancil Hall......T. W. Rosdale
Evans, Susannah, and Sutton, John, Sept. 9, 1814. Thomas Taylor....Abraham Six
Evans, Thomas, and Neel, Rebecca, Jan. 8, 1821. Benj. Burden....Solomon Kitenger
Evens, Francis, and Axton, Nancy, Aug. 31, 1818. Benj. Kelley......Philip Axton
Evens, Henry, and Miller, Mary, March 7, 1816. Thomas Taylor....John Anderson
Evens, Thomas, and Neel, Lalrinah, Feb. 10, 1820. Thomas Taylor........
Ezel, Greenberry, and Sharp, Eliza, Nov. 22, 1832. Wm. Hart.........H. D. Taylor
Ezel, Jeremiah, and Keown, Elizabeth, March 25, 1834. Paul Abney. William Keown
Ezel, Thomas, and Autory, Elizabeth, Jan. 11, 1822. William Harlt.....John Autory
Ezell, Levice, and Dougherty, Chesterfield, Jan. 7, 1835. _____.....Wiley Peasley
Far, Sarah, and Atherton, Benjamin, Jan. 15, 1806. Benj. Talbert....Henry Brown
Farley, Wm., and Wakeland, Sarah, Sept. 9, 1819. Loderic Davis .....Filbert Newton
Faught, Thomas, and Iler, Eliza Ann, Dec. 2, 1840. _____..........John Iler
Felix, Elizabeth, and Carter, Abraham, Feb. 7, 1828. D. J. Kelley.....Philip Felix
Felix, Phillip, and Haynes, Judith, April 11, 1824. John James........Hardin Haynes
Ferguson, Samuel, and Owen, Leccice, April 19, 1834. Wm. Sandefur....C. M. Baker
Ferguson, Julia, and Hale, Armstrong, Jan. 8, 1829. Wm. Harlt......Harrison Taylor
Field, Almenda, and Barnard, Milton E., Sept. 20, 1836. John Phipps....Jack Field
Field, Aquilla, and Tichenor, Sarah, March 25, 1800. Benj. Talbert........
Field, Aquilla, and Tichenor, Sarah, March 11, 1820. _____.....Timothy Tichenor
Field, Elizabeth, and Gibson, John, May 18, 1802. James Keele......Barnett Field
Field, Elizabeth M., and Landrum, Wm. Tom, April 24, 1837. J. Pinkston. H. Taylor
Field, Hannah, and Ashby, Horiteo, March 28, 1804. Thomas Taylor....Sally Field
Field, Henry, and Ball, Tucky, June 23, 1805. John Davis............Mark Florence
Field, Lucy, and Davis, James, Feb. 20, 1810. John Davis.........William Field
Field, Nancy, and Odum, William, Aug. 28, 1809. John Davis.........Henry Field
Field, Thomas, and Newcome, Eliza, Sept. 17, 1835. William Harlt.......H. Briant
Field, William, and Horren, Jane Henry, Sept. 27, 1832. Wm. Harlt....Jeff. Bennett
Field, Willis, and Moore, Polly Ann Sophia, Aug. 16, 1838. B. Ward.....Isaac Brown
Field, Zachariah, and Ford, Sebrina, Feb. 28, 1814. Joseph Faulks....... James Ford
Files, Polly, and Moody, John, April 13, 1812. Loney Jackson........William Libbs
Finley, Sam, and Bigger, Widow Sarah, July 6, 1805. T. Taylor.......G. Willingway
Firneman, William, and Matherson, Nancy, Feb. 6, 1810. John Cragg. Adam Galloway
Fitzhugh, James, and Barrett, Matilda, Oct. 3, 1825. Wm. Harlt......Samuel Pate
Floyd, Jasper, and Dunn, Mrs. Lebina, May 28, 1800. Carter Tarrent....Wm. Jones
Fogle, Charles, and Pender, Elizabeth, Sept. 22, 1818. Loderic Davis....Wm. Leach
Ford, Ann, and Hoover, Leonard, Dec. 19, 1812. Benj. Talbert......Steven Shoemaker
Ford, Cassandra, and Ward, Bassett, April 1, 1822. Wm. Harlt..... Jeffries Bennett
Ford, Dolly, and Likens, Thomas, Dec. 10, 1838. Ancil Hall..........John Ford
Ford, Francis, and Woodward, Eliza, Nov. 20, 1838. Basil Ward .....Alex. Rowe
Ford, Harriet, and Lynn, Nathan, Nov. 4, 1822. Wm. Hart ....Leonard Hoover

Ford, John, and Keown, Martha, Oct. 12, 1840. John Phipps..........W. S. Keown
Ford, Mahala, and Ward, Jesse, June 2, 1825. Wm. Harlt............Lewis Ford
Ford, Martha, and Miller, Reuben, Feb. 14, 1835. Ancil Hall............—
Ford, Nancy, and Wallace, Benjamin, June 19, 1823. Wm. Harlt......John A. Taylor
Ford, Sebrina, and Field, Zachariah, Feb. 28, 1814. Joseph Faulks.....James Ford
Ford, William, and Chapman, Sally, Feb. 10, 1813. Thomas Taylor....Samuel Lewis
Foster, Peter, and Hocker, Polly, May 18, 1819. Loderic Davis.......Weaver Hocker
Foster, Polly, and Gibson, Moses, Sept. 7, 1805. John Davis..........Noratic Gibson
Fowler, Nancy, and Garner, Ephraim, June 28, 1802. Ignatius Pigman. Ben Fowler
Fraze, Robert, and Berryman, Isabelle, July 15, 1837. Jacob Miller....J. B. Rogers
French, David, and Hudson, Ann, Dec. 20, 1820. Thomas Downs......Morton Hudson
French, George, and Hudson, Sally, Dec. 3, 1827. Wm. Harlt.........Thomas Hudson
French, Margaret, and Hudson, Wm., Aug. 20, 1821. Thomas Downs. Samuel French
French, Samuel, and Hudson, Fanny, Aug. 29, 1821. Thomas Downs....Thos. Hudson
French, Sarah, and Westerfield, James, June 9, 1824. Benj. Kelley......Dillis Dyer
Fulkerson, Alfred, and Taylor, Hannah, April 25, 1835. Geo. Render....Sept. Taylor
Fulkerson, Fulkerd, and Coleman, Polly, March 30, 1818. Loderic Davis....H. Coleman
Fulkerson, Fulkivin, and Gropsby, Nancy, Feb. 3, 1808. Wm. Anderson.....C. Shultz
Fulkerson, John, and Hocker, Nancy, Feb. 3, 1801. Ignatius Pigman....Geo. Hocker
Fulkerson, Margaret, and Smith, George, Nov. 30, 1829. Geo. Render. Adam Fulkerson
Fulkerson, Margaret, and Graves, Geo., Feb. 24, 1834. Geo. Render....Philip Fulkerson
Fulkerson, Mary Jane, and Fulkerson, Philip, Jan. 21, 1839. G. Render. G. H. Graves
Fulkerson, Milly, and Wise, Levi, Dec. 25, 1823. Thomas Taylor........J. Fulkerson
Fulkerson, Molly, and Wise, Levi, Dec. 25, 1823. Benj. Talbert......Adam Fulkerson
Fulkerson, Nancy, and Benton, James, July 25, 1829. Chas. Henderson. A. Fulkerson
Fulkerson, Philip, and Fulkerson, Mary Jane, Jan. 21, 1839. G. Render. G. H. Graves
Fulkerson, Rachel, and Wilson, Thomas, March 21, 1814. Thomas Taylor...Geo. Smith
Fulkerson, Rachel, and Yontz, Lemuel, Sept. 18, 1839. A. Taylor.....Philip Fulkerson
Fulkerson, Rebecca, and Covington, Edward, Oct. 25, 1836. Geo. Render. Geo. Smith
Fulkerson, Susan, and Fulkerson, Thomas, Dec. 12, 1836. Alfred Taylor. J. Fulkerson
Fulkerson, Thomas, and Fulkerson, Susan, Dec. 12, 1836. Alfred Taylor. J. Fulkerson
Funk, Nancy H., and Davenport, Sam A., Sept. 18, 1840. Alfred Taylor....—
Funkhauser, Isaac, and Young, Polly, Aug. 8, 1807. Benj. Talbert......James Young
Fuqua, Eliza, and Bennett, Lewis, Sept. 3, 1831. Ancil Hall........William Fuqua
Fuqua, Emeline, and Staples, James, Sept. 28, 1839. Ancil Hall.......James Fuqua
Fuqua, Lucretia, and Bennett, Nelson, Sept. 29, 1831. David Kelley....Wm. Fuqua
Fuqua, William, and Smith, Polly, Jan. 23, 1834. Ancil Hall........James Fuqua
Gabbert, William, and Hunt, Delilah, April 15, 1814. Nath. Pulliam....Valentine Hunt
Gallespy, Nancy A., and Royal, Richard, Feb. 27, 1836. Ancil Hall.....Wm. Gallespy
Galloway, Adam, and Leach, Sarah, Nov. 20, 1811. Benj. Talbert....James Hubbard
Galloway, David, and Johnson, Elizabeth, Dec. 8, 1809. Warren Cox....Jas. Holida
Galloway, John, and Martwick, Elizabeth, Feb. 7, 1806. Benj. Talbert....Z. Galloway
Galloway, Mary, and Jordan, Adam, Feb. 6, 1804. John Davis........David Glenn
Gardner, Fanny, and Anderson, John, March 7, 1817. Thomas Taylor. Henry Evans
Garner, Ephraim, and Fowler, Nancy, June 28, 1802. Ignatius Pigman....Ben Fowler
Garther, John, and Tilford, Louisa Ann, Oct. 17, 1840. Basil Ward....Andrew Tilford
Gary, Elijah, and Likens, Rosanna, Dec. 22, 1834. Wm. Anderson......Mark Likens

Marriage Records, 1799 to 1840

Gentry, Benjamin, and Johnson, Ann, Dec. 14, 1839. Basil Ward......Jones Johnson
Gentry, Cicey, and Neighbors, John C., Oct. 13, 1829. J. Phipps....Garrison Hoover
Gentry, Eliza, and Lynn, Nathan, Oct. 17, 1835. Wm. Sandefur....William Jones
Gentry, Elizabeth, and Petty, John, Dec. 18, 1835. Ancil Hall......Benjamin Gentry
Gentry, James, and Hornbeck, Elizabeth, July 21, 1803. John Davis....Elijah Myers
Gentry, James, and Leach, Sally, Feb. 2, 1835. Wm. Hart..............John Hall
Gentry, Joseph, and Thomas, Rhoda, Jan. 8, 1801. Ignatius Pigman......Wm. Carter
Gentry, Mopey, and Jones, Elizabeth, April 3, 1829. David Kelley......Wm. Jones
Gentry, Nancy, and Pinkston, Pattie, July 2, 1838. Ancil Hall..........Joe Gentry
Gentry, Polly, and Davis, Owen, Nov. 8, 1834. William Sandefur......Jas. Atherton
Gentry, Sally, and Hoover, Garrison, Sept. 15, 1829. Wm. Harlt......Joseph Gentry
Gentry, Samuel, and Miller, Dorcas, Sept. 21, 1829. John Denham.....Wm. M. Miller
Gentry, William, and Hodges, Mary, March 18, 1816. Benj. Kelley......Henry Evans
Gibbons, Lydia, and Barnett, William, April 30, 1812. Thos. Taylor....Wm. Wallace
Gibson, Daniel, and Cravens, Dorcas, April 22, 1832. John Phipps......Jesse Cravens
Gibson, Elizabeth, and Tanner, Salkins, Oct. 18, 1809. John Davis.....Wm. Tanner
Gibson, John, and Field, Elizabeth, May 18, 1802. James Keele........Barnett Field
Gibson, Jordan, and Wakeland, Nancy, Jan. 13, 1810. Loderic Davis....Gideon Gibson
Gibson, Mary, and Wall, Robert, Oct. 13, 1809. John Davis............Joe McFarland
Gibson, Moses, and Foster, Polly, Sept. 7, 1805. John Davis.........Noratic Gibson
Gibson, Nancy, and Hunter, Reuben, Sept. 29, 1817. Benj. Kelley....Adam Fulkerson
Gibson, Polly, and Shultz, Jacob, March 22, 1800. Robert Moseley....William Gibson
Gibson, William, and Shirtley, Polly, March 28, 1890. _____
Gilbert, Elizabeth, and Calloway, Chester, Oct. 24, 1809. John Davis....A. Hepsley
Gilbert, John, and Turner, Jemima, Feb. 18, 1802. James Keele..........
Gill, Thomas, and Shayer, Frances, Dec. 13, 1806. John Colvert......Jeremiah Ranal
Gillispie, James, and Gillispie, Margaret, Dec. 21, 1831. Ancil Hall....Wm. Gillispie
Gillispie, Lucy, and McKendly, Benjamin, May 15, 1840. Ancil Hall...Wm. Gillespie
Gillispie, Margaret, and Gillispie, Jas., Dec. 21, 1831. Ancil Hall.....Wm. Gillispie
Gilmore, Thomas, and Marlow, Mahala, Jan. 31, 1827. David Kelley....Thos. Marlow
Givins, John, and Bryant, Margaret, Dec. 2, 1810. John Davis.........John Bryant
Glen, William, and McFarland, Leah, Dec. 16, 1809. John Davis......Wm. McFarland
Glenn, Martha, and Anderson, Nelson, Dec. 17, 1808. John Davis......Wm. Glenn
Glever, Sally, and Bozarth, Jeremiah, Feb. 28, 1814. Joseph Faulks....Geo. Matthews
Glover, Betsy, and McFarland, William, Feb. 10, 1812. John Davis....John McFarland
Glover, Phebe, and McFarland, Robert, Sept. 18, 1812. John Davis....Robt. Moseley
Goff, Betsy, and Donaldson, Patrick, Aug. 6, 1805. _____........Robt. Mosely
Gold, Nancy, and Little, Thomas, Dec. 25, 1807. John Davis..........John Baird
Goldsmith, Elizabeth, and Lee, Samuel, Oct. 21, 1824. Thomas Taylor....Thos. Wilson
Goldsmith, John, and Taber, Rebecca, July 14, 1824. Thomas Taylor....Pardon Taber
Gosset, Eliza Ann, and Staples, William, Oct. 5, 1840. Basil Ward......Jesse Ross
Gosset, Elmira, and Smith, John C., March 10, 1840. Basil Ward.........Dan Hix
Grant, Eliza, and Smith, Thomas, Nov. 14, 1821. James Porter..........Wm. Belt
Grant, Elizabeth, and Borer, Valentine, Dec. 2, 1824. Benj. Talbert......Elijah Phipps
Grant, Sally, and Hudson, David, Feb. 1, 1816. Loney Jackson........James Lewallen
Graves, George, and Fulkerson, Margaret, Feb. 24, 1834. Geo. Render...Phil Fulkerson
Graves, Mary, and Robinson, John, Aug. 1, 1836. Adlai Boyd........George Graves

Ohio County in the Olden Days

Gray, Nellie, and Blevins, John, Dec. 28, 1819. John Phipps............——————
Greaver, Patsy, and Medley, Samuel, Jan. 21, 1813. John Davis......Meredith Cox
Green, John, and Burden, Jemima, Sept. 12, 1832. Benjamin Burden....Absalom Peace
Green, William, and Cox, Sally, Jan. 2, 1836. George Render..........James Cox
Greenwood, Walcott, and Leddington, Nancy, July 21, 1816. Thos. Taylor..Thos. Ralph
Greenwood, Walcott, and Reeves, Polly Ann, Dec. 22, 1840. Wm. Downey. J. Warden
Greer, George, and Benton, Elizabeth, Sept. 17, 1811. Thomas Taylor....Silas Benton
Greer, Mary, and Barkin, Sanders, Nov. 5, 1833. John Phipps........George Greer
Grey, Ellender, and Griffith, Edward, May 30, 1807. Benj. Talbert......Chas. Grey
Grey, Nancy, and Blevins, John, Jan. 6, 182(_). Lodowick Davis.........——————
Grey, Sally, and Wakeland, John, Nov. 25, 1819. Loderic Davis..........Benj. Gray
Grider, Henderson, and Ireland, Jane, Nov. 11, 1822. John Ridgeway....Benj. Newton
Griffith, Edward, and Grey, Ellender, May 30, 1807. Benj. Talbert.....Charles Grey
Griffith, Remus, and Handley, Sally, March 5, 1809. Wm. Anderson....Aquilla Field
Griffith, Ruth, and Cummins, Moses, Oct. 23, 1810. John Davis........J. Thompson
Grigsby, Aaron, and Chapman, Levina, Aug. 25, 1813. Thomas Taylor...F. Fulkerson
Grigsby, Eliza, and Davis, Nathan, _____, 1840. Alfred Taylor.......John Grigsby
Grigsby, Nathaniel, and Whitmore, Nancy, _____, 1811. Loderic Davis. G. Peteet
Grigsby, Nathaniel, and Blevins, Charlotte, Jan. 17, 1825. L. Davis......J. Blevins
Gropsby, Nancy, and Fulkerson, Fulkivin, Feb. 3, 1808. Wm. Anderson.....C. Shultz
Gross, Daniel, and Smeathers, Jane, Feb. 1, 1800. Benj. Talbert........Wm. Smothers
Groves, William, and Black, Lucinda, Nov. 29, 1822. Benj. Kelley....Willis J. Black
Hale, Ama, and Jones, William, March 23, 1828. Ancil Hall............Joseph Hale
Hale, Armstrong, and Ferguson, Julia, Jan. 8, 1829. Wm. Harlt......Harrison Taylor
Hale, Caleb, and Huff, Sally, March 11, 1817. Thomas Taylor........Charles Huff
Hale, Jane, and Thomas, John, March 8, 1813. Benj. Kelly..........Thomas Moseley
Hale, John, and Winkler, Polly, Jan. 15, 1814. Benj. Kelly............Wm. Galloway
Hale, William, and Bannon, Sally, Oct. 25, 1825. ——————..........John Bannon
Hale, Zamira, and Johnson, John, Nov. 6, 1835. Ancil Hall..............——————
Hall, Ancil, and Chapman, Rachel, Feb. 7, 1840. J. Bristow..........Squire Whittaker
Hall, Bazlip, and Williams, Aggie Jane, Aug. 15, 1839. J. G. Ward........G. Bryant
Hall, Betsy, and Baize, Nathan, Feb. 10, 1825. Loderic Davis..........Samuel Lee
Hall, Betsy, and Matthews, Lawson, Feb. 23, 1829. Ancil Hall..........John Henry
Hall, David, and Morgan, Susan, Oct. 19, 1812. William Rogers.....Charles Morgan
Hall, Dosha, and Dehaven, Edward, May 15, 1828. Ancil Hall......Armstrong Hale
Hall, James, and Baize, Polly, Sept. 13, 1823. Loderic Davis.........Nathan Baize
Hall, John, and Cobbs, Forbetha, Feb. 3, 1835. Ancil Hall..............Henry Cobbs
Hall, Mingo, and Brooks, Leah, Jan. 18, 1806. Thomas Taylor........Joseph Dunlap
Hall, Patsy, and Marlow, Tobias, May 10, 1831. Ancil Hall..............Jesse Cobb
Hall, Peggy, and Crockin, John, March 26, 1820. Benj. Kelley.........——————
Hall, Polly, and Wilson, Joseph, Jr., Oct. 20, 1824. Joseph Wilson, Sr.......John Hall
Hall, Samuel, and Taylor, Leanah, Jan. 8, 1822. Warner Crowe..........James Hall
Hamilton, George, and Smith, Jane, Oct. 25, 1833. William Sandefur....John Smith
Hamilton, Harrison, and Jones, Sarah, June 28, 1835. William Hart.....Isaac Morton
Hamilton, Samuel, and Crowe, Louise, April 17, 1834. Wm. Hart......Geo. Hamilton
Hamilton, William, and Paget, Eliza, Oct. 25, 1830. Ancil Hall..........Thos. Smith
Handley, John, and Lynn, Nancy, Feb. 3, 1807. John Davis............Henry Jones

Marriage Records, 1799 to 1840

Handley, Sally, and Griffith, Remus, March 9, 1809. Wm. Anderson...Aquilla Field
Handy, William, and Neal, Diana, Jan. 8, 1824. Loderic Davis........Nathan Howard
Hanks, Charles, and Martin, Hannah, March 7, 1822. Warner Crowe...James Martin
Hanshaw, William, and Davis, Lucy, Oct. 12, 1814. Thomas Taylor....Matthew Adams
Hardeste, Rebecca, and Porter, Thompson, July 13, 1804. Wm. Anderson. S. Cleaver
Hardin, David R., and Banks, Nancy, May 18, 1839. Ancil Hall.......David Banks
Harding, Polly, and Ward, Reuben, June 28, 1814. ———.......Moses Chapman
Harlin, Polly, and Raley, William, June 16, 1839. ———..........Jesse Ward
Harlong, Mitalda, and Allen, Alfred, Jan. 31, 1840. Paul Brey..........James Izel
Harrington, Ellen, and Williams, Wm. B., Sept. 24, 1840. Jos. Miller....Francis Miller
Harris, Betsy, and Brant, John, Feb. 10, 1811. John Davis.............Jesse Harris
Harris, Culsey, and Monroe, Martin Andrew, Oct. 30, 1828. Wm. Harlt..Richard Nall
Harris, James, and Edmunds, Jane, Nov. 17, 1825. Loderic Davis.....James Hamilton
Harris, Mahala, and Thompson, Henry, July 23, 1832. Bluford Henry. Thos. Berryman
Harris, Sally, and Acker, William, March 5, 1813. John Davis..........Jesse Harris
Harsha, Jean, and Six, John, April 3, 1812. Thomas Taylor.........Nathaniel Downs
Hart, Elvira, and Duke, John, June 4, 1831. William Hart..........John H. Mason
Hart, William, and Milton, Frances, Feb. 6, 1834. Wm. B. Landrum....Elijah Phipps
Haskins, Charles, and Ashby, Tanna, Dec. 9, 1836. Geo. Render......Jesse Ashby
Hatcher, Eleanor, and Davis, Hezekiah, July 21, 1813. Loderic Davis....Philip Hocker
Hatcher, Elizabeth, and Anderson, Amos, Feb. 5, 1820. Davis Loderic....Wm. Hatcher
Hatcher, Lindsey, and Roberts, Techarih, April 11, 1819. Loderic Davis. C. McCreney
Hatcher, William, and Morton, Sally, April 10, 1821. L. Davis........Thomas Morton
Hatfield, Ann, and Springton, Moses, Jan. 21, 1804. John Davis......Wm. Springton
Hayden, Moorman, and Jackson, Providence, Dec. 29, 1828. Wm. Harlt. Jas. Eidson
Hayden, Nancy, and Taber, Philip, Jan. 19, 1829. John Denham......John Hayden
Haynes, Belinda, and Haynes, Mason, Aug. 16, 1838. W. B. Taber......Josiah Haynes
Haynes, Charles, and Tilford, Lucy, Jan. 1, 1836. Ancil Hall........Walker Daniel
Haynes, Edy, and Willis, James K., Feb. 3, 1834. David Kelley........John Haynes
Haynes, Elizabeth, and Miller, Christopher, Feb. 5, 1809. Wm. Anderson. Jas. Haynes
Haynes, Elizabeth, and Davis, Wm., Jan. 11, 1832. David Kelley......Dixon Baker
Haynes, Francis, and Moberly, Mary Ann, Dec. 22, 1834. David Taber. Wm. Moberly
Haynes, Hannah, and Carter, William, May 2, 1824. Benj. Kelley......Alex. Barnett
Haynes, Hannah, and Kimball, Wm. Allen, Aug. 25, 1825. M. Utterback. Hardin Haynes
Haynes, Hardin, and Haynes, Polly, Feb. 17, 1822. Benj. Kelley.......James Martin
Haynes, James, and Rains, Jane, Feb. 11, 1839. J. L. Burrows.......Jeremiah Izel
Haynes, Judith, and Felix, Phillip, April 11, 1824. John James......Hardin Haynes
Haynes, Lucy, and Newberry, Parks, Aug. 26, 1837. James Holding....Geo. McDaniel
Haynes, Mason, and Haynes, Belinda, Aug. 16, 1838. W. B. Taber....Josiah Haynes
Haynes, Nancy, and Nicholas, William, Oct. 11, 1817. Thomas Downs....John New
Haynes, Nancy, and Deweese, Farmer, Feb. 25, 1837. John Pinkston....John Haynes
Haynes, Polly, and Wallace, Joseph, Oct. 11, 1817. Thomas Taylor......John New
Haynes, Polly, and Haynes, Hardin, Feb. 17, 1822. Benj. Kelley........Jas. Martin
Haynes, Polly, and Huff, Lewis, Feb. 17, 1829. David Kelley........Samuel Haynes
Haynes, Paulina, and Kelly, Carter, Jan. 7, 1832. David J. Kelley....Francis Haynes
Haynes, Sarah, and Miller, David, Dec. 3, 1839. S. Buchorn........Joseph Haynes
Haynes, Susanna, and May, Isaac, Feb. 3, 1835. David Kelley.......Robert Walker

Ohio County in the Olden Days

Haynes, William, and Taylor, Lucy, Dec. 6, 1830. David J. Kelley....Samuel Huston
Head, Polly, and Armstrong, Thomas, Aug. 8, 1832. Ancil Hall..........B. Barnett
Hearing, Elizabeth, and Taylor, Sullen, May 15, 1831. John Phipps. George Brown
Hearing, Nancy, and Taylor, Philip, May 15, 1831. John Phipps......George Brown
Hearrel, Ann, and McCrey, Alexander, March 23, 1813. Benj. Malone....Ennis Ury
Hearst, Isaac, and Hocker, Nancy, June 15, 1802. John Davis........John Hubbard
Heck, Randall, and Chapman, Eliza, Aug. 22, 1839. Alfred Taylor....Ezekiel Chapman
Hedden, Jesse, and Whittinghill, Rebecca, March 2, 1829. Wm. Long....Geo. Hedden
Hedges, James, and Ashby, Charlotte, Oct. 23, 1806. John Davis....Warren Ashby
Hedges, James, and Dexter, Rebecca, Nov. 8, 1809. John Davis......James Dexter
Hedges, James, and Tanner, Jane, Aug. 19, 1826. Jared Tichenor.....Peter Hedges
Hedges, Josiah, and Brown, Ann, March 11, 1818. George Render.....Joshua Brown
Hedges, Mary, and Ashby, Warren, Feb. 18, 1807. John Davis......Josiah Hedges
Hedges, Mary, and Brown, Thomas, June 11, 1834. _____.........James Hedges
Hedges, Peter, and Tichenor, Sally, Aug. 25, 1826. Jared Tichenor.....Richard Tanner
Hedges, Ruth, and Taylor, Henry, Sept. 27, 1809. John Davis......Thomas Bennett
Hedges, William, and Tanner, Jane, Sept. 21, 1805. John Davis.....William Tanner
Heet, Nicholas, and Ervin, Jane, June 2, 1813. Thomas Taylor......Richard Barnett
Heet, Samuel, and McKinney, Fanny, May 21, 1827. Wm. Harlt.....John Daniel
Henderson, Charles, and Rogers, Margaret, Feb. 2, 1811. Thomas Taylor. J. Hockley
Henderson, Emily, and Nall, J. G., March 27, 1831. Bluford Henry. R. W. McCreery
Henderson, Henry, and Logan, Sally, Jan. 1, 1823. Thos. Taylor......Henry Pirtle
Henderson, Linetta, and Robertson, Powhatan, June 25, 1834. F. H. Blades. W. Bradley
Hendricks, Harrison, and Lewallen, Hannah, Feb. 27, 1814. N. Pulliam. J. Lewallen
Hendricks, Patsy, and Jones, Francis, March 23, 1810. Wm. Anderson. Eli. Hendrix
Hendricks, Samuel, and Lucas, Sally, May 16, 1825. Wm. Harlt.......John Lucas
Henman, Maria, and Bennett, Jesse, Nov. 2, 1804. Thomas Taylor.......A. Henman
Henman, Rhoda, and Perigo, Romey, Oct. 1, 1801. James Keele......Samuel Henman
Herrald, Richard, and Compton, Winney, July 25, 1800. John Grammar. Jas. Skiman
Higgins, Williams, and Maddox, Elizabeth, Dec. 1, 1819. Aquilla Davis. Aquilla Field
Hillman, Benj., and Davis, Elizabeth, Sept. 19, 1809. Thomas Taylor...Forrest Davis
Hilt, Elizabeth, and Jacob, Elisha, Feb. 27, 1813. Thomas Taylor......Sam Crawford
Himmon, George, and Stewart, Nancy, Feb. 22, 1813. John Davis. Moses Cummings
Hipshey, Amos, and Hudson, Providence, Dec. 5, 1808. Wm. Anderson. W. E. Hudson
Hipsley, Elizabeth, and Hudson, John, March 8, 1821. James Porter....Amos Hipsley
Hobby, James, and Rogers, Nancy, Feb. 19, 1824. Loderic Davis. Jonathan Rogers
Hobly, James, and Lynn, Hannah, Oct. 11, 1811. Benj. Talbert........James Lynn
Hoboy, Betsy Coffee, and Moseley, James, Dec. 25, 1832. B. W. Reynolds. J. Hoboy
Hocker, Advisa, and Shields, John, March 31, 1836. George Render....Nathan Hocker
Hocker, Charles, and Rowe, Cynthia, Feb. 28, 1835. _____..........John Phipps
Hocker, Dorcas, and Barnard, Josiah, Dec. 24, 1805. Thomas Taylor....Philip Harker
Hocker, Henry, and Mitchell, Mary H., Feb. 19, 1829. Wm. Harlt.......Abel Mitchell
Hocker, John B., and Ashby, Susannah, Dec. 10, 1831. John Phipps....Thomas Ashby
Hocker, John B., and Leach, Ellen, Nov. 26, 1834. Thomas Davis......H. D. Taylor
Hocker, Martin, and Davis, Nelly, April 12, 1829. Loderic Davis........Dillis Dyer
Hocker, Nancy, and Fulkerson, John, Feb. 3, 1801. Ignatius Pigman....Geo. Hocker
Hocker, Nancy, and Hearst, Isaac, June 15, 1802. John Davis.......John Hubbard

Marriage Records, 1799 to 1840

Hocker, Nancy, and Barnard, Lloyd, Jan. 30, 1824. Loderic Davis......Martin Hocker
Hocker, Nicholas, and Render, Hester, Aug. 14, 1813. Loderic Davis. Matthew Adams
Hocker, Nicholas, and Cooper, Clarissa, Sept. 25, 1827. Loderic Davis....H. Cooper
Hocker, Philip, and Leddington, Nancy, Mar. 4, 1816. _____......Thos. Pendor
Hocker, Philip, and Hughes, Nancy, May 4, 1816. _____..........James Ford
Hocker, Philip, and Cochran, Rachel, June 1, 1816. Loderic Davis....Hezekiah Davis
Hocker, Polly, and Redmond, Felix, June 26, 1812. Loderic Davis......Phil Hocker
Hocker, Polly, and Foster, Peter, May 18, 1819. Loderic Davis........Weaver Hocker
Hocker, Quisenberry, and Cooper, Betsy A. I., April 13, 1840. J. Phipps. W. Phipps
Hocker, Rebecca, and Coleman, Richard, Jan. 23, 1823. William Harlt....N. Hocker
Hocker, Richard Weaver, and Davis, Mary Ann, July 30, 1836. _____ S. Huston
Hocker, Sally, and Barnes, John, Jan. 5, 1836. John Phipps........Charles Lawton
Hocker, Sarah, and Hogan, Charles, Dec. 20, 1800. Ignatius Pigman. George Hocker
Hodden, Rosey, and Alm, James, May 21, 1808. John Grower.......... Jones Alm
Hodges, John, and Liner, Ally, Oct. 3, 1818. Benj. Kelley............Amos Hodges
Hodges, Mary, and Gentry, William, March 18, 1816. Benj. Kelley....Henry Evans
Hogan, Charles, and Hocker, Sarah, Dec. 20, 1800. Ignatius Pigman...George Hocker
Holeman, Anthony, and Young, Nancy, Oct. 29, 1835. George Render. Polly Young
Holeman, Polly, and Victories, Jacob, May 3, 1828. Wm. Anderson....Jas. Holman
Holman, James, and Tong, Rebecca, April 14, 1809. Wm. Anderson....Stephen Clever
Holman, Patsy, and Ward, Jacob, Dec. 22, 1827. Thos. Taylor........Wm. Eidson
Hoover, Elizabeth, and Jones, James, Dec. 20, 1822. William Hart....William Jones
Hoover, Garrison, and Gentry, Sally, Sept. 15, 1829. William Harlt....Joseph Gentry
Hoover, Jacob, and Jones, Polly, June 15, 1822. William Hart......William Jones
Hoover, John, and Kelley, Salina, March 7, 1833. Ancil Hall........Jonathan Hoover
Hoover, Jonathan, and Roach, Mahala Ann, July 8, 1828. Wm. Harlt....Robt. Wilson
Hoover, Leonard, and Ford, Ann, Dec. 19, 1812. Benj. Talbert....Steven Shoemaker
Hoover, Mille, and Eatherington, Aaron, March 24, 1819. Thos. Taylor...._____
Hoover, Millie, and Atherton, Aaron, Mar. 21, 1819. Thos. Taylor......Jacob Hoover
Hoover, Milly, and Cooper, Jacob, Nov. 18, 1839. Basil Ward......Leonard Hoover
Hoover, Polly, and Neighbors, Thomas, May 4, 1821. Thomas Taylor....Jacob Hoover
Hoover, Sally, and Ambrose, John, July 28, 1828. Wm. Hart........James Jones
Hoover, Susan, and Maddox, William, Nov. 22, 1834. Wm. Hart....James Jones
Hopkins, James, and Baird, Polly Dec. 17, 1803. John Davis........James Baird
Hopkins, Ruth, and Boyle, Alexander, July 13, 1820. Joseph Tichenor....Wm. Hill
Hornbeck, Elizabeth, and Gentry, James, July 21, 1803. John Davis....Elijah Myers
Hornbeck, Mary, and Sallee, Thomas, Dec. 2, 1809. Thomas Taylor....Alin Hornbeck
Horren, Jane Henry, and Field, Wm., Sept. 27, 1832. Wm. Harlt....Jeffries Bennett
Horseman, Jesse, and Johnson, Nancy, Oct. 7, 1837. Wm. Anderson....James Johnson
Hostute, Catherine, and Condit, Allen, April 14, 1810. John Davis......James Lin
House, Jacob, and Reed, Sarah, Aug. 3, 1836. A. Fuqua............Septimus Taylor
Houseley, Dosby, and Taylor, Johnson, Feb. 2, 1833. John Phipps......Wm. Houseley
Housley, Elizabeth, and Condit, Peter, Dec. 7, 1826. Jared Tichenor....Robt. Housley
Housley, Robert, and Condit, Abigail, Feb. 6, 1832. Wm. Sandefur......G. Condit
Houston, Sally, and Wickliffe, Isaac, Nov. 4, 1824. Benj. Kelley......Robt. Houston
Houtchins, Jesse, and Clifford, Betsy, April 8, 1818. Geo. Render....Mitchell Clifford
Howard, Allen, and Owen, Patsy L., Oct. 5, 1829. William C. Long.....Henry Owen

Ohio County in the Olden Days

Howard, Elizabeth, and Benton, Erasmus, Mar. 27, 1830. Wm. Harlt. Wm. Leach
Howard, James, and Whittinghill, Polly, Jan. 6, 1838. Ancil Hall......R. Whittinghill
Howard, Nancy, and Shultz, Joseph, Aug. 31, 1822. William Hart......Isaac Malin
Howard, Nathaniel, and Stewart, Elizabeth, Oct. 16, 1822. Wm. Hart....John Smith
Howard, Samuel, and Montgomery, Nancy, Dec. 11, 1822. William Hart.._____
Howard, Samuel, and Johnson, Polly, April 19, 1838. Ancil Hall......James Willis
Howard, Susan, and Wilson, James, April 5, 1835. _____........Benjamin Wilson
Howell, Frankie, and Nanny, James, Sept. 29, 1829. John Phipps....Matthew Nanny
Howell, John, and Bates, Winifred, May 30, 1813. Loney Jackson....Chas. Nothington
Hoyle, Levi, and _____, March 8, 1813. John Davis........Benjamin Duncan
Hudson, Ann, and French, David, Dec. 20, 1820. Thomas Downs......Morton Hudson
Hudson, Barnett, and Hudson, Susannah, May 22, 1810. John Davis....Samuel Ross
Hudson, David, and Grant, Sally, Feb. 1, 1816. Loney Jackson....James Lewallen
Hudson, Edmund, and Makin, Isyphena, Oct. 12, 1838. John Pinkston...Abel Bennett
Hudson, Fanny, and French, Samuel, Aug. 29, 1821. Thomas Brown....Thomas Hudson
Hudson, John, and Hipsley, Elizabeth, March 8, 1821. James Porter....Amos Hipsley
Hudson, Joseph, and Stewart, Rebecca, Oct. 26, 1813. John Davis........_____
Hudson, Joshua, and Mills, Virginia, March 28, 1831. Wm. Downs.....John Patton
Hudson, Lewis, and Hudson, Nancy, _____, 1830. Wm. Downs........
Hudson, Lewis, and Hudson, Nancy, Feb. 17, 1836. Wm. Downs........
Hudson, Nancy, and Patton, John, Aug. 29, 1821. Thomas Downs....Thomas Hudson
Hudson, Nancy, and Hudson, Lewis, _____, 1830. Wm. Downs........
Hudson, Nancy, and Hudson, Lewis, Feb. 17, 1836. Wm. Downs........
Hudson, Patsy, and Simmons, Charles, Dec. 16, 1833. Wm. Downs....Thos. Hudson
Hudson, Providence, and Hipshey, Amos, Dec. 5, 1808. Wm. Anderson. W. E. Hudson
Hudson, Sally, and French, George, Dec. 3, 1827. Wm. Harlt..........Thos. Hudson
Hudson, Susan, and Tarlton, Townstead, Oct. 29, 1812. John Davis. Robt. Tarlton
Hudson, Susannah, and Hudson, Barnett, May 22, 1810. John Davis....Samuel Ross
Hudson, William, and Coffee, Cleo, Aug. 29, 1810. John Craig.......Philip Coffee
Hudson, William, and French, Margaret, Aug. 20, 1821. T. Downs....Samuel French
Huff, Aquilla, and White, Elizabeth, March 25, 1805. _____........Wm. White
Huff, Charles, and Whitler, Polly, March 12, 1835. Ancil Hall......Bradford Whitler
Huff, Elizabeth, and Richards, Thomas, Oct. 17, 1829. Wm. Long....Goldsburg Huff
Huff, Gallsburry, and Richards, Matilda, Sept. 1, 1818. Nall Overale......E. Marlowe
Huff, Lewis, and Haynes, Polly, Feb. 17, 1829. David Kelley........Samuel Haynes
Huff, Nancy, and Henry H. Cobb, Feb. 10, 1840. John Kelley............
Huff, Sally, and Hale, Caleb, March 11, 1817. Thos. Taylor............Chas. Huff
Huff, William, and Marlowe, Eliza, Nov. 12, 1835. Ancil Hall..........Levi Marlowe
Hughes, Joel, and Atherton, Amelia, Oct. 6, 1825. Loderic Davis.....Nicholas Hocker
Hughes, Nancy, and Hocker, Philip, May 4, 1816. _____..........James Ford
Hughes, Sally, and Lanham, John, Jan. 12, 1826. Jared Tichenor....Thomas Ashby
Hughston, John, and Shoemaker, Mary, Nov. 14, 1809. Thos. Taylor. Adam Shoemaker
Humphrey, Catherine, and Humphrey, James, May 24, 1832. Wm. Downs. R. Tichenor
Humphrey, Eliza, and Humphrey, William, Aug. 4, 1837. _____....Wm. Humphrey
Humphrey, James, and Humphrey, Catherine, May 24, 1832. Wm. Downs. R. Tichenor
Humphrey, Margaret, and Brashers, Emanuel, Jan. 9, 1830. J. Phipps. Benj. Humphrey
Humphrey, Matilda, and Neely, M. S., Nov. 16, 1833. R. J. Reynolds. B. Humphrey

Marriage Records, 1799 to 1840

Humphrey, Raughley, and Cain, Jane, Feb. 15, 1827. Wm. Kincheloe....Amos Davis
Humphrey, Sally, and Ingleheart, James, March 8, 1813. John Davis. Dan Humphrey
Humphrey, Sarah, and Brown, Presley, Sept. 24, 1829. Wm. Downs. Benj. Humphrey
Humphrey, William, and Humphrey, Eliza, Aug. 4, 1837. _____...Wm. Humphrey
Hunt, Christine, and Perry, Thomas, Oct. 12, 1807. John Davis.......Henry Perry
Hunt, Delilah, and Gabbert, William, April 15, 1814. Nath. Pulliam. Valentine Hunt
Hunter, Abigail, and Young, William, Jan 23, 1822. Thos. Taylor....Morgan Young
Hunter, Anderson, and Wakeland, Nancy, Mar. 16, 1835. Geo. Render. Wm. Wakeland
Hunter, Elizabeth, and Peak, Alexander, Dec. 7, 1823. Wm. Harlt....Alex Hunter
Hunter, Elizabeth, and Smith, Jesse, Sept. 22, 1830. John Phipps.....Reuben Hunter
Hunter, Jane, and Peak, Alexander, Oct. 22, 1832. Wm. Hart........Samuel Peyton
Hunter, Mary, and Kimble, John, Aug. 6, 1832. George Render........Jesse Smith
Hunter, Nancy, and Powers, John, June 29, 1801. James Keele....Moses Springton
Hunter, Nancy, and Matthews, Alfred, Dec. 21, 1826. Wm. Harlt....Joseph Smith
Hunter, Nancy, and Wakeland, John, Dec. 30, 1828. George Render. Reuben Hunter
Hunter, Reuben, and Bryant, Mary, April 2, 1810. William Anderson...John Bryant
Hunter, Reuben, and Gibson, Nancy, Sept. 29, 1817. Benj. Kelley....Adam Fulkerson
Hurton, Caleb, and Matthews, Lusanna, July 4, 1803. Ignatius Pigman. Geo. Wilson
Huston, Ann, and Allen, William, Feb. 8, 1813. Job Hobbs .....Nathaniel Hamilton
Huston, Samuel, and Stevens, Lydia, April 18, 1831. Wm. Hart......John G. Nall
Hynes, Sally, and Carson, John, Oct. 21, 1812. Francis Travis..........Levi Hynes
Igelheart, Sarah, and Thomson, John, Feb. 1, 1820. Thomas Taylor.....Jacob Iglehart
Iglehart, Sarah, and Tanner, Samuel, Dec. 9, 1824. Jared Tichenor....Joseph Iglehart
Iglehart, Thomas, and Warden, Nancy, Feb. 17, 1835. Wm. Downs....Jas. Warden
Iglehart, Ann, and Southard, Robert, Oct. 16, 1839. Geo. Render.....Isaac Brown
Iglehart, Eliza, and Iglehart, Thomas, March 11, 1826. J. Tichenor......J. Iglehart
Iglehart, Henry D., and Bennett, Amelia Ann, Dec. 10, 1834. Wm. Sandefur. _____
Iglehart, Jacob, and Tichenor, Ann, Sept. 17, 1829. Wm. Downs.....Timothy Tichenor
Iglehart, Janet, and Muller, Jesse, March 17, 1825. Wm. Kincheloe.....Jacob Iglehart
Iglehart, John, and Condit, Emeline, Nov. 28, 1832. Wm. Downs.....Jacob Condit
Iglehart, Matilda, and Miller, Hiram, Aug. 30, 1828. J. Tichenor......Jacob Iglehart
Iglehart, Rebecca, and Moore, David, May 22, 1833. Wm. Downs.....Jacob Iglehart
Iglehart, Thomas, and Iglehart, Eliza, March 11, 1826. J. Tichenor......J. Iglehart
Iglehart, William B., and Condit, Rhoda, Oct. 00, 1827. Geo. McNelly. Wm. Condit
Iler, Eliza Ann, and Faught, Thomas, Dec. 2, 1840. _____..........John Iler
Iler, Elizabeth, and Pierce, Benjamin, Mar. 13, 1826. Geo. Render....John Cannon
Iler, Jacob, and Leach, Elizabeth, Sept. 28, 1813. Loderic Davis......Leonard Leach
Iler, Jacob, and Miller, Polly, Jan. 28, 1818. Loderic Davis........John B. Miller
Iler, Jane, and Pearce, Solomon, Oct. 19, 1832. David Kelley..........Perry Iler
Iler, John, and Leach, Sarah, Sept. 22, 1818. Loderic Davis..........Wm. Leach
Iler, Mary Ann, and Keown, Nathan, Sept. 25, 1836. John Phipps......Henly Iler
Iler, Nancy, and Cannon, John, Jan. 5, 1826. Wm. Harlt............L. McReynolds
Iler, Patsy, and Izel, James, Oct. 29, 1827. Paul Abney..........Wm. M. Miller
Iler, Perry, and Cooksey, Eliza, Feb. 11, 1831. Wm. Hart............Lewis Smith
Iler, Sally, and Lewell, Samuel, Feb. 20, 1812. Benj. Kelley..............John Ilar
Imleber, David, and Tichenor, Peggy, March 20, 1830. Geo. Render. Jas. Tichenor
Ingleheart, Eliza, and Ashley, Jesse, June 27, 1800. William Davis....William Dauney

Ohio County in the Olden Days

Ingleheart, Elizabeth, and Ashby, Jesse, March 22, 1830. Wm. Downs....J. Inglehart
Ingleheart, James, and Humphrey, Sally, March 8, 1813. John Davis. Dan Humphrey
Ingleheart, Julian, and Barnett, James, Sept. 14, 1817. Benj. Kelley. Jared Tichenor
Ingleheart, Polly, and Bell, David, Feb. 12, 1824. Jared Tichenor....John Ingleheart
Ingleheart, Rhoda, and Davis, Thomas, April 18, 1836. Wm. Green......Wm. Condit
Ingleheart, Sally, and Addington, Joshua, Oct. 7, 1834. Wm. Sandefur. H. Addington
Ireland, Jane, and Grider, Henderson, Nov. 11, 1822. John Ridgeway. Benj. Newton
Isler, Polly, and Leach, William, Nov. 11, 1811. Loderic Davis........David Isler
Izel, James, and Iler, Patsy, Oct. 29, 1827. Paul Abney............Wm. M. Miller
Izel, Jeremiah, and Jemison, Eliza, Nov. 24, 1836. _____............Jesse Reno
Jackson, Ann, and Jackson, Elias, Dec. 1, 1817. Thos. Taylor........Wm. Williams
Jackson, Catherine, and Arnold, John, Dec. 2, 1818. Thos. Taylor....Julius Jackson
Jackson, Cesna, and Landrum, Sally, March 14, 1819. Benj. Kelley....Josh. Chapman
Jackson, Chris. E., and Shanks, Camilla, Dec. 18, 1827. Geo. McNelly. M. A. Shanks
Jackson, Elias, and Jackson, Ann, Dec. 1, 1817. Thos. Taylor........Wm. Williams
Jackson, Eliza, and Mason, John, Sept. 26, 1808. Wm. Anderson.......C. Jackson
Jackson, Hannah, and White, John, Aug. 22, 1822. Thomas Taylor....Julius Jackson
Jackson, Hannah, and Whitman, John, Aug. 22, 1822. Thomas Taylor. Alex Barnett
Jackson, Polly, and Crowe, John, July 8, 1835. Wm. Hart..........John Smith
Jackson, Polly, and Render, Joshua, Dec. 23, 1812. Thos. Taylor.........Jas. Rogers
Jackson, Providence, and Hayden, Moorman, Dec. 29, 1828. Wm. Harlt. Jas. Eidson
Jackson, Rebecca, and Mooreman, Jesse, Dec. 29, 1828. Wm. Harlt....Jas. Edison
Jackson, Roby, and Carter, Peggy, March 4, 1814. Loderic Davis....Wm. Carter
Jackson, Sally, and Thomas, William, Nov. 16, 1824. T. Taylor. Christopher Jackson
Jackson, Samuel, and Taylor, Ada Priscilla, Feb. 24, 1828. J. Bristow....Thos. Taylor
Jacob, Elisha, and Hilt, Elizabeth, Feb. 27, 1813. Thos. Taylor........Sam Crawford
James, Fleming, and Rogers, Margaret Ann, Nov. 24, 1839. _____James Rogers
James, John, and Taylor, Margaret, Aug. 29, 1803. John Davis....Richard Taylor
James, Lucy, and Rogers, William Cass, April 22, 1822. Loderic Davis....Wm. James
James, Mariah, and Ambrose, Jacob, June 18, 1823. William Hart.......John Calhoun
James, Moseley, and Rogers, Elizabeth, Nov. 8, 1813. Jas. Rogers....Chas. Henderson
James, Polly, and Lugg, Joel, Feb. 28, 1800. John Davis...............John James
James, Samuel, and Rogers, Patsy, Oct. 19, 1818. John Phipps......James Rogers
James, Susannah, and Taylor, Thomas, Jan. 17, 1814. Loderic Davis. Samuel James
James, William, and Parker, Catherine, April 16, 1801. Jas. Keele.....Thos. Parker
James, William, and Cravens, Jane, July 28, 1825. L. Davis..........Jesse Cravens
Jemison, Eliza, and Izel, Jeremiah, Nov. 24, 1836. _____...........Jesse Reno
Johnson, Ann, and Gentry, Benjamin, Dec. 14, 1839. Basil Ward......Jones Johnson
Johnson, Cyrus, and Taber, Eliza, June 4, 1838. Basil Ward........James Johnson
Johnson, Elizabeth, and Galloway, David, Dec. 8, 1809. Warren Cox....Jas. Holida
Johnson, Elizabeth, and Brown, William, June 9, 1817. Geo. Render. Moses Johnson
Johnson, Elizabeth Ann, and Benton, Nath., Jan. 5, 1826. Wm. Harlt. Reuben Bennett
Johnson, James, and Bruce, Polly, March 13, 1809. Wm. Anderson....Moses Cummings
Johnson, James, and Taber, Deborah, July 16, 1833. Wm. Hart........John Senate
Johnson, Jane, and Taber, Ambers, May 9, 1833. Wm. Hart..........Cyrus Johnson
Johnson, John, and Underwood, Elizabeth, Jan. 12, 1809. John Davis. Charles Scott
Johnson, John, and Malin, Ann, April 3, 1833. Wm. Sandefur........Isaac Malin

Marriage Records, 1799 to 1840

Johnson, John, and Hale, Zamira, Nov. 6, 1835. Ancil Hall..............——
Johnson, Judy, and Crowe, Elijah, Jan. 2, 1814. Benj. Kelley........James Johnson
Johnson, Julian, and Thomas, John, Jan. 11, 1835. Ancil Hall......Clement Johnson
Johnson, Katy, and Trafford, John, March 7, 1811. Loderic Davis....Henry Cooper
Johnson, Marcus, and Brown, Susanna, May 6, 1818. Geo. Render......Ancil Brown
Johnson, Nancy, and Horseman, Jesse, Oct. 7, 1837. Wm. Anderson....Jas. Johnson
Johnson, Nathan, and Taber, Mary, Nov. 19, 1831. John J. Kelley........A. Taber
Johnson, Philip, and Barnett, Rebecca, Aug. 18, 1820. Wm. Harlt....Jeffries Barnett
Johnson, Polly, and Sherman, Thomas, Dec. 5, 1836. J. Pinkston....David Westerfield
Johnson, Polly, and Howard, Samuel, April 19, 1838. Ancil Hall........Jas. Willis
Johnson, Susan, and Owen, John, Oct. 20, 1838. Thomas Downs....Abraham Owen
Johnston, Cemlia, and Morgan, Charles, Sept. 7, 1812. Benj. Talbert. Moses Johnston
Johnston, James, and Taylor, Lucinda, Sept. 10, 1829. Wm. Downs. Gant Johnson
Johnston, Maley, and Taylor, Henry, Sept. 25, 1804. John Davis....James Morton
Johnston, Margaret, and Morgan, Arnold, Aug. 27, 1812. Benj. Kelley....J. Luellan
Johnston, Nancy, and Moore, John, July 14, 1825. Elijah Durbin....Clement Johnson
Jones, Achiles, and King, America, March 1, 1840. James Bristow.....James King
Jones, Elizabeth, and Gentry, Mopey, April 3, 1829. David Kelley......Wm. Jones
Jones, Fielding, and Milton, Harriet, Sept. 21, 1831. Benj. Talbert......Jas. Milton
Jones, Francis, and Hendricks, Patsy, March 23, 1810. Wm. Anderson. Eli. Hendrix
Jones, Gabriel, and Bellance, Cynthia, May 3, 1809. John Davis........Wm. Johnson
Jones, James, and Hoover, Elizabeth, Dec. 20, 1822. Wm. Hart..........Wm. Jones
Jones, John, and Woods, Elizabeth, Aug. 10, 1810. Wm. Anderson........Wm. Wood
Jones, Jos., and Rogers, Elizabeth, Sept. 20, 1822. J. James.........Jonathan Rogers
Jones, Lawrence, and Winkler, Mary, Oct. 9, 1810. James Rogers.....Welcher David
Jones, Nelly, and Philps, James, Dec. 31, 1807. John Davis........William Phelps
Jones, Polly, and Hoover, Jacob, June 15, 1822. William Hart.......William Jones
Jones, Rebecca, and Patton, Thornton, Aug. 5, 1833. David Kelly.....John Patton
Jones, Sarah, and Vittitoe, Daniel, Nov. 5, 1810. Wm. Anderson......Thomas Jones
Jones, Sarah, and Hamilton, Harrison, June 28, 1835. Wm. Hart......Isaac Morton
Jones, William, and Brown, Theby, Oct. 10, 1804. ————.........Reuben Brown
Jones, William, and Hale, Ama, March 23, 1828. Ancil Hall............Joseph Hale
Jordan, Adams, and Galloway, Mary, Feb. 6, 1804. John Davis........David Glenn
Jordan, Susan, and Williams, William, Nov. 3, 1813. Thomas Taylor. Joshua Crowe
Keath, Elizabeth Ann, and Barrett, Thomas, June 21, 1837. John Phipps..B. Malin
Keele, James, and Pen, Peggy, Sept. 14, 1801. James Keele.............——
Keele, James, and Pugh, Margaret, Sept. 15, 1801. James Keele......John Taylor
Keith, Benjamin, and Mills, Elizabeth, July 23, 1828. Wm. Harlt.....Anderson Mills
Kelly, Amy, and Calhoon, John, _____, 1800. Benj. Talbert............——
Kelly, Amy, and Carter, John, March 11, 1809. Wm. Anderson........Joe Haynes
Kelly, Ann Eliza, and Roach, Cornelius, Sept. 6, 1834. Ancil Hall.......John Hoover
Kelly, Belima, and Sharp, Charles, Nov. 8, 1834. Ancil Hall..............——
Kelly, Benjamin, and Thorp, Rebecca, Nov. 11, 1816. Benj. Kelley......Terry Thorp
Kelly, Carter, and Haynes, Paulina, Jan. 7, 1832. David J. Kelley.....Francis Haynes
Kelly, David, and Carter, Fanny, Feb. 16, 1810. Thomas Taylor........John Carter
Kelly, John, and Whittinghill, Sarah, July 5, 1814. Benj. Kelley....Wm. Whittinghill
Kelly, John B., and Rogers, Polly, May 21, 1814. John Weldon.........Clark Hall

Ohio County in the Olden Days

Kelly, Lendon C., and Carter, Delilah, Oct. 5, 1825. David Kelley........Wm. Carter
Kelly, Moses, and Paxton, Eliza Ann, March 3, 1838. Ancil Hall........John Axton
Kelly, Patsy, and Kelly, William, Feb. 24, 1823. John Ridgeway......Landon Kelley
Kelly, Salina, and Hoover, John, March 7, 1833. Ancil Hall..........Jonathan Hoover
Kelly, Sarah, and Whittinghill, William, April 18, 1814. Benj. Kelley. Benj. Kelley
Kelly, William, and Kelly, Patsy, Feb. 24, 1823. John Ridgeway......Landon Kelley
Keown, Elizabeth, and Elms, Thomas, Sept. 12, 1833. Benj. Burden......Ab. Pearce
Keown, Elizabeth, and Ezel, Jeremiah, Mar. 25, 1834. Paul Baney......Wm. Keown
Keown, Martha, and Ford, John, Oct. 12, 1840. John Phipps..........W. S. Keown
Keown, Nathan, and Iler, Mary Ann, Sept. 25, 1836. John Phipps......Henly Iler
Keown, William, and Thomas, Mary Ann, Dec. 14, 1839. C. Taylor....Harrison Taylor
Kerfold, Ann, and Bishop, Erasmus, Feb. 12, 1812. Joe Anderson.......John Taylor
Kigel, Solomon, and Spence, Susan, May 21, 1839. Alfred Taylor........Martin Bailey
Kimball, William Allen, and Haynes, Hannah, Aug. 25, 1825. M. Utterback. H. Haynes
Kimble, John, and Hunter, Mary, Aug. 6, 1832. George Render........Jesse Smith
King, America, and Jones, Achiles, March 1, 1840. James Bristow......James King
King, Deborah, and Dodson, George, Nov. 13, 1828. Thomas Downs....Ashum King
King, Libela, and Purcell, Lewis, Dec. 16, 1828. John Pinkston..........Asbum King
King, Mary Ellen, and Mills, Anderson, Jan. 25, 1836. James Downs...Osburn King
King, Nancy, and Stewart, John, Jan. 28, 1834. William Downs.........
King, Penelope, and Downs, William, Jan. 5, 1836. Thomas Downs......
Kuykendoll, Louise, and Duweese, Dan., Oct. 12, 1840. A. H. Shown....A. Kuykendoll
Lamb, Charlotte, and Pray, Elijah, Feb. 9, 1824. Thos. Taylor.........Wm. Gillespy
Lamb, John P., and Atterberry, Rebecca, Jan. 3, 1831. Ancil Hall.....Henry Edison
Lamb, Sally, and Crabtree, Isaac, March 5, 1814. John Davis..........Robert Lamb
Lamb, Sally Ann, and Cobb, Jesse, Sept. 30, 1831. Ancil Hall...........John Lamb
Lamb, Sarah, and Calhoun, John, Dec. 25, 1806. John Davis........Henry Jones
Land, Polly, and Duposter, William, July 17, 1827. Loderic Davis.......Joseph Land
Landrum, Emily, and O'Connor, William, March 10, 1836. J. Phipps. Nath. Howard
Landrum, Nancy, and Blacklock, Edmond, Aug. 30, 1814. Nathan Pulliam. Sam Burch
Landrum, Priscilla, and Davis, Beverly, Dec. 8, 1825. Ancil Hall........Wm. Winter
Landrum, Ruby, and Scott, Daniel, Jan. 12, 1814. Benj. Kelley........Wm. Nichles
Landrum, Sally, and Jackson, Cesna, March 14, 1819. Benj. Kelley.....Josh. Chapman
Landrum, William Tom, and Field, Elizabeth M., April 24, 1837. J. Pinkston. H. Taylor
Langley, Bartholemew, and Burden, Jane, Jan. 7, 1837. Ancil Hall.....Clem Langley
Langley, Clement, and Sutton, Jane, Aug. 13, 1835. Wm. Sandefur......Jas. Sutton
Langley, Susan, and Clark, Wilford, Jan. 9, 1837. John Wathen.........James Langley
Lanham, Copinder, and McKindley, William, April 6, 1825. Thos. Downs. Eli Lanham
Lanham, Easter, and Dragoo, John, Jan. 9, 1809. Wm. Anderson....Andrew Campbell
Lanham, Elias, and White, Anna, April 20, 1805. John Davis. ....Richard Lanham
Lanham, Henrietta, and Austin, William, March 29, 1826. Thos. Taylor. W. M. Davis
Lanham, Hester, and Pearson, Thomas, April 20, 1825. Thos. Taylor. Elijah Lanham
Lanham, John, and Hughes, Sally, Jan. 12, 1826. Jared Tichenor......Thomas Ashby
Lanham, Lewis, and Plumer, Ann, Dec. 25, 1819. Benj. Kelley........John Grigsby
Lanham, Polly, and Campbell, Andrew, Sept. 8, 1804. Thos. Taylor....Richard Lanham
Lanham, Rachel, and Nicholas, Valentine, Mar. 26, 1812. Benj. Talbert. Elias Lanham
Lanson, John, and Davis, Betsy, June 29, 1820. Loderic Davis......Ignatius Barnard

Marriage Records, 1799 to 1840

Lapp, John, and Turnbaugh, Nanny, Dec. 24, 1806. Thomas Taylor....John Downs
Larrels, William, and Spagner, Peggy, Aug. 7, 1817. _____......Theophilus Petty
Lashbrook, John, and Burton, Rebecca, Oct. 6, 1826. David Kelley....James Burton
Lawton, Amanda M., and Moseley, Robt., Oct. 21, 1840. C. H. Shaver....C. J. Lawton
Lawton, Ann, and Davis, Willis, Aug. 9, 1839. T. J. Ward............Thomas Lawton
Lawton, Caroline, and Moseley, Daniel, Dec. 12, 1836. _____......Wesley Phipps
Laymonds, Jacob, and Wilson, Sally, May 4, 1835. _____..........James Wilson
Layton, Christine, and Myers, Thomas, May 10, 1811. Thomas Taylor. Jonathan Isom
Leach, Altha, and Taylor, Septimus, Dec. 18, 1828. Jasper Bristow....Leonard Leach
Leach, Elizabeth, and Cox, John, May 13, 1806. Thomas Taylor........John Cox
Leach, Elizabeth, and Iler, Jacob, Sept. 28, 1813. Loderic Davis......Leonard Leach
Leach, Ellen, and Hocker, John B., Nov. 26, 1834. Thomas Davis......H. D. Taylor
Leach, James, and Taylor, Rebecca, Dec. 23, 1823. Thos. Taylor....Jonathan Raley
Leach, John, and Taylor, Martha, March 30, 1835. _____........Richard Duke
Leach, Joseph, and Miller, Atha, May 4, 1819. Loderic Davis.......John D. Miller
Leach, Leonard, and Cole, Mary, Feb. 4, 1824. Thos. Taylor.......Septimus Taylor
Leach, Martha Ann, and Coleman, Martin, Feb. 25, 1840. Alfred Taylor. Jos. Leach
Leach, Miranda, and Cox, Thomas, Dec. 24, 1829. Loderic Davis......John Crowe
Leach, Nancy, and Leach, William, Dec. 21, 1813. Thos. Taylor......Wm. Leach, Sr.
Leach, Nancy, and Taylor, Ignatius Pigman, Oct. 13, 1825. J. James. Leonard Leach
Leach, Polly, and Peak, Hezekiah, Aug. 13, 1816. Thos. Taylor..........Wm. Leach
Leach, Sally, and Gentry, James, Feb. 2, 1835. William Hart..........John Hall
Leach, Sarah, and Galloway, Adam, Nov. 20, 1811. Benj. Talbert......Jas. Hubbard
Leach, Sarah, and Iler, John, Sept. 22, 1818. Loderic Davis........William Leach
Leach, Sarah, and Wooley, Richard, Oct. 3, 1832. R. Y. Reynolds....Nathaniel Howard
Leach, Susannah, and Taylor, Richard, April 8, 1834. Loderic Davis. Leonard Leach
Leach, Talbert, and Austin, Margaret, March 25, 1839. _____......T. J. Burton
Leach, William, and Taylor, Jane, Jan. 31, 1804. Thomas Taylor......John Leach
Leach, William, and Isler, Polly, Nov. 11, 1811. Loderic Davis........David Isler
Leach, William, and Leach, Nancy, Dec. 21, 1813. Thomas Taylor....Wm. Leach, Sr.
Leach, William, and Thomas, Mary Ann, June 15, 1840. P. Abney.....Jos. Renfrow
Leaf, Jane, and Newton, Isaac, Dec. 29, 1836. William Brown..........John Leaf
Leatherman, Jane, and Allen, Henry, Feb. 28, 1821. Benj. Burden. Theophelum Allen
Leathermon, Polly, and Evans, Hatfield, March 26, 1821. Benj. Burden. E. Kennedy
Leddington, Nancy, and Hocker, Philip, March 4, 1816. _____......Thos. Pendor
Leddington, Nancy, and Greenwood, Walcott, July 21, 1816. Thos. Taylor. Thos. Ralph
Leddington, Polly, and Underwood, James, April 20, 1826. Geo. Render....John Lane
Lee, Abner, and Adams, Sally, May 19, 1807. John Davis ....Lewis Adams
Lee, Abner, and Barnett, Margaret, Feb. 22, 1810. John Davis......Robert Wall
Lee, Ann, and Shultz, Charles, May 25, 1820. Loderic Davis............John Baize
Lee, Jesse, and Taylor, Hannah, Aug. 28, 1808. John Davis..........Morris Taylor
Lee, Polly, and Sands, James, April 18, 1820. Jacob Miller..........Henry Crowe
Lee, Mrs. Sally, and Narcarron, John, July 20, 1805. John Davis......James Martin
Lee, Samuel, and Goldsmith, Elizabeth, Oct. 21, 1824. Thos. Taylor....Thos. Wilson
Lee, Samuel, and Morand, Nancy, July 10, 1830. Loderic Davis......James Morand
Lee, Talbert, and Brown, Jane, Sept. 29, 1835. Wm. Sandefur....Archibald Taylor
Leggit, William, and Raymond, Betty, Dec. 3, 1812. Thomas Taylor....Elijah Frank

Ohio County in the Olden Days

Lemon, Amy, and Storm, Peter, March 18, 1804. Thomas Taylor....Jacobin Lemon
Lemon, John, and Rogers, Sarah, Oct. 1, 1807. John Davis.............Nat Rogers
Lemon, John, and Rogers, Sarah, Nov. 9, 1807. John Davis............Nat Rogers
Lenham, Elizabeth, and Lewellan, John, ———, 1820. Benj. Kelley. Leonard Leach
Lewallen, Hannah, and Hendricks, Harrison, Feb. 27, 1814. N. Pulliam. J. Lewallen
Lewallen, Samuel, and White, Elizabeth, Aug. 15, 1805. John Davis. Jacob Lewallen
Lewell, James, and Wyles, Polly, Feb. 5, 1817. George Render......David Lindley
Lewell, Jobish, and Midkiff, Peggy, Aug. 10, 1817. Thomas Taylor....Benj. Midkiff
Lewell, Samuel, and Iler, Sally, Feb. 20, 1812. Benj. Kelley............John Iler
Lewellan, Jacob, and Rockerby, Eliza, May 21, 1816. Loney Jackson....Jas. Lewellan
Lewellan, Jobish, and Taylor, Sally, Oct. 22, 1826. Wm. Hart.......Thomas Taylor
Lewellan, John, and Campbell, Martha, Sept. 17, 1810. John Davis.....Jacob Lewellan
Lewellan, John, and Lenham, Elizabeth, ———, 1820. Benj. Kelley. Leonard Leach
Lewellan, Josiah, and Thomas, Jane, Oct. 23, 1819. ——————..........Alex Barnett
Lewellan, Martha, and Barnett, Jacob, Aug. 27, 1812. Benj. Kelley....Jacob Lewellen
Lightfoot, Pendleton, and Crowe, Caroline, Feb. 21, 1832. Wm. Hart. Robt. McCreery
Likens, Rosanna, and Gary, Elijah, Dec. 22, 1834. Wm. Anderson......Mark Likens
Likens, Sally, and Aubrey, Benjamin, Feb. 1, 1836. John Phipps....Mark Likens
Likens, Thomas, and Ford, Dolly, Dec. 10, 1838. Ancil Hall.............John Ford
Lindley, Daniel, and McGill, Sally, Aug. 8, 1809. Wm. Anderson....Daniel Pruden
Lindley, Elizabeth, and Barrett, Thomas, June 27, 1840. Basil Ward....Wm. Lindley
Lindley, Elizabeth Jane, and Tichenor, Haron, Sept. 5, 1838. G. Vaught. Edmond Rowe
Lindley, Margaret, and Bennett, Chas., Dec. 23, 1835. Wm. Sandefur. Dan Lindley
Lindley, Mary, and Condit, Uzal, Nov. 1, 1832. William Kincheloe....David Lindley
Lindsey, Samuel, and Williams, Elizabeth, Oct. 25, 1820. Jared Tichenor. A. Bishop
Lindsey, Thomas, and Six, Catherine, March 12, 1821. Benj. Burden. Daniel Six
Lindsey, William, and Ashby, Rebecca, April 22, 1819. John Phipps.....Wm. Ashby
Liner, Ally, and Hodges, John, Oct. 3, 1818. Benj. Kelley.............Amos Hodges
Linn, James, and Armstrong, Polly, May 15, 1810. John Davis.........Wm. Wright
Linn, Jacob, and Parker, Peggy, Feb. 12, 1810. Thomas Taylor..........Joe Parker
Little, David, and Ashby, Polly, Jan. 15, 1808. John Grower........Warren Ashby
Little, Thomas, and Gold, Nancy, Dec. 25, 1807. John Davis..........John Baird
Logan, Sally, and Henderson, Henry, Jan. 1, 1823. Thos. Taylor.......Henry Pirtle
Logston, Philip and Bryant, Amelia, April 29, 1840. John Phipps........F. R. Hall
Loney, James, and Brown, Ann, May 29, 1821. Jared Tichenor.......Armstead Brown
Loney, John, and Brown, Judy, Aug. 18, 1821. Jared Tichenor........Robert Brown
Loyal, Leticia, and Brandon, Robert, Sept. 23, 1827. Ancil Hall......Wm. B. Charley
Lucas, Elizabeth, and Woodward, William, Feb. 23, 1836. Wm. Sandefur. ———
Lucas, Ingram, and Moore, Eliza Jane, Oct. 19, 1840. Basil Ward......John Farris
Lucas, Polly, and Brown, James, March 30, 1837. Jacob Miller............I. Lucas
Lucas, Sally, and Hendricks, Samuel, May 16, 1825. Wm. Harlt........John Lucas
Lucas, Samuel, and Stewart, Mary, Oct. 26, 1815. John Davis..........———
Lue, John, and Milton, Nancy, April 18, 1822. Wm. Kincheloe.....Jacob Herrsinger
Lugg, Joel, and James, Polly, Feb. 28, 1800. John Davis..............John James
Lynn, Hannah, and Hobly, James, Oct. 11, 1811. Benj. Talbert.......James Lynn
Lynn, Nancy, and Handley, John, Feb. 3, 1807. John Davis..........Henry Jones
Lynn, Nathan, and Ford, Harriet, Nov. 4, 1822. Wm. Hart.......Leonard Hoover

Marriage Records, 1799 to 1840

Lynn, Nathan, and Gentry, Eliza, Oct. 17, 1835. Wm. Sandefur..........Wm. Jones
Lynn, William, and Wallace, Elizabeth, Dec. 25, 1826. Wm. Shelby....Wm. G. Wallace
McCary, Mary Polly, and Crawford, Mason, Feb. 10, 1805. Wm. Davis....N. Ross
McClain, John, and Eatherington, Polly, Oct. 14, 1805. John Davis...A. Eatherington
McClain, Matthew, and Brevins, Polly, April 27, 1809. Wm. Anderson....J. Crowe
McClure, Thomas, and Pinkston, Nancy, April 26, 1813. Benj. Kelley. Thos. Motter
McCormick, Sally Y., and Wooley, Jacob, Nov. 5, 1832. Wm. Hart. John McCormick
McCreery, Charles, and Crowe, Ann, Oct. 28, 1811. Thos. Taylor......Samuel Lewis
McCreery, Slutina, and McGury, G. H., Nov. 26, 1829. Wm. Harlt....Daniel McGury
McCreery, Vitula, and Daniel, Vivian, Sept. 25, 1836. Jas. Taylor....Robt. Brown
McCrey, Alexander, and Hearrel, Ann, March 23, 1813. Benj. Malone.....Ennis Ury
McCroclin, Dolly, and Woodward, Ashford, Feb. 12, 1821. J. Tichenor....J. Calloway
McCrocklin, Sally, and Taylor, Thomas, Oct. 12, 1826. J. Gillespy....Joshua Chapman
McDaniel, Collen, and Avery, Milly, July 12, 1808. Wm. Anderson......John Pult
McDaniel, Gobel M., and Carter, Martha, Nov. 15, 1832. Ancil Hall. Chas. McDaniel
McDaniel, Jesse, and Robertson, Ann, Nov. 18, 1824. Wm. Harlt....Jos. Robertson
McDonald, Charles, and Thompson, Nancy, Oct. 22, 1834. Wm. Hart. Francis Black
McFabes, Betsy, and Dozier, James, Dec. 29, 1813. Thos. Taylor......Joshua Crowe
McFarland, Leah, and Glen, William, Dec. 16, 1809. John Davis....Wm. McFarland
McFarland, Robert, and Glover, Phebe, Sept. 18, 1812. John Davis....Robt. Moseley
McFarland, Walter, and Nall, Sarah Elizabeth, Jan. 2, 1837. J. Pinkston. Richard Nall
McFarland, William, and Glover, Betsy, Feb. 10, 1812. John Davis....John McFarland
McFerrin, John, and Wilson, Sabina, May 5, 1838. Ancil Hall..........John Ford
McGee, Polly, and Eastland, Robert, April 10, 1810. John Davis.....James Mosely
McGill, Ann, and Pruden, Daniel, Nov. 8, 1813. John Davis...........Uzal Condit
McGill, Ann, and Ritchey, John, Sept. 1, 1817. Geo. Render........Daniel Lindley
McGill, Letty, and Miller, Nelson, Oct. 6, 1828. Jared Tichenor..........S. Lindey
McGill, Sally, and Lindley, Daniel, Aug. 8, 1809. Wm. Anderson......Daniel Pruden
McGury, G. H., and McCreery, Slutina, Nov. 26, 1829. Wm. Harlt...Daniel McGury
McIlwain, Jane, and Smith, Hugh, March 13, 1823. Wm. Hart..........
McIntire, William, and Burch, Mary, Jan. 3, 1830. Jacob Miller......Wm. S. Barrett
McKay, Allen, and Davis, Malinda, April 17, 1822. Jared Tichenor......Caleb Hedge
McKendly, Benjamin, and Gillespy, Lucy, May 15, 1840. Ancil Hall....Wm. Gillespy
McKenzie, William, and Webb, Eliza, Jan. 8, 1822. John Ridgeway....Wm. Daniel
McKindley, William, and Lanham, Copinder, April 6, 1825. Thos. Downs. E. Lanham
McKinley, William, and Midkiff, Betsy, Jan. 4, 1830. J. Bristow......John Bozarth
McKinney, Fanny, and Heet, Samuel, May 21, 1827. Wm. Harlt......John Daniel
McNeely, Ezekiel, and Ashby, Polly, Sept. 30, 1819. John Phipps......Wm. Ashby
McSherry, Henry, and Baird, Martha Isabel, Sept. 22, 1840. Basil Ward. Thos. Baird
McSherry, Hiram, and Baird, Martha Jane, Jan. 14, 1840. Basil Ward....Thos. Baird
McWain, Lewis, and Morton, Ann, May 31, 1823. Wm. Harlt.....Alexander Cox
Maddox, Elizabeth, and Higgins, Wm., Dec. 1, 1819. A. Davis..........A. Field
Maddox, James, and Stewart, Elizabeth, Oct. 12, 1833. John Phipps. Wm. Stewart
Maddox, John, and Render, Amelia, July 1, 1819. Loderic Davis....Robert Render
Maddox, Joshua, and Cotter, Nancy, Sept. 5, 1833. Wm. Landrum....Alex Powers
Maddox, Mary Boyd, and Rowe, Thomas, July 15, 1836. Adlai Boyd.....John Maddox
Maddox, Sally, and Southard, Robert, Dec. 6, 1827. Jared Tichenor. John Maddox

Ohio County in the Olden Days

Maddox, Samuel, and Wakeland, Harriet, Sept. 3, 1823. Wm. Harlt. Nath. Howard
Maddox, Thomas, and Shepherd, Delilah, May 25, 1840. _____ _____. Wm. Shepherd
Maddox, William, and Hoover, Susan, Nov. 22, 1834. Wm. Hart........Jas. Jones
Magan, Polly, and Tanner, James, May 15, 1835. Wm. Sandefur......Geo. Brown
Maheurer, Fred..., and Atterberry, Eliza, Sept. 18, 1828. A. Hall....W. Atterberry
Makin, Isyphena, and Judson, Edmund, Oct. 12, 1838. John Pinkston Abel Bennett
Malin, Ann, and Johnson, John, April 3, 1833. Wm. Sandefur..........Isaac Malin
Malin, Elizabeth, and Tichenor, Benj., Dec. 23, 1838. Alfred Taylor. Byron Tichenor
Malin, Isaac, and Shultz, Mary, Sept. 12, 1812. Francis Travis......Chas. Atherton
Malin, John, and Askins, Elizabeth, Aug. 29, 1812. Loney Jackson...Harrison Askins
Malin, Lydia, and Stewart, Carter, April 4, 1828. Loderic Davis........Bazil Malin
Malin, Mariah, and Williams, Samuel, Mar. 6, 1821. Loderic Davis.....Isaac Malin
Malin, Sarah, and Stewart, William, Sept. 17, 1822. Wm. Hart........Jacob Malin
Malin, Susannah, and Moseley, Presby, Feb. 17, 1816. Geo. Render. Thos. Morgan
Marletts, Mabel, and Austin, Philner, April 27, 1837. Wm. Sandefur......J. Hoover
Marlin, Bazil B., and Stewart, Ann, Sept. 17, 1821. Loderic Davis....Thomas Smith
Marlow, Anson, and Marlow, Nancy, Oct. 18, 1821. Thos. Taylor....Edward Marlow
Marlow, Mahala, and Gilmore, Thomas, Jan. 31, 1827. David Kelley. Thomas Marlow
Marlow, Nancy, and Marlow, Anson, Oct. 18, 1821. Thos. Taylor....Edward Marlow
Marlow, Tobias, and Hall, Patsy, May 10, 1831. Ancil Hall..........Jesse Cobb
Marlowe, Eliza, and Huff, William, Nov. 12, 1835. Ancil Hall........Levi Marlowe
Marlowe, Mary, and Rusher, Minor, Jan. 19, 1826. Ancil Hall..........John Marlowe
Marlowe, Thomas, and Albin, Rebecca, Nov. 25, 1837. Ancil Hall.....Absalom Albin
Martin, Anne, and Memvain, Lewis, July 27, 1800. Benj. Talbert........_____
Martin, Cela, and Stone, Daniel W., Nov. 21, 1824. J. Pinkston..........Wm. Huff
Martin, Elias, and New, Nancy, June 4, 1822. Benj. Kelley............James Martin
Martin, Hannah, and Hanks, Charles, March 7, 1822. W. Crowe........Jas. Martin
Martin, Monroe, and Dodson, Dolly, Jan. 4, 1827. John Pinkston......Geo. Dodson
Martin, Reuben, and Brandon, Polly, Feb. 7, 1828. Ancil Hall.....John H. McHenry
Martin, Sally, and Milmay, Thomas, Aug. 22, 1810. Loderic Davis........John Six
Martin, Sally, and Milay, Thomas, Aug. 22, 1814. _____ _____.....Jas. Hallenhead
Martwick, Elizabeth, and Galloway, John, Feb. 7, 1806. Benj. Talbert....Z. Galloway
Mason, Augustus, and Render, Eliza, Aug. 12, 1839. Geo. Render....Robt. Render
Mason, Catherine, and Chapman, Ezekiel, Oct. 15, 1840. Alfred Taylor. John. Mason
Mason, John, and Jackson, Eliza, Sept. 26, 1808. Wm. Anderson........C. Jackson
Mason, Joseph, and Burch, Elenor, Sept. 3, 1825. Thos. Taylor........Benj. Burch
Matherson, Nancy, and Fireman, William, Feb. 6, 1810. John Crags. A. Galloway
Matthews, Alfred, and Hunter, Nancy, Dec. 21, 1836. Wm. Harlt.....Joseph Smith
Matthews, Alfred, and Powers, Eliza, March 5, 1832. Wm. Landrum. Alex. Powers
Matthews, David, and Wilson, Sarah, June 28, 1804. Wm. Anderson...Geo. Matthews
Matthews, George, and Moore, Elizabeth, June 4, 1805. Jas. Keele....John Wilson
Matthews, James, and Crash, Phebe, Aug. 22, 1812. Joseph Wilson....Wm. Matthews
Matthews, Lawson, and Hall, Betsy, Feb. 23, 1829. Ancil Hall........John Henry
Matthews, Lusanna, and Hurton, Caleb, July 4, 1803. Ignatius Pigman. Geo. Wilson
Matthews, Mary, and Overton, Jonathan, Feb. 23, 1814. Thos. Taylor. Geo. Matthews
Matthews, Nancy, and Burch, Henley, Nov. 9, 1829. Ancil Hall......John Johnson
Matthews, Samuel, and Maxwell, Nelly, Sept. , 1822. Joseph Wilson....Wm. Maxwell

Marriage Records, 1799 to 1840

Matthews, William, and Brown, Janet, Aug. 22, 1827. Geo. McNeeley. Philman Moore
Mattox, Susan, and Coleman, Elisha, _____, 1826. Wm. Harlt......Wm. N. Davis
Maxwell, Hamilton and Meadows, Emeline, Sept. 3, 1838. Ancil Hall....John Potter
Maxwell, Nelly, and Matthews, Samuel, Sept. 5, 1822. Joseph Wilson....Wm. Maxwell
Maxwell, William, and Wilson, Elizabeth, Aug. 8, 1831. D. J. Kelley....W. Christian
May, Isaac, and Haynes, Susanna, Feb. 3, 1835. David Kelley........Robert Walker
Meadows, Emeline, and Maxwell, Hamilton, Sept. 3, 1838. Ancil Hall..John Potter
Metcalf, John, and Winkler, Fanny, Sept. 18, 1813. Benj. Kelley......Wm. Galloway
Medley, Samuel, and Greaver, Patsy, Jan. 21, 1813. John Davis....Meredith Cox
Meeks, Hardin, and Agle, Nancy, Oct. 5, 1829. Ancil Hall..........James Adle
Menvain, Lewis, and Martin, Anne, July 27, 1800. Benj. Talbert........._____
Meyers, Elijah, and Barnett, Hannah, June 24, 1801. Ignatius Pigman....J. Mosely
Meyers, Ellen, and Davenport, Wm., Feb. 21, 1838. Basil Ward.....Richard Tarfa
Meyrs, Edward, and Nail, Lucy, Oct. 18, 1836. John Phipps..........Wm. Peyton
Midkiff, Benjamin, and Ward, Elizabeth, March 15, 1834. F. S. Blades...John Phipps
Midkiff, Betsy, and McKinley, William, Jan. 4, 1830. John Bristow. John Bozarth
Midkiff, James, and Taylor, Elizabeth, Dec. 15, 1825. Wm. Harlt....Jonathan Rogers
Midkiff, John, and Smith, Charlotte, March 29, 1827. Wm. Harlt. James Fitzhugh
Midkiff, Joseph, and Taylor, Ann, Nov. 10, 1823. Thomas Taylor.....Benj. Vancleve
Midkiff, Peggy, and Jewell, Jobish, Aug. 10, 1817. Thos. Taylor......Benj. Midkiff
Midkiff, Polly, and Barnett, Joseph, Nov. 30, 1817. Thos. Taylor....Joseph Midkiff
Midkiff, Rebecca, and Pate, William, Nov. 23, 1826. Wm. Harlt....John Midkiff
Milay, Thomas, and Martin, Sally, Aug. 22, 1814. _____.....James Hallenhand
Miller, Amanda, and Arnold, William, Jan. 12, 1835. Wm. Hart......John D. Miller
Miller, Ara Ann, and Mitchell, Thompson, July 25, 1836. _____.......John Miller
Miller, Atha, and Leach, Joseph, May 4, 1819. Loderic Davis........John D. Miller
Miller, Betsy, and Barnes, Weaver, April 6, 1809. Thos. Taylor....Thos. Worthington
Miller, Charlotte, and Pate, Mason C., May 11, 1837. Wm. Brown....James Miller
Miller, Christopher, and Haynes, Elizabeth, Feb. 5, 1809. Wm. Anderson. Jas. Haynes
Miller, David, and Cooper, Jane, Jan. 25, 1810. Wm. Anderson.......Sam Cooper
Miller, David, and Williams, Maria, Aug. 4, 1824. Loderic Davis....Elijah Williams
Miller, David, and Boswell, Polly, Oct. 10, 1825. Wm. Harlt..........Caleb Boswell
Miller, David, and Haynes, Sarah, Dec. 3, 1839. J. Buchorn......Joseph Haynes
Miller, Dorcas, and Gentry, Samuel, Sept. 21, 1829. John Denham. Wm. M. Miller
Miller, Dorcas Jane, and Barnes, Joseph H., April 20, 1840. J. Phipps.....J. Miller
Miller, Eliza, and Myers, Francis, March 15, 1827. Wm. Harlt.....John D. Miller
Miller, Eliza Ann, and Wilcox, Jacob, Aug. 13, 1832. John Phipps......Fred Miller
Miller, Elizabeth, and Thomas, James, April 2, 1809. Wm. Anderson....Thos. Moseley
Miller, Elizabeth Ann, and Ashby, Tanner, June 30, 1836. John Phipps....W. Phipps
Miller, Hiram, and Igleheart, Matilda, Aug. 30, 1828. J. Tichenor....Jacob Igleheart
Miller, Joe, and Smith, Lucy, Sept. 26, 1808. Wm. Anderson......Robert Cates
Miller, Joseph, and Austin, Helen, Nov. 10, 1818. Loderic Davis......John Austin
Miller, Mahala, and Rowan, William, May 9, 1835. Wm. Hart......William Miller
Miller, Mary, and Evens, Henry, March 7, 1816. Thomas Taylor.....John Anderson
Miller, Mary Ann, and Burton, Horace, Nov. 25, 1837. John Pinkston....Robt. Miller
Miller, Mary Catty, and Borough, John, April 11, 1809. John Davis....John Armstrong
Miller, Nelson, and McGill, Letty, Oct. 6, 1828. Jared Tichenor.........S. Lindey

Ohio County in the Olden Days

Miller, Polly, and Iler, Jacob, Jan. 28, 1818. Loderic Davis..........John B. Miller
Miller, Reuben, and Ford, Martha, Feb. 14, 1835. Ancil Hall............——
Miller, Sally, and Cooper, Alexander, June 7, 1814. John Weldon........Wm. Cooper
Miller, Sally, and Chambers, Abrin, July 2, 1828. Ancil Hall..........Jacob Miller
Miller, Siticia, and Autory, Giles, March 28, 1822. Wm. Hart..........John Miller
Miller, William, and Mitchell, Polly, March 24, 1828. Wm. Harlt....Nicholas Hocker
Mills, Anderson, and King, Mary Ellen, Jan. 25, 1836. James Downs....Osburn King
Mills, Elizabeth, and Keith, Benjamin, July 23, 1828. Wm. Harlt....Anderson Mills
Mills, Harvey, and Richards, Catherine, March 1, 1827. Wm. Hart....Craven Peyton
Mills, Mehila, and Calloway, James, March 23, 1823. Wm. Harlt......Abe R. Rowan
Mills, Virginia, and Hudson, Joshua, March 28, 1831. Wm. Downs....John Patton
Milmay, Thomas, and Martin, Sally, Aug. 22, 1810. Loderic Davis......John Six
Milton, Frances, and Hart, William, Feb. 6, 1834. Wm. B. Landrum. Elijah Phipps
Milton, Harriet, and Jones, Fielding, Sept. 21, 1831. Benj. Talbert.....James Milton
Milton, Nancy, and Lue, John, April 18, 1822. Wm. Kincheloe. Jacob Herrsinger
Milton, Sally, and Taylor, John A., Oct. 15, 1823. Thos. Taylor....Wesley Taylor
Mitchell, John, and Smith, Sarah Ann, Aug. 15, 1831. D. J. Kelley....Leonard Bean
Mitchell, Jonathan, and Smith, Jenny A., Sept. 5, 1840. John Phipps. T. Mitchell
Mitchell, Julian, and White, Walker, Oct. 21, 1839. Jacob Miller....Jon. Mitchell
Mitchell, Mary H., and Hocker, Henry, Feb. 19, 1829. Wm. Harlt....Abel Mitchell
Mitchell, Polly, and Miller, William, March 24, 1828. Wm. Harlt....Nicholas Hocker
Mitchell, Rhoda, and Six, Isaac, April 11, 1822. Benj. Kelley.............E. Dean
Mitchell, Sally, and Cox, Anderson, April 27, 1820. Benj. Burden......Jesse Craddox
Mitchell, Sally, and Duvall, Nicholas, April 3, 1824. Thomas Taylor....Isaac Six
Mitchell, Thompson, and Miller, Ara Ann, July 25, 1836. ————......John Miller
Mobberly, John, and Baynes, Mary, March 21, 1832. David Kelley......Dillis Dyer
Mobberly, Mary Ann, and Haynes, Francis, Dec. 22, 1834. D. Taber. Wm. Mobberly
Monroe, Martin Andrew, and Harris, Culsey, Oct. 30, 1828. Wm. Harlt. Richard Nall
Montgomery, Margaret, and Brown, Wm., Jan. 22, 1828. Alex. Chapman. J. Montgomery
Montgomery, Nancy, and Howard, Samuel, Dec. 11, 1822. Wm. Hart....——
Moody, John, and Files, Polly, April 13, 1812. Loney Jackson......William Libbs
Moore, David, and Igleheart, Rebecca, May 22, 1833. Wm. Downs....Jacob Igleheart
Moore, Eliza Jane, and Lucas, Ingram, Oct. 19, 1840. Basil Ward......John Farris
Moore, Elizabeth, and Matthews, George, June 4, 1805. Jas. Keele......John Wilson
Moore, John, and Johnston, Nancy, July 14, 1825. Elijah Durbin....Clement Johnson
Moore, Patsy, and Atterburry, Richard, April 19, 1807. John Davis....Walker Moore
Moore, Polly Ann Sophia, and Fields, Willis, Aug. 16, 1838. B. Ward....Isaac Brown
Moore, Rebecca, and Bennett, James, Jan. 13, 1838. B. Burdon....Jacob Inglehart
Moore, Sally, and Atterberry, David, April 6, 1809. John Grower....Geo. Matthews
Mooreman, James L., and Morris, Eliza, March 5, 1832. Wm. Brown. Thos. B. Morris
Mooreman, James V., and Bureman, Nancy, Sept. 30, 1823. Ben H. Johnson. J. Edison
Mooreman, Jesse, and Jackson, Rebecca, Dec. 29, 1828. Wm. Harlt....James Edison
Morand, Nancy, and Lee, Samuel, July 10, 1830. Loderic Davis.....James Morand
Morgan, Arnold, and Johnston, Margaret, Aug. 27, 1812. Benj. Kelley...J. Luellan
Morgan, Charles, and Johnston, Cemlia, Sept. 7, 1812. Benj. Talbert. Moses Johnston
Morgan, Elizabeth, and Atherton, John, March 4, 1837. Ancil Hall....James Tanner
Morgan, Jane, and Brown, John, Oct. 10, 1835. Wm. Sandefur......Geo. Brown

Marriage Records, 1799 to 1840

Morgan, John, and Eidson, Molly, Feb. 10, 1834. Wm. Hart............John Eidson
Morgan, Susan, and Hall, David, Oct. 19, 1812. Wm. Rogers.........Charles Morgan
Morris, Amos, and Crabtree, Isabel Elizabeth, Aug. 13, 1827. Paul Abney....Wm. Six
Morris, Eliza, and Mooreman, James L., March 5, 1832. Wm. Brown....Thos. B. Morris
Morris, Nancy, and Barnett, Martin, April 1, 1826. Ancil Hall.......James Miller
Morrison, Daniel, and Pigman, Sally, June 12, 1805. Thomas Taylor. Ignatius Pigman
Morton, Ann, and McWain, Lewis, May 31, 1823. Wm. Harlt......Alexander Cox
Morton, Ann, and Barnard, Jared, Nov. 27, 1833. Wm. Downs......Thomas Morton
Morton, Cynthia Ann, and Williams, Jeremiah, Feb. 16, 1835. J. Phipps. Thos. Morton
Morton, Delia, and Robertson, John, Sept. 3, 1838. J. G. Ward......Richard Duke
Morton, Elizabeth, and Rhodes, Henry, Nov. 14, 1831. Wm. Downs. Thos. Morton
Morton, Isaac, and Shanks, Sally H., May 27, 1823. Wm. Harlt.....Richard Walker
Morton, Jesse, and Paxton, Sally Walker, April 13, 1835. _____....Samuel Paxton
Morton, Margaret, and Ross, Joseph, July 18, 1812. Joe Anderson......Thos. Morton
Morton, Polly, and Calhoun, John, Dec. 25, 1819. _____........Chas. McCreney
Morton, Sally, and Hatcher, Wm., April 10, 1821. Loderic Davis....Thomas Morton
Moseley, Daniel, and Lawton, Caroline, Dec. 12, 1836. _____......Wesley Phipps
Moseley, Elijah, and Barnes, Mary, Jan. 24, 1811. Thos. Taylor....Higgerson Belt
Moseley, Elijah, and Westerfield, Phebe Jane, Oct. 19, 1834. M. Ford. C. Westerfield
Moseley, James, and Hoboy, Betsy Coffee, Dec. 25, 1832. B. W. Reynolds. J. Hoboy
Moseley, Jesse, and Curd, Mary, Aug. 12, 1824. Richard Neal......Robt. Lightfoot
Moseley, John, and Westerfield, Nancy, March 28, 1834. J. Benden...Geo. Westerfield
Moseley, Mary, and Wakeland, Allen, Jan. 25, 1840. John Phipps. Alexander Barnett
Moseley, Presby, and Malin, Susannah, Feb. 17, 1816. Geo. Render....Thos. Morgan
Moseley, Robert, and Allen, Mary, Sept. 16, 1823. Wm. Harlt........Jacob Wood
Moseley, Robert, and Curlet, Margaret, Jan. 22, 1829. Thos. Taylor....Thos. Taylor
Moseley, Robert, and Lawton, Amanda M., Oct. 21, 1840. C. H. Shaver. C. J. Lawton
Moseley, Robert C., and Archibald, Nancy, Jan. 10, 1837. Ancil Hall....B. B. Malin
Muller, Jesse, and Igleheart, Janet, March 17, 1825. Wm. Kincheloe....Jacob Iglehart
Myers, Benjamin, and Erwin, Elizabeth, Dec. 26, 1816. Benj. Kelley. Francis Erwin
Myers, Francis, and Miller, Eliza, March 15, 1827. Wm. Harlt......John D. Miller
Myers, Margaret, and Robertson, Daniel, Dec. 6, 1828. Wm. Harlt. Joseph Robertson
Myers, Nancy, and Robertson, Joseph, Nov. 19, 1828. Wm. Harlt...Daniel Robertson
Myers, Thomas, and Layton, Christine, May 10, 1811. Thos. Taylor. Jonathan Isom
Nall, Gatewood, and Berryman, Frances, Sept. 2, 1828. Wm. Harlt...Richard Nall
Nall, John Gatewood, and Henderson, Emily, Mar. 27, 1831. B. Henry. R. W. McCreery
Nall, Lucy, and Meyrs, Edward, Oct. 18, 1836. John Phipps.......William Peyton
Nall, Margaret P., and Bland, Slaughter E., Oct. 9, 1834. Wm. Hart.....Richard Nall
Nall, Martha Jane, and Deering, S. S., Sept. 22, 1840. A. H. Shown........John Nall
Nall, Sarah Elizabeth, and McFarland, Walter, Jan. 2, 1837. J. Pinkston. Rich. Nall
Nanny, Ann, and Cravens, Jesse, Aug. 23, 1832. John Phipps..........Edward Nanny
Nanny, James, and Howell, Frankie, Sept. 29, 1829. John Phipps.....Matthew Nanny
Napier, Mary, and Cox, Finis, Feb. 17, 1807. Benj. Talbert..........Rene Napier
Narcarron, John, and Lee, Mrs. Sally, July 20, 1805. John Davis....James Martin
Nash, Peggy, and Edwards, William, March 25, 1800. Benj. Talbert......
Neal, Delilah, and Cooper, Robert, March 28, 1809. Wm. Anderson....Sam Cooper
Neal, Diana, and Handy, William, Jan. 8, 1824. Loderic Davis.......Nathan Howard

Neal, Elizabeth, and Davis, Richard, Nov. 4, 1824. Loderic Davis....Wm. Handy
Neal, Lytle, and Shultz, Diana, Aug. 20, 1817. Geo. Render..........John Shultz
Neal, Peggy, and Williams, Edwin, April 14, 1810. Wm. Anderson......J. Atheveon
Neel, Lalrinah, and Evens, Thomas, Feb. 10, 1820. Thomas Taylor......
Neel, Rebecca, and Evans, Thomas, Jan. 8, 1821. Benj. Burden....Solomon Kitenger
Neely, Julian, and Duke, William, Feb. 28, 1836. Wm. Davis..........J. L. Condit
Neely, Math. S., and Humphrey, Matilda, Nov. 16, 1833. R. J. Reynolds. B. Humphrey
Neighbors, Elizabeth, and Shepherd, Wm., Aug. 1, 1811. T. Taylor. J. Whittinghill
Neighbors, John C., and Gentry, Cicey, Oct. 13, 1829. J. Phipps....Garrison Hoover
Neighbors, Thomas, and Hoover, Polly, May 4, 1821. Thos. Taylor....Jacob Hoover
Nelson, William, and Shown, Rhea, Jan. 7, 1811. Thos. Taylor.....Arthur Wallace
Nelson, William, and Westerfield, Betsy, Sept. 25, 1836. J. Pinkston. C. Westerfield
Neville, Emeline, and Carter, George, May 3, 1839. John Pinkston. Ed. Turner
New, James, and Austin, Nancy, Jan. 19, 1818. Benj. Kelley........Joseph Wallace
New, Nancy, and Martin, Elias, June 4, 1822. Benj. Kelley..........James Martin
Newberry, Parks, and Haynes, Lucy, Aug. 26, 1837. James Holding....Geo. McDaniel
Newcomb, Mrs. Sally, and Welch, Thomas, Jan. 26, 1837. _____....J. Taylor
Newcome, Eliza, and Field, Thomas, Sept. 17, 1835. Wm. Harlt..........H. Briant
Newcome, Samuel, and Brian, Sarah, Feb. 4, 1825. Wm. Harlt.....Jeffries Bennett
Newton, Isaac, and Leaf, Jane, Dec. 29, 1836. Wm. Brown............John Leaf
Newton, Mildred, and Wells, William, March 5, 1840. J. L. Burrows. John Newton
Nicholas, Ellen, and Chapman, Wilson, Jan. 31, 1838. Ancil Hall....Squire Whittaker
Nicholas, Valentine, and Lanham, Rachel, Mar. 26, 1812. Benj. Talbert. Elias Lanham
Nicholas, William, and Haynes, Nancy, Oct. 11, 1817. Thos. Downs.....John New
Nichols, John, and Theckles, Kitty, April 28, 1808. Benj. Talbert.....Wm. Phipps
Nichols, Polly, and Ellis, William, June 18, 1838. Ancil Hall..........Jesse Chapman
Niffice, Isabel, and Perigo, Jonathan, Nov. 4, 1817. George Render......D. Lindley
Norris, Meriah, and Burden, Eli D., July 8, 1830. Benj. Burden.......V. W. Peyton
North, Elizabeth, and Taylor, Simon, Dec. 31, 1801. Ignatius Pigman....Jesse Kede
O'Connor, William, and Landrum, Emily, Mar. 10, 1836. J. Phipps. Nathaniel Howard
Odum, William, and Field, Nancy, Aug. 28, 1809. John Davis.........Henry Field
Oldham, George, and Chambers, Elizabeth, Feb. 14, 1818. J. Bristow. J. L. Smith
Oldham, Martha, and Sutton, John, June 6, 1831. Wm. Sandefur......Levi Rollings
Oldham, Orpha, and Westerfield, George, June 20, 1840. Thos. T. Ellis. _____
Oldham, Susannah, and Sharp, Isaac, Oct. 18, 1839. Basil Ward....Nimrod Marlin
Overlin, Lebiba, and Baker, Wm., Nov. 4, 1826. Wm. Harlt..........Wm. Overlin
Overtin, Delilah, and Clark, William, July 8, 1806. Thos. Taylor......Wm. Overtin
Overton, James, and Williams, Levinica, Aug. 5, 1806. John Grammar. _____
Overton, Jonathan, and Matthews, Mary, Feb. 28, 1814. Thos. Taylor. Geo. Matthews
Owen, Elenor, and Ward, Hezekiah, Nov. 1, 1827. Geo. McNelly....Higgerson Belt
Owen, Elizabeth, and Stevens, Richard, Nov. 10, 1830. Wm. Harlt. Hezekiah Ward
Owen, Frances, and Davis, Baxter, July 12, 1830. James Miller.......Henry Owen
Owen, John, and Johnson, Susan, Oct. 20, 1838. Thomas Downs....Abraham Owen
Owen, Leccice, and Ferguson, Samuel, April 19, 1834. Wm. Sandefur. C. M. Baker
Owen, Patsy L., and Howard, Allen, Oct. 5, 1829. Wm. C. Long......Henry Owen
Owen, Sarah J., and Bennett, William J., Jan. 17, 1840. R. Holding. Richard Stevens
Paget, Eliza, and Hamilton, William, Oct. 25, 1830. Ancil Hall......Thomas Smith

Marriage Records, 1799 to 1840

Paine, John, and Robertson, Kitty, Oct. 1, 1819. ———————....... William Day
Park, David, and Ross, Sarah, April 16, 1839. T. Buchanan........ Castleman Ross
Parker, Bazell, and Tilford, Mrs. Elizabeth, Oct. 17, 1833. Benj. Burden. Wm. Daniel
Parker, Catherine, and James, William, April 16, 1801. Jas. Keele.... Thomas Parker
Parker, Peggy, and Linn, Jacob, Feb. 12, 1810. Thomas Taylor.......... Joe Parker
Parker, William, and Six, Elizabeth, April 10, 1812. Thomas Taylor....... John Six
Parks, Quinton, and Shown, Margaret, Aug. 20, 1826. Thos. Taylor..... Peter Shown
Pate, Jane, and Smith, Thomas, April 26, 1827. John Pinkston.... James Fitzhugh
Pate, Mason C., and Miller, Charlotte, May 11, 1837. Wm. Brown.... Jas. Miller
Pate, Samuel, and Thrasher, Auretta, March 11, 1824. Wm. Harlt.... Nicholas Hocker
Pate, William, and Midkiff, Rebecca, Nov. 23, 1826. Wm. Harlt..... John Midkiff
Patton, John, and Hudson, Nancy, Aug. 29, 1821. Thos. Downs...... Thomas Hudson
Patton, Thornton, and Jones, Rebecca, Aug. 5, 1833. David Kelly.... John Patton
Paxton, Eliza Ann, and Kelly, Moses, March 3, 1838. Ancil Hall....... John Paxton
Paxton, Sally Walker, and Morton, Jesse, April 13, 1835. ——————.... Samuel Paxton
Paxton, Samuel, and Williams, Elizabeth, Mar. 4, 1817. L. Davis. Elijah Williams
Payne, Emily Ann, and Cox, R. E., Sept. 28, 1840. John Phipps.... F. R. Robertson
Payner, Mitchell, and Brown, Pretius, Dec. 19, 1800. Ignatius Pigman.... Jon. Brown
Payton, Elisha, and Underwood, Eliza, Jan. 12, 1808. John Davis.... Joe McFarland
Payton, Frances, and Thomas, Peter, Dec. 22, 1840. ———————...... F. R. Robertson
Peak, Alexander, and Hunter, Elizabeth, Dec. 7, 1823. Wm. Harlt...... Alex Hunter
Peak, Alexander, and Hunter, Jane, Oct. 22, 1832. Wm. Hart........ Samuel Peyton
Peak, Hezekiah, and Leach, Polly, Aug. 13, 1816. Thos. Taylor....... Wm. Leach
Pearce, Aborn, and White, Ruth, Oct. 8, 1838. Benj. Burden.......... H. D. Taylor
Pearce, Jacharah, and White, Dorcas, July 29, 1840. Paul Abney...... John White
Pearce, Nancy, and Renfrow, Alfred, Oct. 14, 1832. Jacob Miller...... Absalom Pearce
Pearce, Solomon, and Iler, Jane, Oct. 19, 1832. David Kelley.......... Perry Iler
Pearce, Susan, and Burden, Osaah, Oct. 2, 1837. Wm. Anderson....... Absalom Pearce
Pearce, William, and Burden, Cynthia Ann, June 18, 1833. B. Burden. J. W. Crowe
Pearson, Thomas, and Lanham, Hester, April 20, 1825. Thos. Taylor.... Elijah Lanham
Peddicord, Eliza, and Bozarth, Washington, Dec. 12, 1838. Ancil Hall.... L. Peddicord
Peddicord, Jonathan, and Barnard, Minerva, Aug. 24, 1836. ———————, Ignatius Barnard
Pemberton, Beny, and Brown, Robert, March 9, 1835. Ancil Hall...... Wm. Brooks
Pemberton, William, and Barnett, Sarah, April 2, 1839. Wm. Brown. Robert Brown
Pen, Peggy, and Keele, James, Sept. 14, 1801. James Keele............
Pender, Elizabeth, and Fogle, Charles, Sept. 22, 1818. Loderic Davis.... Wm. Leach
Pender, Thomas, and Atherton, Ann, Oct. 14, 1817. Loderic Davis. Abednego Baize
Perigo, Jonathan, and Niffice, Isabel, Nov. 4, 1817. Geo. Pender........ D. Lindley
Perigo, Romey, and Henman, Rhoda, Oct. 1, 1801. James Keele.... Samuel Henman
Perry, Thomas, and Hunt, Christine, Oct. 12, 1807. John Davis....... Henry Perry
Petty, John, and Gentry, Elizabeth, Dec. 18, 1835. Ancil Hall........ Benj. Gentry
Peyton, Ellen, and Balmain, Henry, Sept. 28, 1833. Wm. Hart.... Lucien Peyton
Peyton, Mary Ann, and Sheffer, Anthony, Sept. 14, 1837. J. D. Holding. Wm. Peyton
Phelps, Lucinda, and White, Davey, Feb. 8, 1839. ———————...... Thomas Phelps
Phillipes, Philip, and Carter, Carolina, Oct. 22, 1827. Ancil Hall.... Henry Crowe
Phillips, Betsy, and Carter, Alford, July 15, 1835. Ancil Hall...... Nathan Howard
Phillips, Polly, and Black, Willis, June 5, 1828. Ancil Hall........ Solomon Phillips

Ohio County in the Olden Days

Philps, James, and Jones, Nelly, Dec. 31, 1807. John Davis............Wm. Phelps
Phipps, Ann, and Render, Thomas, Jan. 27, 1820. Loderic Davis......John Phipps
Phipps, Elijah, and Robertson, Harriet, Dec. 15, 1827. Wm. Harlt....Wm. Austin
Phipps, John, and Barnard, Ann, Nov. 18, 1819. Loderic Davis....Ignatius Barnard
Phipps, Lucinda, and Render, Christopher, Dec. 22, 1840. John Phipps. Wash. Phipps
Phipps, Martha, and Dent, Peters, Aug. 23, 1838. C. J. Ward..........Henry Board
Phipps, Nancy, and Cooper, Henry, Oct. 31, 1803. Ignatius Pigman.....Wm. Phipps
Phipps, Polly, and Rowe, Edmund, Jan. 30, 1811. Loderic Davis....Thomas Phipps
Phipps, Rebecca, and Bright, William, Jan. 5, 1805. John Granmer....Wm. Phipps
Phipps, Thomas, and Barnard, Sally, Nov. 2, 1829. John Phipps........John Phipps
Pierce, Benjamin, and Iler, Elizabeth, Mar. 13, 1826. Geo. Render....John Cannon
Pigman, Amy, and Work, Samuel, Jan. 13, 1801. Ignatius Pigman....Levy Pigman
Pigman, Levi, and Taylor, Jane, Aug. 1, 1801. Ignatius Pigman......Joseph Barnes
Pigman, Phelena, and Taylor, Harrison, Oct. 6, 1813. T. Taylor....Steven Statler
Pigman, Sally, and Morrison, Daniel, June 12, 1805. T. Taylor....Ignatius Pigman
Pigman, Sidney, and Rice, John, June 29, 1809. Thomas Taylor......Charles Scott
Pinkston, John, and Tilly, Polly, May 8, 1832. R. Y. Reynolds.......Thomas Hall
Pinkston, Nancy, and McClure, Thomas, April 26, 1813. Benj. Kelley....Thos. Motter
Pinkston, Pattie, and Gentry, Nancy, July 2, 1838. Ancil Hall..........Joe Gentry
Plain, John, and Ross, Tanner, Sept. 22, 1823. Jared Tichenor........Thos. Ross
Plumer, Ann, and Lanham, Lewis, Dec. 25, 1819. Benj. Kelley........John Grigsby
Plumer, Caleb, and Daniel, Mary Ann, June 3, 1819. Thos. Taylor. Jeremiah Tilford
Pool, Allen P., and Cox, Elizabeth, Nov. 29, 1836. _____..........Thomas Cox
Pool, William, and Brown, Jane, Dec. 25, 1826. Charles Tanks.....William McLough
Porter, Sally, and Chapman, Robert, Jan. 12, 1836. John Phipps......Virgil Porter
Porter, Thompson, and Hardeste, Rebecca, July 13, 1804. Wm. Anderson. S. Cleaver
Potect, Job, and Whiteacre, Molly, May 16, 1812. Loney Jackson.....Simon Taylor
Potts, Isabel, and Rogers, John, June 13, 1808. Wm. Anderson........Roger Potts
Potts, Johanna, and Crabtree, Abraham, Dec. 13, 1810. Loderic Davis. Ralph Hunt
Potts, Martha, and Bristoe, Lovey, April 22, 1809. Wm. Anderson.....Jesse Potts
Potts, Rachel, and Tanner, William, Dec. 2, 1804. John Davis........Samuel Work
Potts, Rachel, and Conner, William, March 7, 1807. John Davis.......John Conner
Powers, Alexander, and Sutton, Matilda, Aug. 12, 1831. Thos. Taylor. Jas. Johnson
Powers, Hannah, and Breshoro, John, May 24, 1813. Benj. Kelly......Isaac Covens
Powers, John, and Hunter, Nancy, June 29, 1801. Jas. Keele......Moses Springton
Powers, John, and Taber, Matilda, Feb. 18, 1839. Basil Ward.......Jas. Johnson
Powers, Judith, and Brashiers, Thomas, Nov. 16, 1814. Benj. Kelly......John Powers
Pray, Elijah, and Lamb, Charlotte, Feb. 9, 1824. Thos. Taylor....Wm. Gillespy
Preston, Sanford, and Rogers, Mary Ann, Nov. 1, 1837. John Pinkston. Jas. B. Rogers
Preston, William, and Shroeter, Mary Ann, Jan 13, 1840. J. Phipps....Jesse Breant
Prudden, James, and Barnett, Rachel, Nov. 4, 1839. Basil Ward....Joseph Barnett
Pruden, Ann, and Woodward, Thomas, Jan. 12, 1820. Wm. Harris....Benj. Woodward
Pruden, Daniel, and McGill, Ann, Nov. 8, 1813. John Davis..........Uzal Condit
Pugh, Margaret, and Keele, James, Sept. 15, 1801. James Keele......John Taylor
Purcell, Lewis, and King, Libela, Dec. 16, 1828. John Pinkston.......Asbum King
Railey, Benjamin, and Campbell, Rebecca, Dec. 19, 1825. Wm. Harlt.....Jon. Railey
Railey, Elizabeth, and Ward, Jesse, Sept. 8, 1836. Adlai Boyd..........R. Walker

Marriage Records, 1799 to 1840

Railey, John, and Wilson, Nancy, July 14, 1828. Wm. Harlt......Robert Wilson
Railey, Polly, and Wilson, James, April 25, 1827. Wm. Harlt....Jonathan Railey
Rains, Jane, and Haynes, James, Feb. 11, 1839. J. L. Burrows.......Jeremiah Izel
Raley, James, and Wilson, Sally, July 30, 1838. Wm. Hart......Nimrod Wilson
Raley, William, and Harlin, Polly, June 16, 1839. _____...........Jesse Ward
Ralph, Catherine, and Sutton, William, Oct. 26, 1835. Wm. Hart......Wm. C. Leach
Ralph, Nancy Jane, and Burks, Davis, May 18, 1839. Thomas Downs. Wm. Ralph
Raymond, Betty, and Leggit, William, Dec. 3, 1812. Thomas Taylor....Elijah Frank
Reddecood, Mary, and Brown, Isaac C., March 20, 1840. Basil Ward...L. Reddecood
Redding, Amanda Elvina, and Wallace, Wm. G., Dec. 9, 1839. Wm. Loney. J. Fitzhugh
Redman, Polly, and Austin, John, Oct. 9, 1832. John Phipps..........John Phipps
Redmond, Ann, and Austin, John, Oct. 25, 1837. John Phipps........John Phipps
Redmond, Felix, and Hocker, Polly, June 26, 1812. Loderic Davis....Phil Hocker
Redmond, Robert, and Davis, Harriet, March 2, 1811. Thomas Taylor. Forrest Davis
Reed, George, and Breamer, Mary, June 25, 1807. Samuel Hodge......Samuel Hodge
Reed, James, and Clutter, Delilah, July 18, 1804. Thos. Taylor........Stephen Taylor
Reed, Margaret, and Shull, David, Aug. 25, 1830. John Phipp ....James Reed
Reed, Sarah, and House, Jacob, Aug. 3, 1836. A. Fuqua..........Septimus Taylor
Reeds, Jacob, and Rogers, Martha B., Sept. 12, 1833. David Kelley. Jonathan Rogers
Reeds, Moses, and Render, Elenor, July 1, 1833. David Kelley......Robert Render
Reeves, Polly Ann, and Greenwood, Walcott, Dec. 22, 1840. Wm. Downey. J. Warden
Render, Amelia, and Maddox, Joseph, July 1, 1819. Loderic Davis...Robert Render
Render, Amelia, and Render, Robert, Jan. 23, 1836. Geo. Render......Thos. Render
Render, Catherine, and Borah, Lee, June 18, 1831. Geo. Render........Nat. Howard
Render, Christopher, and Phipps, Lucinda, Dec. 22, 1840. J. Phipps. Wash. Phipps
Render, Elenor, and Reeds, Moses, July 1, 1833. David Kelley......Robert Render
Render, Eliza, and Mason, Augustus, Aug. 12, 1839. Geo. Render......Robt. Render
Render, Hester, and Hocker, Nicholas, Aug. 14, 1813. Loderic Davis....Matthew Adams
Render, John, and Tichenor, Jane, Jan. 16, 1839. Geo. Render........Elisha Coleman
Render, Joshua, and Jackson, Polly, Dec. 23, 1812. Thomas Taylor.....James Rogers
Render, Mary, and Austin, Robert, March 17, 1829. Geo. Render......Robt. Render
Render, Nancy, and Chapman, Willis, Dec. 13, 1805. Benj. Talbert....Robt. Render
Render, Polly, and Austin, Barnch, Aug. 10, 1818. John Phipps......George Render
Render, Robert, and Brown, Charlotte, Dec. 9, 1801. Ignatius Pigman...Jos. Barnes
Render, Robert, and Render, Amelia, Jan. 23, 1836. Geo. Render........Thos. Render
Render, Sarah, and Ward, Edward, May 28, 1814. Loderic Davis......Joshua Render
Render, Sarah, and Chapman, Solomon, June 4, 1824. Wm. Harlt......Robt. Render
Render, Tally, and Rowe, George, July 13, 1840. F. D. Garrett......Thomas Davis
Render, Thomas, and Phipps, Ann, Jan. 27, 1820. Loderic Davis......John Phipps
Renfrow, Alfred, and Pearce, Nancy, Oct. 14, 1832. Jacob Miller.....Absalom Pearce
Renfrow, Kellion, and Thomas, Emily, Sept. 4, 1836. Jacob Miller....Nathan Thomas
Rhodes, Henry, and Morton, Elizabeth, Nov. 14, 1831. Wm. Downs....Thos. Morton
Rhodes, Presley, and Ross, Sally, Dec. 31, 1838. _____...........Joseph Ross
Rice, John, and Pigman, Sidney, June 29, 1809. Thomas Taylor........Charles Scott
Rice, Nelly, and Clifford, Michael, Jan. 6, 1820. John Pinkston........Peter Foster
Richard, Elizabeth, and Crowe, Henry, Feb. 24, 1820. Benj. Kelley. Edward Marlow
Richard, William, and Beardon, Nancy, July 15, 1826. Ancil Hall.....Elijah Phipps

Ohio County in the Olden Days

Richards, Catherine, and Mills, Harvey, March 1, 1827. Wm. Hart....Craven Peyton
Richards, Matilda, and Huff, Gallsburry, Sept. 1, 1818. Nall Overale......E. Marlowe
Richards, Thomas, and Huff, Elizabeth, Oct. 17, 1829. Wm. Long. Goldsbury Huff
Riggs, Isaac, and Atherton, Delilah, Dec. 29, 1823. Jared Tichenor....Joseph Riggs
Riley, Elijah, and Rogers, Nancy, April 22, 1805. John Davis..........Noel Hanal
Riley, Higginson, and Barnard, Sarah, March 30, 1840. John Phipps....J. Reddison
Rinney, John, and Runney, Maria M., Oct. 9, 1823. Wm. Harlt..........L. Rogers
Ritchey, John, and McGill, Ann, Sept. 1, 1817. George Render......Daniel Lindley
Roach, Cornelius, and Westerfield, Mary, Oct. 3, 1831. Ancil Hall......J. Westerfield
Roach, Cornelius, and Kelly, Ann Eliza, Sept. 6, 1834. Ancil Hall......John Hoover
Roach, Eliza, and Burkes, John, Nov. 17, 1836. Ancil Hall............Edward Roach
Roach, Mahala Ann, and Hoover, Jonathan, July 8, 1828. Wm. Harlt. Robt. Wilson
Robel, Logustain P., and Cox, Elizabeth, April 5, 1828. Jasper Bristow. Wm. Barrett
Roberts, Techarih, and Hatcher, Lindsey, April 11, 1819. Loderic Davis. C. McCreney
Roberts, Willis, and Adle, Margaret, June 28, 1814. John Weldon.....Chas. Thrift
Robertson, Amanda, and Dean, Summers, April 30, 1826. Ancil Hall....Wm. Austin
Robertson, Ann, and McDaniel, Jesse, Nov. 18, 1824. Wm. Harlt.....Joseph Robertson
Robertson, Daniel, and Myers, Margaret, Dec. 6, 1828. Wm. Harlt....J. Robertson
Robertson, Harriet, and Phipps, Elijah, Dec. 15, 1827. Wm. Harlt. Wm. Austin
Robertson, Henry, and Axton, Margaret, Aug. 25, 1825. Benj. Talbert. Benj. Axton
Robertson, John, and Morton, Delia, Sept. 3, 1838. J. G. Ward......Richard Duke
Robertson, Joseph, and Myers, Nancy, Nov. 19, 1828. Wm. Harlt....Daniel Robertson
Robertson, Kitty, and Paine, John, Oct., 1819. _____..........William Day
Robertson, Powhatan, and Henderson, Linetta, June 25, 1834. F. H. Blades. W. Bradley
Robinson, John, and Graves, Mary, Aug. 1, 1836. Adlai Boyd..........George Graves
Robinson, Margaret, and Wilkins, Samuel, April 9, 1807. John Davis. Barnett Clark
Robinson, Philip, and Blevins, Patsy, Dec. 26, 1822. Loderic Davis....Phil Fulkerson
Robtree, Polly, and Rogers, Asa, Dec. 2, 1810. John Davis.............Adam Robtree
Rock, Elizabeth, and Spurrier, Elijah, March 21, 1804. Thomas Taylor. Benj. Owens
Rockerby, Eliza, and Lewellan, Jacob, May 21, 1816. Loney Jackson. Jas. Lewellan
Rogers, Asa, and Robtree, Polly, Dec. 2, 1810. John Davis..........Adam Robtree
Rogers, Cindrella, and Wilson, Simon, Oct. 9, 1837. _____......Jonathan Rogers
Rogers, Edward, and Chapman, Nancy, Jan. 22, 1818. John Phipps....Jas. Chapman
Rogers, Elizabeth, and James, Moseley, Nov. 8, 1813. Jas. Rogers....Chas. Henderson
Rogers, Elizabeth, and Jones, Joseph, Sept. 20, 1822. J. James......Jonathan Rogers
Rogers, John, and Potts, Isabel, June 13, 1808. Wm. Anderson.........Roger Potts
Rogers, Margaret, and Henderson, Charles, Feb. 2, 1811. Thos. Taylor....J. Hockley
Rogers, Margaret Ann, and James, Fleming, Nov. 24, 1839. _____. James Rogers
Rogers, Martha B., and Reeds, Jacob, Sept. 12, 1833. David Kelley. Jonathan Rogers
Rogers, Mary Ann, and Preston, Sanford, Nov. 1, 1837. John Pinkston. Jas. B. Rogers
Rogers, Nancy, and Riley, Elijah, April 22, 1805. John Davis..........Noel Hanal
Rogers, Nancy, and Hobby, James, Feb. 19, 1824. Loderic Davis....Jonathan Rogers
Rogers, Nancy Ray, and Butler, John, June 16, 1839. Alfred Taylor....Fleming James
Rogers, Patsy, and James, Samuel, Oct. 19, 1818. John Phipps......James Rogers
Rogers, Polly, and Kelly, John B., May 21, 1814. John Weldon..........Clark Hall
Rogers, Sarah, and Lemon, John, Nov. 9, 1807. John Davis..........Nat Rogers
Rogers, Sarah, and Lemon, John, Oct. 1, 1807. John Davis.............Nat Rogers

Marriage Records, 1799 to 1840

Rogers, William Cass, and James, Lucy, April 22, 1822. Loderic Davis....Wm. James
Rosdale, Tucker, and Shown, Elizabeth, March 31, 1822. Wm. Hart....Peter Shown
Rosedale, Tucker, and Eidson, Morning, July 20, 1823. Wm. Harlt....John Eidson
Ross, Aaron, and Davis, Jerimiah, Dec. 23, 1819. Loderic Davis........Amos Davis
Ross, Ervin, and Ashby, Katy, Sept. 5, 1804. John Davis............Jesse Ashby
Ross, Jemima, and Davis, Solomon, Nov. 29, 1829. Loderic Davis.......John Cox
Ross, John, and Daniel, Doranda, March 30, 1840. ———........William Daniel
Ross, Joseph, and Morton, Margaret, July 18, 1812. Joe Anderson....Thos. Morton
Ross, Joseph, and Ross, Martha Ann, March 6, 1836. Ancil Hall........John Phipps
Ross, Louisa Ann, and Taylor, James, Jan. 10, 1838. James Ward......Thomas Ross
Ross, Lucinda, and Borah, Noah, Oct. 31, 1835. George Render......Thomas Ross
Ross, Martha Ann, and Ross, Joseph, March 6, 1836. Ancil Hall.......John Phipps
Ross, Nancy, and Rowe, Robert, Jan. 26, 1830. William Downs........Jesse Ross
Ross, Sally, and Rhodes, Presley, Dec. 31, 1838. ———..........Joseph Ross
Ross, Sarah, and Park, David, April 16, 1839. T. Buchanan........Castleman Ross
Ross, Tanner, and Plain, John, Sept. 22, 1823. Jared Tichenor........Thomas Ross
Ross, Thomas, and Stewart, Levinia, May 11, 1824. Thomas Downs....John Bozarth
Ross, Willis, and Blevins, Keturah, June 24, 1821. Thomas Taylor....Barnett Clouch
Rothrock, Henry, and Young, Mary, May 12, 1838. George Render. Andrew Glenn
Roundtree, James, and Williams, Viney, July 31, 1806. John Davis. Benj. Farmer
Rowan, Alexander, and Simmons, Marcia, Dec. 23, 1828. Wm. Harlt. Asbum Simmons
Rowan, William, and Miller, Mahala, May 9, 1835. William Hart....William Miller
Rowan, William C., and Barnett, Abigail, Dec. 24, 1829. Wm. Harlt. Robt. Barnett
Rowe, Amelia, and Tichenor, Alney, Oct. 6, 1834. Geo. Render........Geo. Rowe
Rowe, Broxton, and Bishop, Ann, June 2, 1831. William Downs. Eramus Bishop
Rowe, Cynthia, and Hocker, Charles, Feb. 28, 1835. ———......John Phipps
Rowe, Edmund, and Phelps, Polly, Jan. 30, 1811. Loderic Davis....Thomas Phelps
Rowe, Elizabeth, and Ashby, David, March 25, 1812. Joe Anderson. Edward Rowe
Rowe, Elizabeth Crowe, and Ashby, George, Sept. 13, 1836. Geo. Render. J. Stewart
Rowe, Emila, and Taylor, John T., ———, 1830. Wm. Downs.........
Rowe, George, and Render, Tally, July 13, 1840. F. D. Garrett......Thomas Davis
Rowe, Judith, and Stewart, James, April 15, 1835. ———........Robert Rowe
Rowe, Judy, and Brown, Robert, Nov. 8, 1816. George Render........
Rowe, Nancy, and Ashby, William, March 29, 1816. George Render....Thomas Rowe
Rowe, Randolph, and Bozarth, Rebecca, Sept. 24, 1808. Wm. Anderson. J. Bozarth
Rowe, Robert, and Underwood, Matilda, July 10, 1820. Jared Tichenor. ———
Rowe, Robert, and Ross, Nancy, Jan. 26, 1830. William Downs.......Jesse Ross
Rowe, Sally, and Ashby, Peter, Aug. 7, 1817. George Render........Robert Rowe
Rowe, Thomas, and Brown, Margaret, Feb. 1, 1817. Geo. Render. Armstrong Brown
Rowe, Thomas, and Maddox, Mary Boyd, July 15, 1836. Adlai Boyd. Jno. Maddox
Royal, James, and Cravens, Jessie, Aug. 4, 1831. Ancil Hall.........Jesse Cravens
Royal, John, and Davis, Isabella, Jan. 14, 1830. Thos. Taylor........Wm. Royal
Royal, Richard, and Gallespy, Nancy A., Feb. 27, 1836. Ancil Hall. Wm. Gallespy
Royal, Samuel, and Wade, Purmeley, July 17, 1836. Ancil Hall.....Ballenger Wade
Runney, Maria M., and Rinney, John, Oct. 9, 1823. Wm. Harlt.........L. Rogers
Rusher, Elizabeth, and Barker, Elisha, Aug. 19, 1839. Ancil Hall......John Banner
Rusher, Minor, and Marlow, Mary, Jan. 19, 1826. Ancil Hall........John Marlowe

Sallee, Thomas, and Hornbeck, Mary, Dec. 2, 1809. Thomas Taylor...Alin Hornbeck
Sandefur, Francis, and Bennett, Mary, Nov. 7, 1822. Wm. Hart........Jeff Bennett
Sandefur, John, and Bennett, Sarah, Sept. 21, 1832. Wm. Hart......Jeffries Bennett
Sandefur, Wm., and Bennett, Elizabeth, Sept. 9, 1825. S. Julian....Alford Bennett
Sands, James, and Lee, Polly, April 18, 1820. Jacob Miller..........Henry Crowe
Scott, Daniel, and Landrum, Ruby, Jan. 12, 1814. Benj. Kelley.......Wm. Nichles
Shane, James, and Cumpton, Theodocia, Jan. 9, 1809. Wm. Anderson. Charles Scott
Shane, Mary, and Furpin, Phillip, Feb. 1, 1800. Ignatius Pigman.....John Shane
Shanks, Camilla, and Jackson, Chris. E., Dec. 18, 1827. Geo. McNelly. M. A. Shanks
Shanks, Quintus, and Taylor, Lucinda, Aug. 30, 1838. J. G. Ward....Edmund Rowe
Shanks, Sally H., and Morton, Isaac, May 27, 1823. Wm. Harlt.....Richard Walker
Sharp, Charles, and Kelly, Belima, Nov. 8, 1834. Ancil Hall.............
Sharp, Eliza, and Greenberry, Ezel, Nov. 22, 1832. Wm. Hart..........H. D. Taylor
Sharp, Isaac, and Oldham, Susannah, Oct. 18, 1839. Basil Ward.....Nimrod Martin
Sharp, William T., and Shoemaker, Nancy, June 23, 1831. Wm. Downs. Thomas King
Shayer, Thomas, and Gill, Frances, Dec. 13, 1806. John Colvert.....Jeremiah Ranal
Shayn, John, and Turpin, Mary, Dec. 8, 1800. Ignatius Pigman......Aquilla Davis
Sheffer, Anthony, and Peyton, Mary Ann, Sept. 14, 1837. J. D. Holding. Wm. Peyton
Shepherd, Delilah, and Maddox, Thomas, May 25, 1840. _____, William Shepherd
Shepherd, Nancy, and Davis, Joseph, Jan. 25, 1840. John Phipps........
Shepherd, Polly, and Shultz, Nathan, Sept. 9, 1830. John Phipps.....John Shepherd
Shepherd, Sarah, and Baize, Isaac, Dec. 5, 1840. Basil Ward...........J. Shepherd
Shepherd, William, and Neighbors, Elizabeth, Aug. 1, 1811. T. Taylor. J. Whittinghill
Shepherd, William, and Davis, Margaret, Feb. 26, 1840. J. Phipps......T. Davis
Sherman, Thomas, and Johnson, Polly, Dec. 5, 1836. J. Pinkston....David Westerfield
Shields, James, and Autry, Emeline, Sept. 3, 1839. _____..........Simon Ashby
Shields, John, and Hocker, Advisa, March 31, 1836. Geo. Render....Nathan Hocker
Shirtley, Polly, and Gibson, William, March 28, 1800. _____ ....
Shiveley, John L., and Cooper, Sarah, Feb. 9, 1830. J. Bristow......David French
Shoemaker, Mary, and Hughston, John, Nov. 14, 1809. Thos. Taylor. Adam Shoemaker
Shoemaker, Nancy, and Sharp, William T., June 23, 1831. Wm. Downs...Thos. King
Shown, Edith, and Corn, William, Dec. 31, 1831. Wm. Downs........John Bozarth
Shown, Elizabeth, and Rosdale, Tucker, March 31, 1822. Wm. Hart....Peter Shown
Shown, Margaret, and Parks, Quinton, Aug. 20, 1826. Thos. Taylor....Peter Shown
Shown, Peter, and Bennett, Elizabeth, Aug. 30, 1820. Thos. Taylor....John Bennett
Shown, Rhea, and Nelson, William, Jan. 7, 1811. Thos. Taylor......Arthur Wallace
Shown, Sarah, and Wallace, Hugh William, Dec. 8, 1823. Wm. Harlt. Peter Shown
Shroeter, Mary Ann, and Preston, Wm., Jan. 13, 1840. John Phipps....Jesse Breant
Shull, David, and Reed, Margaret, Aug. 25, 1830. John Phipps........James Reed
Shultz, Charles, and Lee, Ann, May 25, 1820. Loderic Davis..........John Baize
Shultz, Diana, and Neal, Lytle, Aug. 20, 1817. Geo. Render..........John Shultz
Shultz, Jacob, and Gibson, Polly, March 22, 1800. Robt. Moseley......Wm. Gibson
Shultz, John, and Towels, Comfort, Oct. 23, 1821. Loderic Davis....Isaac Malin
Shultz, John, and Elms, Jane, June 10, 1829. Loderic Davis.......Charles Shultz
Shultz, John, and Cox, Ann, Sept. 18, 1831. John Phipps..........William Cox
Shultz, Joseph, and Howard, Nancy, Aug. 31, 1822. Wm. Hart......Isaac Malin
Shultz, Mary, and Malin, Isaac, Sept. 12, 1812. Francis Travis....Charles Atherton

Marriage Records, 1799 to 1840

Shultz, Nancy, and Boys, John, Oct. 7, 1801. James Keele.............——————
Shultz, Nancy, and Baze, John, Oct. 6, 1807. John Davis........Matthew Shultz
Shultz, Nathan, and Shepherd, Polly, Sept. 9, 1830. John Phipps....John Shepherd
Shultz, Nicholas, and Davis, Cynthia Ann, Oct. 6, 1832. John Phipps. Gideon Davis
Simmons, Albeun S., and Barnard, Miranda, Dec. 16, 1833. Wm. Downs. Thos. Hudson
Simmons, Charles, and Hudson, Patsy, Dec. 16, 1833. Wm. Downs....Thos. Hudson
Simmons, Charlotte, and Woodward, John M., Sept. 29, 1827. —————, John C. Rogers
Simmons, Marcia, and Rowan, Alexander, Dec. 23, 1828. Wm. Harlt. Asbum Simmons
Simmons, William, and Calloway, Tomzay, Feb. 18, 1820. Wm. Harris. Dillis Dyer
Six, Catherine, and Lindsey, Thomas, March 12, 1821. Benj. Burden. Daniel Six
Six, David, and Cox, Elizabeth, Dec. 23, 1819. Benj. Burden.......Frederic Trunell
Six, Elizabeth, and Parker, William, April 10, 1812. Thos. Taylor........John Six
Six, Isaac, and Mitchell, Rhoda, April 11, 1822. Benj. Kelley............E. Dean
Six, John, and Harsha, Jean, April 3, 1812. Thos. Taylor........Nathaniel Downs
Six, Nancy, and Taylor, Thomas, ————, 1821. Thomas Taylor......Isaac Six
Six, William, and Crabtree, Jane, Dec. 26, 1821. Benj. Burden........David Six
Smeathers, Archibald, and Taylor, Dolly, Sept. 29, 1828. T. Taylor. Harrison Taylor
Smeathers, Archibald, and Taylor, Margaret, Nov. 16, 1840. J. Phipps....T. P. Taylor
Smeathers, Eliza, and Statler, George, Aug. 8, 1808. Thos. Taylor....Wm. Smeathers
Smeathers, James, and Bell, Elizabeth, April 4, 1805. John Davis.........——————
Smeathers, Jane, and Gross, Daniel, Feb. 1, 1800. Benj. Talbert....Wm. Smeathers
Smith, Caroline, and Sutton, Ishmael, March 14, 1839. Jno. Pinkston. Samuel Mills
Smith, Charlotte, and Midkiff, John, March 29, 1827. Wm. Harlt....Jas. Fitzhugh
Smith, Eliza, and Christian, Walter, Sept. 26, 1833. Benj. Burden....Andrew Balmain
Smith, Elizabeth, and Wise, Levi, Sept. 5, 1840. ——————............Remus Gibson
Smith, George, and Fulkerson, Margaret, Nov. 30, 1829. Geo. Render. Adam Fulkerson
Smith, Hardy, and Taylor, Amy, June 8, 1801. James Keele............Benj. Taylor
Smith, Hugh, and McIlwain, Jane, March 13, 1823. Wm. Hart..........——————
Smith, Jane, and Hamilton, George, Oct. 25, 1833. Wm. Sandefur......John Smith
Smith, Jenny A., and Mitchell, Jonathan, Sept. 5, 1840. John Phipps. T. Mitchell
Smith, Jesse, and Hunter, Elizabeth, Sept. 22, 1830. John Phipps....Reuben Hunter
Smith, John, and Stewart, Elizabeth, May 20, 1820. Benj. Kelley......John Smith
Smith, John C., and Gosset, Elmira, March 10, 1840. Basil Ward..........Dan Hix
Smith, John J., and Crowe, Nancy, Feb. 22, 1832. Wm. Sandefur......Dillis Dyer
Smith, Joseph, and Anderson, Sarah, April 19, 1813. Thos. Taylor....Leonard Hoover
Smith, Lewis, and Tilford, Eliza Jane, Feb. 4, 1832. D. J. Kelley......Walker Daniel
Smith, Lucinda, and Stedam, Isaac, Dec. 20, 1836. Ancil Hall..........James Mason
Smith, Lucy, and Miller, Joe, Sept. 26, 1808. Wm. Anderson........Robt. Cates
Smith, Maryan, and Daniel, Walker, Aug. 22, 1825. Wm. Harlt......James Smith
Smith, Nancy, and Stephens, Thomas, Aug. 28, 1816. Thos. Taylor......Thos. Moore
Smith, Nancy, and Westerfield, Hayden, Jan. 7, 1832. Ancil Hall........J. S. Hoover
Smith, Polly, and Fuqua, William, Jan. 23, 1834. Ancil Hall............James Fuqua
Smith, Sarah Ann, and Mitchell, John, Aug. 15, 1831. D. J. Kelley....Leonard Bean
Smith, Thomas, and Grant, Eliza, Nov. 14, 1821. Jas. Porter............Wm. Belt
Smith, Thomas, and Pate, Jane, April 26, 1827. John Pinkston......James Fitzhugh
Smith, Thomas, and Daniel, Ann, Dec. 10, 1831. John Phipps........Thos. Ashby
Smith, William, and Chapman, Sally, Dec. 19, 1832. John Phipps......Robt. Chapman

Southard, Nancy, and Chapman, Ellis, Sept. 14, 1820. Loderic Davis....Amos Davis
Southard, Robert, and Maddox, Sally, Dec. 6, 1827. Jared Tichenor. John Maddox
Southard, Robert, and Igleheart, Ann, Oct. 16, 1839. Geo. Render.....Isaac Brown
Southard, Thomas, and Brown, Eliza, March 26, 1838. Geo. Render....Jas. Brown
Spagner, Peggy, and Larrels, William, Aug. 7, 1817. _____....Theophilus Petty
Spence, Sarah, and Bailey, Martin, Sept. 8, 1834. Allen Boyd........John Spence
Spence, Susan, and Kigel, Solomon, May 21, 1839. Alfred Taylor......Martin Bailey
Spray, George, and Stanley, Polly, March 2, 1813. Loderic Davis....Isaac Crabtree
Sprigg, Thomas, and Barnett, Rachel, Jan. 20, 1803. Ignatius Pigman. Robt. Baird
Springton, Moses, and Hatfield, Ann, Jan. 21, 1804. John Davis......Wm. Springton
Spurrier, Elijah, and Rock, Elizabeth, March 21, 1804. Thos. Taylor....Benj. Owens
Stanley, Polly, and Spray, George, March 2, 1813. Loderic Davis...Isaac Crabtree
Staples, James, and Fuqua, Emeline, Sept. 28, 1839. Ancil Hall.......James Fuqua
Staples, William, and Gosset, Eliza Ann, Oct. 5, 1840. Basil Ward.....Jesse Ross
Statler, Eliza, and Taylor, Nicholas C., March 13, 1817. Benj. Malone....Ennis Ury
Statler, George, and Smeathers, Eliza, Aug. 8, 1808. Thos. Taylor....Wm. Smeathers
Statler, Ignatius Pigman, and Stevens, Siney, Dec. 19, 1825. W. Harlt. John Duke
Statler, Matty, and Duke, William, _____, 1818. Thos. Taylor....Nicholas Taylor
Statler, Sally, and Duke, Richard, Feb. 24, 1823. Wm. Harlt........Caleb Boswell
Statler, Susanna L., and Stevens, Henry, Nov. 21, 1831. Wm. Hart. Sam Houston
Stedam, Isaac, and Smith, Lucinda, Dec. 20, 1836. Ancil Hall.........James Mason
Stephens, Ann, and Boswell, Alex. H., Oct. 11, 1819. Thos. Taylor....Jas. Johnson
Stephens, Joseph, and Smith, Nancy, Aug. 28, 1816. Thos. Taylor....Thos. Moore
Stevens, Charles W., and Wallace, Polly, May 29, 1830. Thos. C. Cooper. H. Stevens
Stevens, Charlotte, and Belt, Higginson, Jan. 10, 1805. Thos. Taylor. Wm. Stevens
Stevens, Charlotte, and Barnett, Joseph, Oct. 28, 1821. Wm. Foulks....M. McClean
Stevens, Charlotte, and Taylor, Benjamin, Nov. 17, 1836. _____....Wesley Stevens
Stevens, David, and Taylor, Henrietta, Nov. 4, 1818. Loderic Davis....Sep. Taylor
Stevens, Elizabeth, and Carson, Lindsey, Oct. 24, 1826. Wm. Harlt....Thos. Stevens
Stevens, Elvira, and Taylor, John, March 27, 1837. J. D. Holding....Wesley Stevens
Stevens, Henry, and Statler, Susanna L., Nov. 21, 1831. Wm. Hart. Sam Houston
Stevens, James, and Austin, Sarah Emily, Oct. 14, 1839. Mino Ford. Brooks Austin
Stevens, John, and Duke, Dolly, Sept. 17, 1819. Loderic Davis.....Richard Duke
Stevens, John, and Baird, Jane, March 10, 1830. Wm. Harlt........James Baird
Stevens, John, and Stevens, Susan, Sept. 3, 1838. _____........Richard Duke
Stevens, John, and Blacklock, Adeline, Mar. 4, 1839. Basil Ward. Richard Blacklock
Stevens, Joshua, and Allen, Mahala, Jan. 13, 1838. Basil Ward......Isaac Keown
Stevens, Lydia, and Huston, Samuel, April 18, 1831. Wm. Hart......John G. Nall
Stevens, Mahala, and Stevens, Taylor, March 4, 1839. Basil Ward....John Stevens
Stevens, Minerva, and Austin, Wisas, Nov. 6, 1838. John Pinkston....David Stevens
Stevens, Nathaniel, and Bennett, Mary Jane, Mar. 25, 1833. R. Y. Reynolds. S. Bennett
Stevens, Richard, and Bennett, Maria, Aug. 3, 1805. Thos. Taylor....Aquilla Field
Stevens, Richard, and Owen, Elizabeth, Nov. 10, 1830. Wm. Harlt...Hezekiah Ward
Stevens, Sally, and Taylor, Richard, Jan. 10, 1822. John James......John G. Stevens
Stevens, Sarah Ann, and Wallace, Talbert, May 9, 1830. T. C. Cropper. H. Stevens
Stevens, Siney, and Statler, Ignatius Pigman, Dec. 19, 1825. Wm. Harlt. John Duke
Stevens, Susan, and Stevens, John, Sept. 3, 1838. _____......Richard Duke

Marriage Records, 1799 to 1840

Stevens, Taylor, and Stevens, Mahala, March 4, 1839. Basil Ward....John Stevens
Stevens, William M., and Baird, Mary, Feb. 25, 1833. R. Y. Reynolds. Jas. Baird
Stewart, Ann, and Marlin, Bazil B., Sept. 17, 1821. Loderic Davis......Thos. Smith
Stewart, Carter, and Malin, Lydia, April 4, 1828. Loderic Davis......Bazil Malin
Stewart, Cornelius, and Crowder, Ann, Jan. 24, 1835. W. Sandefur....Thos. Crowder
Stewart, Elizabeth, and Bozarth, Wm., Nov. 14, 1817. John Pinkston. Alex Stewart
Stewart, Elizabeth, and Smith, John, May 20, 1820. Benj. Kelley......John Smith
Stewart, Elizabeth, and Howard, Nathaniel, Oct. 16, 1822. Wm. Hart. John Smith
Stewart, Elizabeth, and Maddox, James, Oct. 12, 1833. John Phipps....Wm. Stewart
Stewart, Henry, and Cooper, Martha, March 22, 1837. Wm. Anderson. Jas. Campbell
Stewart, James, and Campbell, Maria Jane, Jan. 22, 1827. L. Davis....Alex. Cooper
Stewart, James, and Rowe, Judith, April 15, 1835. _____..........Robert Rowe
Stewart, John, and King, Nancy, Jan. 28, 1834. Wm. Downs............_____
Stewart, John, and Campbell, Elizabeth, March 18, 1839. J. G. Ward. Richard Stevens
Stewart, Levinia, and Ross, Thomas, May 11, 1824. Thomas Downs....John Bozarth
Stewart, Mary, and Locus, Samuel, Oct. 26, 1815. John Davis.........._____
Stewart, Nancy, and Himmon, George, Feb. 22, 1813. John Davis....Moses Cummings
Stewart, Rebecca, and Hudson, Joseph, Oct. 26, 1813. John Davis........_____
Stewart, Richard, and Campbell, Mary, Jan. 14, 1837. Ancil Hall....Wm. J. Stewart
Stewart, William, and Malin, Sarah, Sept. 17, 1822. Wm. Hart........Jacob Malin
Stocumband, Samuel, and Beck, Polly, March 20, 1804. John Davis...Stephen Beck
Stone, Celia, and Dover, Abraham, Aug. 20, 1805. _____.........Wm. Watson
Stone, Daniel W., and Martin, Cela, Nov. 21, 1824. John Pinkston........Wm. Huff
Storm, Abigail, Earp, Nicholas, Dec. 19, 1836. Jas. Holding............L. D. Earp
Storm, Elizabeth, and Earp, Josiah, April 17, 1837. Jas. Holding....Nicholas Earp
Storm, Peter, and Lemon, Amy, March 18, 1804. Thomas Taylor....Jacobin Lemon
Stovall, Elizabeth, and Watson, William, June 1, 1805. Thos. Taylor. John Watson
Streets, Samuel, and Whitaker, Elizabeth, Oct. 28, 1799. Wm. Rowan. Matthew Shultz
Sullenger, Birch, and Bell, Elenor M., Sept. 27, 1836. John Phipps.....Robt. T. Bell
Sullenger, Francis, and Duke, Susannah, Feb. 19, 1840. John Crouch. John Huston
Sutherland, Susanne, and Bryant, William, Sept. 12, 1804. Thos. Taylor. Benj. Benton
Sutton, Ishmael, and Smith, Caroline, Mar. 14, 1839. John Pinkston....Samuel Mills
Sutton, Jane, and Langley, Clement, Aug. 13, 1835. Wm. Sandefur....Jas. Sutton
Sutton, John, and Evans, Susannah, Sept. 9, 1814. Thos. Taylor......Abraham Six
Sutton, John, and Oldham, Martha, June 6, 1831. Wm. Sandefur....Levi Rollings
Sutton, Matilda, and Powers, Alexander, Aug. 12, 1831. Thos. Taylor. Jas. Johnson
Sutton, William, and Ralph, Catherine, Oct. 26, 1835. Wm. Hart....Wm. C. Leach
Swain, James, and Terrence, Nancy, July 5, 1833. Wm. Hart....Washington Brown
Swearingen, Elimilech, and Weeks, Angeline, July 21, 1827. D. Kelley....Jas. Smith
Taber, Ambers, and Johnson, Jane, May 9, 1833. Wm. Hart.......Cyrus Johnson
Taber, Deborah, and Johnson, James, July 16, 1833. Wm. Hart......John Senate
Taber, Eliza, and Johnson, Cyrus, June 4, 1838. Basil Ward........James Johnson
Taber, Mary, and Johnson, Nathan, Nov. 19, 1831. John J. Kelley........A. Taber
Taber, Matilda, and Powers, John, Feb. 18, 1839. Basil Ward........Jas. Johnson
Taber, Pardon, and White, Rachel, March 24, 1800. Thos. Taylor....Joseph White
Taber, Philip, and Hayden, Nancy, Jan. 19, 1829. John Denham....John Hayden
Taber, Rebecca, and Goldsmith, John, July 14, 1824. Thomas Taylor. Pardon Taber

Ohio County in the Olden Days

Talbert, Benjamin, and Davis, Amelia, Dec. 7, 1838. Wm. Hart......James Albin
Tally, Perry, and Willis, Elizabeth, Oct. 17, 1807. Benj. Talbert....Joseph Haynes
Talmon, Sally Ann, and Cortland, John, Oct. 22, 1824. Wm. Harlt....James Talmon
Tanner, Eliza, and Atherton, Moses, Dec. 21, 1830. Wm. Downs....Zachariah Field
Tanner, James, and Magan, Polly, May 15, 1835. Wm. Sandefur....George Brown
Tanner, Jane, and Hedges, William, Sept. 21, 1805. John Davis......Wm. Tanner
Tanner, Jane, and Hedges, James, Aug. 19, 1826. Jared Tichenor......Peter Hedges
Tanner, Salkins, and Gibson, Elizabeth, Oct. 18, 1809. John Davis....Wm. Tanner
Tanner, Samuel, and Iglehart, Sarah, Dec. 9, 1824. Jared Tichenor....Joseph Iglehart
Tanner, William, and Potts, Rachel, Dec. 2, 1804. John Davis.........Samuel Work
Tanson, Elizabeth, and Cox, Joseph, Jan. 17, 1825. Loderic Davis.....Thomas Davis
Tarlton, Charles, and Taylor, Margaret, Jan. 15, 1801. I. Pigman. Richard Moseley
Tarlton, Rebecca, and Cravens, Jesse, Sept. 17, 1802. Ignatius Pigman. John Mosely
Tarlton, Robert, and Calloway, Sarah, Feb. 10, 1810. John Davis....Chas. Calloway
Tarlton, Townstead, and Hudson, Susan, Oct. 29, 1812. John Davis. Robert Tarlton
Taylor, Absalom, and Burton, Polly, Nov. 8, 1826. Thos. Downs....Redding Taylor
Taylor, Ada Priscilla, and Jackson, Sam, Feb. 24, 1828. J. Bristow....Thos. Taylor
Taylor, Amy, and Smith, Hardy, June 8, 1801. James Keele.........Benj. Taylor
Taylor, Ann, and Midkiff, Joseph, Nov. 10, 1823. Thos. Taylor......Benj. Vancleve
Taylor, Ann, and Downey, Alex., April 14, 1826. H. B. Hunter......John A. Taylor
Taylor, Ann Marie, and Wallace, Arthur, Aug. 5, 1831. T. Taylor. Septimus Taylor
Taylor, Archibald, and Brown, Mary Ann, Oct. 23, 1826. _____....John Brown
Taylor, Arnold, and Welsher, Elizabeth, June 26, 1802. Jas. Keele. Benj. Taylor
Taylor, Benjamin, and Stevens, Charlotte, Nov. 17, 1836. _____. Wesley Stevens
Taylor, Blackstone, and Austin, Elizabeth, Jan. 10, 1828. Wm. Harlt. Thos. Austin
Taylor, Catherine, and Martin, Coleman, Oct. 2, 1799. John Moseley. Henry Coleman
Taylor, Clarice, and Barrett, Ignatius, May 17, 1826. T. Taylor....Richard Taylor
Taylor, Dolly, and Smeathers, Archibald, Sept. 29, 1828. T. Taylor. Harrison Taylor
Taylor, Eliza Jane, and Taylor, H. C., July 9, 1838. Wm. Kincheloe. Sept. Taylor
Taylor, Elizabeth, and Midkiff, James, Dec. 15, 1825. Wm. Harlt. Jonathan Rogers
Taylor, Elizabeth, and Duke, Thomas, Sept. 6, 1832. Bluford Henry....Thos. Barnett
Taylor, H. C., and Taylor, Eliza Jane, July 9, 1838. Wm. Kincheloe. Sept. Taylor
Taylor, Hannah, and Lee, Jesse, Aug. 29, 1808. John Davis.........Morris Taylor
Taylor, Hannah, and Fulkerson, Alfred, April 25, 1835. Geo. Render. Sept. Taylor
Taylor, Harrison, and Pigman, Phelena, Oct. 6, 1813. T. Taylor....Stephen Stratton
Taylor, Harrison D., and Davis, Mary, Nov. 11, 1828. W. Kincheloe. Christ. Jackson
Taylor, Henrietta, and Stevens, David, Nov. 4, 1818. Loderic Davis. Sept. Taylor
Taylor, Henry, and Johnston, Maley, Sept. 25, 1804. John Davis......Jas. Morton
Taylor, Henry, and Hedges, Ruth, Sept. 27, 1809. John Davis......James Dexter
Taylor, Hester Ann, and Davis, Thomas Y., Dec. 23, 1840. C. J. Ward......J. Mason
Taylor, Hilly Caroline, and Taylor, Levi, Dec. 26, 1831. Thos. Taylor. Sept. Taylor
Taylor, Ignatius Pigman, and Leach, Nancy, Oct. 13, 1825. J. James. Leonard Leach
Taylor, James, and Ross, Louisa Ann, Jan. 10, 1838. Jas. Ward......Thomas Ross
Taylor, Jane, and Pigman, Levi, Aug. 1, 1801. Ignatius Pigman....Joseph Barnes
Taylor, Jane, and Leach, William, Jan. 31, 1804. Thos. Taylor......John Leach
Taylor, Jane, and Wallace, John, Aug. 10, 1818. John Phipps........Geo. Render
Taylor, Jane, and Brown, Samuel, Nov. 22, 1831. Ancil Hall.........Levi Taylor

Marriage Records, 1799 to 1840

Taylor, Jane, and Ellis, Joseph, Sept. 15, 1835. Wm. Hart......Washington Phipps
Taylor, John, and Clifford, Nancy, June 22, 1813. John Davis........James Marks
Taylor, John, and Berryman, Elvina, July 4, 1833. R. Y. Reynolds....John Calhoun
Taylor, John, and Stevens, Elvira, March 27, 1837. J. D. Holding. Wesley Stevens
Taylor, John A., and Milton, Sally, Oct. 15, 1823. Thos. Taylor......Wesley Taylor
Taylor, John T., and Rowe, Emila, _____, 1830. Wm. Downs.........._____
Taylor, Johnson, and Houseley, Dosby, Feb. 2, 1833. John Phipps....Wm. Houseley
Taylor, Joseph, and Bennett, Susan, July 18, 1809. T. Taylor.......Thomas Bennett
Taylor, Leanah, and Hall, Samuel, Jan. 8, 1822. Warner Crowe........James Hall
Taylor, Levi, and Taylor, Hilly Caroline, Dec. 26, 1831. T. Taylor....Sept. Taylor
Taylor, Lucinda, and Johnston, James, Sept. 10, 1829. Wm. Downs....Gant Johnson
Taylor, Lucinda, and Shanks, Quintus, Aug. 30, 1838. J. G. Ward....Edmund Rowe
Taylor, Lucy, and Haynes, William, Dec. 6, 1830. David J. Kelley....Samuel Huston
Taylor, Margaret, and Tarlton, Charles, Jan. 15, 1801. I. Pigman....Richard Moseley
Taylor, Margaret, and James, John, Aug. 29, 1803. John Davis.....Richard Taylor
Taylor, Margaret, and Smothers, Archibald, Nov. 16, 1840. J. Phipps....T. P. Taylor
Taylor, Margarie, and Chapman, James, Feb. 4, 1819. John Phipps. Richard Taylor
Taylor, Martha, and Alphine, Sutton, Aug. 23, 1810. John Davis.....Henry Taylor
Taylor, Martha, and Leach, John, March 30, 1835. _____......Richard Duke
Taylor, Mason, and Blacklock, Clarissa, Oct. 18, 1830. D. Kelley....Thos. Blacklock
Taylor, Nicholas, and Craddock, Margaret, Oct. 8, 1833. Thos. Taylor...Richard Taylor
Taylor, Nicholas C., and Statler, Eliza, March 13, 1817. Benj. Malone....Ennis Ury
Taylor, Philip, and Welsher, Mary, Aug. 17, 1799. James Keele......John Douglas
Taylor, Philip, and Hearing, Nancy, May 15, 1831. John Phipps....George Brown
Taylor, Rebecca, and Dupoy, James, Dec. 19, 1801. James Keele.....Philip Taylor
Taylor, Rebecca, and Leach, James, Dec. 23, 1823. Thos. Taylor....Jonathan Raley
Taylor, Richard, and Wise, Delilah, March 19, 1819. John Phipps....Jacob Fulkerson
Taylor, Richard, and Stevens, Sally, Jan. 10, 1822. John James.......John G. Stevens
Taylor, Richard, and Leach, Susannah, April 8, 1834. L. Davis....Leonard Leach
Taylor, Sally, and Lewellan, Jobish, Oct. 22, 1826. Wm. Hart.......Thomas Taylor
Taylor, Sarah, and Chamberlin, Liles, Feb. 10, 1824. Warner Crowe. Arch. Davis
Taylor, Sarah Ann, and Bean, Wm. R., Aug. 29, 1833. Wm. Downs. Thos. Taylor
Taylor, Sarah Ann, and Austin, Wm., Oct. 31, 1836. Geo. Render......John Phipps
Taylor, Septimus, and Leach, Altha, Dec. 18, 1828. Jasper Bristow. Leonard Leach
Taylor, Silas, and Brown, Eliza, April 15, 1832. John Phipps.......George Brown
Taylor, Simon, and North, Elizabeth, Dec. 31, 1801. Ignatius Pigman. Jesse Kede
Taylor, Simon, and Six, Nancy, _____, 1821. Thomas Taylor........Isaac Six
Taylor, Sullen, and Hearing, Elizabeth, May 15, 1831. John Phipps. George Brown
Taylor, Susan, and Borah, Jacob E., Sept. 30, 1833. J. Phipps....Harrison Taylor
Taylor, Thomas, and James, Susannah, Jan. 17, 1814. Loderic Davis....Samuel James
Taylor, Thomas, and McCrocklin, Sally, Oct. 12, 1826. J. Gillespy. Joshua Chapman
Taylor, William, and Brown, Ann, Jan. 20, 1825. Thomas Taylor.....John Kenney
Terrence, Nancy, and Swain, James, July 5, 1833. Wm. Hart......Washington Brown
Thealkil, Paten, and Weeks, Polly, May 10, 1804. Thomas Taylor........._____
Theckles, Kitty, and Nichols, John, April 28, 1808. Benj. Talbert......Wm. Phipps
Thomas, David E., and Wallace, Mary Ann, May 11, 1840. J. G. Ward. Thorn. Wallace
Thomas, Emily, and Renfrow, Kellion, Sept. 4, 1836. Jacob Miller....Nathan Thomas

Thomas, James, and Miller, Elizabeth, April 2, 1809. Wm. Anderson. Thos. Moseley
Thomas, Jane, and Lewellan, Josiah, Oct. 23, 1819. ———........Alex Barnett
Thomas, John, and Hale, Jane, March 8, 1813. Benj. Kelly......Thomas Moseley
Thomas, John, and Johnson, Julian, Jan. 11, 1835. Ancil Hall......Clement Johnson
Thomas, Mary Ann, and Keown, Wm., Dec. 14, 1839. Craw. Taylor. Harrison Taylor
Thomas, Mary Ann, and Leach, Wm., June 15, 1840. Paul Abney....Joseph Renfrow
Thomas, Nathan, and Underwood, Sally, Aug. 5, 1819. John Phipps......———
Thomas, Nathaniel, and Daniel, Martha, April 18, 1833. Wm. Downs. John Daniel
Thomas, Peter, and Payton, Frances, Dec. 22, 1840. ———......F. R. Robertson
Thomas, Rhoda, and Gentry, Joseph, Jan. 8, 1801. Ignatius Pigman. Wm. Carter
Thomas, William, and Jackson, Sally, Nov. 16, 1824. T. Taylor......Christ. Jackson
Thompson, Catherine, and Duncan, Samuel, Dec. 15, 1810. Jas. Rogers. Joe Thompson
Thompson, Henry, and Harris, Mahala, July 23, 1832. Bluford Henry. T. Berryman
Thompson, Margaret, and Berryman, Thomas, Aug. 8, 1831. Wm. Hart. Francis Black
Thompson, Nancy, and McDonald, Charles, Oct. 22, 1834. Wm. Hart. Francis Black
Thomson, John, and Igelheart, Sarah, Feb. 1, 1820. T. Taylor....Jacob Iglehart
Thornback, Phoebe, and Brown, John, Feb. 21, 1814. Benj. Kelly.....James Sallee
Thorp, Ann, and Carter, Moses, Dec. 23, 1817. Benj. Kelley........Terry Thorp
Thorp, Rebecca, and Kelly, Benjamin, Nov. 11, 1816. Benj. Kelley....Terry Thorp
Thorp, Sally, and Clement, Wm., April 3, 1812. Lon. Jackson......Stephen Thorp
Thrasher, Auretta, and Pate, Samuel, March 11, 1824. Wm. Harlt...Nicholas Hocker
Thrasher, Eli, and Crawford, Mary Elizabeth, Nov. 3, 1822. J. Hart. Ed Blacklock
Tichenor, Alney, and Rowe, Amelia, Oct. 6, 1834. George Render....George Rowe
Tichenor, Ann, and Tichenor, Collier, Aug. 19, 1826. P. Warner......Silas Tichenor
Tichenor, Ann, and Igleheart, Jacob, Sept. 17, 1829. Wm. Downs....Tim. Tichenor
Tichenor, Benj., and Malin, Elizabeth, Dec. 23, 1838. Alf. Taylor....Byron Tichenor
Tichenor, Bennett, and Condit, Angelina, Aug. 30, 1831. Wm. Hart....Jacob Condit
Tichenor, Collier, and Tichenor, Ann, Aug. 19, 1826. P. Warner......Silas Tichenor
Tichenor, Elizabeth, and Drake, Rice, Oct. 27, 1840. ———......Dan Tichenor
Tichenor, Haron, and Lindley, Elizabeth Jane, Sept. 5, 1838. G. Vaught. Ed Rowe
Tichenor, James, and Bennett, Margaret, March 28, 1814. Geo. Render. J. Tichenor
Tichenor, Jane, and Render, John, Jan. 16, 1839. Geo. Render.......Elisha Coleman
Tichenor, John, and Blevins, Sally, Oct. 15, 1823. Jared Tichenor....James Hatcher
Tichenor, Lydia, and Tichenor, Warren, Sept. 5, 1836. Adlai Boyd. James Tichenor
Tichenor, Peggy, and Imleber, David, March 20, 1830. Geo. Render. James Tichenor
Tichenor, Polly, and Bennett, Thomas, July 24, 1819. John Phipps....Tim. Tichenor
Tichenor, Polly, and Bennett, Thomas, ———, 1820. Benj. Talbert....———
Tichenor, Sally, and Hedges, Peter, Aug. 25, 1826. Jared Tichenor.....Rich. Tanner
Tichenor, Sally, and Brown, Isaac, Dec. 23, 1833. T. Taylor........Jared Tichenor
Tichenor, Sarah, and Fields, Aquilla, March 25, 1800. Benj. Talbert......———
Tichenor, Sarah, and Fields, Aquilla, March 11, 1820. ———...Timothy Tichenor
Tichenor, Warren, and Tichenor, Lydia, Sept. 5, 1836. Adlai Boyd....Jas. Tichenor
Tilford, Eliza Jane, and Smith, Lewis, Feb. 4, 1832. D. J. Kelley......Walker Daniel
Tilford, Mrs. Elizabeth, and Parker, Bazzell, Oct. 17, 1833. Benj. Burden. Wm. Daniel
Tilford, Louisa Ann, and Garther, John, Oct. 17, 1840. B. Ward.......Andrew Tilford
Tilford, Lucy, and Haynes, Charles, Jan. 1, 1836. Ancil Hall........Walker Daniel
Tilford, Mary, and Combs, Eden, May 8, 1839. John Phipps..........Jesse Ward

Marriage Records, 1799 to 1840

Tilford, Nancy, and Daniel, George, March 18, 1827. David Kelley....Walker Daniel
Tilly, Polly, and Pinkston, John, May 8, 1832. R. Y. Reynolds.......Thomas Hall
Tinsley, Martha, and Duke, Washington, March 21, 1840. Basil Ward....J. Tinsley
Tong, Rebecca, and Holman, James, April 14, 1809. Wm. Anderson.....Stephen Clever
Tongon, Priscilla, and Barret, Joshua, April 1, 1819. T. Taylor.....Richard Barret
Topsley, Elenor, and Clever, Stephen, April 22, 1810. John Davis.........J. Crowe
Towels, Comfort, and Shultz, John, Oct. 23, 1821. Loderic Davis......Isaac Malin
Towns, John, and Utterback, Margaret, Dec. 4, 1838. Jas. G. Ward. Wm. H. Griffin
Trafford, John, and Johnson, Katy, March 7, 1811. Loderic Davis......Henry Cooper
Travel, John, and Brown, Sally, Sept. 13, 1809. Thos. Taylor.........Henry Brown
Troxal, Frederic, and Cox, Jane, April 13, 1818. _____........Solomon Kissinger
Trumboo, Peggy, and Wally, Levy, Oct. 6, 1807. John Trumboo......Jacob Myers
Tuell, Matilda, and Campbell, James, May 1, 1838. Ancil Hall......Archibald Stewart
Tumbaugh, William, and Bell, Abigail, Oct. 14, 1817. Benj. Kelley......Joe Allen
Tumnondy, William, and Condit, Jemima, July 28, 1818. Nall Overale. Moses Condit
Turnbaugh, Nanny, and Lapp, John, Dec. 24, 1806. Thomas Taylor.....John Downs
Turner, Jemima, and Gilbert, John, Feb 18, 1802. James Keele........._____
Turner, Nancy, and Davenport, S. A., Sept. 18, 1840. Alfred Taylor....Wm. Turner
Turpin, Mary, and Shayn, John, Dec. 8, 1800. Ignatius Pigman......Aquilla Davis
Turpin, Phillip, and Shane, Mary, Feb. 1, 1800. Ignatius Pigman.......John Shane
Turpin, Sarah, and Walker, William, Feb. 16, 1804. Thomas Taylor. Philip Turpin
Tuttle, William, and Bunch, Margaret, Dec. 23, 1831. Ancil Hall......Wm. McIntire
Underwood, Eliza, and Payton, Elisha, Jan. 12, 1808. John Davis....Joe McFarland
Underwood, Elizabeth, and Johnson, John, Jan. 12, 1809. John Davis. Chas. Scott
Underwood, Elizabeth, and Barry, Abraham, May 10, 1813. T. Taylor. Joshua Crowe
Underwood, Elizabeth, and Bennett, John, Aug. 14, 1823. Wm. Hart. Richard Elliot
Underwood, James, and Leddington, Polly, April 20, 1826. George Render. John Lane
Underwood, John, and Campbell, Lucinda, Aug. 20, 1827. Jared Tichenor. Jno. Loney
Underwood, Matilda, and Rowe, Robert, July 10, 1820. Jared Tichenor. _____
Underwood, Sally, and Thomas, Nathan, Aug. 5, 1819. John Phipps......_____
Upton, Edvina, and Curd, Daniel, Nov. 11, 1830. Wm. Downs.......S. G. H. McGary
Utterback, Margaret, and Towns, John, Dec. 4, 1838. Jas. G. Ward....Wm. H. Griffin
Vannada, Margaret, and Winifree, Charles, Dec. 30, 1807. John Davis. John Vannada
Vickory, Rosa, and Blevins, William, Jan. 5, 1819. Loderic Davis......John Shultz
Victories, Jacob, and Holeman, Polly, May 3, 1828. Wm. Anderson. James Holeman
Vittitoe, Daniel, and Jones, Sarah, Nov. 5, 1810. Wm. Anderson......Thomas Jones
Wade, Ballanger, and Erwin, Mrs. Mary, Oct. 20, 1833. Wm. Hart....Edmund Roach
Wade, Purmeley, and Royal, Samuel, July 17, 1836. Ancil Hall.....Ballenger Wade
Wade, William, and Warden, Garden, Sept. 12, 1835. _____......James Warden
Wafford, Wm., and Atherton, Peggy, Aug. 16, 1810. Joe Anderson....Moses Atherton
Wakeland, Allen, and Moseley, Mary, Jan. 25, 1840. John Phipps....Alexander Barnett
Wakeland, George, and Wise, Milly, Nov. 25, 1833. Geo. Render.....Tobias Wise
Wakeland, Harriet, and Maddox, Samuel, Sept. 3, 1823. Wm. Harlt. Nathaniel Howard
Wakeland, John, and Grey, Sally, Nov. 25, 1819. Loderic Davis......Benj. Gray
Wakeland, John, and Hunter, Nancy, Dec. 30, 1828. Geo. Render....Reuben Hunter
Wakeland, Nancy, and Gibson, Jordan, Jan. 13, 1810. Loderic Davis. Gideon Gibson
Wakeland, Nancy, and Hunter, Anderson, March 16, 1835. Geo. Render. W. Wakeland

Ohio County in the Olden Days

Wakeland, Plemelia, and Carter, Wren, Dec. 9, 1831. Geo. Render......Allen Wakefield
Wakeland, Polly, and Brown, James, Oct. 5, 1820. Loderic Davis....Wm. Wakeland
Wakeland, Sarah, and Farley, Wm., Sept. 9, 1819. Loderic Davis.....Filbert Newton
Walker, Sarah Ann Martha, and Berry, William, July 20, 1838. J. G. Ward. R. Walker
Walker, William, and Bell, Mary, Sept. 14, 1804. T. Davis........H. Petticunard
Walker, William, and Turpin, Sarah, Feb. 16, 1804. Thomas Taylor....Philip Turpin
Wall, Robert, and Gibson, Mary, Oct. 13, 1809. John Davis..........Joe McFarland
Wallace, Arthur, and Taylor, Ann Marie, Aug. 5, 1831. T. Taylor. Septimus Taylor
Wallace, Benjamin, and Ford, Nancy, June 19, 1823. Wm. Harlt....John A. Taylor
Wallace, Chas. Franklin, and Wooley, Dicey, Nov. 5, 1828. Wm. Harlt. Higgerson Belt
Wallace, Elizabeth, and Lynn, William, Dec. 25, 1826. Wm. Shelby....Wm. G. Wallace
Wallace, Elizabeth, and Benton, Nicholas, Nov. 8, 1830. Wm. Harlt....Peter Shown
Wallace, Franklin, and Bennett, Matilda, Jan. 25, 1836. Wm. Sandefur. Jas. Bennett
Wallace, Hugh William, and Shown, Sarah, Dec. 8, 1823. Wm. Harlt. Peter Shown
Wallace, James S., and Ward, Matilda L., May 24, 1840. Basil Ward. Nathan Bennett
Wallace, John, and Taylor, Jane, Aug. 10, 1818. John Phipps......Geo. Render
Wallace, John Benton, and Bishop, Annie Marie, July 29, 1828. Wm. Harlt. Josh Bishop
Wallace, Joseph, and Haynes, Polly, Oct. 11, 1817. Thomas Taylor.....John New
Wallace, Mary Ann, and Thomas, David E., May 11, 1840. J. G. Ward. T. Wallace
Wallace, Nancy, and Bryant, Horatis, Aug. 22, 1829. Wm. Harlt......John Wallace
Wallace, Nancy, and Baird, Wm. L., Oct. 22, 1837. John Pinkston. Richard Walker
Wallace, Polly, and Stevens, Charles W., May 29, 1830. Thos. C. Cooper. H. Stevens
Wallace, Talbert, and Stevens, Sarah Ann, May 9, 1830. T. C. Cropper. Henry Stevens
Wallace, Washington, and Cox, Lucinda, Aug. 29, 1833. Wm. Hart....Robt. Johnson
Wallace, William, and Cooper, Elenor, June 8, 1803. _____........Henry Cooper
Wallace, Wm. G., and Redding, Amanda Elvina, Dec. 9, 1839. Wm. Loney. J. Fitzhugh
Wally, Levy, and Trumboo, Peggy, Oct. 6, 1807. John Trumboo......Jacob Myers
Ward, Bassett, and Ford, Cassandra, April 1, 1822. Wm. Harlt....Jeffries Bennett
Ward, Delilah, and Ambrose, Michael, March 18, 1840. Basil Ward. Nathan Bennett
Ward, Edward, and Render, Sarah, May 28, 1814. Loderic Davis....Joshua Render
Ward, Elizabeth, and Midkiff, Benjamin, March 15, 1834. F. S. Blades. John Phipps
Ward, Hezekiah, and Owen, Elenor, Nov. 1, 1827. Geo. McNelly. Higgerson Belt
Ward, Jacob, and Holman, Patsy, Dec. 22, 1827. Thos. Taylor........Wm. Eidson
Ward, Jesse, and Ford, Mahala, June 2, 1825. Wm. Harlt............Lewis Ford
Ward, Jesse, and Railey, Elizabeth, Sept. 8, 1836. Adlai Boyd..........R. Walker
Ward, John, and Bennett, Minerva, June 17, 1835. Wm. Hart.......Joseph Bennett
Ward, Martha, and Bennett, Nathan, Jan. 5, 1831. Wm. Sandefur......Ezra Ward
Ward, Matilda L., and Wallace, James S., May 24, 1840. Basil Ward. Nathan Bennett
Ward, Rebecca, and Benton, Allen, March 16, 1820. Benj. Kelly......William Carter
Ward, Reuben, and Harding, Polly, June 28, 1814. _____........Moses Chapman
Ward, Susan, and Benton, James, Jan. 9, 1827. John Pinkston........John Ward
Warden, Betsy, and Dexter, Benj., Jan. 29, 1827. Jared Tichenor....Joseph Warden
Warden, Ella, and Calvert, Payton, Feb. 14, 1835. Geo. Render......James Warden
Warden, Even, and Blevins, Linsey, Aug. 22, 1820. Benj. Talbert.....Wm. Ashby
Warden, Garden, and Wade, William, Sept. 12, 1835. _____......James Warden
Warden, Nancy, and Iglehart, Thomas, Feb. 17, 1835. Wm. Downs....James Warden
Warnell, Richard, and Cochran, Polly, Feb. 19, 1818. Loderic Davis....John Shultz

Marriage Records, 1799 to 1840

Warren, Moses, and Brant, Hannah, Oct. 15, 1807. John Davis.........Ed Brant
Watson, Cynthia, and Boswell, Caleb, April 29, 1840. John Phipps......B. Watson
Watson, Elizabeth, and Abner, Edward, Dec. 31, 1806. John Davis....Robt. Watson
Watson, John, and English, Betsy, May 1, 1806. John Grammar......John Powers
Watson, William, and Stovall, Elizabeth, June 1, 1805. Thos. Taylor...John Watson
Webb, Eliza, and McKenzie, William, Jan. 8, 1822. John Ridgeway. Wm. Daniel
Webb, Titha, and Allen, Nathan, May 3, 1829. John Denham..........John Webb
Webb, William, and Eidson, Lucy, Jan. 23, 1839. J. G. Ward....William Mooreman
Wedding, Leo, and Wright, Mary, Feb. 10, 1840. John Phipps....William Wright
Wedding, Mary, and Barrett, Richard, May 1, 1820. John Rillney....John Ridgeway
Weeks, Angeline, and Swearingen, Elimilech, July 21, 1827. D. Kelley. Jas. Smith
Weeks, Catherine, and Atterberry, Reuben, Jan. 1, 1814. Joseph Wilson. _____
Weeks, Catherine, and Atterberry, Reuben, Dec. 22, 1823. Joseph Wilson. R. Eskridge
Weeks, Elizabeth, and Eskridge, Robinson, Oct. 7, 1818. Jos. Wilson. Jas. Mathews
Weeks, Polly, and Thealkil, Paten, May 10, 1804. Thomas Taylor........_____
Weeks, Polly, and Young, John, Feb. 9, 1807. Thomas Taylor.........John Weeks
Welch, Thomas, and Newcomb, Mrs. Sally, Jan. 26, 1837. _____.Johnson Taylor
Welcher, Malinda, and Christian, William, Aug. 7, 1821. _____....F. Fulkerson
Welcher, William, and Davis, Dorcas, Sept. 5, 1810. John Davis......Henry Davis
Wells, William, and Newton, Mildred, March 5, 1840. J. L. Burrows....John Newton
Welsher, Elizabeth, and Taylor, Arnold, June 26, 1802. James Keele....Benj. Taylor
Welsher, Mary, and Taylor, Philip, Aug. 17, 1799. James Keele......John Douglas
Westerfield, Betsy, and Nelson, William, Sept. 25, 1836. J. Pinkston. C. Westerfield
Westerfield, D., and Whittinghill, Cath. H. L., July 12, '34. A. Hall. W. Whittinghill
Westerfield, George, and Oldham, Orpha, June 20, 1840. Thos. T. Ellis. _____
Westerfield, Hayden, and Smith, Nancy, Jan. 7, 1832. Ancil Hall......J. S. Hoover
Westerfield, James, and French, Sarah, June 9, 1824. Benj. Kelley.....Dillis Dyer
Westerfield, Mary, and Roach, Cornelius, Oct. 3, 1831. Ancil Hall....J. Westerfield
Westerfield, Nancy, and Moseley, John, March 28, 1834. J. Benden. Geo. Westerfield
Westerfield, Phebe Jane, and Moseley, Elijah, Oct. 19, 1834. M. Ford. C. Westerfield
Whitaker, Elizabeth, and Streets, Samuel, Oct. 28, 1799. Wm. Rowan. Matt. Shultz
White, Abagile, and Dougherty, William, March 17, 1836. _____....Lewis White
White, Alfred, and Clark, Sarah Ann, July 11, 1839. Alfred Taylor....James Clark
White, Anna, and Lanham, Elias, April 20, 1805. John Davis......Richard Lanham
White, Davey, and Phelps, Lucinda, Feb. 8, 1839. _____.......Thomas Phelps
White, Dorcas, and Pearce, Jacharah, July 29, 1840. Paul Abney......John White
White, Elizabeth, and Huff, Aquilla, March 25, 1805. _____....William White
White, Elizabeth, and Lewallen, Samuel, Aug. 15, 1805. John Davis. Jacob Lewallen
White, John, and Jackson, Hannah, Aug. 22, 1822. Thomas Taylor....Julius Jackson
White, Lewis, and Andsey, Emilie, Aug. 19, 1831. David Kelley.......John A. White
White, Mary Ann, and Burton, James, Oct. 18, 1838. Ancil Hall........Dewey White
White, Rachel, and Taber, Pardon, March 24, 1800. Thomas Taylor....Joseph White
White, Ruth, and Pearce, Aborn, Oct. 8, 1838. Benj. Burden..........H. D. Taylor
White, Sarah, and Deweese, Martin, Jan. 25, 1830. Paul Abney.....Thomas White
White, Temperance, and Wilson, Henry, Jan. 30, 1834. _____Thompson Mitchell
White, Walker, and Mitchell, Julian, Oct. 21, 1839. J. Miller......Jon. Mitchell
Whiteacre, Molly, and Potect, Job, May 16, 1812. Loney Jackson...Simon Taylor

Ohio County in the Olden Days

Whitler, Polly, and Huff, Charles, March 12, 1835. Ancil Hall.....Bradford Whitler
Whitman, John, and Jackson, Hannah, Aug. 22, 1822. Thos. Taylor. Alex. Barnett
Whitmore, Nancy, and Grigsby, Nathaniel, ———, 1811. Loderic Davis. G. Petect
Whittaker, Lee, and Benton, Miranda, Dec. 8, 1817. Thos. Taylor. Benj. Benton
Whittehill, Elizabeth, and Ervin, William, Dec. 1, 1815. Benj. Kelley......———
Whittier, Elizabeth, and Crowe, Hyram, July 25, 1827. Ancil Hall......Jacob Miller
Whittinghill, Cath. H. L., and Westerfield, D., July 12, '34. A. Hall. W. Whittinghill
Whittinghill, Polly, and Howard, James, Jan. 6, 1838. Ancil Hall.....R. Whittinghill
Whittinghill, Rebecca, and Hedden, Jesse, March 2, 1829. Wm. Long. George Hedden
Whittinghill, Sarah, and Kelley, John, July 5, 1814. Benj. Kelley....W. Whittinghill
Whittinghill, William, and Kelly, Sarah, April 18, 1814. Benj. Kelley. Benj. Kelley
Wickliffe, Isaac, and Houston, Sally, Nov. 4, 1824. Benj. Kelley....Robert Houston
Wilcher, Nancy, and Brown, Joshua, Sept. 14, 1812. John Davis....William Wilcher
Wilcher, Nancy, and Christian, James, Sept. 18, 1813. Benj. Kelly. Wm. Galloway
Wilcox, Jacob, and Miller, Eliza Ann, Aug. 13, 1832. John Phipps....Fred Miller
Wiley, Lucinda, and Autry, Burrel, March 10, 1834. John Phipps......Simon Autry
Wiley, Mahala, and Evans, Jefferson, Jan. 4, 1830. Philip Abney......Wm. Campbell
Wilkins, Elizabeth, and Biggerstall, John, Oct. 10, 1807. Benj. Talbert. M. Atherton
Wilkins, James, and Boas, Sally, Sept. 29, 1825. Thomas Taylor......W. E. Probert
Wilkins, Samuel, and Robinson, Margaret, April 9, 1807. John Davis. Barnett Clark
Williams, Aggie Jane, and Hall, Bazlip, Aug. 15, 1839. J. G. Ward........G. Bryant
Williams, Amos, and Coleman, Christine, Feb. 22, 1825. Loderic Davis. H. Coleman
Williams, Edwin, and Neal, Peggy, April 14, 1810. Wm. Anderson.....J. Atherton
Williams, Elizabeth, and Paxton, Samuel, March 4, 1817. L. Davis....E. Williams
Williams, Elizabeth, and Lindsey, Samuel, Oct. 25, 1820. J. Tichenor....A. Bishop
Williams, Erezine, and Coleman, Ann, Nov. 7, 1831. John Phipps. Mallam Coleman
Williams, Evan, and Ashby, Fronie, March 14, 1807. Benj. Talbert....Jesse Ashby
Williams, Evan, and Cain, Rebecca, Aug. 8, 1808. Wm. Anderson.....James Baird
Williams, Harriet, and Coleman, Martin, Nov. 7, 1831. John Phipps....E. Williams
Williams, Isaac, and Coleman, Sally, Feb. 10, 1824. Loderic Davis......Henry Coleman
Williams, Jeremiah, and Morton, Cynthia Ann, Feb. 16, 1835. J. Phipps. T. Morton
Williams, Levinica, and Overton, James, Aug. 5, 1806. John Grammar......———
Williams, Maria, and Miller, David, Aug. 4, 1824. Loderic Davis. Elijah Williams
Williams, Mary, and Barnett, Isaac, July 30, 1814. Benj. Kelly......Wm. Whitt
Williams, Philip, and Wise, Rachel, Aug. 5, 1816. Loney Jackson....Slip Williams
Williams, Polly, and Cummins, Jacob, March 11, 1824. J. Tichenor. Jas. Williams
Williams, Rebecca, and Dubois, Stephen, May 23, 1819. B. Talbert....Nat Thomas
Williams, Rebecca, and Calloway, Wm., June 2, 1836. Wm. Downs. David Williams
Williams, Samuel, and Malin, Mariah, March 6, 1821. Loderic Davis. Isaac Malin
Williams, Taylor, and Brown, Ann L., ———, 1825. Thos. Taylor.....John Kenney
Williams, Viney, and Roundtree, James, July 31, 1806. John Davis. Benj. Farmer
Williams, Warden, and Ashby, Rebecca, Sept. 25, 1839. Thos. Downs. Wm. Ashby
Williams, William, and Jordan, Susan, Nov. 3, 1813. Thos. Taylor....Joshua Crowe
Williams, William B., and Harrington, Ellen, Sept. 24, 1840. J. Miller. F. Miller
Willis, Elizabeth, and Tally, Perry, Oct. 17, 1807. Benj. Talbert........Jos. Haynes
Willis, James K., and Haynes, Edy, Feb. 3, 1834. David Kelley........John Haynes
Wilson, Betsy, and Aubrey, William, May 13, 1828. Wm. Hart......Robert Wilson

Marriage Records, 1799 to 1840

Wilson, Elizabeth, and Maxwell, William, Aug. 8, 1831. D. J. Kelley....W. Christian
Wilson, George, and Clark, Elenor, Aug. 26, 1808. Wm. Anderson...Sarah Clark
Wilson, Henry, and White, Temperance, Jan. 30, 1835. _____. Thompson Mitchell
Wilson, James, and Railey, Polly, April 25, 1827. Wm. Harlt......Jonathan Railey
Wilson, James, and Howard, Susan, April 5, 1835. _____......Benjamin Wilson
Wilson, John, and Albin, Polly, April 5, 1823. William Harlt......Absalom Albin
Wilson, Joseph, Jr., and Hall, Polly, Oct. 20, 1824. Jos. Wilson, Sr.........John Hall
Wilson, Martha, and Douglas, Jonathan, Nov. 11, 1809. John Davis....Geo. Wilson
Wilson, Mary Jane, and Adams, John, Dec. 9, 1839. John Phipps.....Thomas Wilson
Wilson, Nancy, and Railey, John, July 14, 1828. Wm. Harlt.........Robert Wilson
Wilson, Rhoda, and Allen, William, July 4, 1831. Thos. Taylor......James McKenzie
Wilson, Sabina, and McFerrin, John, May 5, 1838. Ancil Hall..........John Ford
Wilson, Sally, and Laymonds, Jacob, May 4, 1835. _____.........James Wilson
Wilson, Sally, and Raley, James, July 30, 1838. William Hart.........Nimrod Wilson
Wilson, Sarah, and Matthews, Davis, June 28, 1809. Wm. Anderson.....Geo. Matthews
Wilson, Simon, and Rogers, Cindrella, Oct. 9, 1837. _____......Jonathan Rogers
Wilson, Thomas, and Fulkerson, Rachel, March 21, 1814. Thos. Taylor...Geo. Smith
Wilson, Warren, and Cobb, Elizabeth L., Nov. 6, 1832. Ancil Hall....Warren Cobb
Winifree, Charles, and Vannada, Margaret, Dec. 30, 1807. John Davis. Jno. Vannada
Winkler, Mary, and Jones, Lawrence, Oct. 9, 1810. Jas. Rogers......Welcher David
Winkler, Polly, and Hale, John, Jan. 15, 1814. Benj. Kelly..........Wm. Galloway
Wise, Daniel, and Brown, Milly, July 26, 1840. T. Garrett.............
Wise, Delilah, and Taylor, Richard, March 19, 1819. John Phipps....Jacob Fulkerson
Wise, James, and Coleman, Sarah, Jan. 5, 1828. Jared Tichenor......Philip Williams
Wise, Katie, and Davenport, Robert, Nov. 13, 1817. Geo. Render....Philip Fulkerson
Wise, Levi, and Fulkerson, Milly, Dec. 25, 1823. Thos. Taylor........J. Fulkerson
Wise, Levi, and Fulkerson, Molly, Dec. 25, 1823. Benj. Talbert......Adam Fulkerson
Wise, Levi, and Smith, Elizabeth, Sept. 5, 1840. _____..........Remus Gibson
Wise, Milly, and Wakeland, George, Nov. 25, 1833. Geo. Render....Tobias Wise
Wise, Rachel, and Williams, Philip, Aug. 5, 1816. Loney Jackson....Slip Williams
Wise, William, and Blevins, Irene, March 10, 1831. John Phipps.....J. R. Williams
Woods, Elizabeth, and Jones, John, Aug. 10, 1810. Wm. Anderson......Wm. Wood
Woodward, Ann, and Dexter, Silas, July 4, 1825. Wm. Harlt..........John Barnett
Woodward, Ashford, and McCroclin, Dolly, Feb. 12, 1821. J. Tichenor. Jas. Calloway
Woodward, Benjamin, and Bennett, Polly, May 23, 1820. W. Barnett. Reuben Bennett
Woodward, Delilah, and Bennett, Asa, Feb. 9, 1817. George Render. Hezekiah Ford
Woodward, Eliza, and Ford, Francis, Nov. 20, 1838. Basil Ward.......Alex. Rowe
Woodward, James H., and Crowe, Elizabeth, April 8, 1833. W. Hart. Elijah Crowe
Woodward, John M., and Simmons, Charlotte, Sept. 29, 1827. _____John C. Rogers
Woodward, Matilda, and Benton, Joseph, Feb. 24, 1835. Wm. Hart. Richard Walker
Woodward, Stephen, and Crowe, Sarah Ann, Oct. 24, 1838. J. Phipps. Quintus Shanks
Woodward, Thomas, and Pruden, Ann, Jan. 12, 1820. Wm. Harris. Benj. Woodward
Woodward, William, and Lucas, Elizabeth, Feb. 23, 1836. William Sandefur....
Wooley, Dicey, and Wallace, Chas. Franklin, Nov. 5, 1828. Wm. Harlt. Higgerson Belt
Wooley, Jacob, and McCormick, Sally Young, Nov. 5, 1832. W. Hart. J. McCormick
Wooley, Levi, and Crawford, Jossie, Aug. 1, 1814. Benj. Kelley......Thomas Baird
Wooley, Richard, and Leach, Sarah, Oct. 3, 1832. R. Y. Reynolds. Nathaniel Howard

Ohio County in the Olden Days

Work, Samuel, and Pigman, Amy, Jan. 13, 1801. Ignatius Pigman......Levy Pigman
Worthington, Thomas, and Barnes, Elenor, Nov. 18, 1806. J. Davis....Weaver Barnes
Wright, Aaron, and Baize, Margaret, Jan. 7, 1830. Thos. Taylor. Emanuel Bracher
Wright, Mary, and Wedding, Leo, Feb. 10, 1840. John Phipps........Wm. Wright
Wunkler, Fanny, and Medcalf, John, Sept. 18, 1813. Benj. Kelley......Wm. Galloway
Wylee, Dolly, and Christian, Charles, Dec. 23, 1816. Benj. Malone....Wm. Wylee
Wyles, Polly, and Lewell, James, Feb. 5, 1817. George Render.....David Lindley
Yontz, Lemuel, and Fulkerson, Rachel, Sept. 18, 1839. A. Taylor.....Phil Fulkerson
Young, John, and Weeks, Polly, Feb. 9, 1807. Thomas Taylor.........John Weeks
Young, Mary, and Rothrock, Henry, May 12, 1838. Geo. Render....Andrew Glenn
Young, Nancy, and Holeman, Anthony, Oct. 29, 1835. Geo. Render....Polly Young
Young, Polly, and Funkhauser, Isaac, Aug. 8, 1807. Benj. Talbert....James Young
Young, William, and Cumpton, Molly, March 13, 1806. John Davis. John Barnett
Young, William, and Hunter, Abigail, Jan. 23, 1822. Thos. Taylor.....Morgan Young

Index

Index

This Index does not include Appendix F: Ohio County Marriage Records, 1799 to 1840, pages 135 to 190

Acton, Wm. Henry, 131.
Adair, Gen. John, 31.
Adams Fork Settlement, 53.
Addingtons, pioneers, 64.
Alexander, Prof. Wayland, 74 n.
Allen, Elizabeth (Mrs. Harrison Taylor), 130 n.
Allen, Joseph, 54, 55, 55 n.
Allen, William Porter, 131.
Ambrose, James Ferdinand, 131.
Ambroses, pioneers, 64.
Anderson, Mrs., scalped by Indians, 11, 122.
Anderson children, killed by Indians, 10, 11, 117 n., 122.
Anderson, John, 122.
Anderson, Nath. D., 121.
Armendt, Henry Frederick, 131.
Arnold, Zebra, 118 n.
Ashby, Thomas, 106.
Ashley, George, 22.
Ashley, Hardin, 131.
Ashleys, pioneers, 64, 69.
Athertons, pioneers, 69.
Aull, Albert S., 131.
Austin, Edward G., 131.
Austin, Rev. James, 66.
Austin, John M., 68.
Awtry, Wm. McKendree, 131.
Axley, James, 106.
Axton, Levi Marion, 131.

Baird, Alexander B., 131.
Baird, James, 20.
Baird, Robert, 122.
Baird, Samuel L., 131.
Bairds, pioneers, 4, 64.
Baker, Augustus, 131.
Baker, Isaac H., 131.
Baker, J. W., 131.
Bank of Hartford, Commonwealth, 62.
Banking, early, 60.
Bardstown, 39 n., 58, 59.
Barnard, George W., 131.
Barnard, Ignatius P., 131.
Barnard, Joshua, 20.
Barnard, Wm., 23.
Barnard, Wm. L., 118 n.
Barnards, pioneers, 64.
Barnes, Hamilton, 105.
Barnes, James, 25.

Barneses, pioneers, 64.
Barnett, Alex., 20.
Barnett, Amanda Phipps, 131.
Barnett, Amelia May (Mrs. W. W. Rogers), 135.
Barnett, Hannah, captured by Indians, 11, 122.
Barnett, James M., 131.
Barnett, John L., 131.
Barnett, Joseph, 7 n., 8, 13, 22, 122; land troubles, 42.
Barnett, Joseph C., 131.
Barnett, Rachel, 22.
Barnett, Robert, 19, 22.
Barnett, Capt. Robert, 29.
Barnetts, pioneers, 4, 64, 71.
Barnett's Creek, 119.
Barnett's Station, 4, 6, 7 n., 8, 11, 69, 122.
Barrett, Ignatius, 107.
Barrett, James P., 2 n.
Barrett, Lycurgus, 2 n.
Barrett, Lyman G., 2 n.
Barrow, Harrison Taylor, 130 n.
Barrow, Mary, 130 n.
Barrow, Dr. Woolfolk, 130 n.
Barrow, Woolfolk, Jr., 130 n.
Barry, Daniel, 23, 24 n., 74, 74 n.
Battle, J. H.(W. H. Perrin, and G. C. Kniffin), "Kentucky, a History of the State," 76 n., 131-134, 134 n.
Bean, Dr. Henry F., 131.
Bean, Henry William, 131.
Bean Family, 131.
Bear Creek, 19, 115.
Beardley, Horace, 23.
Beaver Dam, 119, 101 n., 120 n.
Beaver Dam Baptist Church, 69.
Beda, 120 n.
Bell, John D., 131.
Bell, Robert T., 121.
Bells, pioneers, 64.
Bell's Run Church, 120 n.
Belt, Higginson, 65.
"Ben Hardin, His Times and Contemporaries" (Little), 7 n., 74 n.
Bennett, Alexander B., 131.
Bennett, Asa, 64.
Bennett, B. M., 131.
Bennett, Charles N., 131.
Bennett, George, 64.
Bennett, Jacob T., 131.
Bennett, Jeffries, 64.

Bennett, John, "Governor," 64.
Bennett, John (Jr.), 64.
Bennett, Obed., 64.
Bennett, Reuben, 31, 64, 65, 68.
Bennett, Samuel, 64.
Bennett, Titus, 64.
Bennetts, pioneers, 64, 65.
Berry, John, 6.
Berry, Dr. Wm. J., 76 n.; sketch of, 77 n.; 121.
Bethel Baptist Church, 70.
"Bibb's Reports," 48.
Biographies published in 1885, 131-134.
Blackford, pioneer, 6.
Blackford's Creek, 6, 19, 115.
Bland, Richard Parks, 74 n.
Blankenship, John B., 131.
Blankenship, Wm. H., 131.
Bodley, Temple, and Samuel M. Wilson, "History of Kentucky," 134 n.
Boone, Daniel, 4, 5.
Borah's Ferry, 120 n.
Bordley, Rev. Nathan (colored), 72 n.
Botts, A. G., 1 n.
Bowles, Thomas, 131.
Brackin, W. L. S., 131.
Brandon, Peter, 118 n.
Breckinridge County, 19, 23, 70, 89, 116.
Briant, James, 20.
Briant, Zachariah, 118 n.
Broadnax, Judge Henry P., 21, 23, 24, 27, 34 n.
Brown, George A., 131.
Brown, Isaac, 131.
Brown, Isaac Sylvester, 131.
Brown, James B., 131.
Brown, John Sep., 131.
Brown, Samuel, 109.
Browns, pioneers, 64.
Bryan, William Jennings, 74 n.
Bryant, Asberry Anderson, 131.
Buck Horn, 119, 120 n.
Buford, 119, 120 n.
Bullitt's Lick, 59.
Burch, Benjamin, 118 n.
Burr, Aaron, 28.
Burton, Lillie B., 2 n.
Burton, Seley, 118 n.
Butler, Charles W., 131.
Butler County, 19, 70, 116, 119, 131 n.
Byers, William Spurrier, 131.

Cain, Marcy T., 131.
Calhoon, George (Revolutionary soldier), 118 n.
Calhoun, 6, 7 n., 87.
Calhoun, George, 85.

Calhoun, Judge John, 7 n., 77; sketch, 84-87; 91, 121.
Calloway, Chesley, 118 n.
Campbell, William, 118n., 121.
Canebrakes, 3, 4.
Caney Creek, 4, 85, 119.
Cannan, John Wesley, 131.
"Carey's Atlas of the World and Quarters"(1814), see early Map of Ohio County, 20.
Carter, Sarah Jane (Mrs. Wm. Foster), 95 n.
Carter, William (Sr.), 118 n.
Casebier, Wm., 6.
Centretown (Centertown), 120 n.
Ceralvo, 119, 120, 120 n.
Chapman, Mrs. James, 24 n.
Chapman, Old Mr., model Christian, 71.
Chapmans, pioneers, 71.
Charles, Wm. B., 68.
Chase, Myers, and John Dorsey's heirs, 6.
Chick, Archie Little, 131.
Childs, Robert Enos, 131.
Chinn, John, 131.
Chinn, Josias, 131.
Christian, Charles Val., 131.
Christian, Samuel Meritt, 131.
Clark, James, 6.
Clay, Henry, 86, 98, 109, 129.
Cleaver, pioneer, 6.
Cleaver, Stephen, 19, 20, 22, 42.
Cleavers, pioneers, 4.
Clerk's Office, Old Brick, see text under picture of Courthouse, 100.
Clinton, Thomas, 86.
Coal and iron ore, 50, 65, 117, 119.
Coffman, Alfred T., 121.
Cold Friday, 82.
Cole, Squire Wm. Stewart, 131.
Coleman, William D., 131.
Colemans, pioneers, 69.
Collins, James Luther, 130 n.
Collins, Lewis, and Richard H., "History of Kentucky," 7 n., 10, 117 n., 120 n., 117-124.
Collins, Randall Taylor, 129 n.
Commercial Hotel, 31, 59.
Compass and chain, old, 121.
Concord Church, 12.
Condit, Timothy, 54, 55 n.
Condits, pioneers, 64.
Cook, Marie (Mrs. John Pendleton Taylor), 130 n.
Cool Spring, 119, 120 n.
Coombs, W. H., n 2.
Cooper, J. Will, 132.
Cooper, Lorenzo Dow, 132.
Cooper, William, 23, 118 n.

Index

Coppage, James R., 132.
Cotton gin, 44.
Couch, Mrs. Calvin, 24 n.
County officers, first, 19-27.
"Courier-Journal," 24 n., 94 n.
Court, Old and New, parties, 88.
Courthouse: first, 21, 32; old Clerk's Office, and present Courthouse, see text under picture of Courthouse, 100.
Courts, first, 19-27.
Cox, Isaac, 6.
Cox, Dr. Leonard Thomas, 132.
Cox, Samuel K., 132.
Craig, Robert, 92 n.
Cravens, Jesse, 19, 20.
Criss, Col., of Bullitt's Lick, 59.
Cromes, Charles W., 132.
Cromwell, 119, 120, 120 n.
Crowe, Ann Wayman, wife of Dr. McCreery, 78 n.
Crowe, Elijah, 88, 121.
Crowe, John W., 121.
Crowe, Joshua, 20, 22, 23, 77.
Crowe and Taylor, merchants, 63.
Crowe Tavern, 32, 59.
Crowe's militia district, 20.
Crowes, pioneers, 64.
Crutchers, belles, 68.
Cummins, Moses: sketch, 82, 83; 121.
Cummins, Tula Pendleton, 95 n.
Curlet, Jane, wife of Old Harrison Taylor, 82, 102-106, 127.
Curlet, Margaret (wife of Rev. Thomas Taylor), 129 n.
Curlet, Nicholas (father of Margaret Curlet), 129 n.
Curran, Charles Courtney, 74 n.
Curran, Ulysses T., 74 n.

Daniel, Joseph, 132.
Daniel, Robert J., 132.
Daveiss, John, 27 n.; sketch, 81; 121.
Daveiss, Joseph Hamilton, 26, 27 n., 81, 84.
Davidge, Judge Henry, 19; sketch, 80; 121.
Daviess County, 19, 68, 70, 81, 83, 84, 89, 116 n., 118, 119, 134 n.
"Daviess County, An Illustrated Historical Atlas Map of," 27 n.
"Daviess County, History of," 2 n., 27 n., 84 n., 134 n.
Davis, Hannah, 89, 92 n.
Davis, James Clinton, 132.
Davis, John, and wife, Elizabeth Davis, 130 n.
Davis, John F., 132.
Davis, Rev. Lodowick, 70.

Davis, Margaret Young (Mrs. Thomas Taylor), 129 n.
Davis, Mary (Mrs. Harrison D. Taylor), 129, 129 n.
Davis, Thomas, 129 n.
Davis, Wm. M., 68, 88, 121.
Davises, belles, 68.
Davison, Edward, 132.
Dean, Mrs. Mary Hale, 135.
Dickey, Mrs. F. P., "Blades of Blue grass," 95 n.
Doherty, John, 132.
Dorsey, John (heirs), 6.
Dorsey, Larkin, 7.
Downs, Mr., at Vienna, 12.
Downs, Rev. Thomas, 70.
Downs, Rev. William, 22, 70.
Draper Manuscripts, 184 n.
Duff, Robert J., 132.
Duke, Isaac N., 132.
Duke, John, 65.
Duke, John D. T., 132.
Duke, Richard, 18 n.
Duke, Robert N., 132.
Duke, Captain Wm , 18 n.
Duke, William Henry, 132.
Duncan, Ben, 68.
Duncan, David, 132.
Duncan, William G., 132.
Dunn, Mr., Indian fighter, 59.
Dutch ancestry, 15, 17.
Dutch Bible, 17.
"Dutch Root Doctor," Houseman, 76.
Duvall, Wm., 5.
Duvall, Gov. Wm. P., 5, 33, 34.
Dyer, Dillis, 68, 84; sketch, 88; 89, 121.

Elizabethtown, 4, 57.
Elizabethtown and Paducah Railway, 119.
Elliott, Richard, 62, 63, 68.
Ellis, Alexander C., 132.
Elm Lick, 102 n.
Eskridge, Henry M., 132.
Eudaley, James, 132.
Everly, William J., 132.
Excelsior School House, 34 n.

Faith, Mr., wounded by Indians, 122.
Faiths, pioneers, 64.
Falheron, Philip, 107.
Farms and forests, 50-52; products, 118, 120.
Fayette County, 116.
Federalist party, 28.
Felix, Charles B. B., 132.
Felix, Frank L., 2 n., 132.

195

Felix, James Thomas, 132.
Felix, William Logan, 132.
Ferguson, Joshua, 68.
Fergusons, belles, 68.
Fetherton, Wm., 23.
Field, Aquilla, 22, 24 n., 69.
Field, Benjamin, 22, 23, 118 n.
Field, Charles L., 132.
Field, Henry, 20.
Fields, pioneers, 64.
Filson Club, The, 13 n., 32 n., 49 n., 128, 134 n.
Fitzhugh and Rose, merchants, 59.
Flat Clay Lick, 19, 115.
Fogle, McDowell A., 2 n.
Ford, Elisha M., 121.
Ford, James W., 132.
Ford, John A., 132.
Ford, Joshua G., 1 n.
Ford, William, 132.
Fordsville, 119, 120 n.
Foreman, Elizabeth, 24 n.
Forests and farms, 3, 50-52; products, 118, 120.
"Forget Me Not" (McHenry), 94 n.
Fort Hill Farm, 8.
Foster, Isaac, 132.
Foster, William, 95 n., 132.
Foster, Dr. William, 95 n.
Frankfort, 118, 125.
"Frankfort Cemetery, History of" (Johnson), 125 n.
Frazier, Absalom, 132.
Fulkerson, Septimus P., 132.
Fulkerson, William H., 132.

Gaines, William W., 132.
Gardner, Thomas, 6.
Garrard, Gov. James, 19.
Geological Survey Maps, 120 n.
Gibson, Remus, 121.
Gill, Thos., 22.
Gillstrap, Thomas, 132.
Glenn, David, 19, 20, 22.
Glenn, James S., 2 n.
Glenns, pioneers, 64.
Goodlet, Dr., of Bardstown, 78 n.
Gordon, George W., 132.
Gordon, William A., 132.
Goshen Church, 70.
Grass, Henry, 6.
Grayson County, 19, 70, 116, 119.
Green River, 1, 3, 4, 6, 7, 8, 17, 19, 22, 34, 50, 88, 115, 116, 117, 119, 122, 123, 128.
"Green River and Its People, Old Stories of" (Little), 74 n.
Green River Country, 4, 5, 7 n., 33, 34 n., 91, 117.
"Green River Country from Bowling Green to Evansville" (Greene), 134 n.
Greene, W. P., "Green River Country from Bowling Green to Evansville," 134 n.
Greenup, Christopher, 23.
Greep, J. W., 2 n.
Greer, Bluford C., 132.
Greer, John C., 132.
Greer, Samuel H., 132.
Gregory, Rev. Joseph L., 72 n.
Gregory, William F., 132.
Griffin, Frank, 74 n.
Griffin, Lucy (Mrs. Randall Taylor), 129 n.
Griffin, Warren, 50.
Griffith, Remus, 81, 121.
Griffiths, pioneers, 64.
Grissom, Mr., 129 n.
Gross, Dr. S. A., "A Report on Kentucky Surgery," 78 n.
Gruelle, Wallace, 2 n.

Haden, Louis G., 132.
Hale, Dr. Josiah, 92 n.
Hall, James, 118 n.
Hancock County, 19, 70, 116, 119, 131 n.
Handley, John, 6, 7, 23, 121.
Handleys, pioneers, 4, 64.
Hanging, the first, 53-56.
Hansford, Charles, 118 n.
Harbison, William, 129 n.
Hardin, Ben, 74.
Hardin, Martin D., 89.
Hardin County, 1, 4, 19, 47, 116, 119.
"Hardin's Reports," 48.
Hardinsburg, 20, 53, 62, 86.
Hardwick, Clarence, 132.
Harrises, pioneers, 71.
Harrison, Hannah (Mrs. John Taylor), of Colonial Virginia, 129 n.
Harrison family of Va., 101, 127, 129 n.
Harris's Fork, 19, 115.
Harrod, James, 8.
Harsha, James, 109.
Hart, Eli Milton, 132.
Hartford, 6, 8-11, 13, 16, 20, 25, 29, 31, 32, 34, 44, 50, 57-63, 67, 68, 69, 84, 88, 110, 118, 119, 120, 120 n., 122, 123, 128; origin of name, 9.
Hartford Academy, also Seminary, 73, 74, 74 n.
"Hartford and Ohio County," by Mrs. F. E. Merriman, 134 n.
"Hartford Herald," 2 n., 92 n., 93 n. See Introduction.
"Hartford Republican," 2 n.
Hartford Station, 4, 6, 7 n., 122.
Hatfield, Henry, 6.

Index

Hatler, Francis M., 132.
Hawkins, John A., 132.
Hay, Adam, 6.
Hay, Michael, 6.
Haynes, John, 121.
Hayneses, pioneers, 64.
Haynesville, 120 n.
Hayward, Prof. Wm. B., 74 n., 132.
Hedges, Josiah, 23.
Helm, Leonard, 3, 4.
Henderson, Beverly, 24 n.
Henderson, Charles; sketch, 24 n.; 25, 68, 82, 117 n., 135.
Henderson, Elizabeth, 24 n.
Henderson, Emily A., 24 n.
Henderson, Miss Gabrielle, 24 n.
Henderson, James, 24 n.
Henderson, Jeannette, 24 n.
Henderson, John, 24 n.
Henderson, Richard, and Co., 116.
Henderson, Thomas, 24 n.
Henderson County, 19, 89, 116.
"Henderson County, History of" (Starling), 116 n.
Henderson, Town of, 65.
Hendersons, pioneers, 64; belles, 68.
Henry, Patrick, 5.
Hill, Samuel E., 132.
Hillyer, James, 121.
Hines, Alfred Thomas, 132.
Hines, John Birks, 132.
Hines, John W., 132.
Hines, Thomas Henry, 132.
Hines' Mills, 119, 120 n.
Hocker, George B., 132.
Hocker, James B., 132.
Hocker, Philip M., 132.
Hocker, Richard P., 121, 132.
Hodges, Asa W., 132.
Hogarth, John, 6.
Hogg's Fall, 120 n.
Holbrook, John D., 132.
Hopkins, Gen. Samuel, 29, 59.
Hopkins County, 89.
Horse Branch, 120 n.
Horton, 34 n., 120 n.
Houseman, a "Dutch Root Doctor," 76.
Howell, Capt. John, 19, 20, 118 n.; sketch of, 125, 126; remains removed to Frankfort, 125, 126.
Hubbard, Edward Clarence, 132.
Hudnall, Joseph A., 132.
Huff, Benj., 6.
Hunley, Elias Gress, 132.
Hunter, William M., 132.
Hunters, pioneers, 71.
Hussey, Charles W., 132.
Hustons, pioneers, 64.

Iglehart, Rev. Benj. T., 132.
Iglehart, James B., 132.
Indian depredations, 7, 10-14, 18, 59, 122, 123, 124.
Indians and Moundbuilders, evidences of prehistoric, 1, 2, 121.
Infares and weddings, 38, 39.
Irvin, Mr., surgical operation on, 78 n.
Irvin, Francis, hanging of, 53-56.
Irving, Washington: "Ralph Ringwood," 30, 34, 35, 57, 106.
Isaacs, John, 8.
Isaacs, pioneers, 4.

Jackson, Gen. Andrew, 14, 29, 31, 65, 86, 87.
Jackson, Christopher, 19, 20.
Jackson, George, 23.
Jackson, Samuel, 20.
Jacksons, pioneers, 4.
Jail, first, 20, 32, 53.
James, Eugene P., 132.
James, Rev. John, 70, 106.
Jefferson County, 1, 4, 13 n., 47, 116.
Jenkins, Rev. Benj. F., 132.
"Jerks," 71, 72.
Jett, Thaddeus S., 132.
Jewell, John H., 132.
Jillson, Willard Rouse, 13 n.; "Kentucky Land Grants," 49 n., "Old Kentucky Entries and Deeds," 49 n.
Johnson, Elijah, 132.
Johnson, J. Polk, "A History of Kentucky and Kentuckians,"134 n.
Johnson, John M., 132.
Johnson, L. Frank, "A History of the Frankfort Cemetery," 125 n.
Johnson, Moses, 118 n.
Johnson, Samuel (Sr.), 118 n.
Johnston, Major James, 31, 60, 121.
Jones, Churchill, 55 n.
Jones, Rev. Geo. W., 34 n.
Jones, James, 118 n.
Jones, Nancy Jane, 2 n.
Jones, Richard A., 60.
Jones, Samuel, 132.

Keal, James, 19.
Keele, James, 106.
Keith, John, 6.
Kelley, David J., 121.
Kelley, James, 118 n.
Kelly, Dr. Howard A., "American Medical Biography," 78 n.
Kelly, William, 6.
Kennedy, Ezekiel, 55 n.
"Kentucky and Kentuckians, a History of" (Johnson), 134 n.

"Kentucky, Biographical Cyclopedia of the Commonwealth of," 92 n., 127 n., 134 n.
"Kentucky, Biographical Encyclopedia of," 77 n., 92 n., 127 n., 134 n.
"Kentucky, Bluegrass State, The, History of" (Bodley and Wilson), 134 n.
Kentucky District, 116.
"Kentucky Entries and Deeds, Old" (Jillson), 49 n.
Kentucky Geological Survey, maps, 120 n.
"Kentucky, History of the State" (Battle), 76 n., 131-134, 134 n.
"Kentucky, History of" (Collins), 7 n., 10, 117 n., 120 n., 117-124.
"Kentucky, History of" (Kerr), 134 n.
"Kentucky Land Grants" (Jillson), 49 n.
"Kentucky, Methodism in, History of" (Redford), 72 n.
Kentucky State Historical Society, 94 n., 129 n.
"Kentucky Surgery, A Report on" (Gross), 78 n.
Kerr, Charles, "History of Kentucky," 134 n.
Kiel, Jemmy, 34 n.
Killam, Rev. Hiram, 72 n.
Kimbley, Ezekiel V., 132.
Kimbley, Isaac F., 132.
King, Nichols, 6.
King, W. T., 132.
Kinnimonth, Robert E., 132.
Kinsolving, Herbert B., 132.
Knight, Jacob, 6.
Know-Nothing Party, 1 n., 99.

Lamar, John, 44 n.
Lamar, Susannah (Mrs. Ignatius Pigman), 44 n., 129 n.
Land and products, valuation of, 117, 118, 119, 120, 120 n.
Land titles, 42-44, 47-49, 49 n.
Lawyers, ten well-known, 80-92; 118.
Layton, Dr. Charles W., 132.
Layton, John Jay, 132.
Leach, Alfred K., 132.
Leach, Henry Clay, 132.
Leach, Leonard H., 132.
Leach (William), 107.
Leaches, pioneers, 64.
Lee, James Stone, 132.
Legislature, members of, 121.
Leitchfield, 89, 120 n.
Lewellin, Jacob, 22, 23.
Lewis, John W., 132.
Lewis and Rogers, merchants, 59.
Lexington, 25.
Life in olden days, 35-41, 57, 67, 68.

Lincoln County, 116.
Lindley, Henry J. C., 132.
Liter, Adam, 132.
Literary clubs, 94, 94 n., 95 n.
Little, Lucius P., "Ben Hardin, His Times and Contemporaries," 7 n., 74 n.; "Local Preachers in Old Times," 72 n.; "Old Stories of Green River and Its People," 74 n.
Lock and Dam, Green River, 7 n., 88.
Logan, Abram Winter, 130 n.
Logan, Mrs. Mary Taylor, 130 n. See Introduction.
Logan County, 64, 116, 131.
Long Falls on Green River, 6, 7 n., 13.
"Lonz Powers" (Weir), 38 n.
Lopez Expedition, 129 n.
Louisville, 78, 121.
Loves, pioneers, 4.
Lyon, Gen. Hylan B., see text under picture of Courthouse, 100.
Lyon House, 3', 59.
Lyons, William, 132.

McAdoo, J. F., see McHenry's Map of Ohio County, 68.
McCoy, Daniel, 6.
McCreary, Gov. James B., 78 n.
McCreery, Dr. Charles, 68; sketch of, 76-78, 78 n.; 121.
McCreery, Harold, 68.
McCreery, James, 78 n.
McCreery, Robert, 78 n.
McCreery, Thomas Clay, 78 n.
McCreerys, belles, 68.
McElroy, Kittie, 24 n.
McFarland, Joseph D., 55 n.
McFarlands, pioneers, 64.
McGrady's militia district, 20.
McHenry, 65, 120 n.
McHenry, Barnabas, 89, 92 n.
McHenry, Emma (Mrs. J. Hale), 92 n.
McHenry, Henry D., 92 n., 94 n., 121, 132.
McHenry, Mrs. Jennie T., "Rosine," 94 n.; "Forget Me Not," 94 n.
McHenry, Jenny (Mrs. R. Craig), 92 n.
McHenry, John H. (Jr.), 1 n., 92 n.
McHenry, John H. (Sr.), 68; sketch, 89-92, 92 n.; 121.
McHenry, John J., Map, 68; statistics, 120, 120 n.
McHenry, Lemuel S., 92 n.
McHenry, Martin D., 68.
McHenry, W. Estill, 92 n., 121.
McHenry, William H., 92n.
McIlmurray, John, killed by Indians, 122.
McIntyre, Prof. Malcolm, 74 n.
McKendrick, Rev. Wm., 70.
McKenzie, Daniel, 59.

Index

McKenzie, Wm., 59.
McLean, Judge Alney, 42, 54, 87.
McLean County, 7 n., 19, 70, 116, 119, 131 n.
McQuown, H. C., 72 n.
Maddox, Azariah Peck, 132.
Maddox, David J. K., 132.
Maddox, John, 23.
Maddox, John (Sr.), 118 n.
Maddoxes, pioneers, 64.
Madison, Gabriel, 8.
Malin, Jacob, 55 n.
Marriage Records, 1799 to 1840, 135–190.
Martin, George M., 132.
Martin, Wade N., 133.
Mason, Robert J., 133.
Massie, Charles W., 133.
Matthews, Heber, 2 n.
Maxey, Chamburs I., 133.
Maxey, Rev. Wilburn A., 133.
Maxwell, Wm., killed by Irvin, 53.
May, Allen, 55 n.
May, Junius, 129 n., 130 n.
May, Sarah Mildred (Mrs. Henry Pirtle Taylor), 130 n.
Mays, pioneers, 4, 64.
Meador, Dr. James W., 133.
"Medical Biography, a Cyclopedia of American" (Kelly), 78 n.
Medkiff, Wm. Paton, 133.
Mercer, William, 133.
Merchants, early, 57–63.
Merriman, Mrs. Frances E., "History of Hartford and Ohio County," 134 n.
Metcalf, Henry S., 133.
"Methodism in Kentucky, History of" (Redford), 72 n.
Militia musters, 20, 37, 38, 38 n.
Miller, David, 23.
Miller, Elijah, 133.
Miller, Jacob, 33.
Miller, James, 133.
Miller, James Barney, 133.
Miller, James P., 133.
Miller, John, "Tick-eyed John," "Bluebeard," 11, 18, 33, 34 n., 122.
Miller, Joseph, 129 n.
Miller, Rev. Joseph, 72 n.
Miller, Joseph T., 133.
Miller, W. H., 121.
Millers, pioneers, 64.
Milligan's Ferry, 20.
Mitchell, Dr. G. F., 133.
Mitchell, Dr. J. J., 133.
Mitchell, Thomas, 129 n.
Monroe, John, 118 n.
Monroe, John H., 133.
Montague, Mrs. Nancy I., 133.
Moore, Elias, 6.

Moore, John Wilson, 133.
Morehead, Robert Y., 133.
Morgan, Gen. David, 30.
Morgantown, 119.
Morrison, Daniel, 39 n., 45 n.
Morrison, Isaac, 6.
Morton, David, 32, 59, 61, 62, 133.
Morton, Isaac, 11, 32, 59, 61, 62, 94 n.
Morton, Dr. James S., 133.
Morton, Mrs. Jennie C., 94 n.
Morton, John C., 94 n.
Morton, John P., 133.
Morton, Louis C., 133.
Morton, Richard, 23.
Morton, Samuel, 32, 59, 61, 62.
Morton, Timoleon, 133.
Morton, Wm., 62.
Mortons, merchants (Samuel, Isaac, and David), 32, 59, 60, 61, 62.
Mortons, pioneers, 64, 69.
Moseley, John, 23.
Moseley, Robert, 59, 73, 89, 121.
Moseley, Robert, or Bob, 21, 33, 34, 34 n., 115, 118 n.
Moseley and Thompson, merchants, 60.
Moseleys, pioneers, 64.
Mott, Dr. Valentine, 78 n.
Muddy Creek, 1, 6, 20, 22, 34 n., 45, 67, 106, 119.
Muddy Run, 8.
Muhlenberg County, 68, 70, 78 n., 89, 116, 131 n.
"Muhlenberg County, History of" (Rothert), 7 n., 38 n.
Murray, Mr., Indian fighter, 59.
Murray and Walker, merchants, 60.
Myers, Chase, and John Dorsey's heirs, 6.
Myers, Jacob, 6.
Myers, Michael, 23, 55 n.

Nall, Dr. Burr F., 8, 129 n.
Nall, Mrs. John G., 24 n.
Nall, John Gatewood, 24 n., 63.
Nall, Larkin G., 63, 121.
Nashville, 16.
"National American," 1 n.
Neal, Samuel, 11.
Nelson County, 1, 4, 47, 64, 116.
New Orleans, 61, 64, 68.
New Orleans, Battle of, 29, 32, 32 n., 45 n., 59.
"New Orleans, Battle of" (Smith), 32 n.
Newton, Benjamin, 133.
Newton, George W., 133.
No Creek, 16, 64.
No Creek Baptist Church, 70.
"Not Altogether Fanciful" (Walker), 95 n.

O'Brien, Mrs. Catherine, 133.
O'Brien, Edward J., "Best Short Stories, 1915," 95 n.
O'Flaherty, John, 2 n.
Ohio County, formation of, 1, 4, 115, 116; origin of name, 117.
"Ohio County News," 2 n.
Ohio River, 6, 10, 12, 15, 18, 19, 22, 70, 115, 122.
Oldham, George, 55 n.
Oldham, John, 22.
"Orphan Brigade, History of the" (Porter), 77 n.
Owen, Abraham, 84.
Owensboro, 16, 26, 39 n., 62, 68, 84, 91.

Panther Creek, 16, 20, 22, 50, 119.
Paradise, 120 n.
Paradise Road, 70.
Park, James A., 133.
Park, William H. H., 133.
Parks, Peter, 118 n.
Patterson, Dr. Beverly N., 133.
Patterson, George W., 133.
Patterson, Jonathan H., 133.
Patterson, Langston M., 133.
Patton, James H., 133.
Patton, Dr. John Wm., 133.
Paxton, Joseph, 55 n.
Payton, Joel, 133.
Pemberton, Wm. Dawson, 133.
Pender, Thomas, 118 n.
Pendleton, Dr. John E., sketch of, 76 n.; 95 n., 130 n., 133.
Pendleton, Mary (Mrs. Harrison Pirtle Taylor), 130 n.
Pendleton, T. D. (pen name of Tula Pendleton Cummins), 95 n.
Perry's Victory, 32.
Petty, Francis, 118 n.
Petty, John William, 133.
Peyton, Craven, 78.
Peyton, Dr. Samuel O., 24 n., 68; sketch of, 78, 79; 121; see text under picture of Courthouse, 100.
Peyton, Wm., 24 n., 78, 121.
Pharis, Francis M., 133.
Phipps, John, 63.
Phipps, W. W., 63.
Phippses, pioneers, 64.
Physicians, early, 76-79, 118.
Pigeon Roost Fork of Muddy Creek, 34, 34 n., 45, 106.
Pigman, Anne (Mrs. Samuel Work), 45 n.
Pigman, Ignatius, 18, 19, 39 n.; land troubles, 42, 43, 44; life of, 44 n.; 129 n.
Pigman, Levi, 44, 45, 46, 109.

Pigman, Philena (wife of Harrison Taylor, son of Richard), 45 n.
Pigman, Miss Polly, 45 n.
Pigman, Rhoda (Mrs. Stephen Statler), 18, 18 n., 45 n., 129 n.
Pigman, Sallie (Mrs. Daniel Morrison), 34 n., 39 n., 45 n.
Pigman, Sidney (Mrs. John Rice), 45 n.
Pigman, Wesley, 43, 34 n., 45 n.
Pigmans, pioneers, 4.
Pinkston, Rev. Daniel, 70.
Pinkston, Rev. John, 70, 72 n.
Pioneers, families, some, 4, 64-68.
Pirtle, Ferdinand W., 133.
Pirtle, Judge Henry; sketch, 88, 89; 126, 128.
Pirtle, Rev. John, 88.
Pirtle, Timothy C. F., 133.
Pleasant Ridge, 120 n.
Point Pleasant, 119, 120 n.
Point Precinct, 116.
Popes, pioneers, 69.
Population, 118, 119, 120, 120 n.
Porter, William H., 133.
Powers, John, 23.
"Preachers, Local, in Old Times" (Little), 72 n.
Price, Robert, 23.
"Pue" (Pugh), Peggy (Mrs. Keele), 106.
Pugh, Peggy, 34 n.

"Quits" (Mrs. James Chapman), 24 n.

Ragland, John Walker, 133.
Ragland, Moses Smith, 133.
Raley, James, 133.
Ralph, John L., 133.
"Ralph Ringwood" (Irving), 33, 34, 35, 57, 106.
Redford, Rev. Albion H., "History of Methodism in Kentucky," 72 n.
Reid, George W., 133.
Reid, Mosby J., 133.
Religion, 44 n., 65, 66, 69-72, 72 n., 118.
Render, Elijah Franklin, 133.
Render, George, 66.
Render, Rev. George, 65, 66, 69.
Render, George W., 133.
Render, Greene, 66.
Render, John, 133.
Render, Joshua, 65, 66.
Render, Joshua, Sr., 65.
Render, Joshua L., 133.
Render, Robert, 65, 66.
Render, Robert, Sr., 1, 2.

Index

Render, William P., 133.
Render Coal Mines, 65, 120 n.
Renders, pioneers, 64, 65, 69.
Renfrow, Mark, 133.
Renfrow, Virgil, 133.
Representatives, Member of the House of, 121.
"Revolution, American, Kentucky Society Sons of," 118 n.
Revolutionary soldiers, list of, 118 n.
Reynolds, William H., 133.
Rhoads, Daniel, 6.
Rhoads, Daniel James, 133.
Rhoads, Henry, 6, 42, 121.
Rhoads, McHenry, 2 n., 133.
Rhoads, Solomon, 7 n.
Rhoadses, pioneers, 4, 64.
Rhoadsville (later Vienna, now Calhoun), 6.
Rice, Mrs. John, 45 n.
Richland Creek, 4.
Riley, John C., 133.
Rileys, pioneers, 64.
Ringo, Ben D., 2 n.
Risbey, John, 23.
Roach, Cornelius, 55 n.
Robertson, B. P., 2 n.
Robertson, Mrs. Powhatan, 24 n.
Robertson, Sylvester W., 133.
Rochester, 120 n.
Rock Lick Creek, 19, 115.
Rockport, 119, 120, 120 n., 121.
Rogers, John, 55.
Rogers, John Butler, 133.
Rogers, Mrs. Whittier W., 135.
"Roland Trevor" (Triplett), 84 n.
Rollins, Aaron, 6.
Rone, Christopher C., 133.
Rose, Samuel, 59.
Rose and Fitzhugh, merchants, 59.
"Rosine" (Mrs. Jennie T. McHenry,) 94 n.
Rosine, post office, 120 n.
Rosine Tunnel, 34 n.
Rothert, Otto A., "A History of Muhlenberg County," 7 n., 38 n. See Introduction.
Rough Creek, 8, 9, 13, 16, 19, 22, 34, 40, 50, 73, 115, 117, 118, 119, 128.
Rowan, Dr. Alex. R., 10, 121.
Rowan, John, 10.
Rowan, Judge John, 13 n., 20, 88.
Rowan, Stephen, 10, 12, 55 n.
Rowan, William, 10.
Rowan, William, 13 n., 19, 20, 24 n.
Rowan County, 13 n.
Rowans, pioneers, 64.
Rowe, Edmund, 66, 67.
Rowe, George, 66, 67.
Rowe, George, 133.

Rowe, Robert, 66.
Rowe, William L., 133.
Rowes, pioneers, 64, 66, 67, 69.
Rumsey, 88.
Rumsey, Wm. H., 121.
Russell, Robert S., 121.

Sanders, Dr. George R., 133.
Sandifur's Crossing, 34 n.
Schachner, Dr. August, 78 n.
Schools, Old-time, 73, 74, 74 n., 75, 78 n.
Schultz, Patty and Polly, 34 n.
Schultz, Simon, 34 n.
Science Hill, Tevis School, 77.
Select, 120 n.
Senators, State, 121.
Shanks, James, 73, 121.
Shanks, Quintus C., 73, 121.
Shankses, pioneers, 64; belles, 68.
Sharp, Dr. Samuel F., 133.
Sharpe, Wm., first child born at Hartford, 13.
Shelby, Gov. Isaac, 29, 30, 84.
Shelbyville, 77, 129 n.
Shepherd, Adam, 6.
Sherrod, Wm. Henry, 133.
"Shield, The," also "Ford's Southern Shield," 1, 1 n., 2 n. See Introduction.
Shively, Wm. Henry, 133.
Shown, Peter, 40, 41.
Showns, pioneers, 64.
Shrewsbury, Wm. D., 133.
Shultz, George C., 133.
Shultz, Matthias, 8, 118 n.
Shultzes, pioneers, 64.
Shutts, Diadama, 118 n.
Sipple, Nath., 23.
Slaves and slavery, 71, 93-96.
Smith, Dr. Benjamin, 68; sketch of, 78.
Smith, David L., 133.
Smith, George N., 133.
Smith, James, 68.
Smith, John K., 133.
Smith, Joseph H., 133.
Smith, Thomas J., 133.
Smith, William, 20.
Smith, Z. F., "Battle of New Orleans," 82 n.
Smiths, pioneers, 64.
Smith's Ferry, 20.
Smothers, William, or Bill Smothers or Smithers, 23, 25-27, 33, 34 n., 82.
Sorrels, John, 118 n.
South Carrollton, 119, 120 n.
"Southern Shield, Ford's," 2 n.
Spanish Conspiracy, 28.
Spanish Domain, 64.

Stackhouse, an outlaw, 104, 105.
Starling, Edmund L., "History of Henderson County," 116 n.
Statistics, 118-122, 120 n.
Statler, Eliza (Mrs. Nicholas C. Taylor), 18 n., 129 n.
Statler, Ignatius P., 18 n.
Statler, Rev. L. B., 18 n.
Statler, Mattie (Mrs. Wm. Duke), 18 n.
Statler, Sallie (Mrs. Richard Duke), 18 n.
Statler, Stephen: comes to Hartford, 15-18; family of, 18 n.; 19, 20, 26, 45 n., 117 n., 122, 129 n.
Statler, Susan Lamar (Mrs. Henry Stevens), 18 n.
Statlers, pioneers, 64.
Stephens, Daniel [David?], 107.
Stevens, Henry, 18 n., 65.
Stevens, John, 65.
Stevens, John A., 7 n.
Stevens, Rev. R. Thomas, 72.
Stevens, Richard, 65, 107.
Stevens, Richard Henry, 133.
Stevens, Thomas, 65.
Stevens, William, 23, 65.
Stevenses, pioneers, 64, 65.
Stewart, Rev. James C., 133.
Stock marks, recorded, 20.
Sublett, Lafayette, 133.
Sugar Camp, Maple, 70.
Sulphur Springs, 120 n.
Sutton, 120 n.
Sutton, Cicero Truman, 2 n., 133.
Sutton, John T., 133.

Tabor, Pardon, 133.
Talbott, Rev. Benjamin, 69.
Tannehill, James, 118 n.
Tarleton, Bob, 34 n.
Tarleton [Charles?], 107.
Tayloe, Benjamin, 118 n.
Taylor, A. Donnie, 133.
Taylor, Ann, 108.
Taylor, Benjamin, 118 n.
Taylor, Benjamin (son of John), 108.
Taylor, Blackstone, 107.
Taylor, Christina, 108.
Taylor, Clarissa (Mrs. Ignatius Barrett), 107.
Taylor, Cynthia, 108.
Taylor, Elizabeth (daughter of John Taylor), 108.
Taylor, Elizabeth (daughter of Old Harrison Taylor), 106.
Taylor, Esther Stuart Cook, 130 n.
Taylor, Fleming, 108.
Taylor, Frances, Miss, 107, 129 n.
Taylor, Frances (Mrs. Burr F. Nall), 129 n.

Taylor, Hannah (daughter of John), 108.
Taylor, Hannah (Mrs. Samuel Brown, daughter of Old Harrison Taylor), 109.
Taylor, Harrison (infant), 129 n.
Taylor, Harrison, Old, 82, 101-109, 107 n., 127, 129 n.
Taylor, Harrison (son of Old Harrison Taylor), 11, 19, 42, 59, 68, 103, 107, 107 n., 108, 130 n.
Taylor, Harrison (son of Richard), 45 n., 106.
Taylor, Harrison (son of Wm.), 108.
Taylor, Harrison D., 72 n., 101 n., 107, 117 n., 125, 126; autobiographical notes, 97-100, 110, 111; biographical, 127-130, 129 n., 130 n., 134 n., "History of the Taylor Family," 101-111.
Taylor, Harrison Pirtle, 130 n.; sketch, 130 n.
Taylor, Harvey (son of Sep.), 108.
Taylor, Henrietta (Mrs. Daniel [David?] Stevens), 107.
Taylor, Dr. Henry Pirtle, 129 n., 130.
Taylor, Hester Ann (Mrs. Davis; Mrs. Grissom), 129 n.
Taylor, Ignatius, 108.
Taylor, J. S., 121.
Taylor, Jane (daughter of Septimus), 108.
Taylor, Jane (Mrs. John Wallace), 108, 130 n.
Taylor, Jane (Mrs. Levi Pigman), 45, 109.
Taylor, Joe, 34 n.
Taylor, John, of Colonial Virginia, 129 n.
Taylor, John (son of Old Harrison), 45, 46, 108.
Taylor, John (son of Richard), 107.
Taylor, John A. (son of second Harrison), 108.
Taylor, John Alexander, [108], 133.
Taylor, John, "Coffee," 108, 133.
Taylor, John Junius (infant), 130 n.
Taylor, John McHenry (infant), 129 n.
Taylor, John Pendleton, 130 n.
Taylor, Joseph (son of Old Harrison), 108.
Taylor, Julia (Mrs. Th. Mitchell), 129 n.
Taylor, Katy (Mrs. Coleman; Mrs. Thomas Ashby), 106.
Taylor, Leonard L., 133.
Taylor, Levi, 108.
Taylor, Lorenzo, 108.
Taylor, Margaret (daughter of John), 108.
Taylor, Margaret (Mrs. James Harsha), 109.
Taylor, Margaret (Mrs. Junius May), 129 n.
Taylor, Margaret Curlet, (Mrs. William Harbison), 129 n.

Index

Taylor, Marion C., sketch, 129 n.
Taylor, Mary (Mrs. Abram Winter Logan), (Mrs. Mary Taylor Logan), 130 n. See Introduction.
Taylor, Mason, 107.
Taylor, Milton, 70, 107, 129 n.
Taylor, Nicholas C., 18 n., 55, 107, 129 n.
Taylor, Peggy (Mrs. John James), 106.
Taylor, Rachel, 108.
Taylor, Randall, 129 n.
Taylor, Richard, of England and Colonial Virginia, 129 n.
Taylor, Richard (son of Old Harrison), 59, 104, 106, 107, 107 n., 121.
Taylor, Richard (son of Wm.), 108.
Taylor, Richard (son of Richard), 107.
Taylor, Richard M. (son of Sep.), 108.
Taylor, Richard Stevens, 133.
Taylor, S. Calvin, 133.
Taylor, Sallie (daughter of John), 108.
Taylor, Sallie (Mrs. Philip Falheron), 107.
Taylor, Sallie M. (Mrs. Woolfolk Barrow), 130 n.
Taylor, Mrs. Sarah A., 133.
Taylor, Septimus (Jr.), 108.
Taylor, Septimus (son of Old Harrison), 23, 108.
Taylor, Septimus (son of Wm.), 108.
Taylor, Simon, of Colonial Virginia, 129 n.
Taylor, Simon (son of Old Harrison), 108.
Taylor, Squire L., 133.
Taylor, Stephen (son of John), 108.
Taylor, Susan (Mrs. Joseph Miller), 129 n.
Taylor, Susan (Mrs. Richard Stevens), 107.
Taylor, Rev. Thomas, 45, 68, 70, 104, 105, 106, 107, 107 n., 127, 129 n.
Taylor, Thomas (son of Harrison D.), 129 n.
Taylor, Thomas (son of Rev. Thomas), 107, 129 n.
Taylor, Thomas Alfred, 108.
Taylor, Virgil, 133.
Taylor, Washington, 108.
Taylor, Wesley, 107, 129 n.
Taylor, Wm. (son of Old Harrison), 108.
Taylor, Wm. (son of Wm.), 108.
Taylor, Wm. A., 133.
Taylor, Wm. S., 108.
Taylor and Crowe, merchants, 63.
Taylor Cemetery, The Milton, 129 n.
"Taylor Family, History of" (Taylor), 101-111, 101 n.
Taylor Family Reunion at Beaver Dam, 101 n.

Taylors, pioneers, 4, 64, 68.
Tevis School, Science Hill, 77.
Thames, Battle of the, 29, 30, 32 n.
"Thames, Battle of the" (Young), 32 n.
Thomas, Christopher, 133.
Thomas, James A., 134.
Thomas, James William, 134.
Thomas, John, 32.
Thomas, Massey, 23.
Thomas, Sukey, 34 n.
Thomas Family, The, 133.
Thomases, pioneers, 64.
Thompson, Anthony, 22, 23, 118 n.
Thompson, Rev. Anthony, 70, 72 n.
Thompson, Ed Porter, "History of the Orphan Brigade," 77 n.
Thompson, Henry, 121.
Thompson, Philip, 30, 82; sketch, 83, 84; 90, 121.
Thompson and Moseley, merchants, 60.
Thomson, George Bell, 134.
Tichenor, James A., 134.
Tichenor, John W., 134.
Tichenor, Lavega W., 134.
Tichenor, Silas N., 134.
Tichenor, Squire W., 134.
Tichenors, pioneers, 64, 69.
Tinsley, Henry, 134.
Tippecanoe, Battle of, 84.
Tobacco, 52, 60, 61.
Tracy, Daniel F., 134.
Travis, Charles, 22.
Travis's militia district, 20.
Trible, Barnett, 130 n.
Trible, Mrs. Kittie (Mrs. Harrison D. Taylor), 130, 130 n.
Trible, Mary Ellen (Mrs. Clarence E. Walker), 130 n.
Triplett, Philip, 91.
Triplett, Robert, 82, 84 n.
Triplett, Robert, "Roland Trevor, or The Pilot of Human Life," 84 n.
Trout, Daniel B., 134.
Tyler, Capt. James, 29, 30.

Undel, Abel, 6.
Union County, 89, 131 n.
"Union Regiments of Kentucky" (1897), 129 n.

Vannada, Martin, captured by Indians, 117 n., 122.
Van Nort, Green Berry, 134.
Vantrace, Isaac, 6.
Vaughan, David, 134.
Vienna (now Calhoun), 6, 7, 7 n., 10, 12.
Vincent, Post, 64.

Walker, Clarence E., 130 n.
Walker, E. Dudley, 95 n., 121, 134.
Walker, E. Helm, 130 n.
Walker, Rev. Jesse, 70.
Walker, Miss Lizzie, "Not Altogether Fanciful," 95 n.
Walker, Logan, 63.
Walker, R. L., 77.
Walker, Sarah M., 77 n.
Walker and Murray, merchants, 60.
Walkers, pioneers, 64.
Wallace, Charles, 20.
Wallace, John, 130 n.
Wallace, Samuel, 134.
Wallace, Wm., 25, 58.
Wallaces, pioneers, 64.
Walle, John, 134.
Walton Creek Baptist Church, 69.
Walton's Creek, 66, 119.
War of 1812, 14, 28-32, 32-n., 45 n., 59, 60, 65, 84.
Warden, Barnett C., 134.
Washington, Baily, 5.
Watkins, Ansel, 55 n.
Wattie, Mr., 45, 46.
Webb, Thomas E., 134.
Wedding, Dr. Sylvester J., 134.
Wedding Family, The, 134.
Weddings and infares, 38, 39.
Weir, James, "Lonz Powers," 38 n.
Weller, Jacob, 134.
Westerfield, Cornelius, 20.
Westerfield, John C., 134.
Westerfield, Uriah J., 134.
Westerfield, Wm. H., 134.
White, Joseph, 23.
White's Fork, 119.

Whitescarver, Rev. Diocles, 72 n.
Wickliffe, Martin H., 25.
Wickliffe, Nathaniel, 31, 58.
Williams, Edward R., 134.
Williams, Elijah, 67.
Williams, Cross B., 134.
Williams, James H., 62.
Williams, Jerry, 67.
Williams, Jesse S., 134.
Williams, Rev. Otho, 70.
Williams, Samuel A., 134.
Williams, Thomas, 134.
Williams, W. H., 134.
Willis, Felix G., 134.
Wilson, Ansel, 134.
Wilson, Judge John B., 27 n., 34 n., 55 n.
Wilson, John Calvin, 134.
Wilson, Samuel Martin, 134.
Wilson, Samuel M., and Temple Bodley, "History of Kentucky," 134 n.
Wing, Charles Fox, 78.
Wise, Daniel, 134.
Wolf scalps, 19.
Work, Samuel, 20, 24 n., 45 n.; sketch, 80, 81.

Yates, Marion, 134.
Yeaman, George H., 1 n.
Yellow Banks (Owensboro), 39 n.
Yellow Creek, 9.
York, Samuel, 19.
Young, Bennett H., "Battle of the Thames," 32 n.
Young, Thomas Adam, 6.
Young, Dr. Wm. S., 86.